NEW PERSPECTIVES
ON HISTORICAL THEOLOGY

John Meyendorff

New Perspectives on Historical Theology

Essays in Memory of John Meyendorff

Edited by

Bradley Nassif

WILLIAM B. EERDMANS PUBLISHING COMPANY
GRAND RAPIDS, MICHIGAN / CAMBRIDGE, U.K.

© 1996 Wm. B. Eerdmans Publishing Co.
255 Jefferson Ave. S.E., Grand Rapids, Michigan 49503 /
P. O. Box 163, Cambridge CB3 9PU U.K.

Printed in the United States of America

02 01 00 99 98 97 96   7 6 5 4 3 2 1

Library of Congress Cataloging-in-Publication Data

New perspectives on historical theology: essays in memory
of John Meyendorff / edited by Bradley Nassif.
p.   cm.
Includes bibliographical references.
ISBN 0-8028-0704-6 (pbk.: alk. paper)
1. Theology, Doctrinal — History. 2. Church history. 3. Orthodox
Eastern Church. 4. Spirituality. 5. Liturgics.
I. Meyendorff, John, 1926-   . II. Nassif, Bradley.
BT21.2.N48   1995
230 — dc20   95-46085
                              CIP

Contents

John Meyendorff

History

Theology

Spirituality and Liturgy

Scripture and Exegesis

Foreword

John Meyendorff was, for his generation, among the most distinguished representatives and exponents of the Orthodox tradition in theology and historiography. But at the same time by his ecumenical labors and by his learning, as well as by the warm humanity of his character and personality, he had close friends and numerous admirers far beyond the ordinary confines of his own tradition. The present collection of essays in his memory attests that wideness in the circle of scholars who profoundly valued the man, the priest, the theologian, the most learned historian. The news of his premature death on July 22, 1992, left lumps in a large number of throats.

In the unceasing dialogue between the Christian traditions of East and West, between the Orthodox and the rest — whether Roman Catholic or Anglican or Reformed — his cheerful and serene voice responded with grace, firmness, and total integrity. For Western theologians, once he had published his seminal volumes on Gregory Palamas in 1959, it was unthinkable to hold an international conference on top-level ecumenical issues without inviting him to deliver a major paper. Indeed the pressures and demands made upon him must at times have felt almost insupportable, when one recalls what responsibilities he also carried at Dumbarton Oaks, at Fordham University, and lastly as Dean of St. Vladimir's Seminary in Crestwood, where he and his wife were the soul of hospitality to visitors. Partnered for many years at the Seminary by the powerful mind of Alexander Schmemann, he simply embodied both for his own people and for Western Christians the finest scholarship and the best thinking of the

Orthodox Churches. He equipped himself with a masterly knowledge of the historical sources — in several languages — and could move with apparent effortlessness through the tangled thickets not only of Byzantine Church affairs but also of such critical moments in East-West relations as the Council of Florence. Among the personalities of Florence, as one would expect, he felt bound to regard the unbending Mark Eugenicus as the authentic voice of the Palamite theology, in preference to the softer humanism of Bessarion, on behalf of whose sincerity Fr. Joseph Gill once had to write a notable plea. At the same time he could write warmly and gratefully of the evident fact that at Florence Pope Eugenius IV made substantial concessions to the Orthodox understanding of primacy and conciliarity and, no doubt to the consternation of Torquemada and his more hard-line advisers, did not at all insist on the older imperialism of the medieval monarchy. His last book on *Imperial Unity and Christian Divisions* illustrates how his concern about the unity of East and West contributed to the way in which he put questions to the historical evidence.

Requiescat in pace.

HENRY CHADWICK
Christ Church
Oxford

Introduction

BRADLEY NASSIF

"There is no Orthodoxy without Holy Tradition, which implies communion in Spirit and in truth with the witness of the apostles and the fathers, based upon the belief that, by the power of God and in spite of all historical human weaknesses, there was and there is an uninterrupted, consistent and continuous Holy Tradition of faith held by the Church throughout the centuries. This belief in Tradition is not identical with simple conservatism. Holy Tradition is a living tradition. It is a witness to the unchanging Truth in a changing world."[1]

John Meyendorff

This book is dedicated to John Meyendorff, one of the most insightful ecclesiastical historians of the twentieth century. The quote above expresses an underlying conviction that governed the entire course of his career. His belief in consistency and continuity in the theological history of the church inspired a significant portion of his work. He proceeded on the assumption that the Christian Church, despite its great diversity, preserved an identifiable core of apostolic tradition that was passed down

1. John Meyendorff in *The Legacy of St. Vladimir's*, ed. J. Breck, J. Meyendorff, and E. Silk (Crestwood, NY: St. Vladimir's Press, 1990), 15.

intact from generation to generation. Identifying that core of apostolic tradition, however, is seldom easy. The problem is variegated and complex. It requires that it be viewed from a variety of angles, periods, and disciplines.

In memory of their friend and colleague, an international team of scholars from Europe and America have gathered together in this memorial volume to carry forward that vision that was so central to Father John's work. To be sure, not all the authors would agree with his belief that the Orthodox Church is the only church that has preserved the apostolic tradition in its fullness. Nevertheless, Meyendorff was a moderate in this regard, eager to affirm whatever he could find of the apostolic faith in other confessions. Reflecting his ecumenical outlook, the authors come from Orthodox, Catholic, and Protestant traditions. Most knew him personally, a few only through his publications. All, however, are experts in their fields. Only the stature of a man like John Meyendorff could have solicited such a distinguished roster of theologians!

The goal of the present volume is to offer "New Perspectives on Historical Theology." It seeks to examine the theme of continuity and change in Christian history through fresh interpretations of more established landmarks, and less-traveled paths. The authors visit vital issues, old and new, that have shaped the identity of the Christian tradition in historical and contemporary perspective. Classical themes and contemporary challenges are brought together in one volume to speak compellingly to the needs of Christianity today. An important by-product of the essays will lead readers to consider more carefully the supportive role that historical theology has played in our understanding of the biblical text (to be discussed below).

The scope of the project spans diverse historical periods (Rome, Byzantium, Europe, and America), and integrates several academic disciplines (history, theology, Bible, patristics, liturgy, and spirituality). Admittedly, such a methodology has both advantages and disadvantages. The chief disadvantage is that it results in uneven coverage of the book's theme. The combination of different periods and disciplines has resulted in obvious lacunae of important issues. But the risk of this criticism seems worth taking in the face of the fragmented approach to theology that prevails today. Far too often in academia the theological disciplines are studied in isolation from each other as though each was at odds with the others. This has had the effect of creating disciplinary tunnel vision. The inclusive methodology that has been adopted here has the advantage of advocating a maximalist approach to theology. In a few instances, special topics were solicited to fill gaps in present-day scholarship; but the majority of authors were given the guiding theme for the project and then asked to create their own ideas. Consequently, the book can make no pretense of covering all the important subjects, or even most of them. It is simply a modest effort to examine a limited number of key issues over the centuries from an integrated perspective.

The volume is intended for both the academy and the church. It is designed for students and professionals across denominational lines and in diverse academic disciplines. The authors hope that it will be especially profitable for classroom and ecumenical settings. Religion professors, students, church leaders, and the Faith and Order Commission of the World Council of Churches are the ones who may possibly profit the most from it. The book may serve as a companion text to illuminate special topics in survey courses on church history, theology, worship, or the history of exegesis. Professors may find it useful for highlighting historical trends and doctrinal themes that cannot be fully addressed in their class lectures or the students' textbook. In every case, the contributors have sought to advance the field of historical theology by providing original or revised interpretations, challenging older cherished views, assessing and advancing the current state of scholarship in their disciplines, or exploring timely issues of today. The articles presume that the reader possesses a general knowledge of church history in the ancient, medieval, and modern worlds.[2]

A survey of the table of contents will identify the areas (collectively, not chronologically) in which each author has developed a new perspective on a classical or contemporary subject. Classical topics include the continuing relevance of tradition, a fresh evaluation of the accomplishments and limits of the Council of Chalcedon (C.E. 451), the relationship between grace and the knowledge of God, perceptions of Paul in the history of exegesis, a reinterpretation of charisma versus institution in one of the greatest medieval mystics (East and West), Dionysius the Areopagite, the perplexing problem of the text and boundaries of the Old Testament canon in the Byzantine

---

2. Those for whom this assumption does not apply can fill the gaps in their knowledge by consulting an introductory survey of Christian history, such as the one by Justo Gonzalez, *The Story of Christianity* (two volumes; New York: Harper & Row, 1984 and 1985), and by the same author, *A History of Christian Thought* (three volumes; Nashville: Abingdon, 1970-1975).

Church, revised models of patristic methods of Scriptural exegesis, a re-formulation of the relationship between *agape* and *eros* in Christian mysti-cism of the ancient and medieval worlds, and a lively liturgical debate that has divided the Orthodox and Catholic churches since the fourteenth century over the "moment of consecration" of the communion elements. Contem-porary challenges focus on the concept of "communion" as a description of the church, the background of events leading to the current crisis in Bosnia-Herzegovina, and a recent phenomenon in American Orthodoxy concerning an intriguing merger between evangelical and Orthodox churches. I believe it is safe to postulate that as a result of the scholarship presented here, several obstacles that have divided Christians heretofore will no longer be considered valid barriers to theological unity today. Every person who wrestles with these issues, even if they disagree with the conclusions presented, will have to deal with the research presented here.

It is impractical to comment on the particular value of all the essays since each one has made a very different contribution to modern scholar-ship. Collectively, however, they impact our interpretation of the most important source of Christian truth, namely, the Bible itself. It is a maxim that the Scriptures form the basis for all Christian history, doctrine, worship and spirituality. For the church Fathers, theology was based upon Scripture, and their ways of theologizing reflected that conviction.[3] Through the

---

3. This is especially important to underscore for those of us who labor in the Orthodox Church. Over the past hundred years Eastern Orthodoxy has witnessed a theological revival first in the area of patristics, then in liturgics. While this has been a positive development, it has also tended to overemphasize the role of these disciplines in contemporary formulations of the faith. Many (it is hard to quantify but easy to identify) working in the fields of dogmatic theology, canon law, church history, and liturgics have tended to define Orthodoxy chiefly in terms of its historical development in Byzantium and Russia more than in terms of its biblical and apostolic foundations. The use of the Bible by authors within these disciplines has often been shallow and exegetically unpersuasive. More than anything else, what is most urgently needed today is balanced recovery of Orthodox dogmatic values through a revival in the field of biblical studies. Happily, the situation is beginning to change, but serious problems remain over the rightful appropriation of modern exegetical methods. The most valu-able dialogue partner for the Orthodox to pursue in evaluating the strengths and weaknesses of higher criticism appears to be the work of evanglical biblical scholars (such as Ralph P. Martin, F. F. Bruce, Murray Harris, Donald Hagner, Craig Evans, Walter Liefeld, Grant Osborne, Gordon Fee, I. Howard Marshall, Moíses Silva, Craig Blomberg, Bruce Waltke, John Sailhamer, and others).

medium of historical theology, it is hoped that this book will contribute in some small way to a recovery of that biblical priority. Specifically, the categories of "History" and "Theology" provide perspectives on the origin, development, and spread of aspects of biblical doctrine from apostolic times to the present. The articles under "Spirituality and Liturgy" are concerned with the outworking of individual and corporate communion with God, i.e., with mystical theology and with the moral and liturgical life that grows out of the Scriptural teachings. The section on "Scripture and Exegesis" enables us to see what the biblical text is and how other interpreters in the past have exegeted it. Their conclusions provide a valuable commentary on the biblical text that can serve as a type of grid for checking and challenging our own exegetical methods and conclusions. All of this implies the need to recognize that history, theology, and exegesis are distinct but complementary approaches to Christian truth; yet any rigid separation of them results in a failure to keep text and community together (which is precisely what has occurred in our post-Enlightenment era). We find ourselves encouraged to adopt a methodology that gives biblical theology top priority in the formulation of the faith, but one that is carried out within the context of a community of believers, within what Meyendorff called the "living tradition" of the church.

Finally, some reflections on Father John himself. The pieces by Henry Chadwick, Jaroslav Pelikan, and especially Lewis Shaw outline his life and work and are fitting tributes to his accomplishments. The episcopal commentaries on Father John also eloquently testify to the scope of his influence on world Orthodoxy. The bishops' warm appreciation for his dedicated service will go far to reinforce his permanent memory in the life of the church. To each bishop I offer my sincere thanks for your contributions to this volume. I should note that every effort was made to invite His Holiness Alexis II, Patriarch of Moscow, to share his personal thoughts. The administrative complications of the Moscow patriarchate, however, prevented success. For that we are all disappointed, but knowing Father John's close relationship with the patriarch and members of his cabinet, I can say with all confidence that His Holiness would have given his blessing on Father John's work had he been aware of the opportunity of doing so.

As Father John's student and friend for ten years, I had the privilege of closely observing his behavior in a number of educational and ecclesial contexts. The first time I met him was at St. Vladimir's Orthodox Seminary, then later he became my doctoral mentor at Fordham University, where I

was one of his last students. I took practically every class he offered to learn
as much as I could from his expansive knowledge of the Orthodox tradition.
My last conversation with him was over the crackling telephones in Moscow
as he set up an appointment for me with the patriarch's office. I was trying
to build a bridge between the Orthodox and Protestant evangelical communities through the establishment of a Russian chapter of the "Society
for the Study of Eastern Orthodoxy and Evangelicalism."[4] Little did I know
that that would be our last conversation. After returning to America I
received a follow-up letter from him two weeks before he passed away.
Then, suddenly, he was gone. His death was soon announced in all the
churches. I shall never forget the feeling I had when I heard the news. It
was as though a mighty oak tree had quietly fallen to the ground. Pondering
the loss of his presence, I felt a keen sense of indebtedness to all that he
had done for me and so many others. It was then that the idea for this book
was born. A small way to honor his memory was to organize a project that
would carry on his lifelong concerns.

It is my sincere hope that the Orthodox community throughout the
world will recognize him for what he truly was — a contemporary church
Father. Along with the late Georges Florovsky and Alexander Schmemann,
John Meyendorff forms a trilogy of what can possibly be termed the "American Fathers," an epitaph reminiscent of the three great Cappadocian
Fathers of the fourth century. Father John bequeathed to future generations
the historical facts and interpretive insights needed to guide us through the
rich complexities of the Christian East. But more than a man of uncommon
brilliance, he was also a man of uncommon humility. He reminds us that
the ultimate purpose of historical theology is not the acquisition of knowledge. Foundational as knowledge is, the goal of historical inquiry is to move
us beyond the mere intellect to a personal encounter with the living God.

---

4. An academic organization of Orthodox and evangelical scholars and church
leaders that gathers annually at the Billy Graham Center at Wheaton College, Wheaton,
Illinois. Through its meetings and published papers, it seeks to make the theological
histories of the two traditions known and understood in relation to each other.

Acknowledgments

I would like to express very warmest appreciation to my wife, Barbara. Her constant love, prayers, and support have been a divine source of sustaining grace. Her unfailing confidence in my work has been a tremendous encouragement through the challenges of this project and those now underway (Psalm 34:3).

In addition to honoring John Meyendorff, this memorial volume is also for his wife Marie and their children. Gratitude is due to Paul Meyendorff for providng valuable feedback and bibliographic information. Their loss has been deeply felt, yet comforted in anticipation of "the resurrection of the dead and the life of the age to come" (Nicene Creed).

Permission has been graciously granted by John Breck, Elaina Silk, and the editorial staff of St. Vladimir's Theological Quarterly to use a draft of a complete bibliography of John Meyendorff that they will publish in the coming months and the article by Alexander Golitzin in SVTQ (vol. 38:2, 1994). The Christian Century gave permission to reprint the memorial piece by Jaroslav Pelikan that appeared in their September 22-30, 1992 issue, as did the Anglican Theological Review to reproduce an earlier form of my article on Antiochene exegesis (vol. 70:4, 1993).

Contributors

HENRY CHADWICK Honorary Student of Christ Church, Oxford University; formerly Master of Peterhouse, Cambridge University

AVERY DULLES, S.J. Laurence J. McGinley Professor of Religion and Society, Fordham University

GERARD H. ETTLINGER, S.J. Professor and Chairperson of the Department of Theology and Religious Studies, St. John's University, Jamaica, New York

KARLFRIED FROEHLICH Benjamin B. Warfield Professor of Ecclesiastical History, Emeritus, Princeton Theological Seminary

ALEXANDER GOLITZEN (HIEROMONK) Assistant Professor of Theology, Marquette University, Milwaukee, Wisconsin

VESELIN KESICH Professor of New Testament, Emeritus, St. Viadimir's Orthodox Seminary

BERNARD McGINN Naomi Shenstone Donnelley Professor of Historical Theology, Divinity School, University of Chicago

BRADLEY NASSIF Professor of Orthodox Theology and New Testament,

Antiochian House of Studies, Ligonier, Pennsylvania; Visiting Professor of Eastern Orthodoxy at Trinity Evangelical Divinity School, Deerfield, Illinois; president of the Society for the Study of Eastern Orthodoxy and Evangelicalism

RICHARD A. NORRIS, JR. Professor of Church History, Union Theological Seminary, New York

JAROSLAV PELIKAN Sterling Professor of History, Yale University

HAROLD P. SCANLIN Translation Advisor, United Bible Societies, New York

LEWIS SHAW Specialist on Russian Orthodoxy, Ph.D. Cambridge University

ROBERT TAFT Ordinary Professor of Oriental Liturgy, Pontifical Oriental Institute, Rome

JEAN TILLARD, O.P. Professor of Theology, Dominican College of Theology and Philosophy, Ottawa, Canada

DEMETRIOS TRAKATELLIS Metropolitan of Vresthena; Distinguished Professor of Biblical Studies and Christian Origins, Hellenic College, Holy Cross Greek Orthodox School of Theology, Brookline, Massachusetts

GEOFFREY WAINWRIGHT Robert Earl Cushman Professor of Christian Theology, Divinity School, Duke University

TIMOTHY P. WEBER David T. Porter Professor of Church History, Southern Baptist Seminary, Louisville, Kentucky

ROBERT WILKIN William R. Kenan, Jr. Professor of the History of Christianity, University of Virginia

JOHN MEYENDORFF

Pastoral Reflections

In the footsteps of the Greek Fathers of the Church, the late Rev. Dr. John Meyendorff of blessed memory dedicated his life to scholarship and knowledge for the purpose of enlightening Orthodox faithful. He reintroduced many faithful, particularly in the Diaspora, to the fundamental tenets of their faith, but more importantly he made them aware of their history, be it Byzantine, Russian, or otherwise. Through his consummate scholarship he presented fresh and sound Orthodox interpretation, often squarely laying to rest myths and misconceptions. Through his priesthood he added the dimension of loving pastor and devoted teacher. Through his personal zeal and vision he inspired the lives of many who thirsted for a deeper understanding and instilled in them a rekindling of their Orthodox faith. Through his prolific works, a great many, once strangers to Orthodoxy, came to know and embrace the holy Orthodox Church.

We offer thanks to God Almighty for giving us John Meyendorff. He was a devoted son of the Church, a sterling churchman. He was highly esteemed by this venerable Ecumenical Throne, about which he lectured and authored countless pages. He recognized, wrote, and taught about the Primacy of Honor of the Ecumenical Patriarchate and its right to take initiative and to play the role of coordinator among all Orthodox as seen within the catholicity and ecumenicity of Orthodoxy. His thinking, inherited from his mentor, the late Very Rev. Fr. Georges Florovsky, was solidly founded in the Ecumenical Councils, sacred canons, history, praxis, and Tradition of the Church. Furthermore, he displayed an unmistakeable and

3

devout respect for and attachment to the Holy Great Church of Christ and the Queen of Cities. We offer these few words in solemn tribute to him without hesitation or hyperbole, and we pray that his blessed memory be eternal.

The Ecumenical Patriarch of
Constantinople
BARTHOLOMEW I

I was privileged to have known John Meyendorff as both my teacher and a close personal friend. He was deeply devoted to the service of the academy and the Church. As a scholar, the scope of his work was expansive. Few have equaled his ability to move across the vast landscape of Byzantine and Russian religious history, yet engage in a technical discussion of the fine points of Greek and Latin texts. Scholars at the dawn of the third millennium and beyond simply cannot study the Orthodox Church without relying on John Meyendorff as a safe guide through the rich complexities of the Christian East.

The See of Antioch humbly offers its thanks to Almighty God for giving us Fr. John as a churchman. For many years we enjoyed the fruit of his labors, which can be seen today in the lives of hundreds of students he prepared for academic or pastoral ministries. In his interpretation of the Orthodox faith he was always a "moderate" — true to Holy Tradition and therefore avoiding the extremes of theological relativism and triumphalism. He was never content to stop at the theoretical level of truth but earnestly strived for its practical application to the contemporary needs and challenges of the Church. In all of his endeavors, his driving concern was for the glory of the lifegiving Trinity and the spiritual growth and unity of the "one, holy, catholic and apostolic Church." May that goal be further advanced in this book dedicated to John Meyendorff, whose memory is blessed forever.

His Beatitude, IGNATIUS IV
Patriarch of Antioch and All the East
Damascus, Syria

Father John Meyendorff's life and work revealed him as a man of the Church. For him, theology and the pastoral ministry and practical witness of the Orthodox Church were essential dimensions of the one life of faith. He understood — and taught — that the authentic vision of the Orthodox Church is that both the human intellect and the human heart are fully alive in Christ, in Christ's truth and Christ's love, and that the light of Christ illumines all. The word *integrity* most fully conveys the quality of Father John's priestly and academic ministries. As his brother in the priesthood and then as his bishop and coworker in St. Vladimir's Seminary, I am grateful for Father John's life and work, and I experience his death as a personal loss.

> Metropolitan THEODOSIUS
> President, St. Vladimir's Orthodox
> Theological Seminary
> Primate, Orthodox Church in America

Protopresbyter John Meyendorff was truly a unique person. He was a theologian, historian, patristics expert, and great scholar. His many books on all aspects of church life and order will live long after many of his contemporaries have departed this life. As Dean of St. Vladimir's Seminary he showed much pastoral concern for his students. The history of Orthodoxy in North America cannot be written properly without such luminaries as Father John, of blessed memory, gracing that history.

> Metropolitan PHILIP
> Primate, Antiochian Orthodox
> Christian Archdiocese of North America

Fr. John Meyendorff will go down in the annals of Orthodoxy in America as one of the great theologians of our time, following in the footsteps of Frs. Florovsky and Schmemann. Not only do his literary contributions remain the standard for future generations, but his tenure as Dean of St. Vladimir's Theological Seminary and his leadership in the various Orthodox dialogues with various denominations will also leave its mark on American Orthodoxy. He always adhered to the traditions of the one Holy

Catholic and Apostolic Church, whether he was writing about the history of the Church, her theology, or her ecclesiology.

May his memory be eternal!

Archbishop IAKOVOS
Primate of the Greek Orthodox Church
of North and South America

In the life of each one of us, there have been a few books — perhaps very few indeed — which have made a permanent difference to our lives, opening our eyes to a new world and transforming our inner vision. Two such books in my life were Fr. John's early works, *St Grégoire Palamas et la mystique orthodoxe* and *Introduction à l'étude de Grégoire Palamas* (both later translated into English), which I read at Oxford in the winter of 1960-61. They came to me as a revelation. For the first time I began to appreciate the rich complexity, the underlying unity, and the unbroken continuity of the Orthodox spiritual tradition — from St. Gregory of Nyssa, Evagrius, and the Desert Fathers, through St. Dionysius the Areopagite and St. Maximos the Confessor, to its fulfillment in St. Gregory Palamas and the fourteenth-century Hesychasts. Ever since then the mystery of Christ's Transfiguration and the extension of that mystery in the lives of the saints have remained central to my own theological reflection. Alike in these two books and in his later writings, Fr. John spoke to us not only as a scholarly specialist, rigorous in his academic standards, but as a persuasive and inspiring interpreter of Orthodox history and spirituality. His own personal faith, while never obtrusive, was plainly manifest in what he wrote.

Bishop KALLISTOS (Timothy) Ware
Bishop of Diokleia
Oxford University

In Memory of John Meyendorff

JAROSLAV PELIKAN

Protopresbyter John Meyendorff, whose earthly life ended on July 22, 1992, at the age of 66, came from a family with a tradition of public service in Czarist Russia. He was born at Neuilly-sur-Seine in France, was graduated in 1949 from the Orthodox Theological Seminary Saint Sergius in Paris (the "Russkaya") and in 1958 from the Sorbonne, taught and lectured chiefly in the U.S., and died in Canada. That international odyssey is matched by the international significance of the man and his work as scholar and churchman.

As a scholar, Meyendorff made a major contribution to this century's renewal of understanding of the history of Byzantine culture and of the Byzantine Church. His critical edition and French translation of the *Triads of Gregory Palamas* (published at Louvain in 1959), which was originally his dissertation at the Sorbonne, together with his monograph on Gregory of that same year, opened up to Western scholars for the first time the spirituality and speculation of this frequently misunderstood and maligned fourteenth-century monastic and "Hesychast" thinker. A volume titled *Christ in Eastern Christian Thought* (1969), which I am proud to have proposed as an editor for Corpus Books, found in the person of the God-man the leitmotiv that makes sense of Eastern theological metaphysics, church councils, iconoclastic debates, and mystical devotion. *Byzantine Theology* (1974) is the road map for any English-speaking inquirer to begin exploring that important but uncharted territory.

When I read the galleys of the last book Meyendorff published before his death, *Imperial Unity and Christian Divisions,* which came out in 1989 from St. Vladimir's Seminary Press, I broke my usual embargo on writing jacket blurbs to say:

> There are very few scholars in the East or West who would be in a position to undertake this assignment. In fact, it would take an Eastern scholar who is in the West to do it right. And that is, of course, what John Meryendorff is. With a firm grasp on the complicated primary sources and a thorough but critical knowledge of the modern scholarly literature, he skillfully takes the reader through the maze of these centuries, and he does so with fairness, objectivity, and sympathy. I cannot imagine any student of church history who would not benefit from this remarkable achievement.

That assessment still stands.

Although he had a term as acting director of Harvard University's Dumbarton Oaks Center for Byzantine Studies in Washington and served for a long time as adjunct professor at Fordham University, it was his assocation with St. Vladimir's Seminary for a third of a century, from 1959 to 1992, that represented his scholarly identity. At a time when many of us felt obliged to choose between the study and the seminary, he managed to combine the two, staying with the seminary and even becoming its dean in 1984 at the death of Alexander Schmemann, who had succeeded Georges Florovsky. He also carried a crushing load of responsibilities in the newly reconstituted Orthodox Church in America, which he served as adviser to the Holy Synod, as editor of the monthly newspaper, and as preacher and lecturer. He worked to heal jurisdictional disputes and schisms and to foster a sense of the Orthodox Church as a cohesive force in American life.

In many respects Meyendorff was the last representative of the émigré Russian Orthodox community, with roots in and a strong hold on Russian culture. At the same time he was the most American of that generation — American and French and Russian and Greek! There will be need for some future historian to give a full-length account of the story of Eastern Orthodoxy in the Western Hemisphere, a story that turned exactly two centuries old on September 24, 1994, the bicentennial of the Kodiak mission. It begins with ethnic groups isolated from one another no less than from the rest of American life, but it has now reached the point at which the reality of the Orthodox experience occupies a place of honor within the total religious community of North and South America. In that story the transitional generation has featured a remarkable group of leaders, including Archbishop Iakovos and the triad of Fathers Florovsky, Schmemann, and Meyendorff. American Orthodoxy — and American Christianity — will never be the same, thanks to their work.

Among my many cherished colleagues and dear friends over the past forty-six years John Meyendorff occupied a unique place. We used to joke about the historical irony that had made someone with a Germanic name like his a member of the Orthodox Church and someone with a Slavic name like mine a member of the Lutheran Church. When a group of my students, under the editorship of Patrick Henry, assembled a volume of essays for my sixtieth birthday, it was natural that Father John should be one of the two from among my colleagues whom they invited to join them (the other being Albert Outler). And so when, on July 17, St. Vladimir's Seminary telephoned that Father John had suddenly and gravely taken ill in Montreal, I immediately called the hospital and spoke with his wife Marie — and, thank God, was able to speak briefly also with him. (Typically, he wanted to know how my book about the Cappadocian Fathers was coming along.) A week later, I lit a candle and joined in the chants for his funeral at St. Vladimir's. Those chants, thanks to what he and his colleagues have done, were now in English, but the *cantus firmus* beneath them was also Greek and Church Slavonic. As the *Liturgy of St. John Chrysostom* petitions, *Christiana ta telē tēs zōēs hēmōn, Christianskija konĕiň života našego:* "For a Christian end of our life, without pain, without shame, and peaceful; and for a good account before the Judgment Seat of Christ: let us pray."

John Meyendorff and the Heritage of the Russian Theological Tradition

LEWIS SHAW

T he thought of the late Protopresbyter John Meyendorff evolved in relation to a complex web of intellectual tendencies emerging in Russia during the twilight of the Romanov dynasty. In order to understand his thinking, therefore, it is necessary to sketch out a brief intellectual genealogy of sorts. It is our hope and intention that this succinct essay will encourage more detailed study.

The thought of the "Paris School" of Russian theology, which had its roots in what Nicholas Zernov called the "Russian Religious Renaissance,"[1] is still virgin land that has only begun to be cleared. Following the twin cataclysms of the October (Bolshevik) Revolution and the Civil War, the Russian "Diaspora" settled first in Serbia, next in Germany, and finally in France, pushed westward by the unstable political and economic conditions in Central Europe after the First World War.[2] The presence in Paris of a

---

1. N. Zernov, *The Russian Religious Renaissance of the Twentieth Century* (London, 1963).

2. Space does not permit a detailed description of the intellectual and theological climate the émigrés found during their journey westward. For such, cf. the excellent discussion in Aidan Nichols, O.P., *Theology in the Russian Diaspora* (Cambridge, 1989), pp. 48-61. It is worth saying that Meyendorff ("Mission, Unity, Diaspora," *Catholicity and the Church* [Crestwood, New York, 1983], pp. 103-10) thought the term "Diaspora" inappropriate to any group of Christians, who are *prima facie*, and by definition, so-journers on earth and pilgrims in time. They look to their home beyond time from the Church, a "colony of heaven on earth." Their "citizenship is in heaven" (Philippians

group of talented theologians and the need to train priests for the Russian Orthodox in the West prompted the founding in 1926 of a theological school, the Orthodox Theological Institute; in 1940 the school became the *Institut Saint Serge.* Its aim was to keep alive the best of the prerevolutionary Russian theological tradition, in the expectation that one day its leaders would be called back to Russia to help re-create the Russian Church from the ashes; émigrés confidently asserted well into the 1920s that the Communist system would collapse of its own internal problems within a few years. The Institute became the outstanding center of Orthodox theology in this century, serving as the locus of the "Paris school," which combined theological originality with respect for tradition.

The "Paris school" attempted to combine two prerevolutionary theological traditions. On the one hand, there was a tradition stemming from the four prerevolutionary academies, those of Moscow, St. Petersburg, Kiev, and Kazan. This stream survived at *Saint Serge* in an emphasis on patristics, liturgics, and church history. On the other hand, there was another tradition stemming from lay circles returning to orthodoxy on the eve of the Revolution. These thinkers were interested in the philosophy of religion and philosophical theology. This element also survived at *Saint Serge* and, led by Sergei Bulgakov, developed as an emphasis on speculative dogmatics.

The principal representatives of the traditionalist current were, *inter alios,* Georges Florovsky, Vladimir Lossky, Nikolai Afanasiev, Alexander Schmemann, Paul Evdokimov, and John Meyendorff. These men sought the *telos* and fulfillment of the Church in what Florovsky called "Christian Hellenism," a commitment to the Greek character and origins of dogmatic language, of the liturgy, and of Orthodox iconography, especially as they evolved in Byzantium. Out of this genius grew these scholars' attempts to present the thought of the Fathers in modern idiom, which Florovsky called the "neo-patristic synthesis."

3:17-21). This does not devalue time and history; to the contrary, it frees humanity from cosmic and temporal determinism by limiting, circumscribing, and defining time and the history occurring within it.

I. The Patristic Revival in Russia[3]

Florovsky[4] held that the work of Philaret (Drozdov), Metropolitan of Moscow, was the crucial factor in the Church's "return to the Fathers." Philaret's career extended from the reign of Alexander I to that of his namesake Alexander II, the "Tsar-Liberator." He had been weaned on the ideas of a Ukrainian prelate and favorite of Peter the Great, Feofan Prokopovich. Peter was drawn to Prokopovich's enthusiastic promotion of Lutheran and Reformed Scholasticism,[5] a Protestantization[6] that provided the Tsar with some theological rationale for his general overhaul of the Russian Church. Clearly aware of the twin influences of Protestantism and Roman Catholicism upon contemporary Russian Orthodoxy, Philaret undertook a return to the very biblical and patristic sources of the Christian faith. There he recovered the ecclesiological themes of the Church as the mystical Body of Christ and the Church as the extension into the present of Pentecost.[7] His weighty *Katikhizis* unites, in its conclusive 1839 edition, these motifs with Peter of Mogila's concept of the Church as a supernatural society.[8] Inspired by the superb Second Sophistic rhetoricians Saints Gregory Nazianzen and John Chrysostom, Philaret viewed preaching as integral to theology, the only aim of which is the constant nurture of the Body of Christ.

In the nineteenth century, for the first time in the history of Russian theology,[9] Church history and the history of dogma were made the

---

3. For parts of this section I am indebted to research I did for my thesis on Georges Florovsky; to research I did in the spring and summer of 1988 for the revision of *Theology in the Russian Diaspora;* and to the insights of my friend and colleague Aidan Nichols, O.P.

4. Cf. Florovsky, "Westliche Einflüsse in der russischen Theologie," *Kyrios* 2 (1937), 15.

5 . Cf. T. Chaistovich, *Feofan Prokopovich i ego vremia* (St. Petersburg, 1868).

6. *Contra* the ideas of the Jesuit-trained Stefan Iavorsky, in whose monument *Kamen' very* one detects the unmistakable Roman Catholic Scholastic influence of Robert Bellarmine.

7. Cf. M. Jugie, "Philarete Drozdov," *Dictionnaire de Theologie Catholique* 12A, columns 1376-96.

8. Cf. C. Golubiev, *K. Mitropolit Petr Mogila i ego spodvizhniki* (Kiev, 1883, 1898); M. Jugie, "Mogila, Pierre," *Dictionnaire de Theologie Catholique,* 10/8, columns 2063-81.

9. For an in-depth treatment of the overall sweep and development of Russian theology, cf. Florovsky, *Puti Russkogo bogosloviia* (Paris, 1937), translated into English as *The Ways of Russian Theology,* 2 volumes (Belmont, Massachusetts, 1979 and 1987),

objects of special scholarly consideration, as in contemporary Germany, France, and England. Among the educated classes generally, Romanticism stoked the fires of a zeal and ardor for anything having to do with antiquity. More specifically, scholars of the theological academies of Russia grew impassioned about the study of early Church history. Originally, they had read Mefody Smirnov's 1805 *Liber Historicus de rebus in primitiva sive trium primorum et quarti ineuntis saeculorum ecclesia christiana,* as well as translations of the seminal scholarship of L. S. Le Nain de Tillemont and J. Bingham. Nevertheless, by the middle of the century they had printed far more primary and secondary source material. Patristic studies, particularly, made great advances through the important investigations of Philaret Gumilevsky, Rector of the Moscow Academy and later Archbishop of Chernigov.[10] He, together with his former teacher I. Korsunsky, founded in 1843 at Moscow a patristic series called *Tverniia sviatikh ottsev.* The premier historian of Russian patristic study, Kiprian Kern, writes:

> The fruits of these labors were truly remarkable. From 1843 on the Moscow Academy will continue to translate texts, and to reedit those already published, right up to the very end of the Tsardom. Some of the Fathers were edited three or four times. Almost all the writings of the great theologians and Fathers of the Church were translated. The entire series comprised more than eighty volumes. The work of editing was interrupted only in 1917, when it had reached Maximos the Confessor and Nikephoros of Constantinople.[11]

The work of Philaret and Korsunsky engendered a flood of corollary study. The whole body of patristic literature was divided up with great

---

hereinafter referred to as *Ways.* The present essay is deeply indebted to the work of Florovsky.

10. Archbishop Philaret's substantial contributions are summarized in his *Istoricheskoe uchenie ob ottsakh Tserkvi* (Chernigov, 1859). For a full treatment of Philaret, cf. S. Smirnov, *Philaretarkhepiskop Chernigovskii* (Tambov, 1859). Prior to the work of Philaret and others, translation and study of the Fathers in Russia had been happenstance at best. Earlier, patristic texts had been translated and collected in catenae and anthologies at monasteries. This nonsystematic practice lived on into the modern period, particularly at Optina Pustyn and at the monastery of St. Panteleimon on Mount Athos.

11. K. Kern, *Les Traductions russes des textes patristiques* (Chevetogne/Paris, 1957), p. 12.

care and meticulousness among the four theological academies. Moscow took the Greek Fathers of the fourth to seventh centuries, excluding Chrysostom, whom St. Petersburg took. Additionally, St. Petersburg assumed responsibility for Eusebius, Socrates, Sozomen, and Evagrius, as well as the Byzantine historians George Akropolites, Gregory of Cyprus, Gregory Pachymeres, John Kinnamos, Niketas Choniates, Nikephoros Bryennios, Nikephoros Gregoras, and Prokopios of Caesarea, liturgical texts both Eastern and Western, and finally, Theodore the Studite. Kazan promised translation of a mélange of the acts of patristic ecumenical and local councils, the Apocrypha, and Origen, Hippolytus, and Gregory the Great. Kiev took on the Latin Fathers, eminently Cyprian, Tertullian, Arnobius, Ambrose, Jerome, and Augustine. Complementarily, the journal *Pravoslavnoe obozrenie* shouldered the Apostolic Fathers, the Apologists, and Irenaeus. Individual Russian Orientalists devoted themselves to Coptic, Syriac, Armenian, Georgian, and Ethiopic texts.

The scholarly output of Archbishop Philaret was prodigious. He and his contemporary Makary (Bulgakov), Metropolitan of Moscow from 1879, not only attempted a history of Russian theology itself, but wrote considerable treatises of systematic theology as well.[12] These expositions relied heavily on the contemporary Roman Catholic school of Tübingen, particularly F. A. Staudenmaier, J. E. Kuhn, and F. A. Trendelenburg.[13]

Makary and Philaret saw the necessity of integrating thorough patristic study into the *curricula* of the Academies, whose students would determine the course of theological education and thinking throughout the empire. However, the hierarchs and their protégés appreciated the intrinsic worth of patristics. Florovsky celebrated the Moscow Academy teaching career of Philaret (Gumilevsky)'s pupil Alexander Gorsky, whose "audience always remembered his unforgettable characterization of Origen."[14] Gor-

12. Cf. Archbishop Philaret (Gumilevsky), *Obzor ruskkoi dukhovnoi literaturi* (Chernigov, 1859), and *Pravoslavnoe dogmaticheskoe bogoslovie* (Chernigov, 1854 and 1865). Cf. Metropolitan Makary (Bulgakov), *Pravoslavnoe dogmaticheskoe bogoslovie* (St. Petersburg, 1849-53), translated into French as *Theologie dogmatique orthodoxe* (Paris, 1859-60). Metropolitan Makary's writings on the Kievan school, the Old Ritualists (*Raskolniki*), and the general history of the Russian Church up until 1667 are described in detail by T. Titov, *Makarii Bulgakov, mitropolit Moskovskii i Komomenskii* (Kiev, 1895 and 1903). Translations of Archbishop Philaret's works are sorely needed.

13. Florovsky showed a particular fondness for these thinkers as well.

14. Florovsky, *Ways,* vol. II, p. 143.

sky's skills were not limited to oral pedagogy; at the behest of Philaret (Drozdov), he teamed with K. I. Nevostruev in writing a six-volume *Description (Opisanie)* of the Slavic manuscripts in the Moscow Synodal Library, an effort requiring many years of research and work. The work still has great value as a history of the Slavic text of Scripture. Gorsky's enthusiasm was catching. He encouraged his colleague Evgeny Golubensky to examine Byzantine texts relating to the rise and early life of Christianity in Russia. Petersburg, on the other hand, generally restricted the study of Church history to Byzantium.

In the wake of this flurry of the study of Christian antiquity, students of patristics probed the canons of the apostolic, sub-apostolic, patristic, and Byzantine periods. Understandably, their scholarly interests were influenced not a little by the canonical situation of the contemporary Russian Church. Seminal theses were thus related to such crucial questions as "the mutability of canon law" and the "canonicity" of the Holy Synod of Russia.[15] What all this intense activity led to was the creation of Russia's own school of historical theology, with its center at the Moscow Academy, a school which produced the likes of Vasily V. Bolotov and Nikolai N. Glubokovsky.[16] The Holy Synod published new educational statutes in 1869 which divided the *curricula* of the Academies into three sections proper: theology *in ipso,* church history (including the history of doctrine), and pastoralia.[17] This categorization encouraged the evolution of genuine patristic scholarship in late Romanov Russia. The 1869 reform demanded that theologians' exposition of doctrine take full cognizance of the history of dogma.

It is this "return to the Fathers" in nineteenth-century Russia that set the stage for the emergence of the "Paris School" of Orthodox thought in post–World War I France, of which John Meyendorff became a later and integral part.

---

15. Ibid., vol. II, p. 150.

16. Florovsky called Glubokovsky "the Russian Tillemont," because of his precise scientific manuscript research and attention to detail.

17. Ibid., pp. 150ff.

II. Khomiakov and Slavophilism

The Slavophiles[18] were deeply influenced by continental Idealist and "Traditionalist" philosophers.[19] Consequently and ironically, they sought the ideal society in a return to what they understood Russia to have been prior to Peter the Great. Their support for Orthodoxy resulted from their belief that traditional Russian culture was coextensive with the Russian Church. The theologian *par excellence* of the Slavophile movement was A. S. Khomiakov.[20]

Khomiakov was much indebted to I. V. Kireevsky's theory of "integral knowledge." Kireevsky himself returned to Orthodoxy after his wife remarked to him that he could find in the Greek Fathers everything he had found in Schelling. He began to frequent the monastery of Optina Pustyn, where he took part in the institution's program of translating the Fathers. Kireevsky wanted to develop a philosophy rooted in patristic teaching. Unfortunately, he died before completing his work, which he saw as a redemptive Russian response to the shortcomings of Scholasticism.

In the realm of theology, his ideas were taken up by Khomiakov. Briefly put, when all the powers of the mind are brought together in "integral reason," faith emerges as an apprehension of spiritual verity. Faith results from the unity of the mind's powers, which are brought together, and held together, by "integral reason." Faith, in this sense, is not held by the individual as such but by the organic community of which he or she is a member. Here begins Khomiakov's ecclesiology.

The Russian Church, according to Khomiakov, combined freedom and unity — two seemingly opposed phenomena. The Church's oneness is attained through *sobornost'*, a term that will always be associated with

---

18. The mass of literature treating Slavophilism is huge. Especially relevant are N. V. Riasonovsky, *Russia and the West in the Teaching of the Slavophiles* (Cambridge, MA, 1952); F. C. Copleston, S.J., *Philosopy in Russia: From Herzen to Lenin and Berdyaev* (Tunbridge Wells, 1986); A. Gratieux, *Khomiakov et le mouvement slavophil* (Paris, 1939); F. C. Suttner, *Offenbarung, Gnade und Kirche bei A. S. Chomjakov* (Wurzburg, 1967); P. P. O'Leary, *The Triune Church: A Study in the Ecclesiology of A. S. Khomiakov* (Dublin, 1982).

19. Especially the Idealists J. G. Fichte and F. W. J. von Schelling; G. W. F. Hegel; and the so-called "Traditionalists," J. de Maistre and L. de Bonald.

20. Among the philosophers of the movement, it is important to mention I. V. Kireevsky; M. P. Pogodin; and Y. F. Samarin.

Khomiakov. Oddly, he did not use the term in his own works. It occurs only in the Russian translation of the theologian's "French Brochures."[21] The word can be given only a proximate rendering in English. Variously construed as "conciliarity" (though it is only secondarily concerned with institutions), "communion" (though it bears no immediate sacramental reference and is, indeed, the *sine qua non* of all the sacraments, comprehending and informing their totality), and "togetherness" (unlike a purely sociological entity, it defies analysis; it can be seen only with the eyes of faith), it has no one English equivalent.[22]

21. N. Berdyaev, in his *A. S. Khomiakov* (Moscow, 1912), has many astute observations of the thinker. The term *sobornost'* itself is based on the text of a late medieval Old Church Slavonic revision of the Nicene Creed. Originally, the Old Church Slavonic text *tvo edinou sviatou kafolitcheskou i apostolikou tserkov; kafolitcheskou* was replaced by *sobornoou* as a Russian reaction to those who wished reunion with Rome during the twilight of Byzantium.

22. Florovsky, in his 1934 essay " 'Sobornost': The Catholicity of the Church," written for E. L. Mascall's *The Church of God* (London, 1934), translates *sobornost'* with the neologism "catholicity." For Florovsky, the Church is the place where our salvation is accomplished; and catholicity is particularly incarnated in the stuff and action of the sacraments, as Christ the Word was incarnate in the flesh. Here we are in the realm of sustained metaphor — characteristic of Florovsky — rather than that of precise definition. As the mystery of the Person of Jesus Christ eludes definition, so does the catholicity of the Church. One may infer from both Florovsky and John Meyendorff that differentiation and division — the processes that lead to definition — disappear, as does the "natural consciousness" within which they (differentiation and division) happen, in the "concrete union of love." Catholicity is no more external to the Church than is authority. It is only from within the Church, the Body of Christ and place of our salvation, that catholicity can be experienced. Florovsky prefers the adjectival, as opposed to the nominal, usage. This is also true of Meyendorff's 1973 essay, "The Catholicity of the Church" (*St. Vladimir's Theological Quarterly* 17½ [1973], pp. 5-18), where he notes that "if the Fathers had developed — as does modern theology — a special branch of theological science called 'ecclesiology,' they would have come to use the term 'catholicity' as an abstraction or a generalization of the adjective 'catholic,' just as they spoke of 'deity' *(theotēs)*, 'humanity' *(anthropotēs)*, etc., when they were defining the hypostatic union. But it is a fact that patristic thought has somehow avoided speaking of the 'marks' of the Church *in abstracto*" (p. 5). If one were to attempt a definition of catholicity from the neo-patristic viewpoint, one might say it is the inner wholeness and integrity of the Church's life (cf. Florovsky, "The Catholicity of the Church" in vol. I of *The Collected Works of Georges Florovsky*, ed. R. Haugh [Belmont, MA, 1978 and 1987], *Bible, Church, Tradition: An Eastern Orthodox View*, p. 40; *The Collected Works* are hereinafter referred to as *CW*, followed by the appropriate volume number).

Sobornost' represents a "fundamental link between truth and mutual love in the Church."[23] By its disposition to the autocracy of the see of Rome, the Roman Catholic Church substituted totalitarianism for *sobornost'*, both in teaching (the "infallibility" of the *magisterium* of the Pope) and in administration (the "universal jurisdiction" of the bishop of Rome). Thus, to Khomiakov, Roman Catholicism had become an "unnatural tyranny," just as Protestantism was an "unprincipled revolt." However, in Orthodoxy the seeker would find

> A unity . . . more authoritative than the despotism of the Vatican, for it is based on the strength of mutual love. There a liberty is to be found more free than the license of Protestantism, for it is regulated by the humility of mutual love. There is the Rock and the Refuge.[24]

The suggestion that only Orthodoxy can marry the qualities of unity (S. Iavorsky) and of freedom (F. Prokopovich) has been called Khomiakov's "fundamental proposition."[25] The harmony of love, freedom, and oneness form the Church's *regula fidei*.

The traditional organization of *obshchinnost'*[26] — Russian peasant society — emerged, according to this lay theologian, from the genius of Orthodoxy.[27] The Church is not a monolith but a union, one in which the unity natural to the Church does not kill, but nurtures the freedom of persons. It is because the Russian Church is a transfigured *obshchina*, or peasant commune, that Khomiakov sees Orthodoxy as both the beginning and the fullness of the Christian Church. But Khomiakov's theology of the

---

23. P. P. O'Leary, *The Triune Church: A Study in the Ecclesiology of A. S. Khomiakov* (Dublin, 1982), p. 89.

24. P. K. Christoff, *An Introduction to Nineteenth Century Slavophilism: A Study in Ideas*, vol. I: *A. S. Xomjakow* (The Hague, 1961), p. 137.

25. M. Gordillo, "Russie (Pensée religieuse)," *Dictionnaire de Theologie Catholique*, columns 360f.

26. Khomiakov's sociological ideal; it translates as "communality." The attraction of Tolstoy and other Fabianist-Russian aristocrats to peasant society as the paradigm of community, is well known. It was this ideal that inspired the foundation of *kibbutzim* and *moshavim* by Jewish pioneers in nineteenth-century Palestine.

27. The political philosophy of the "Knight of Orthodoxy," as he was called (cf. Florovsky, *Ways*, vol. II, p. 38), owes not a little to Schelling — cf. W. Setschkareff, *Schellings Einfluss in der russischen Theologie der zwanziger und dreissiger Jahre des neunzehnten Jahrhunderts* (Leipzig, 1939).

Church set his political philosophy on a firm dogmatic basis — the Holy Trinity, which had given birth to the Church in the first place.

The Church was born on Pentecost, when the Spirit acted in history so that the Church became the extension of Christ Himself — *Christus Praesens* — in time. As at one time Christ was exterior Truth, now he gives himself "interiorly." Christ is the bond uniting his disciples in mutual affection. Entrée to revealed truth depends on perseverance in this mutual love. Khomiakov does not emphasize the historical role of Christ as compared to his mystical presence within his Spirit-filled Body, the Church. Khomiakov observes and reiterates that the Church's invisible grace becomes visible in the sacraments — especially the Divine Liturgy, the origin and the home of all theology.[28] Interestingly, in Khomiakov's thinking the hierarchy is not essential to the Church's mission — and here one detects the guiding hand of the Romantic and pietistic individualism of Germany. Love-held-in-common, "the depository and the guardian of faith,"[29] is the Church's guarantor of truth — not the Bible, not a single bishop acting in the name of the whole Church, nor a council.

Throughout the remainder of the Romanov years, Khomiakov's ecclesiology drew considerable fire from official Orthodox groups. He was not given permission to print his work until 1879; even then, a colophon was added, stating that the theologian's writing harbored errors due to the fact that he had no "formal theological training." Thus, he did not use "the positive sources of Scripture and Tradition" in his exposition, nor did he assign the visible structures of the Church their rightful and necessary roles. Nevertheless, after the 1917 Revolution, almost all theologians of the Russian "Diaspora" accepted varying versions of Khomiakov's ecclesiology, which would comprise: (1) the whole People of God — including both clergy and laity — as the home of the Church's authority, which cannot be subsumed by the bishops-in-council; (2) the use of the term *sobornost'*; and (3) the disappearance of division and the enhancement of freedom in the concrete union of love. John Meyendorff inherited the "Diaspora's" acceptance of these guiding principles and themes.

28. Cf. J. S. Romanides, "Orthodox Ecclesiology according to Alexis Khomiakov," *The Greek Orthodox Theological Review* 2 (1956), p. 67.

29. Khomiakov, *L'Église latine et le protestantisme au point de vue de l'Église d'Orient* (Lausanne, 1872), p. 381.

III. The Russian Religious Renaissance at the End of the Nineteenth Century: The "Revival" of Contemplative Prayer

V. S. Soloviev was a significant thinker for all the Paris Russians, especially for Bulgakov and his disciples. Meyendorff would have been keenly aware of Soloviev's ideas from a young age. His thought, with its Russianization of German Idealism, was a mélange of concepts and philosophies, including Kabbala, Emmanuel Swedenborg, Freemasonry, and Franz von Baader in which Sophia, the mysterious personification of Eternal Womanhood, and gnostic and theosophical themes predominate.[30] Perhaps the thematic importance of Soloviev was that both the Sophiologists — those for whom the imagery and thought of Soloviev were foundational — and the "neo-patrologues" inferred from his program the need for the development of a comprehensive grammar of discourse/*apologia* for Christianity in the face of modernity, an integral part of which was a religious articulation of history. But Solovievan speculation was so repugnant to Florovsky, Lossky, Afanasiev, Schmemann, Meyendorff, et al. that they felt an urgency to get their own ideas into print as an antidote to that which they regarded as poisonous and seductive. In a sense, the "neo-patristic synthesis" (for so it was called by Florovsky, who watched the "neo-Thomism" of Jacques Maritain develop concurrently in *entre guerre* France) can be read as a "confessionalist" response to Solovievan Sophiology.[31] It is well worth quoting, as a general indicator of opinion among the "neo-patrologues," the judgment of Florovsky on Soloviev:

> [Vladimir] Soloviev claimed to be not only a philosopher but also a "theurgist." He dreamed of a "religious act," and a religious act through art. Soloviev must be judged not only on the basis of his philosophy but also on the merits of his religious life. After all, it is impossible to be a

30. Cf. S. L. Frank, *A Solovyov Anthology* (New York, 1950), p. 13.

31. Another suggested disparity between Parisian Sophiologists — especially Bulgakov — and the "neo-patrologues" concerns their perspectives on the redemptive activity of Christ: Bulgakov's was primarily that of *kenosis* (kenoticism), while that of the "neo-patrologues" was one of *theōsis*. Of course they are not necessarily opposed; but the presuppositions from which they proceed, and the conclusions reached, may differ considerably. Both had considerable antecedents in Russian religious thought. A comparative study showing how, and why, the christologies of these two schools varied would be welcome.

Christian solely by one's worldview. The development of Solovievan themes by [Alexander] Blok and others serves as an immanent critique (and exposure) of his experiment, and calls into question all "religion of romanticism," religious aestheticism, or aesthetic religion. Temptation yields to seduction. Sometimes it does not yield, but is conquered. Some enter the Church not to pray, but to dream. And the religious life of those among the *intelligentsia* who returned to the Church was stricken and poisoned by this temptation.[32]

Of more importance for neo-patristic thought *in se,* from among the Russian religious *intelligentsia,* was the iconographic vision of the brothers E. N. and S. N. Trubetskoy. Focusing on iconography, they brought educated Russians to a new awareness of the country's Byzantine and medieval heritage and showed that love and knowledge should not only be sought from a recovery of the past and the appropriation of European philosophy, but was to be found free for the asking in the Divine Liturgy, *archē* and *telos* of the Church.

Until E. N. Trubetskoy published his *Umozrenie v Kraskakh,*[33] icons per se had not been objects of theological reflection in Russian culture. However, at least as early as St. John Chrysostom, the unbreakable relationship of prayer and grace between Christians and icons was described in written form.[34] Seminally, the Trubetskoys linked the theology of icons and of the liturgy to eschatology.[35] This eschatological emphasis will reappear

---

32. Florovsky, *Ways,* vol. II, p. 251. There is an appreciable literature on Soloviev, of which cf. the following: D. Stremooukhoff, *Vladimir Soloviev and His Messianic Work,* tr. Elizabeth Meyendorff (Belmont, MA, 1980); M. d'Herbigny, *Un Newman russe. Vladimir Soloviev* (Paris, 1911); and E. Munzer, *Solovyev: Prophet of Russian and Western Unity* (London, 1956). The following are English translations of important essays by Soloviev: *War and Christianity from the Russian Point of View* (London, 1915); *The Justification of the Good: An Essay in Moral Philosophy,* tr. Natalie A. Duddington (New York, 1918); *Plato,* tr. R. Gree (London, 1935); *God, Man and the Church: The Spiritual Foundations of Life,* tr. Donald Attwater (London, 1938); *The Meaning of Love,* tr. Jane Marshall (New York, 1947); *Lectures on God-Manhood* (London and Dublin, 1948); *Russia and the Universal Church* (London, 1948); and S. L. Frank, *A Solovyov Anthology* (New York, 1950).

33. *Umozrenie v Kraskakh* was published in Moscow in 1906. It was translated into English as *Icons: Theology in Color* (Crestwood, New York, 1973).

34. Cf. Archbishop Anthony Bloom, *Living Prayer* (London, 1966), p. 68.

35. A study comparing themes central to the Trubetskoys with those of pre–World War I German Expressionism would be welcome.

prominently in the philosophy of Berdyaev and in the theologies of Florovsky, Evdokimov, and Meyendorff, *inter alios*.[36] Florovsky decisively reconfirmed the Byzantine link between the sacraments, ecclesiology, and eschatology; and the eschatological matrix of the liturgy enjoyed brilliant handling by Afanasiev and his student Schmemann.[37]

Umozrenie v Kraskakh reaches a socio-philosophical profundity correlating a theology of icons with eschatology. Trubetskoy's prototypical man is defined by a compassionate, disinterested love, and a christic yearning for the good. He is a subject of the Kingdom of his Beloved, God. He eschews a misanthropic, deadening hedonism that vitiates and enslaves everything to its idol of ultimate self-debasement and decadence. Such pursuit of satiation is the precise opposite of *theōsis*, the magnification of grace in a person's never-ending ascent to the Beloved.[38] Love freely chosen crucifies

---

36. Meyendorff, following the lead of other "neo-patrologues" (with the exception of Evdokimov), does not overtly emphasize eschatology; it functions in his thought as a given or a presupposition. "Eschatology," he writes (in *Byzantine Theology* [New York, 1974], pp. 218f.), "can never really be considered a separate chapter of Christian theology, for it qualifies the character of theology as a whole. This is especially true of Byzantine Christian thought. . . . Not only does it consider man's destiny — and the destiny of all of creation — as *oriented toward an end;* this orientation is the main characteristic of the sacramental doctrines, of its spirituality, and of its attitude toward the 'world.' Furthermore, following Gregory of Nyssa and Maximus the Confessor, it considers the ultimate end itself a *dynamic* state of man and of the whole of creation: the goal of created existence is not, as Origen thought, a static contemplation of divine 'essence,' but a dynamic ascent of love, which never ends, because God's transcendent being is inexhaustible, and which, thus, always contains new things yet to be discovered *(novissima)* through the union of love." Nowhere else is Meyendorff's eschatology summarized more eloquently or concisely.

Indeed, for Meyendorff, "conditional," or "prophetic," eschatology "constitutes the only theologically acceptable basis for the idea of tradition. . . . what we call Holy Tradition is the history of the right choices made by human beings confronted by the prophetic word of God, responding correctly in the concrete historical circumstances of their time. They are those whom we call saints. Accepting tradition actually means to live in the communion of saints, who lived in the past but have also prepared the future. . . . the idea of tradition is therefore inseparable from eschatology — the 'conditional' eschatology revealed to us in scripture" ("Does Christian Tradition Have a Future?" in *Catholicity and the Church* [Crestwood, New York, 1983], pp. 88f.).

37. A study of the use of the term "eschatology" in modern Orthodox theology would be welcome.

38. Cf. Meyendorff's use of Gregory of Nyssa's *In Cant. or. VI* in *Byzantine Theology*, p. 12.

narcissism in the ordeal and struggle of *podvig*, or *askēsis*, the quest for which sharpens the image of the God of our being into the likeness of God in Christ, a way into the new creation ever renewed by sacramental life. In the neo-patristic view, the sacramental and the eschatological are complementary. The Church is a sacramental society of kingly pilgrims both recalling and anticipating ultimate eschatological action, a Body growing into a new creation.[39]

Indeed, several determinative anthropological and sacramental motifs find their sum and nexus in E. N. Trubetskoy's mystical ecclesiology: the Church is God's teleological vision and command, and as God eternally contemplated the image of the world, so with good enjoyment does He intend the transformation of image into the likeness of new life in grace in His Church. The Church unites all believers, through catholicity and grace, in itself. In this mystery of sacramental catholicity, the Church expresses her prescience and anticipation of the mystical conquest of time and the transfiguration of history.

All of these men, and the schools of thought they represented, were part of something much larger: the Orthodoxy of Russia. It was genuinely the Church of the people, a predominantly peasant Church with the sacraments at its center, buoyed by a revived monasticism. It was this revitalized monasticism, a renewal of interest in contemplative prayer, and a reawakening to the Eucharist as the stuff of the Church's life in Christ that recapitulated and enfleshed everything said above, forming the backdrop of the "neo-patrologues'" all-consuming interest in *theōsis*, or deification.

According to Florovsky,[40] this revival may be said to have commenced when, in the late eighteenth century, the Metropolitan of St. Petersburg, Gavriil Petrov, asked the renowned *staretz* Paissy Velichkovsky for a Slavonic version of the Greek spiritual classic, the *Philokalia*. The *Philokalia*, compiled by Macarius of Corinth and the champion of frequent Eucharistic reception, Nicodemus the Hagiorite, both monks of Mount Athos, was a long anthology of primarily Byzantine and Palestinian monastic spiritual counsels. Paissy's Slavonic version was known as the *Dobrotoliubie*. Its in-

---

39. According to an essay of Father Paul Lazor of St. Vladimir's Seminary, the theme of anticipation was a favorite of Meyendorff's; P. Lazor, *Father John Meyendorff — Our Teacher* (Crestwood, New York, 1992), p. 2.

40. Florovsky, *Ways*, vol. I, pp. 156f.

fluence in nineteenth-century Russia, in tandem with British and continental pietistic writings, can scarcely be overestimated.[41]

These three theological strains took root and melded in the life of the extraordinary Bishop of Voronezh, Tikhon Zadonsky. His most famous work, *On True Christianity*, owes its title to a book of the same name authored by the German Lutheran pietist Johann Arndt, whose writings Tikhon "particularly enjoyed reading and re-reading."[42] Another of Tikhon's books, *A Spiritual Treasury Gathered from the World*, is very similar in content to a Latin pamphlet written by Joseph Hall, Anglican Bishop of Norwich, during the reign of Charles I.[43] It was St. Tikhon who fired Dostoyevsky to create "Father Zosima" in his novel *The Brothers Karamazov*.[44] Dostoyevsky, as well as Soloviev and L. Tolstoy — not to mention others prominently associated with the Slavophile movement — had resort to Optina Pustyn, the center of the monastic revival.[45]

The books and writings of the *Dobrotoliubie*, in which *podvig*,[46] or self-denial, as the texture of ascetic holiness, became more available to the reading public as the nineteenth century wore on. This was due largely to Bishop Theophan (Govorov) the Recluse[47] of Vladimir, whose Russian

---

41. The reigns of Catherine the Great (1762-96), Paul I (1796-1801), and Alexander I (1801-25), saw a great influx of pietism, especially in academic and learned aristocratic circles, whose thinking impregnated many levels of Russian life.

42. Florovsky, *Ways*, vol. I, p. 157. Arndt's mystical writings were immensely popular in German-speaking lands. His *Vier Bücher vom wahren Christentum* (1606) was quickly translated into almost all European languages and influenced many Protestants and Roman Catholics, as well as St. Tikhon.

43. Florovsky, *Ways*, vol. I, p. 344.

44. Cf. N. Gorodetzky, *St. Tikhon Zadonsky: Inspirer of Dostoevsky* (London, 1951). It is also likely that Dostoyevsky had in mind *Staretz* Amvrosi (Gremkov, 1812-91) of Optina when he created "Zosima." The monk-philosopher of aristocracy, Konstantin Leontiev, advised Dostoyevsky to visit Amvrosi after Leontiev and his wife Anna Nikolaevna had lost their second child in 1878.

45. Cf. Florovsky, *Ways*, vol. II, p. 164. Soloviev and Dostoyevsky were close friends.

46. The term can bear a variety of meanings in Russian. It had currency among nineteenth-century Russian authors, especially Tolstoy, who found it useful in constructing his demanding moral ethos.

47. Interestingly, Theophan found distasteful others labeling him a *zatvornik* (recluse) or referring to his "seclusion." He writes: "They have made my cloister into a place of seclusion. There is nothing of the solitary hermit about it. I have locked myself away so that I would not be bothered — not with a view to the strictest ascetism, but

(not Slavonic) version of the *Dobrotoliubie* incorporated materials not used by the original Mount Athos compilers of the anthology. Conveniently, Bishop Theophan's text was laid out in the form of a daily manual. The type of spirituality represented by the *Dobrotoliubie* attracted not only intellectuals and writers, but many of the peasantry as well — as evidenced by the publication in 1870 of the renowned *The Way of a Pilgrim*.[48] Like *The Way* were the writings of the famed Bishop Ignaty (Brianchaninov).[49]

This revival in Russia of the Byzantine hesychast tradition, of which both Ignaty and Theophan were integral parts, took strong root in the life and work of a gifted priest whose parish was the naval yards of Kronstadt, Father Ioann Sergiev (1829-1908). He is widely known in the West as Father John of Kronstadt. He was "a genuine and typical continuer of patristic tradition in asceticism and theology."[50]

IV. John Meyendorff: A Brief Précis of His Life and Thought

One of the principal problems of Christian life and thought in the twentieth century has been, and will continue to be in the next century, that of tradition and its corollary, authority. Among Christians everywhere the need for adaptation and self-examination is obvious. Meyendorff points out the problem in his early book, *The Orthodox Church: Its Past and Its Role in the World Today:*

---

in order to ceaselessly concern myself with books" (Florovsky, *Ways*, vol. II, p. 169). Bishop Theophan had a special fondness for English commentaries.

48. Originally published at Kazan as *Otrovennye rasskazy strannika dukhovnomu svoemu otsu.* The English translation was published at London in 1954.

49. Ignaty was originally a monk of Optina Pustyn, and he became head of the Sergiev hermitage near St. Petersburg. Bishop Ignaty was stringently ascetic — one might even say hyper-ascetic — and was inexorably opposed to what Florovsky called the "dreamy" tendency in Russian spirituality. At Optina he was a disciple of *Staretz* Leonid (Nagoulkin, 1768-1841). He engaged in a famous debate with Theophan the Recluse on the nature of spirits and angels. Among his many writings, *Ascetical Experiences* and a remarkable sermon, "On Death," deserve special attention.

50. Florovsky, *Ways*, vol. II, p. 169. Used of Theophan the Recluse, it applies equally to John of Kronstadt.

The Orthodox theologian . . . is under a strict obligation to distinguish carefully in this heritage between that which forms part of the Church's Holy Tradition, unalterable and universally binding, received from the past, and that which is a mere relic of former times, venerable no doubt in many respects but sometimes also sadly out of date and even harmful to the mission of the Church. All modernism of the wrong kind is of course to be condemned, as exemplified recently by the Renovated Church in Russia, but also all narrow conservatism like that of the Russian Old Believers, which tends to canonize the past as such.[51]

Christians could find themselves in a cult of the contemporary, in a concern for the future that would be as lifeless as antiquarianism — lifeless because both antiquarianism and the worship of the future are unable to establish a dynamic relationship to the Church that the Apostles left behind. How can a faith whose identifying antecedents lie in the past live in the present, and open itself to the future? How are we to distinguish between "tradition" and "Tradition," the momentary and the timeless? John Meyendorff, as an heir to the complex flowering of nineteenth and twentieth-century Russian religious thought in the face of modernity, pursued an answer to these questions as his life's vocation and work.

It is no exaggeration to say that Meyendorff was one of this century's leading Orthodox theologians. He was born of Russian émigré parents in Neuilly-sur-Seine, France, on February 17, 1926. At the time of his death in 1992 he was widely known the whole world over for the depth, clarity, and exactness of his scholarship and of his theology. He lived most of his adult life in the United States, where he had been invited in 1959 to join the faculty of St. Vladimir's Orthodox Theological Seminary as Professor of Patristics and Church History. His reputation grew steadily throughout his life.

His works *Byzantine Theology* (1971) and *Christ in Eastern Christian Thought* (1969) are recognized as classical treatments of their subjects. They are works of profound and precise erudition. Meyendorff published other important books: *A Study of Gregory Palamas* (1959), *L'Église orthodoxe: hier et aujourd'hui (1960), Marriage: An Orthodox Perspective* (1975), *Byzantium and the Rise of Russia* (1980), and *Imperial Unity and Christian Divisions: The Church 450-680 A.D.* (1989). Other essays and articles col-

---

51. *The Orthodox Church: Its Past and Its Role in the World Today,* tr. John Chapin (New York, 1962), p. 162. Originally published as *L'Église orthodoxe: hier et aujourd'hui* (Paris, 1960).

lected and published as books include *Orthodoxy and Catholicity* (1966), *Living Tradition* (1978), *The Byzantine Legacy in the Orthodox Church* (1981), *Catholicity and the Church (1983), Witness to the World* (1987), and *Vision of Unity* (1987). He wrote in English, French, and his ancestral Russian. His works appear in at least twelve languages.

Meyendorff's productivity as a scholar and a theologian was prodigious and rigorous. In intellectual matters he was satisfied with nothing but the best. His long years of work in the histories of Byzantium and of Russia had initiated him in the strictest disciplines of scientific research. He despised any suggestion or hint that the Orthodox theological tradition was nebulous or vague. He brought to its exposition vitality, devotion, and clarity. If, as he always declared, the work of the theologian takes him into the domain of the suprarational, this never meant for him that reason and clarity could be abandoned. To the contrary, the way to the "vision glorious" — that knowledge which lies beyond the rational (the "meta-conceptual," as it were) — unfolds through the exactness and humility with which the theologian is prepared to employ the conceptual. The Holy Spirit does not do away with our cognitive powers or swallow them up in his activity. Instead, the Spirit exalts both the powers of "reason" and of "intuition."

Nevertheless, Meyendorff's concerns for precision, for detail, and for reason were not those of a pedant. He was, first and foremost to everyone who knew him, a teacher. For him, theology and life were inexorably interwoven. He was "an avid student of current affairs," who had "substantial knowledge and often profound insight into world leaders and political events."

> He took great satisfaction in the fact that he was in Moscow, celebrating the Liturgy on the feast of the Transfiguration (August 19, Old Style, 1991) in the Kremlin Church of the Dormition, when the coup which eventually led to the collapse of communism in Russia began. He loved to discuss international and particularly Russian and Eastern European political happenings, and in his comments and interpretations about them he was, once more, a teacher.[52]

Any suggestion that theology could be a subject that one could practice as a profession, teach in one's work days, and then lay aside, would have struck him as preposterous. Similarly, any idea that religion could be

---

52. Paul Lazor, "Father John Meyendorff — Our Teacher," Letter from St. Vladimir's Orthodox Theological Seminary, October, 1992, p. 2.

simply a compartment of one's life would have been equally unthinkable to him. His faith, theology, and life formed a whole, a unity that was grounded in a marvelous knowledge and love of the Tradition and customs of the Church and that at the same time was open to every genuinely human experience. He might have buried himself in historical and doctrinal scholarship, secluded from the demands of the twentieth century. The son of exiles, he grew up in a France that, during his adolescence, knew defeat and the agonies of the Nazi Occupation.

Meyendorff's thought developed as a continuation of the "neo-patrologues'" opposition to the school of Sophiology, so prominent during the late Imperial era. A whole line of thinkers had tried to work out a clearly *Russian* Orthodoxy, to a certain extent founded on their borrowings from continental Idealism and Traditionalism. This seemed to the "neo-patrologues" to involve a betrayal of the patristic tradition that gave a distinctive and universal grammar of philosophical-theological discourse to orthodoxy. From the neo-patristic viewpoint, to be Orthodox meant faithfulness to the witness of the Greek patristic tradition. Meyendorff writes:

> On the one hand, [the Church] is committed to the truth which the Fathers preserved in their struggles, and there is no way in which that truth can be known and understood except by entering the "mind" of the Fathers, becoming their contemporaries in spirit and, therefore, allowing oneself to become as Greek as they were. Our theology today must maintain *consistency* with their positions: all Orthodox theologians must therefore become "Greek" in that sense.[53]

It is, therefore, of the essence for the theologian to discover what the Greek patristic witness is.

To be a theologian, then, is not to speculate about God as a philosopher might do. However, both the Sophiologists and the "neo-patrologues" speculated; the difference lay in the nature of their speculations. The "neo-patrologues" primarily conjectured about the shape of history, while the Sophiologists were occupied with the nature of God and of the Trinity. If the Sophiologists can be said to have sought the unitive principle underlying knowledge, the "neo-patrologues" can be said to have searched for the underlying principle of history — a "historiosophy," as it were. To be a

---

53. Meyendorff, "Greek Philosophy and Christian Universality," in *Catholicity and the Church* (Crestwood, New York, 1983), p. 47 (emphasis original).

theologian was to come to know God for oneself, insofar as it is given to humankind to know God. It is to come to meet God where God reveals himself, in the fullness of the Church's Tradition.

Meyendorff's theology was thoroughly grounded in history, full of the words and thoughts of the Bible[54] and of the Church Fathers from the Apostles through the Cappadocians, to Maximus the Confessor, John of Damascus, and Gregory Palamas. This "Traditional" theology was, however, at the same time living in the present, appropriated, real, the result of a decisive commitment in the present, which was a commitment of life:

> In fact, dead traditionalism cannot be truly traditional. It is an essential characteristic of patristic theology that it was able to face the challenges of its own time while remaining consistent with the original apostolic Orthodox faith. . . . thus for us to be "traditional" implies an imitation of the Fathers in their creative work of discernment. Like them we must be dedicated to the task of saving human beings from error, and not just maintaining abstract propositional truths. We must imitate their constant effort to understand their contemporaries and to use words and concepts which could truly reach the minds of the listeners. True tradition is always a *living* tradition. It changes while always remaining the same. It changes because it faces different situations, not because its essential content is modified. This content is not an abstract proposition; it is the Living Christ Himself, who said, "I am the Truth."[55]

> The central theme, or intuition, of Byzantine theology is that man's nature is not a static, "closed," autonomous entity, but a dynamic reality, determined in its very existence by its relationship to God. This relationship is seen as a process of ascent and communion — man created in the image of God, is called to achieve freely a "divine similitude"; his

---

54. EDITOR'S NOTE: By his own admission, Meyendorff was not a Scripture scholar, though he had taken several years of Hebrew and New Testament Greek. In class lectures and writing he seldom grappled with exegetical problems, partly because his Hebrew had become rusty and also because he had only a secondhand knowledge of the exegetical problems posed by contemporary New Testament scholarship. Most often in class he preferred to emphasize patristic views of ecclesiology, sacramental theology, and the role of the episcopate. Yet even when dealing with the Church Fathers he minimized their exegesis and textual criticism of the New Testament.

55. Meyendorff, *Living Tradition* (Crestwood, New York, 1978), pp. 7f. (emphasis original).

relationship with God is both a givenness and a task, an immediate experience and an expectation of even greater vision to be accomplished in a free effort of love.[56]

The dynamism of God's and humankind's mutual movement toward each other weds theology and experience in the transfiguration, or deification, of the whole man; humankind's ascent toward God was ordered by God for human nature from the beginning.[57] Meyendorff's theology is in great part a synthesis emerging from his exposition of the mutually interpretative anthropology and christology of Maximus the Confessor. The comprehensiveness and integrity of the Confessor are key, the *sine qua non* and *summum bonum* of Orthodox theology:

> In fact, Maximus can be called the real father of Byzantine theology. Only through his system, in which the valid traditions of the past found their legitimate place, were the ideas of Origen, Evagrius, the Cappadocians, Cyril, and Pseudo-Dionysius preserved within Eastern Christianity. . . . It remains impossible . . . to understand the whole of Byzantine theology without becoming aware of Maximus' synthesis.[58]

In elucidating Maximus, Meyendorff unites christology and anthropology in a compelling vision:

> By his death and resurrection, Christ destroys the separation that existed since the fall between paradise and the universe. "Today you shall be with me in Paradise," says Christ to the good thief (Lk 23:43) — giving to the human race access to the forbidden garden, coming back himself on

---

56. Meyendorff, *Byzantine Theology* (New York, 1974), p. 2.

57. Meyendorff, *Christ in Eastern Christian Thought* (Crestwood, New York, 1975), p. 140.

58. Ibid., pp. 131f. For this interpretation, Meyendorff is heavily indebted to S. L. Epifanovich's classic treatment of the Confessor, *Prepodobnyi Maksim Ispovednik i vizantiiskoe bogoslovie* (Kiev, 1915); cf. *Christ in Eastern Christian Thought*, p. 231, notes 1 and 2. Indeed, Meyendorff's very usage of the term "Byzantine theology" roots him firmly in the nineteenth- and twentieth-century Russian school of historical theology. In assigning this preeminent role to Maximus, Meyendorff goes further than Florovsky, and the emphases of the two scholars in their descriptions of the Confessor also differ — cf. Florovsky, *The Byzantine Fathers of the Sixth to Eighth Century,* in *CW* IX, pp. 208-53.

earth after his resurrection, and showing that in himself paradise and the universe are henceforth one. By his ascension he unites heaven and earth through the exaltation of the human body, co-natural and consubstantial with ours, which he had assumed. By going beyond the angelic orders with his human soul and body, he restores the unity between the worlds of sense and of mind, and establishes the harmony of the whole creation. Finally, as man, he accomplishes in all truth the true human destiny that he himself had predetermined as God, and from which man had turned: he unites man to God. The ultimate aim of the divine plan is thus man's deification.[59]

This is a theology of ever-growing assent and of the movement of commitment — not only in the present, but also in the future, for it presupposes eschatology.[60] This upward movement toward God, which was ordered by God for human nature (see above), requires participation in God — as does all natural movement. In paradise man needed only to follow his own natural movement of communion with God, the *telos* for which he was destined: "Man's only true destiny was to conform to his nature, that is, to be in communion with God."[61] Maximus "resurrects and exploits the Alexandrian doctrine of the Logos,"[62] and it is the light of the Logos, medium between the Father and man, which bathes the landscape of our existence, promising redemption in the restoration of communion with God. As the harmony of creation is restored in Christ, in conformity with itself, the opposition between our mode of existence and our nature disappears. We will no longer live at war with ourselves.[63]

This essentially dynamic doctrine of salvation supposes a double movement: a divine movement toward man consisting of making God partakable of by creation, and a human movement toward God, willed from the beginning by the Creator, and restored in Christ. The hypostatic union of these two movements in the incarnate Word constitutes the

59. *Christ in Eastern Christian Thought,* p. 143.
60. Meyendorff, *Byzantine Theology,* pp. 218-22.
61. Meyendorff, *Christ in Eastern Christian Thought,* p. 138.
62. Ibid., p. 133.
63. According to Maximus, since the fall, humankind's *tropos* (mode of existence) is at war with its *logos* (nature) — the paradigm of dysfunction. Prior to the fall, the *tropos* followed the blueprint of the *logos.* Every being possesses a preexistent and natural *logos,* which, when the being is given existence, becomes the pattern for its *tropos.*

essence of Maximus' Christolgy: two natures imply two energies or wills meeting one another.[64]

By energy or movement *(kinesis)* we know God, and by movement God draws near to us. The stage is set for the eventual development by Gregory Palamas of a distinction between the divine essence and energies:

> Palamite christocentrism, in direct dependence on St. Maximus, implies, as does also the thought of the Confessor, the doctrine of the energies. It is only within the perspective of the Maximian doctrine of the two energies or wills of Christ that it is possible to understand the terminology of St. Gregory Palamas. Moreover, the council of 1351 presents the Palamite doctrine of the energies as a development *(anaotyxis)* of the decrees of the Sixth Ecumenical Council of 680.[65]

Indeed, a christology thoroughly grounded in anthropology guarantees the integrity of the patristic synthesis, and affirms its conclusions:

> By basing christological thinking on anthropology, one is necessarily led to the other major conclusions of Greek patristics: man does not disappear in contact with God but, on the contrary, becomes more truly and freely man, not only in his similarity to God, but also in what makes him radically different from his Creator. And this is the very meaning of the hypostatic union of divinity and humanity in Christ.[66]

Here the reflections of Georges Florovsky are particularly apposite:

> "Incarnation" and "deification" — *sarkōsis kai theōsis* — are two linked movements. In a certain sense the Logos is always becoming incarnate, and in everything, for everything in the world is a reflection of the Logos, especially in man, who was placed on the edge of the world as the receiver of God's grace. The Incarnation of the Logos crowns God's descent into the world, and creates the possibility for the opposite movement.[67]

---

64. Meyendorff, *Christ in Eastern Christian Thought,* pp. 143f.
65. Ibid., p. 203. The idea of "openness" of persons and the essence/energies distinction have signal and profound ramifications for Meyendorff's understanding of the Trinity; cf. *Byzantine Theology,* pp. 186-88, and this essay, pp. 38-41.
66. *Christ in Eastern Christian Thought,* p. 211.
67. Florovsky, *The Byzantine Fathers of the Sixth to Eighth Century,* p. 227.

Theōsis is the destiny and call of humanity, and all theology is to some extent a commentary on this primary and ultimate divine challenge and summons, the central soteriological and christological affirmation.

We are here at the center of the neo-patristic synthesis, "the infinite pity which reigns in the hearts of those becoming united with God."[68] In the union of humankind with God in Christ and in the Holy Spirit, there is the continual movement and activity of love between the God-like man and the man-like God. The mutual interpenetration of divine and human traits, the simple and complex movement of the divine affection and of loving human response and striving in the *hypostasis* of Christ, is the desire of inGodded *eros* for mutual community and affection. As human and divine met in the "Yes" of Mary in the Annunciation, they join and fuse in the Person of Christ. In the Word humanity is deified through commingling with God.

In the bond uniting his human and divine natures, *agapē*, Christ shows us the way of reconciliation between God and humanity, the supreme example of *theōsis*. Gregory Nazianzus writes:

> God [is] crucified. . . . the dead rose up for a pledge of the final and general resurrection. The miracles before the grave and at the grave — who will worthily sing? But none is like the miracle of my salvation. A few drops of blood recreate the whole world and become to us what rennet is to milk, binding us together and compressing us in unity.[69]

Christ our friend, the pioneer of our *theōsis*, healer of our humanity, and author of divine-human unity, does not annihilate our creaturely condition, but raises it to that communion with the Eternal Creator for which in the beginning we were made. This is the work of the Holy Spirit, who unifies theology and life, objective and subjective, individual and community, and tradition and creativity in the marriage of human freedom to grace. Meyendorff writes:

> The [patristic] references to the presence of the Spirit in the *natural* man rather point to two things:
> — the *openness upwards* of the human person, called to ascend

68. V. Lossky, quoting St. Isaac the Syrian, in *The Mystical Theology of the Eastern Church* (Cambridge, 1957), p. 111.

69. Nazianzus, *Orat.* 45, 29, M.P.G. XXXVI, columns 661, 664.

towards the divine, unending, limitless aim which God has set as
human destiny;

— the *freedom*, which Gregory of Nyssa identifies as the very content
of the image of God, making man similar to his Creator and
different from all other created beings.

The restoration of the Spirit as guiding principle of human existence
in Christ is therefore a return to the ancient dignity of freedom, which
Adam lost through the Fall, by becoming a slave to death, to corrupti-
bility, and to sinfulness. The Spirit restores what Maximus the Confessor
called "natural will," which gives man freedom from all cosmic deter-
minisms and allows him to be truly himself in relation to God and the
world. The human person is authentically free only in unity with the
Spirit of God.

It is at this point that one discovers why, beginning with the author
of the writings attributed to St. Macarius the Great, the entire tradition
of Eastern Christian spirituality insisted upon the *personal*[70] and conscious character of the Christian experience of God.[71]

For the "neo-patrologue," the personal and the corporate are bound together
by the grace of the Holy Spirit; anthropological, christological, eucharistic,
and ecclesiological images are mutually interpretative and definitive, rooted
as they are in the deep and rich soil of a lived trinitarian faith. The Church,
the fulfillment of the Incarnation and icon of the Trinity, is the primary and
ultimate point of reference for anthropology. Meyendorff explains:

> The mystery of the Church, fully realized in the Eucharist, overcomes
> the dilemma of prayer and response, of nature and grace, of the divine

70. Meyendorff seemed interested in the connection between modern personalist
psychology and the psychological implications and explorations of patristic anthropologies. This nexus — that is to say, the idea of using patristic anthropologies and ideas of
person as potential bearers and signifiers for contemporary psychological terms — was
seen and developed in embryo by the Russian philosopher-theologian V. I. Nesmelov.
Meyendorff hoped that a translation of and commentary on Nesmelov's written work
would begin as soon as possible. Similarly, in a 1990 conversation with Meyendorff, we
suggested that Bulgakov hoped that, among other important *desiderata*, the personali-
zation of Sophia would accomplish a similar purpose with regard to the nascent language
of contemporary psychology.

71. Meyendorff, "The Theology of the Holy Spirit," in *Catholicity and the Church*,
pp. 22f. (emphasis original).

as opposed to the human, because the Church, as the Body of Christ, is precisely a communion of God and man, not only where God is present and active, but where humanity becomes fully "acceptable to God," fully adequate to the original divine plan; prayer itself then becomes an act of communion, where there cannot be any question of its not being heard by God. The conflict, the "question," the separateness, and the sinfulness are still present in each individual member of the Church, but only inasmuch as he has not fully appropriated the divine presence and refuses to conform to it; the presence itself, however, is the "new testament in my Blood" (Lk 22:20), and God will not take it away. Thus, all Christians — including the bishop, or the priest — are individually nothing more than sinners, whose prayers are not necessarily heard, but *when gathered together in the name of Christ,* as the "Church of God," they are a part in the New Testament, to which God has eternally committed Himself through the Son and the Spirit. . . . It is the Spirit which makes Christ present in the age between His two comings: when divine action is not imposing itself on humanity, but offering itself for acceptance by human freedom and by communicating itself to man, making him authentically free.[72]

Humanity finds its fullness and wholeness in Christ and his Body. Catholicity is the very affirmation of self, expressed in redeemed character; in the fullness of the communion of saints, the clarity of God's will — the catholic transfiguration of personality — is accomplished. "The Church is the likeness of the existence of the Holy Trinity, a likeness in which many become one."[73] The Church's transfiguration in communion — its *theōsis* — is not absorption into, or dissolution in, a limitless sea of divinity in an abstract Godhead. The Christian is neither united with nor absorbed by, God's *ousia*. On the contrary the life in Christ is an affirmation, and perceptible sculpting-out, of distinct self-consciousnesses with unique tastes, feelings, aspirations, and attributes — or of persons — a glorification of the human person, the "reasonable statue," carved out in the image of Christ. This is *theōsis,* and the joy of that *theōsis* is humanity's given otherness, its creatureliness. Here again, the implications of the doctrines of the incarnation and of the hypostatic union of the two natures in Christ are clear: the *theōsis* of humankind

72. Meyendorff, *Byzantine Theology,* p. 207 (emphasis original).
73. Florovsky, "The Catholicity of the Church," in *CW* I, p. 44.

unfolds with respect to, and is dependent upon, the humanization of God. Christ's humanity is

> a *deified* humanity, which, however, does not in any way lose its human characteristics. Quite to the contrary. These characteristics become even more real and authentic by contact with the divine model according to which they were created. In this deified humanity of Christ's, man is called to participate, and to share in its deification. This is the meaning of sacramental life and the basis of Christian spirituality. The Christian is called . . . as Nicholas Cabasilas puts it, to "life *in* Christ" through baptism, chrismation, and the Eucharist.[74]

Transfiguration does not obliterate the boundary between divine and human; it marks the ultimate degree of communion between divine and human persons and the beginning of the beatific vision of purity of heart. It is this transformation in the divine communion of love that is the sempiternal pattern and foundation of the Church, where humanity becomes one unity, in one Body. The divine conversation of prayer forms, in the Church's renewing deposit of the *charisma veritatis*, a sacramental community enchristing and anointing all who bear Jesus' title as a name, Christians, in history, for all time. Grace is hypostasized and realized in the visible words, the *logoi*, of the sacraments, God's very own sealed energies. The Church is God's teleological vision and command, and as God eternally contemplates the image of the world, so with good enjoyment does he intend the transformation of image into the likeness of new life in grace in his Church: "At all times, Byzantine theologians understood the Eucharist," Meyendorff argues,

> as the center of a soteriological and triadological mystery, not simply as a change of bread and wine. Those who followed Dionysian symbolism approached the Eucharist in the context of a Hellenistic hierarchical cosmos, and understood it as the center of salvific action through mystical "contemplation," which still involved the whole destiny of humanity and the world. Those who held a more Biblical view of man and a more Christocentric understanding of history approached the Eucharist as the key to ecclesiology;[75] the Church, for them, was primarily the place where

---

74. Meyendorff, *Byzantine Theology*, p. 164 (emphasis original).
75. It is important to note that the twin problems of the claims and of the

God and man met in the Eucharist, and the Eucharist became the criterion of ecclesial structure and the inspiration of all Christian action and
responsibility in the world. In both cases the Eucharist was understood
in a cosmological and ecclesiological dimension affirmed in the formula
of the Byzantine oblation: "Thine own of thine own, we offer unto Thee
on behalf of all and for all."[76]

The sacraments are means of divine revelation and are related to God
as a body is related to the soul; they are in the nature of an instrument or a
vehicle of expression, as though a mode of creation in another existence. Just
as the true core of a man's personality, his inapprehensible self, is never
revealed to others but manifests itself through his mind, emotions, and body,
so Christ is made manifest through the sacraments — although his *ousia* is
not revealed. The Church is the icon and vessel of God's grace-filled enflesh-
ment — "God in Man Made Manifest" — in the world. Just as one is called
to sacramental participation in the Church's nature *(katholikotēs)*, one is
called to participate in God's nature, which is redemptive. The Church, the
community of those "acting primarily in the manifest Person of Christ *(in
persona Christi),*" is constituted by the sacraments, the eschatological path
and ladder of mystical ascent in *theōsis*. The paths of revelation and knowledge meet and correspond in the Church, where the Holy Spirit will perfect
and finish knowledge, by the energies of the sacraments transforming cogni-
tion and intellectual comprehension into the *eros*[77] of "meta-knowledge,"

---

authority of the papacy concerned Meyendorff greatly throughout his life. Much of his
reflection about these issues he based on F. Dvornik's monumental critical examination
of the idea of apostolicity, *The Legend of the Apostle Andrew and the Idea of Apostolicity
in Byzantium* (Cambridge, Massachusetts, 1958). This part of Meyendorff's thinking
changed little from the publication of *L'Église orthodoxe: hier et aujourd'hui* to the end
of his life.

76. Meyendorff, *Byzantine Theology*, p. 208. The Eucharist as the key to ecclesiology was a favorite theme of Meyendorff's — cf., e.g., "Church and Ministry," in *Catholicity and the Church*, pp. 52f.

77. Revelation, time, and being are focused on God's election of humanity in
Christ. The human person, the "reasonable statue" (a phrase borrowed from Methodius
of Olympus) is an animate likeness of the eternal Divinity. As God's desire is for
humanity, so is ours for God. We have by nature an *eros* for God and knowledge of him.
This *eros* is not opposed to *agapē*, but is its zenith and brightness. "Divine *eros*," insisted
Georges Florovsky, "blazes up on the very heights of mysterious life" (*The Byzantine
Fathers of the Sixth to Eighth Century*, p. 242).

theognōsia. In the sacraments the truth that is held and preserved by the whole Church is experienced and appropriated personally by each Christian.

Karl Rahner was a theologian who, Meyendorff thought, was suffused with the thinking of the pre-Augustinian Fathers. Meyendorff was drawn to the ideas of Rahner, which communicated the patristic spirit in contemporary language. Nowhere is this more evident than in Rahner's crucially theocentric anthropology. " 'A human being,' writes Karl Rahner, 'is a reality absolutely open upwards; a reality which reaches its highest (though indeed "unexacted") perfection, the realization of the highest possibility of man's being, when in it the Logos himself becomes existent in the world.' "[78]

Appropriating Rahner's compelling patristic existentialism, Meyendorff sees human freedom, grace, and the activity of the Holy Spirit in history as mutually inclusive. He identifies the existential "openness" and freedom of humankind with participation in divine life, a dynamic with a necessarily strong pneumatological underpinning:

> What makes man truly man is the presence of this Spirit of God. Man is not an autonomous and self-sufficient being; his humanity consists firstly in an openness to the Absolute, to immortality, to creativity in the image of the Creator, and secondly in the fact that God met this openness when He created man and that, therefore, communion and participation in divine life and glory is man's *natural* element.[79]

Meyendorff points out that an acceptance of Rahner's christology will necessarily involve a reorientation of one's thinking as to the definition of persons and the implications of such reorientation for an understanding of the Trinity:

78. Meyendorff, *Christ in Eastern Christian Thought*, p. 211. He quotes Rahner's "Current Problems in Christology," in *Theological Investigations*, vol. I (Baltimore, 1965), p. 183; he further refers the reader to Rahner's "Considerations generales sur la christologie," in *Problemes actuels de Christologie. Travaux du Symposium de l'Arbesle 1961*, ed. H. Bouesse and J. J. Latour (Paris, 1965), pp. 21f.

79. Meyendorff, "Orthodox Theology Today" in *Living Tradition* (Crestwood, New York, 1978), p. 175 (emphasis original). Here he has synthesized the anthropologies of Paul (2 Corinthians), of Irenaeus *(Adversus haereses)*, and of Gregory of Nyssa *(De opificio hominis)*. By way of comment, it must be said that an equation between the God of Abraham, Isaac, and Jacob and the Father of our Lord Jesus Christ, on the one hand, and the Absolute of modern European philosophy, on the other hand, does not necessarily hold.

Karl Rahner arrives at challenging the Latin idea that the persons of the Trinity are internal relations in the divine essence, for, indeed, if such were the case, the divine hypostasis of the Logos could neither be the subject of change and passion, nor be seen as the existential center of his human nature. A sound Christology implies, for Rahner, the return to a pre-Augustinian concept of God, where the three hypostases were seen first of all in their personal, irreducible functions, as Father-God, Son-Logos, and the Spirit of God, and not only as expressions of the unique immutable essence.[80]

Meyendorff's rich trinitarian and christological interpretations of the Fathers sprang from the perspective of a committed Orthodox Christian who was deeply sensitive to contemporary canonical and pastoral issues. He was particularly troubled by the lack of Orthodox unity in North America. His powerful words are forthright:

There cannot exist any doctrinal, disciplinary, missionary, or canonical justification for the state of canonical chaos in which the Orthodox Church lives, for example, in America. The situation is made more dramatic by the fact that no one — not even the sister churches, the bishops, the theologians, not to speak of the average priest or layman — seems to recognize that the revealed God-established *norm* of Church unity is being forgotten and, in fact, consciously rejected, when one

---

80. Meyendorff, *Christ in Eastern Christian Thought*, p. 213. Again he refers the reader to Rahner's "Considerations generales sur la christologie," 17, and "Current Problems in Christology," 188. Such a redefinition of what a person is would challenge the almost axiomatic contemporary notion that the person, or self, is continuous and autobiographical. Such a rethinking would very possibly involve the ecclesial anthropology of the neo-patrologues, in which the triune identity, or Trinity, is linked to the Church's radical modification of self, personality, and ego — in short, all that comprises human self-consciousness — into a catholic consciousness. Such a radically converted consciousness has at its core an initial and ultimate movement of self-emptied compassion toward the whole of creation (cf. Rom. 8:18-22 and above, p. 33 and note 68). "This is the sense of the movement ordered by God for man's nature. It is a re-establishment of the natural harmony of creation that constitutes the basis of spiritual life . . ." (Meyendorff, *Christ in Eastern Christian Thought*, p. 140). The deified servant empties himself, with Christ, on behalf of all and for all. Here there is neither competition nor mutual exclusion between the divine and the human (ibid., p. 212); the implied opposition between the *kenosis* and the *theosis* of Christ (cf. above, note 30) disappears in the "uniting unity" of his hypostasis.

admits as normal the existence of several "jurisdictions" side by side in the same place. I have discussed elsewhere the ecclesiological, canonical, and practical issues involved in this question, and others have done it even better. It is obvious that the formal rejection of the territorial norm, the concept that each Orthodox autocephalous or national church has *de jure* a universal jurisdiction over all members of a particular ethnic group wherever they are found (i.e. the Church of Russia over all the Russians, the Church of Constantinople over all the Greeks, etc.) is not unpractical, because it is often impossible to define ethnicity, but also formally racist, and, in fact, heretical. Christ came to establish on earth a new and holy nation, a *tertium genus,* a kingdom which is "not of this world." A church whose only function is to maintain ethnic identification loses the character of [the] true "Church of God." It is unable to fulfill its mission, for it is formally exclusive of those who do not belong to its ethnicity.[81]

His strong Eucharistic ecclesiology was focused and outraged:

To maintain, as is often done, that our ethnic divisions do not prevent us from being in eucharistic communion with each other, and that therefore we keep "spiritual" unity, is obviously insufficient (and often hypocritical) because in Orthodox ecclesiology the Eucharist is the *pattern* of church life and structure. If we celebrate the Eucharist without following the pattern it implies — "one church, one bishop in each place" — we are in fact betraying its meaning, and probably even partake of the Body and Blood of Christ "for our condemnation."[82]

Meyendorff's calling was one of articulation of Orthodoxy in Western idiom, while at the same time encouraging an active, enduring, and strong missionary effort in North America. Poignantly he wrote as a young theologian:

The Orthodox presence in the West is a rather new phenomenon. Following the two world wars large numbers of emigrants from Eastern Europe sought new homes in Western Europe, and particularly in America . . . where several millions of the faithful have largely adopted the

---

81. Meyendorff, "Contemporary Problems of Orthodox Canon Law," in *Living Tradition* (Crestwood, New York, 1978), pp. 105f. (emphasis original).

82. Ibid., p. 106 (emphasis original).

language, culture and ways of thought of their new country, while at the same time remaining faithful to the Church of their forefathers. To some extent, they have even succeeded in breathing into the latter a new missionary spirit and in imbuing it with a new zeal for organization such as it has never known before. By surmounting national differences inherited from the past, by training a clergy that can cope with the new conditions in which the Church finds itself, and by their skill in reconciling a faithfulness to tradition with the needs of the modern world, the Western Orthodox can give an entirely new meaning to their witness to the faith. This is the task to which their Church calls them, a Church which claims to be the true Church of Christ, and it is by this standard that they will be judged by history, by their brothers, by other Christians, and finally by God himself.[83]

These eloquent words guided Meyendorff in his missionary vocation in North America.

The patrimony of John Meyendorff is a theological conception of church history formed by a theological idea of Christian truth. History in his model was always history from the perspective of Christian faith. Only from within the Church could one discern the sacred from the historical. He starts, and ends, with Christian experience — the Trinity, Christ, freedom, and the Church. Because of this, he was able to incorporate into his thinking insights from a number of historians and scholars. If freedom has brought one to Christ, then one knows that all things are summed up in Christ. Through the lens of Meyendorff's christology, one can see the powerful influence not only of those Christian thinkers sanctioned by the Church, but also the impact of those who enjoyed rather less favor or were even condemned — including Origen and Evagrius Ponticus. Christology obviously offered the fullest venue for the expression of his concern with anthropology and freedom. He can also be heard within the broad conversation between the "neo-patrologues" and the French *entre guerre* personalists, or existentialists.

Finally, Meyendorff refers everything human to the judgment and mercy of God in the eschaton.[84] His eschatology was never gloomy, but was always full of hope. He encouraged Christians to see the meaning of

---

83. Meyendorff, *The Orthodox Church,* pp. 230f.
84. Cf. Meyendorff, *Byzantine Theology,* pp. 218-22.

history beyond history and outside time. Meyendorff's doctrine of last things did not emphasize the judgment or wrath of God; he stressed the good things to come and the overwhelming, abundant love of God for humankind, a mercy and love that God is always eager to shower upon us. For Meyendorff eschatology is, in its comprehensiveness, a source of power and of illumination. To experience these things as Meyendorff articulated them is to gain hope. All things are summed up in Christ, and so are charged with eternal meaning. God's eschatological invitation is a calling for people to work with God in the deification, or *theōsis,* of creation.

HISTORY

Tradition and the Spirit of Faith in a Methodist Perspective

GEOFFREY WAINWRIGHT

In June 1992, there took place in Oxford, England, the first in a series of theological conversations sponsored by the Ecumenical Patriarchate and the World Methodist Council with a view to the eventual establishment of an official international dialogue between all the Orthodox Churches and the Churches of Methodism. During that first meeting, the Orthodox and Methodist representatives alike were deeply saddened by the news of Father John Meyendorff's sudden illness and rapid passing. Twenty years earlier, Father John had delivered a memorable lecture on "The Holy Spirit as God" to the Fifth Oxford Institute of Methodist Theological Studies. Now the Orthodox-Methodist ecclesiastical conversations were to take up the pneumatological theme in its ecclesiological and anthropological aspects: how do Orthodox and Methodists understand the work of the Holy Spirit as the shaper of the Christian community across time as well as the source of faith for each believer in every present moment?

Meyendorff had written that the Eastern doctrine of salvation as *theosis* by the Holy Spirit "implies a religion of *personal experience*" and that "the Orthodox East admits the *saints* as authoritative witnesses of truth." The personal faith of the believer and the evidentiary authority of the saints, he continued, are, in Orthodox understanding, located within a community that "the Spirit maintains through history" and in which "the Spirit created the apostolic ministry at Pentecost." "The true, 'catholic' tradition of Christianity," said Meyendorff, "is the one where institutional and charismatic leaderships are able *to recognize in each other the same*

Spirit." For both an episcopal, priestly ministry and a charismatic, prophetic testimony, if authentic, are alike "founded in participation in the same divine Spirit granted to the Church at Pentecost, distributed in baptism, and always working at the 'building-up' of the Body of Christ."[1]

In the Oxford conversations of 1992 it appeared that the Orthodox representatives could hear the Methodist testimony to the present experience of the Holy Spirit in the life of the individual Christian but found it less clear how Methodists as an ecclesial body might see themselves, and indeed be, part of a historic Church founded upon the apostles at Pentecost and indwelt by the Holy Spirit ever since. The present chapter was, therefore, originally prepared for the second Orthodox-Methodist meeting, at Constantinople in July 1993, as an account of how Methodists, as Christians and as a denominational family, view their own relation to the great Tradition of the Church catholic. It is an attempt by a Methodist theologian to describe the sense in which Methodists see the historic Church as the location and instrument of the gospel and the faith, while considering every authentic present experience of faith and testimony to the gospel as the maintenance and renewal of the Tradition — and all of this, of course, in and under the Holy Spirit.[2]

The presentation begins with a statement of the constitutional claims made by Methodist Churches to belong to the Church catholic as the Body of Christ, even while deliberately acknowledging the particular origins of the Methodist movement. Since Methodists ascribe a founding role in their own history to John Wesley, a second section examines the way in which Wesley himself understood Methodism in relation to the patristic Church — a matter of great importance in any Methodist-Orthodox dialogue, given the significance of the early Fathers in the Orthodox understanding of the

---

1. The preceding quotations (italics original) are all taken from John Meyendorff, "The Holy Spirit, as God" in Dow Kirkpatrick, ed., *The Holy Spirit* (Nashville: Tidings, 1974), pp. 76-89; republished in John Meyendorff, *The Byzantine Legacy in the Orthodox Church* (Crestwood, New York: St. Vladimir's Seminary Press, 1982), pp. 153-65.

2. My original text has been nuanced at some points in light of its discussion in Constantinople. I express my gratitude to fellow participants in that conversation, Bishop Kallistos of Diokleia, Protopresbyter George Dragas, Dr. Joe Hale, and Professor Peter Stephens. Much help has also been received from my colleague Karen Westerfield Tucker, who has worked on Wesley's liturgical appropriation and interpretation of the Fathers.

Tradition. A third section then looks at the ways in which John Wesley in turn has assumed the role of a father in the particular Methodist tradition, remembering that the Orthodox have an extended tradition of fatherhood that does not rest only with the great theologians of the early centuries but also includes the later founders of local Churches and the continuing exercise of pastoral (episcopal) and spiritual (monastic and saintly) direction. The fourth part takes examples from the *lex orandi* to illustrate the content of the faith, the manners of its transmission, and the styles of its experience, as these occur characteristically within Methodism; and here the ongoing Wesleyan character again appears. A concluding section summarizes the most recent official theological statement on the theme of Tradition as the United Methodist Church, by far the largest Methodist denomination, has set it in relation to Scripture, experience, and reason as in various senses "sources" and "criteria" of the Christian faith.

I. The Constitutional Self-Understanding of Methodism

The Methodist ecclesial family, which today numbers some sixty million adherents around the world, considers itself part of the entire mystery and history of salvation that begins and ends in the Triune God revealed in Jesus Christ. Methodism's particular origins date from the evangelistic, spiritual, and moral revival led by John Wesley and his brother Charles within the Church of England in the eighteenth century. Both the broader and the narrower aspects of Methodist self-understanding are characteristically expressed in the constitutional documents of the British Methodist Church:

> The Methodist Church claims and cherishes its place in the Holy Catholic Church which is the Body of Christ. It rejoices in the inheritance of the Apostolic Faith and loyally accepts the fundamental principles of the historic creeds and of the Protestant Reformation. It ever remembers that in the Providence of God Methodism was raised up to spread Scriptural Holiness through the land by the proclamation of the Evangelical Faith and declares its unfaltering resolve to be true to its Divinely appointed mission.
>
> The Doctrines of the Evangelical Faith which Methodism has held from the beginning and still holds are based upon the Divine revelation

recorded in the Holy Scriptures. The Methodist Church acknowledges
this revelation as the supreme rule of faith and practice. These Evangelical
Doctrines to which the Preachers of the Methodist Church both Ministers
and Laymen are pledged are contained in Wesley's Notes on the New
Testament and the first four volumes of his sermons.[3]

Similarly, the United Methodist Church, which chiefly results from
the spread of the Wesleyan movement to North America, declares in its
Book of Discipline that

> United Methodists profess the historic Christian faith in God, incarnate
> in Jesus Christ for our salvation and ever at work in human history in
> the Holy Spirit. Living in a covenant of grace under the Lordship of Jesus
> Christ, we participate in the first fruits of God's coming reign and pray
> in hope for its full realization on earth as in heaven.[4]

Claiming "a common heritage with Christians of every age and nation,"
United Methodists find this heritage "grounded in the apostolic witness to
Jesus Christ as Savior and Lord, which is the source and measure of all valid
Christian teaching." In the work of the "leaders of the early Church" to
"specify the core of Christian belief in order to ensure the soundness of
Christian teaching," a special place is recognized to "the determination of
the canon of Christian Scripture and the adoption of ecumenical creeds"
(Nicaea and Chalcedon are mentioned along with the Apostles' Creed). The
Protestant Reformers attempted to "recover the authentic biblical witness"
that had been "classical Christian teaching." Then, in their own day, the
"early Methodists claimed to preach the scriptural doctrines of the Church
of England as contained in the Articles of Religion, the Homilies, and the
Book of Common Prayer." Wesley, it is said, "considered doctrinal matters
primarily in terms of their significance for Christian discipleship." The
"distinctive Wesleyan emphases" include "prevenient grace," "justification

---

3. From the Deed of Union (1932) of the Methodist Church of Great Britain,
clause 30. The "doctrinal clauses" of the Deed, by which the various branches of British
Methodism were reunited in 1932, continue to be protected in *The Constitutional
Practice and Discipline of the Methodist Church*.

4. This statement stands at the head of the rather discursive accounts of "our
doctrinal heritage" and "our doctrinal history" given in the 1992 *Book of Discipline of
the United Methodist Church* (sections 65 and 66), from which the next quotations will
also be drawn.

and assurance," "sanctification and perfection," "faith and good works," "mission and service," and "fellowship in the Church." As "our doctrinal standards and general rules," the *Book of Discipline* then cites the Articles of Religion (based on John Wesley's abbreviation of the Anglican Articles), the Confession of Faith of the Evangelical United Brethren Church,[5] the Standard Sermons of Wesley, Wesley's *Explanatory Notes upon the New Testament,* and the General Rules (based on Wesley's advice in practical ecclesiology and Christian living).[6]

Parts of the extended Methodist family look, in addition, to important figures in their own early history. This is notably true of those originally German-speaking communities in North America deriving from Jacob Albright's Evangelical Association and Philip William Otterbein's United Brethren; and of the African Methodist Episcopal Church, which followed Richard Allen; and of the other historically Black or African American bodies, namely the African Methodist Episcopal Zion and Christian Methodist Episcopal Churches. But the Methodist family as a whole undoubtedly regards John Wesley as its founding father.

II. Wesley on the Fathers

While holding, with the Anglican Articles of Religion, that "Holy Scripture containeth all things necessary to salvation,"[7] Wesley considered the early Christian writers to be "the most authentic commentators on Scripture, as being both nearest the fountain, and eminently endued with that Spirit by whom all Scripture was given."[8] He often supported his own exegesis of

5. Inherited from the body (largely German in ethnic origin) which joined with the Methodist Church to form the United Methodist Church in 1968.

6. The documents listed in this sentence are named in section 67 of the 1992 *Book of Discipline* and are constitutionally protected from change. Section 68 then turns, most discursively of all, to a contemporary statement concerning "our theological task," to which attention will be given in the last part of this paper, since it is the most recent official treatment directed by the United Methodist Church explicitly to the theme of Tradition.

7. Anglican Article VI = Methodist Article V.

8. *An Address to the Clergy* I:2 (*The Works of John Wesley,* ed. Thomas Jackson [3rd ed., London: John Mason, 1829-31], X:484); cf. the sermon of 1777 "On Laying the Foundation of the New Chapel" (Jackson VII:424; Sermon 112 in the Bicentennial Edition of *The Works of John Wesley,* vol. 3, ed. A. C. Outler [Nashville: Abingdon, 1986],

the Scriptures by appeal to patristic interpretations of the biblical passages.[9] The Apostolic Fathers were special favorites of Wesley on the grounds revealed by his endorsement of Archbishop Wake's judgment of them, which he quoted when he published his own translation of them in the first volume of his *Christian Library:* "The authors of the following collection were contemporaries of the holy Apostles. . . . We cannot therefore doubt, but what they deliver to us is the pure Doctrine of the Gospel; what Christ and his Apostles taught, and what these holy men had themselves received from their own mouths."[10] Wesley esteemed "the writings of the first three centuries, not equal with, but next to, the Scriptures."[11] He had learned from the Manchester Non-Jurors[12] that the *"consensus veterum: quod ab omnibus, quod ubique, quod semper creditum"* was "a sure rule of interpreting Scripture," although this should not lead to the mistake of "making antiquity a co-ordinate rather than a subordinate rule with Scripture."[13] In particular, "well-meaning men" had shown "weakness" in relying on what allegedly "had been orally delivered down from the Apostles."[14] Wesley affirmed, as true interpretations of Scripture, the Nicene-Constantinopolitan Creed, the Chalcedonian definition of the one person and two natures of Christ, and the trinitarian theology of the so-called Athanasian Creed.[15] He upheld, and polemically invoked, the teachings of the early

---

p. 585f.). I owe the initial references, though not always the interpretation, to these and many other passages in the following section to Ted A. Campbell, *John Wesley and Christian Antiquity: Religious Vision and Cultural Change* (Nashville: Abingdon/Kingswood Books, 1991).

9. See, for example, *A Farther Appeal to Men of Reason and Religion* I, 5, 15-23 (Jackson VIII:91-101; in the Bicentennial Edition of the *Works,* see volume 11, ed. Gerald R. Cragg, *The Appeals to Men of Reason and Religion* [Oxford: Clarendon Press, 1975], pp. 154-66).

10. See the prefatory material to Wesley's edition of the Apostolic Fathers in his *Christian Library.*

11. Letter of January 4, 1748-49, to Conyers Middleton (Jackson X:14).

12. See Frederick Hunter, "The Manchester Non-Jurors and Wesley's High Churchism," *London Quarterly and Holborn Review* 177 (1947), 56-61.

13. Manuscript of 1737, cited from A. C. Outler, *John Wesley* (New York: Oxford University Press, 1964), p. 46.

14. Letter of January 4, 1748-49, to Conyers Middleton (Jackson X:12).

15. In his irenic *Letter to a Roman Catholic* (1749), Wesley set out the faith of "a true Protestant" in terms of an expansion upon the Nicene-Constantinopolitan Creed (Jackson X:80-86; cf. Geoffrey Wainwright, "Methodism and the Apostolic Faith," in

Church against the revival in his own time of the ancient heresies of Sabellianism and Arianism.[16]

In liturgical matters, Wesley was willing to invoke, first in a precise sense and later rather more generally, the precedent and example of the early Church. In the middle 1730s, when he still accepted the authenticity of the so-called *Apostolic Constitutions* and *Canons,* he wrote in a notebook:

> I believe myself it a duty to observe, so far as I can without breaking communion with my own church:
> 1. To baptize by immersion.
> 2. To use Water [i.e. the mixed chalice], oblation of elements, and alms, invocation [i.e. epiclesis], and a prothesis, in the Eucharist.
> 3. To pray for the faithful departed.
> 4. To pray standing on Sunday and in Pentecost.
> 5. To observe Saturday, Sunday and Pentecost as festival.
> 6. To abstain from blood and things strangled.
>
> I think it prudent (our own church not considered):
> 1. To observe the stations [fasting Wednesday and Friday].
> 2. Lent, especially the Holy Week.
> 3. To turn to the east at the Creed.[17]

It seems that Wesley originally intended to be guided by these practices as part of his attempt in the North American colony of Georgia to restore "primitive Christianity in the wilderness."[18] Later in his career, as the

---

M. Douglas Meeks, ed., *What Should Methodists Teach? Wesleyan Tradition and Modern Diversity* [Nashville: Abingdon/Kingswood Books, 1990], pp. 101-17, 154f.). On Wesley's adherence to Chalcedon, see John Deschner, *Wesley's Christology: An Interpretation* (Dallas: Southern Methodist University Press, 1960). Wesley considered the "explication" of the doctrine of the Trinity in the so-called Athanasian Creed "the best I ever saw" (Sermon "On the Trinity," number 55 in the Bicentennial Edition of *The Works*, vol. 2, ed. A. C. Outler [Nashville: Abingdon, 1985], p. 377; Jackson VI:200).

16. See *Journal* for April 22, 1779 (Jackson IV:149); Sermons "On the Trinity," number 55 in the Bicentennial Edition of *The Works*, vol. 2, ed. A. C. Outler (Nashville: Abingdon, 1985), pp. 378f. (Jackson VI:201), and "On Knowing Christ after the Flesh," number 123, vol. 4, ed. Outler (Nashville: Abingdon, 1987), p. 100 (Jackson VII:292).

17. See Frank Baker, *John Wesley and the Church of England* (London: Epworth/Nashville: Abingdon, 1970), pp. 40-41, 350-54.

18. See Campbell, ch. 3: "Primitive Christianity in the Wilderness."

Methodist movement developed in England, Wesley appealed more generally to the early Church to justify and encourage such practices as the
love-feast (agape) and the watchnight (vigil). Above all, he saw his own
custom of frequent communion as an emulation of the early Church. At
Christmas 1774 he wrote:

> During the twelve festival days we had the Lord's Supper daily; a little
> emblem of the Primitive Church. May we be followers of them in all
> things, as they were of Christ![19]

And at Easter 1777:

> Easter Day was a solemn and comfortable day, wherein God was remark-
> ably present with His people. During the Octave I administered the Lord's
> Supper every morning, after the example of the Primitive Church.[20]

When, in 1784, Wesley was making provision for the Methodist Episcopal
Church in the newly independent United States, he "advise[d] the elders to
administer the Supper of the Lord on every Lord's Day" — thus displaying
awareness of the patristic connection between Sunday and the Eucharist.[21]

In fact, from the very early days of the Methodist movement in
England in the 1740s, John Wesley observed similarities between its
developing organization and the early Church. Sometimes he applied a
patristic model programmatically; sometimes he called attention to the
patristic precedents only *après coup*. Thus in *A Plain Account of the People
Called Methodists* of 1748-49, he noticed that Methodist institutions "generally found, in looking back, something in Christian antiquity likewise, very
nearly parallel": the Methodist societies for "seekers after salvation" corre-

---

19. *Journal* for December 25, 1774 (Jackson IV:38).

20. *Journal* for March 30, 1777 (Jackson IV:95). See John C. Bowmer, *The Sacrament of the Lord's Supper in Early Methodism* (Westminster [London]: Dacre Press, 1951).
In 1787 and 1788, Wesley published a sermon on "The Duty of Constant Communion"
that he had written in 1732 (Sermon 101 in the Bicentennial Edition of *The Works*, vol.
3, ed. A. C. Outler [Nashville: Abingdon, 1986], pp. 427-39; Jackson VII:147-57).
Throughout his life he encouraged his people to press for more frequent communion
in their parish churches at a time when the Anglican custom contented itself with four
celebrations a year.

21. Letter of September 10, 1784, to "Our Brethren in America" (*The Letters of
John Wesley*, ed. J. Telford [London: Epworth, 1931], vol. VII, pp. 237-39).

sponded, he thought, to ancient catechetical classes; Methodist "class tickets" for identification of membership, to "*symbola* or *tesserae,* as the ancients termed them, being of just the same force with the *epistolai systatikai,* commendatory letters, mentioned by the Apostle"; the Methodist penitent bands, to the segregation of penitents in the early Church; the offices of deaconess and widows, to primitive orders.[22] When finally, in 1784, Wesley, a presbyter of the Church of England, felt driven to ordain a ministry to oversee the Methodist work in North America, he appealed to studies of the ancient Church that claimed that bishops and presbyters were essentially of the same order; considering himself "as much a scriptural episcopos as any man in Europe," he judged that the emergency situation in America warranted his exercising the sacramental power of ordination, which had hitherto been held in check only by limits of jurisdiction.[23]

In all of this, Wesley's favor fell chiefly on the Church of the first three centuries. He admired its courage under persecution and its persistence in propagating the gospel.[24] Nevertheless, "before the end of the third century the Church was greatly degenerated from its first purity," and Cyprian's testimony was cited for evidence of degeneration.[25] The greatest fall from grace, however, followed on the conversion of Constantine. A grave moral decline resulted from the Emperor's gifts of wealth and honors to the Church, especially to the clergy.[26] Wesley regretted the building of churches, the homage paid to images, and the multiplication of ritual.[27] He agrees with his correspondent Dr. Conyers Middleton that "after the Empire be-

---

22. *A Plain Account of the People Called Methodists* (Jackson VIII:248-68).

23. See Campbell, pp. 51f., 89-94. The historical studies Wesley relied on were Edward Stillingfleet's *Irenicum* (1659) and Peter King's *Enquiry into the Constitution, Discipline, Unity, and Worship of the Primitive Church* (1712).

24. See Campbell, pp. 48f.

25. Letter of January 4, 1748-49, to Conyers Middleton (Jackson X:12); and (for Cyprian's evidence) the 1787 Sermon "Of Former Times," number 102 in the Bicentennial Edition of *The Works,* vol. 3, ed. A. C. Outler (Nashville: Abingdon, 1986), pp. 450f. (Jackson VII:164).

26. See, for example, in the Bicentennial Edition of *The Works,* the Sermons "The Mystery of Iniquity" (no. 61 of 1783; ed. Outler, 2:462-64; Jackson VII:164), "Of Former Times" (no. 102 of 1787; ed. Outler, 3:449f.; Jackson VII:163f.), "The More Excellent Way" (no. 89 of 1787; ed. Outler 3:263f.; Jackson VII:26f.), "On Attending the Church Service" (no. 104 of 1787; ed. Outler 3:470; Jackson VII:178).

27. See the tract on "The Origin of Image Worship among Christians" (Jackson X:175-77).

came Christian, a general corruption both of faith and morals infected the Christian Church, which, by that revolution, as St. Jerome says, 'lost as much of her virtue, as it had gained of wealth and power.' "[28] Wesley was also disgusted by the polemics and intrigues surrounding conciliar gatherings, even while accepting the dogmatic decisions of the ecumenical councils.[29]

It was doubtless chiefly in reaction against the perceived moral decline of the "great Church" that Wesley showed sympathy with a number of both earlier and later figures and groups on account of their ostensible spiritual and ethical seriousness. Thus he has positive things to say about the Montanists ("real, scriptural Christians"),[30] the Novatianists, and the Donatists ("I suspect they were the real Christians of that age, and were therefore served by St. Augustine and his warm adherents as the Methodists are now by their zealous adversaries").[31] Pelagius, wrote Wesley to his friend John Fletcher, "very probably held no other heresy than you and I do now."[32]

Wesley held that a genuine Christianity remained alive even under the Empire. He recommended for their spiritual quality the reading of St. Basil and St. John Chrysostom, of "Macarius the Egyptian" and "above all, the man of a broken heart, Ephraem Syrus."[33] He recommended familiarity with the lives of early Christians on account of their exemplary moral character in contrast with the sorry state of many professing Christians in his own time.[34]

---

28. Letter of January 4, 1748-49, to Conyers Middleton (Jackson X:1).

29. *Journal* for August 5, 1754 (Jackson II:314).

30. *Journal* for August 15, 1750 (Jackson 2:204).

31. Letter of March 12, 1756 to William Dodd (*Letters,* ed. Telford, 3:170-71).

32. Letter of August 18, 1775, to John Fletcher (Telford 6:175). The comment is illuminated by this: "It is scarce possible at this distance of time to know, what Pelagius really held. All his writings are destroyed; and we have no account of them but from Augustine, his furious implacable enemy. I doubt whether he was any more an heretic than Castellio or Arminius" (Wesley's note in his edition of Mosheim's *Concise Ecclesiastical History*).

33. *An Address to the Clergy* (Jackson X:484); Letter of January 4, 1748-49, to Conyers Middleton (Jackson X:79); Sermon of 1777 "On Laying the Foundation of the New Chapel" (number 112 in the Bicentennial Edition of *The Works,* vol. 3, ed. Outler, p. 586; Jackson VII:424).

34. The sources Wesley turned to were William Cave's *Primitive Christianity* (1672), Claude Fleury's *Moeurs des Chrétiens* (1682), and Johann Lorenz von Mosheim's *Concise Ecclesiastical History.* Wesley made editions of all these three works, excising material that he considered unedifying even among early Christians.

To end this section, let me refer to Wesley's citation of St. John Chrysostom in exegesis of Romans 8:15-16, a favorite passage of Wesley's, concerning the Spirit of faith and adoption. In the *Farther Appeal to Men of Reason and Religion,* Wesley is out to prove that the "testimony of the Spirit," far from being a special miraculous gift reserved to the apostolic age, is "among those ordinary gifts of the Spirit of Christ, which if a man have not he is none of his" (cf. Rom 8:9). He takes Chrysostom's Fourteenth Homily on Romans to show that the Spirit of adoption comes with the New Covenant as such. By the Spirit of adoption we cry "Abba, Father," and Wesley quotes Chrysostom on this Pauline phrase and translates him thus: "This is the first word we utter after those amazing throes (or birth-pangs) and that strange and wonderful manner of bringing forth."[35] This witness of the Holy Spirit is thus, Wesley holds with Chrysostom, "the ordinary privilege of all Christians."

While Orthodox Christians will be gratified by Wesley's evident respect for the earliest Church and its Fathers, they will doubtless have problems with some of his historical interpretations (as, for example, in the matter of episcopacy). Most difficult perhaps will be his insistence on some of the nefarious effects of Constantine's adoption of Christianity, but it should not be forgotten that the Tradition of Orthodoxy also includes the strands of prophetic criticism, spiritual freedom, and moral renewal.

III. Wesley as a Father

A sympathetic observer is able to recognize in the continuing Methodist family the mark of spiritual identity left upon it by John Wesley.[36] In the newly independent United States, the Methodist Episcopal Church was constituted at the Christmas Conference of 1784 held in Baltimore.[37] In

---

35. See *The Appeals to Men of Reason and Religion,* volume 11 (ed. Gerald R. Cragg) of the Bicentennial Edition of *The Works of John Wesley* (Oxford: Clarendon Press, 1975), pp. 157-59; cf. the Letter of July 10, 1747, to "John Smith" (Bicentennial Edition of *The Works,* vol. 26 [Letters II: 1740-1755], ed. Frank Baker [Oxford: Clarendon Press, 1982], p. 251).

36. Francis Frost, "Méthodisme," in G. Jacquemet (ed.), *Catholicisme, hier, aujourd'hui, demain* (1948ff.), volume IX, cols. 48-71: *"Le méthodisme moderne doit en premier lieu cet héritage à John Wesley, tout comme, dans l'Église catholique romaine, un ordre religieux ou une famille spirituelle tient son esprit d'un fondateur."*

37. In the mid-nineteenth century the Methodist Episcopal Church split into the

Britain, the embryonic Methodist denomination emerged more gradually from the Anglican womb, and it was not until the late nineteenth century that the principal Wesleyan body officially called itself the "Wesleyan Methodist Church" as distinct from a "Connexion" (a term deriving from the Conference of Preachers "in connexion with Mr. Wesley"). From early days, however, Methodists on both sides of the Atlantic looked on John Wesley with affection and respect as their "father" (although perhaps Francis Asbury, one of the first two bishops in America, went exceptionally far when he called Wesley "our dear old Daddy").[38]

It may be illuminating in our Methodist-Orthodox dialogue if I can convey a sense of the fatherly position that John Wesley occupies in Methodism. No disrespect is thereby intended to those early Fathers whom Wesley himself held in high regard. In certain ways, Orthodoxy itself has regarded some later-comers as continuing a patristic role in the founding of Churches and the exercise of dogmatic, pastoral, and spiritual teaching and direction. Wesley has in fact been viewed by Methodists as a father in at least four respects: (1) His work of evangelism has begotten us in the gospel; (2) we have sought to be his obedient children and collaborators under God; (3) he has been our teacher in the Christian faith and life; and (4) he has bequeathed us a liturgical heritage.

1. Our Spiritual Progenitor

In the Minutes of the Methodist Conference held at Bristol in 1745, Wesley offers an account of "the origin of church government" that shows how ecclesial order derives from the commission to preach the gospel and the consequent rise of congregations of believers. The passage can be read stereoscopically as a description of both apostolic times and the origins of Methodism:

"Methodist Episcopal Church" and the "Methodist Episcopal Church, South." The two bodies were reunited in 1939 into "The Methodist Church." The name "United Methodist Church" dates from the merger of 1968 with the smaller Evangelical United Brethren.

38. See, for example, *The Journal and Letters of Francis Asbury* (ed. J. Manning Potts, Elmer T. Clark, Jacob S. Payton), vol. 3 (The Letters) (London: Epworth/Nashville: Abingdon, 1958), pp. 60-64 (letter of August 15, 1788, to Jasper Winscom).

Christ sends forth a preacher of the gospel. Some who hear him repent and believe the gospel. They then desire him to watch over them, to build them up in the faith and to guide their souls in the paths of righteousness. . . . If it please God to raise another flock in [a] new place, before [the evangelist] leaves [the first place], he appoint[s] one whom God has fitted for the work to watch over [their] souls also. In like manner, in every place where it pleases God to gather a little flock by His Word, [the evangelist] appoints one in his absence to take the oversight of the rest and to assist them of the ability which God giveth. These . . . look on their first pastor as their common father. And all these congregations regard him in the same light and esteem him still as the shepherd of their souls.[39]

While in the primary sense it is God the Father who begets believers (1 Pet 1:3), the apostle Paul could look on his own work of evangelism as the fathering of faith (1 Cor 4:15). Commenting on the Pauline text in his *Explanatory Notes upon the New Testament,* Wesley remarks that "the relation between a spiritual father and his children brings with it an inexpressible nearness and affection."

It is not surprising that subsequent generations should look on those who evangelized them as their "fathers in the gospel."[40] That is how Methodists have considered John Wesley. A nice early example can be found in the letter written from Baltimore on November 1, 1796 to "The General Conference of the People called Methodists in Great Britain" by Bishops Thomas Coke and Francis Asbury on behalf of "The American General Conference," "Your affectionate and younger Brethren in the Gospel": "We [cannot] possibly," they write, "be too thankful to our adorable Lord, for that highly honoured instrument of his grace, your and our late Father in the Gospel, the Rev. John Wesley."[41]

39. Quoted from A. C. Outler, *John Wesley,* p. 154.

40. Note, for example, the remarks of Bishop Kallistos Ware with regard to Saints Cyril and Methodius: "With Bulgars, Serbs, and Russians as their 'spiritual children,' the two Greeks from Thessalonica abundantly deserve their title 'Apostles of the Slavs' " (Timothy Ware, *The Orthodox Church* [Harmondsworth, Middlesex: Penguin Books, 1963], p. 85).

41. *Minutes of Several Conversations, Between the Rev. John Wesley, A.M., and the Preachers in Connection with Him, from the Year 1744* (Leeds: printed by Edward Baines, 1803), pp. 330-33.

2. Our Senior Evangelist

The spiritual offspring of the evangelist seek to obey their parent. How the matter appeared from Wesley's side emerges from the following question and answer in the Minutes of the Methodist Conference of 1766 meeting at Leeds:

> Q. But what power is this which you exercise over all the Methodists in Great Britain and Ireland?
>
> A. To me the preachers have engaged themselves to submit, to "serve me as sons in the Gospel." But they are not thus engaged to any man, or number of men besides. To me the people in general will submit. But they will not yet submit to any other.[42]

Commenting on Philippians 2:22, from which he made an inexact citation in the text above, Wesley in his *Explanatory Notes upon the New Testament* observed the "elegance" of St. Paul's phrase concerning Timothy: the Apostle speaks of St. Timothy "partly as of a son, partly as of a fellow labourer." That is sufficient to remove any unpleasant edge from the notions of service and obedience to the senior evangelist.

That Wesley's disciplinary oversight was felt to continue after his death appears from a letter written at Leeds by the President (Thomas Coke) and Secretary (Samuel Bradburn) on behalf of the British Methodist Conference of 1797 to the Methodist Societies: the affairs of the Connexion were to be conducted according to "all our ancient rules, which were made before the death of our late venerable Father in the Gospel, the Rev. Mr. Wesley, which are essential rules, or prudential at this present time."[43] This applied even to such matters as the discouragement of complex tunes and anthems in favor of hymns in which "the whole congregation can in general join," on which "our late venerable Father in Christ, Mr. Wesley" first "printed a Minute."[44]

---

42. Ibid., pp. 21, 24.
43. Ibid., pp. 320-26.
44. Conferences of 1796 and 1799 (ibid., pp. 304f., 380).

3. Our Doctrinal and Moral Teacher

Mention has already been made of the constitutional status of texts emanating from Wesley as permanent standards for doctrine and practice in Methodist churches. In the British Methodist Church, all candidates for the preaching ministry, whether ordained or lay, are required to have read, and to undergo examination on, the Standard Sermons of Wesley and his *Explanatory Notes upon the New Testament.* In the United Methodist Church, ordinands and their recommenders must answer a series of questions that derive in large part from the questions that Wesley put to his preachers from the beginning:

> Do they know God as a pardoning God? Have they the love of God abiding in them? Do they desire nothing but God? Are they holy in all manner of conversation? Have they gifts, as well as evidence of God's grace, for the work? Have they a clear, sound understanding; a right judgment in the things of God; a just conception of salvation by faith?

> Have you faith in Christ? Are you going on to perfection? Are you resolved to devote yourself wholly to God and his work? Do you know the General Rules of our Church? Will you keep them? Have you studied the doctrines of the United Methodist Church? Will you preach and maintain them?[45]

In these ways, Wesley continues to instruct the Methodist preachers and members of the Methodist churches.

In academic and even popular theology, Methodists have of course been affected by changing cultural fashions.[46] But periodic Wesleyan revivals arise through returns to the eighteenth-century sources.[47] The more

---

45. From the 1992 *Book of Discipline of the United Methodist Church;* cf. the historic "Large Minutes" (Jackson edition of *The Works,* VIII:324f.).

46. See, for example, Robert E. Chiles, *Theological Transition in American Methodism 1790-1935* (Nashville: Abingdon, 1965).

47. In the immediately preceding generation, an important influence was exercised by Albert C. Outler's florilegium, *John Wesley* (1964), in the Library of Protestant Theology published by the Oxford University Press, New York. Even more significant has been the momentous decision to undertake a Bicentennial Edition of *The Works of John Wesley* in 34 volumes (Oxford: Clarendon Press, 1975-83; Nashville: Abingdon, 1984-). This is the edition, still in process, to which reference has been made wherever possible in this essay.

significant of these revivals invoke not simply a Wesleyan method in theology but Wesleyan doctrinal substance.[48]

4. Our Liturgist and Hymnographer(s)

Ancient Fathers left their names on liturgies that at least in part derive from them: so with St. Basil and St. John Chysostom, not to mention others in the lesser Eastern Churches. Some patristic saints are honored for their hymn writing: so Ambrose, Ephraim, John of Damascus (whose "Day of Resurrection" appears in twentieth-century Methodist hymnals), and even the ninth-century "St. Joseph the Hymnographer" (familar to modern Methodists through his "Happy Band of Pilgrims").

John Wesley provided the Methodists with a *Sunday Service*. Destined first for North America (1784), then for the British Dominions overseas (1786), and finally issued without restriction (1788), it was closely based on the Anglican *Book of Common Prayer* (1662). In the United States, the Methodists between 1784 and 1792 referred to it as "our Prayer Book."[49] In England, it became known as "our venerable father's abridgement" (a phrase used in the "Plan of Pacification" of 1795 as part of the efforts to regulate Methodist liturgical practice in the difficult years of transition after Wesley's death). On both sides of the Atlantic, it underwent several revisions in the nineteenth and twentieth centuries; and although it was overtaken by less formal orders of worship for Sunday morning preaching services, it remained the basis for sacramental rites and pastoral offices.[50] In the second half of the twentieth century, Methodist service books and practice have been greatly influenced by the modern ecumenical and liturgical movements, which have made the ritual structures more patristic in shape while at the same time turning the language of worship more toward

---

48. See Thomas A. Langford, *Practical Divinity: Theology in the Wesleyan Tradition* (Nashville: Abingdon, 1983).

49. See Francis Asbury's letter of April 24, 1786, to George Washington (*The Journal and Letters of Francis Asbury*, 3:47).

50. See Charles R. Hohenstein, "The Revisions of the Rites of Baptism in the Methodist Episcopal Church, 1784-1939" (Ph.D. diss., University of Notre Dame, 1990); Karen B. Westerfield Tucker, " 'Till Death Us Do Part': The Rites of Marriage and Burial Prepared by John Wesley and Their Development in the Methodist Episcopal Church, 1784-1939" (Ph.D. diss., University of Notre Dame, 1992).

contemporary speech patterns. Nevertheless, something of the "Cranmerian" style of Wesley is retained at least in a fragmentary way or as allowed variants (as in the 1784/1882/1936 Order for the Lord's Supper in the British *Methodist Service Book* of 1975 and in Word and Table Service IV in the United Methodist *Book of Worship* of 1992).

It is, however, chiefly through hymnody that the Wesleyan stamp has been put on Methodist worship. Charles Wesley was the principal hymn writer, although John also composed some texts, translated others notably from the German, and edited his brother's when collections appeared under their joint names. Their 166 *Hymns on the Lord's Supper* of 1745 guided the eucharistic understanding and devotion of the early Methodists, and some of the best of these hymns have been maintained or reintroduced in subsequent Methodist hymnals.[51]

Finally, it was the more general *Collection of Hymns for the Use of the People Called Methodists,* which Wesley published in 1780, that provided the structure and the vast bulk of all official hymnals of the British Wesleyans and the Methodist Episcopal Churches in America throughout the nineteenth century. In the preface, Wesley claimed that this collection was sufficient to "contain all the important truths of our most holy religion, whether speculative or practical; yea, to illustrate them all, and to prove them both by Scripture and reason. And this is done in a regular order. The hymns are not carelessly jumbled together, but carefully ranged under proper heads, according to the experience of real Christians. So that this book is in effect a little body of experimental and practical divinity."[52]

In the twentieth century, Methodists have widened the ecumenical range of their hymnody in both time and space, while the Wesleys have remained their chief source (most abundantly so in Britain, where the 1904 *Methodist Hymn Book* contained over 400 Wesleyan texts, the 1933 some 268, and the 1983 *Hymns and Psalms: A Methodist and Ecumenical Hymn*

---

51. See J. Ernest Rattenbury, *The Eucharistic Hymns of John and Charles Wesley* (London: Epworth, 1948); cf. Geoffrey Wainwright, " 'Our Elder Brethren Join': The Wesleys' *Hymns on the Lord's Supper* and the Patristic Revival in England," forthcoming in *Proceedings of the Charles Wesley Society.*

52. Scholarly edition by Franz Hildebrandt and Oliver A. Beckerlegge, *A Collection of Hymns for the Use of the People Called Methodists,* volume 7 in the Bicentennial Edition of *The Works* (Oxford: Clarendon Press, 1983).

Book still some 173). If many Wesleyan hymns from the 1780 *Collection* have been lost to usage, others of a dogmatic and festival kind have been added from other Wesleyan sources.

The *United Methodist Hymnal* of 1989 arranged its hymns according to a structure that follows closely the ancient ecumenical creeds:

The Glory of the Triune God (Praise and Thanksgiving; God's Nature; Providence; Creation)

The Grace of Jesus Christ (In Praise of Christ; Christ's Gracious Life: Promised Coming; Birth and Baptism; Life and Teaching; Passion and Death; Resurrection and Exaltation)

The Power of the Holy Spirit (In Praise of the Holy Spirit; Prevenient Grace; Justifying Grace; Sanctifying and Perfecting Grace).

The Community of Faith (The Nature of the Church; The Book of the Church — Holy Scripture; The Sacraments and Rites of the Church; Particular Times of Worship)

A New Heaven and a New Earth (Death and Eternal Life; Communion of the Saints; Return and Reign of the Lord; The Completion of Creation — The City of God).

It would be a great enrichment if more hymns from the Orthodox Tradition could be made available for singing by Methodists.[53] Might some of the best Wesleyan hymns even find their way into Orthodox worship, so that a Wesleyan voice could contribute to the great symphony?[54] It is, in any case, to the existing Methodist hymnic *lex orandi* that we shall turn for a couple of examples concerning "the Spirit of faith" in the Wesleyan tradition.

---

53. Already some of John Mason Neale's nineteenth-century translations from the Greek were included in earlier twentieth-century Methodist hymnals. More recently, some Russian chant forms have been introduced for occasional use with standard liturgical texts (e.g., the Kyrie).

54. This would be a practical instance of the "exchange of saints" that is necessary to growth in communion among Christian communities. See Geoffrey Wainwright, "Wesley and the Communion of Saints," *One in Christ* 27 (1991), 332-45.

IV. "Spirit of Faith," "Remembrancer Divine"

"Spirit of faith, come down!" This pneumatological epiclesis of a hymn was contained as number 83 of the 525 hymns in the 1780 *Collection*. It has maintained its place in the current British and United Methodist hymnals of 1983 and 1989 respectively.

A full quotation of it will illustrate a number of Wesleyan characteristics. First, the tissue of biblical phrases and allusions demonstrate a use of the Scriptures as the canonical book of the Church's faith and life. Second, the Scriptures are read according to a hermeneutical grid given by the Church's dogmatic understanding concerning the persons and work of the Holy Trinity and the Church's classic proclamation and confession of the gospel of salvation for humankind. Third, this hymn brings together the *fides quae creditur* and the *fides qua creditur* in a fusion of living faith, of incandescent orthodoxy.

Here is invoked the Holy Spirit, whose gift is the fruit of Christ's redemptive work and the beginning of our salvation, who has shaped the Christian community throughout its existence and brings God home in the personal experience of the believer. Let the hymn speak, or sing, for itself:

Spirit of faith, come down,	1 Cor. 2:12;
Reveal the things of God,	2 Cor. 4:13
And make to us the Godhead known,	
And witness with the blood:	1 John 5:8
'Tis Thine the blood to apply,	
And give us eyes to see,	
Who did for every sinner die	Rom. 5:8
Hath surely died for me.	
No man can truly say	1 Cor. 12:3
That Jesus is the Lord	
Unless Thou take the veil away,	2 Cor. 3:12-18
And breathe the living word;	Matt. 4:4; John 20:22
Then, only then, we feel	
Our interest in His blood,	1 John 1:7
And cry with joy unspeakable,	1 Pet. 1:8
Thou art my Lord, my God!	John 20:28
O that the world might know	
The all-atoning Lamb!	John 1:29

Spirit of faith, descend, and show
The virtue of His name;   Acts 4:12
The grace which all may find,
The saving power impart,
And testify to all mankind,
And speak in every heart!

Inspire the living faith
(Which whoso'er receives,
The witness in himself he hath,   1 John 5:10; Rom. 8:15f
And consciously believes),
The faith that conquers all,   1 John 5:4
And doth the mountain move,   Mark 11:23
And saves whoe'er on Jesus call,   Rom. 10:13
And perfects them in love.   1 John 4:17

That is how, at the heart of their life together, Methodists typically preach, receive, teach, learn, confess, and celebrate the Christian faith. That hymn constitutes the "tradition of the faith" in Wesleyan substance and mode.

A second example comes from the Wesley brothers' *Hymns on the Lord's Supper*, where it figured as number 16; it has been included in all British Methodist hymn books of the twentieth century. "Come, Thou Everlasting Spirit" is a eucharistic epiclesis whose key image is drawn from a phrase at the epiclesis in the liturgy of the eighth book of the *Apostolic Constitutions*, where the Holy Spirit is called "the Witness of the sufferings of the Lord Jesus." Invoking the Holy Spirit also as the "Recorder" of Christ's passion and the divine "Remembrancer," the Wesleys link anamnesis and epiclesis in a very traditional way that has also been recovered in such modern ecumenical texts as the Lima document of Faith and Order on *Baptism, Eucharist and Ministry*.[55] Again, the Holy Spirit appears as the bringer of the gospel, the source of living faith, and the power of Christian experience:

Come, Thou everlasting Spirit,
Bring to every thankful mind
All the Saviour's dying merit,
All His sufferings for mankind.

55. See especially *Baptism, Eucharist and Ministry 1982-1990: Report on the Process and Responses* (Geneva: World Council of Churches, 1990), pp. 114-16 (cf. pp. 62-68).

True Recorder of His passion,
Now the living faith impart,
Now reveal His great salvation,
Preach His gospel to our heart.

Come, Thou Witness of His dying,
Come, Remembrancer Divine,
Let us feel Thy power applying
Christ to every soul and mine.

Clearly, for Wesleyans as for the Orthodox, the eucharist embodies the content and a means of the evangelical Tradition and of the Christian faith — all in and under the Holy Spirit. Historically, later Methodists have not been able to match the Wesleys for frequency of sacramental celebration, while the more frequent celebrations in the Orthodox Churches still fail to attract the regular Sunday communion of the faithful such as marked the Church of the earliest centuries. Both Orthodox and Methodists may have something to learn from John Wesley's sermon, written for his Oxford students in 1732 and published by him in 1787-88, on "The Duty of Constant Communion."[56]

V. Scripture, Tradition, Experience, and Reason

The 1972 *Book of Discipline* of the United Methodist Church, in the more discursive parts of its treatment of "Doctrine and Doctrinal Statements and the General Rules," declared, in phraseology widely attributed to Albert C. Outler, that the "living core" of "Christian truth," according to Methodist belief, "stands revealed in Scripture, illumined by tradition, vivified in personal experience, and confirmed by reason." Informally, the four elements of Scripture, tradition, experience, and reason quickly became dubbed "the Methodist, or the Wesleyan, Quadrilateral." Unfortunately, that designation evoked a mental image of four equal sides, with the carefully nuanced verbs of "revealed, illumined, vivified, and confirmed" lost from sight.

The underlying problematic emerged more clearly in the 1980s, when the theological Evangelicals began to ask for a firmer declaration of the

56. *Works,* ed. Jackson, VII:147-57; Sermon 101 in the Bicentennial Edition of the *Works,* vol. 3, ed. A. C. Outler (Nashville: Abingdon, 1986), pp. 427-39.

primacy of Scripture (Wesley called himself *homo unius libri*, which meant
that the Scriptures constituted, in the neat phrase of George Croft Cell, not
so much "the boundary of his reading" as "the center of gravity in his
thinking"), while the theological Liberals prized "reason" and "experience"
for the latitude it allowed their quest for contemporary relevance.[57] That
most parties were keen to show the "Wesleyan" character of the "quadrilateral," or at least of their version of it, is itself an interesting indication of
the role of Wesley among Methodists.

The one element among the four that received by far the least attention
in the recent debate was Tradition.[58] For our present purposes, the most
useful procedure now will be to see what, after the preceding debate, the
General Conference of 1992 put into the *Book of Discipline* concerning
Tradition in its relation to Scripture, experience, and reason. It must be
emphasized that the section on "Our Theological Task" (68) in which this
discursive treatment occurs, like the sections on "Our Doctrinal Heritage"
(65) and "Our Doctrinal History" (66) but unlike "Our Doctrinal Standards
and General Rules" (67), are mere "legislative enactments and neither part of
the Constitution nor under the Restrictive Rules"; in other words, they are
readily subject to improvement. It must further be stressed that the 1992 text
maintains, on the whole, a clearer distinction than the 1972 text did between
(stable) "doctrine" and (more ephemeral) "theology": "the Church considers
its doctrinal affirmations a central feature of its identity," whereas the "theological task" is much more concerned with "interpretation" and "application"
in the changing daily contexts. The theological task serves above all the cause
of authentic Christian witness in particular situations.

---

57. See, chiefly from the Evangelical side, Thomas C. Oden, *Doctrinal Standards
in the Wesleyan Tradition* (Grand Rapids: Zondervan, 1988), and Jerry L. Walls, *The
Problem of Pluralism: Recovering United Methodist Identity* (Wilmore, Kentucky: Good
News Books, 1986, updated 1988).

58. Ted Campbell argued that the modern ecumenical appeal to Tradition could
not be found in Wesley: he lived before the Western recovery of a more organic view
of Tradition that came via the Tübingen Catholic J. A. Moehler and the Englishman
J. H. Newman also into Anglican Tractarianism and even into Protestantism; Wesley
still held the more episodic and discontinuous view of the Church's past that marked
much of older Protestantism (not only on account of the Constantinian "fall" but also
because of the degeneration in the medieval West that had made the sixteenth-century
Reformation necessary). See Ted A. Campbell, "The 'Wesleyan Quadrilateral': The Story
of a Modern Methodist Myth," *Methodist History* 29 (1990-91), pp. 87-95.

This, then, is the gist of what the 1992 General Conference, under "Theological Guidelines: Sources and Criteria," stated particularly with reference to Scripture and to Tradition:[59]

Scripture is primary: Scripture, as the constitutive witness to the well-springs of our faith, occupies a place of primary authority.

Tradition provides both a source and a measure of authentic Christian witness, though its authority derives from its faithfulness to the biblical message.

The Christian witness, even when grounded in Scripture and mediated by tradition, is ineffectual unless understood and appropriated by the individual. To become our witness, it must make sense in terms of our own reason and experience.

More particularly under the heading of "Scripture":

Through Scripture the living Christ meets us in the expereience of re-deeming grace.

The biblical authors, illumined by the Holy Spirit, bear witness that in Christ the world is reconciled to God. The Bible bears authentic testimony to God's self-disclosure in the life, death, and resurrection of Jesus Christ as well as in God's work of creation, in the pilgrimage of Israel, and in the Holy Spirit's ongoing activity in human history.

The Bible is sacred canon for Christian people, formally acknowledged as such by historic ecumenical councils of the Church.

We properly read Scripture within the believing community, informed by the tradition of that community.

The close relationship of tradition, experience, and reason appears in the Bible itself. Scripture witnesses to a variety of diverse traditions, some of which reflect tensions in interpretation within the early Judeo-Christian heritage. However, these traditions are woven together in the Bible in a manner that expresses the fundamental unity of God's rev-

59. *The Book of Discipline of the United Methodist Church,* 1992, quoted from section 68 (pp. 76-80).

elation as received and experienced by people in the diversity of their own lives.

And then directly under the heading of "Tradition":

The theological task does not start anew in each age or each person. Christianity does not leap from New Testament times to the present as though nothing were to be learned from that great cloud of witnesses in between. For centuries Christians have sought to interpret the truth of the gospel for their time.

In these attempts, tradition, understood both in terms of process and form, has played an important role. The passing on and receiving of the gospel among persons, regions, and generations constitutes a dynamic element of Christian history. The formulations and practices that grew out of specific circumstances constitute the legacy of the corporate experience of earlier Christian communities.

These traditions are found in many cultures around the globe. But the history of Christianity includes a mixture of ignorance, misguided zeal, and sin. Scripture remains the norm by which all traditions are judged.

The story of the Church reflects the most basic sense of tradition, the continuing activity of God's Spirit transforming human life. Tradition is the history of that continuing environment of grace in and by which all Christians live, God's self-giving love in Jesus Christ. As such, tradition transcends the story of particular traditions.

In this deeper sense of tradition, all Christians share a common history. Within that history, Christian tradition precedes Scripture, and yet Scripture comes to be the focal expression of the tradition. As United Methodists, we pursue our theological task in openness to the richness of both the form and power of tradition.

The multiplicity of traditions furnishes a richly varied source for theological reflection and construction. For United Methodists, certain strands of tradition have special importance as the historic foundation of our doctrinal heritage and the distinctive expressions of our communal existence.

We are now challenged by traditions from around the world which accent dimensions of Christian understanding that grow out of the sufferings and victories of the downtrodden [and so on for seven or eight more sentences].

Although this United Methodist text contains several important insights, it does not appear to be controlled by what it itself calls the "deeper" or "most basic" sense of Tradition as the entire life of the Church insofar as it bears the gospel — an understanding that has gradually made its way ecumenically since the World Conference on Faith and Order at Montreal in 1963 and is characteristic of Orthodoxy.[60] The Methodist hesitancy in this regard may be due to the more episodic view of Church history that characterizes not only Wesley but Protestants more generally. On the other hand, the United Methodist emphasis on the authoritative primacy of Scripture might valuably prompt Methodists to ask Orthodox Christians what account they, too, can give of how the Scriptures, as a very special part of the Tradition, serve as a critical norm for the entire life of the historical Church — a view that marked the Reformation in the sixteenth century, the Wesleyan revival in the eighteenth, and the confessing Church in the twentieth. How do the Orthodox account for failings in the life of the Church?

Both Orthodox and Methodists will affirm, as the Fathers and Wesley likewise did, that authentic Tradition is found only where the Spirit of faith is present. A subject for exploration in their dialogue may well be the criteria by which the Spirit of faith and authentic Tradition are discerned.

60. I refer to what Montreal called Tradition with a capital T. The United Methodist text concentrates more on what Montreal called tradition with a small t, that is, the act of transmission and the particular traditions (plural).

Bosnia: History and Religion

VESELIN KESICH

The continuing tragedy of Bosnia has been receiving abundant attention in the world press over the last four years. The purpose of this essay is to provide a historical framework and perspective within which the present conflict in Bosnia should be examined.

We can distinguish three historical periods in Bosnian history: The medieval Bosnian state endured repeated attempts to reduce its religious diversity by foreign arms and forced conversion. Turkish dominance led to the distribution of the Muslim population mainly in the towns and the dispersal of Serbs and Croats into mountain regions as a result of "ethnic self-cleansing" as well as forced "ethnic cleansing." Under Austrian rule the official policy was to create as deep a division between Serbs and Croats as possible. It was also the period of the rise of nationalistic aspirations. We will consider here some of the reasons for the fury of what we may call "totalitarian nationalism" that erupted in the post–cold war period.

The knowledge of history, it is true, will not necessarily give us the solution for the present bloodshed among the Bosnian Serbs, Croats, and Muslims, but it may bring to light the consequences of hatred and also those precious moments in Bosnia's long history when common efforts were made for the common good among diverse religious and national groups. The past may serve as a warning not to bury the future by focusing on divisive elements in the past but to search for common ground and to learn from common suffering.

70

I. Bosnia to the Turkish Conquest (1463)

Upon their arrival in the seventh century in what is now known as "former Yugoslavia," then the Roman territory Illyricum, certain Slavic tribes entered the area on the border between the Eastern and Western parts of the Roman Empire. From the start the new invaders came under cultural and religious influences of their better organized and powerful neighbors. With the rise of the Holy Roman Empire under Charlemagne in 800, the division between East and West became even more marked, and the line ran straight through Bosnia, from Lake Skutari in the south to the River Sava in the north. Two centuries later the 1054 division between the Eastern and Western Churches led to the atrocities of the crusades, when Hungary launched Crusades in Bosnia itself. This geographical position of Bosnia, between two worlds, contributed substantially to the complexity of Bosnia's history and spiritual development.

Locked between the two worlds, exposed to religious persecution from the West, deprived of the larger influence of Byzantium, and separated by its inaccessible mountains, Bosnia in isolation developed the so-called Bosnian Church, the nature of which is still a controversial problem for historians.

In Bosnia Serbs and Croats have through the centuries had the most contact, sometimes working together, often fighting each other. To justify their exclusive claims on Bosnia, both groups over the last hundred years have been engaged in interpretation and reinterpretation of Bosnia's medieval past. These arguments often obscure the fundamental fact that Bosnia belonged to both of them.

The first important figure in Bosnian history was Ban (governor) Kulin (1180-1204). He is remembered as one who had deep concern for his people: even today we hear *"Od Kulina Bana, i dobrijeh dana"* ("From Ban Kulin and the good old days"). He brought Bosnia into commercial relations with Ragusa on the Mediterranean and the rising Serbian kingdom in order to weaken Hungarian influence. It is in his reign that there are hints of a "Bosnian Church," considered by the papacy as not conforming to Catholic practice. In an effort to guarantee his loyalty, a Papal legate met in 1203 with Ban Kulin and representatives of his religious community. They solemnly proclaimed: "We renounce the schism of which we are accused." They promised to recognize the Catholic Church as "our mother," as the head of all Churches, and to bring their religious practices into line with the Western rite. But as soon as the prelate departed, the Bosnians, left to themselves, continued the old ways.

Under the pretext of solving the religious problem in Bosnia, Hungary organized several crusades against the Bosnian Church. From 1234 to 1239 the country experienced "all those horrors of fire and sword" that had been visited upon the Albigenses in the south of France.[1] These persecutions did not eliminate the Bosnian Church. In 1322 the Church was very much alive and dominant when Stephen Kotromanić became Ban of Bosnia for thirty years. He absorbed Hum (Herzegovina), which had been under Serbian rule, and established a corridor to the sea. Under Hungarian pressure, however, he abandoned the Bosnian Church in 1340 and adopted the Catholic faith.

Stephen's nephew Tvrtko (1353-91) is hailed as Bosnia's greatest ruler. During his minority, Hungary renewed persecutions of the Bosnian Church. They occupied Hum, but in 1370 Tvrtko recaptured it and reached the Dalmatian coast soon afterward. He married an Orthodox princess in a Catholic ceremony. Crowned king of "Serbia, Bosnia, and the coast" at the Orthodox monastery of Mileševo by its metropolitan, he later added "Dalmatia" to his title. Rome accused him in 1377 of protecting heretics, as Tvrtko refused to persecute the Bosnian Church.[2] After his death the benefits and the hope of his reign dissolved under Hungarian pressure and religious persecution. Tvrtko had a conception of a common state for Serbs and Croats and was thus the first "proto-Yugoslav" ruler. With the death of his son in 1443 his dynasty ended.

As the Turkish conquest approached, there was increasing pressure to eliminate the Bosnian Church by force. The influence of the Franciscans in the affairs of the Bosnian kingdom increased considerably. With the establishment of their vicarate in 1340, they became dominant in missionary work. In the hope of obtaining Western help against the Turks, King Stevan Tomas (1443-61), an adherent of the Bosnian Church, converted to the Catholic faith and initiated a vigorous persecution of the Bosnian Church. Now Bosnians were engaged in the forced conversion of their own people for the first time. A document of 1446 proclaims that the heretics "shall neither build new churches nor restore those that have fallen into decay."[3] At this time the

---

1. William Miller, *Essays on the Latin Orient* (Amsterdam: Hakkert, 1964), p. 471.
2. John V. A. Fine, Jr., *The Bosnian Church: A New Interpretation* (New York: Columbia University Press, 1975), pp. 187-200.
3. Miller, *Essays on the Latin Orient*, pp. 486f.

Bosnian Church suffered great losses of membership, together with the devastation of its property. The son of Tomas was crowned by the papal legate, continuing the religious "cleansing" until the fall of the kingdom in 1463. The disruption of the whole society produced by this policy prepared the ground for easy conquest of the country.

II. The Bosnian Church: Origins and Nature

Debates as to the origins of the Bosnian Church have not yet produced generally accepted conclusions among modern historians. Three distinct views permeate the controversy.

The predominant view has been that the Bosnian Church was a heretical dualistic Church, with characteristics of the Bogomil heresy.[4]

Opposing the "Bogomil" origin of the Bosnian Church, Vaso Glušac, a Serbian historian of medieval Bosnia, offered a contrasting interpretation. He stressed that Rački had relied too heavily on the views of the papal opponents of the Bosnian Church. The Western Church ascribed Manichaeanism to the Bosnian Church to justify the persecution of it. Drawing primarily on domestic sources. Glušac concluded that the Bosnian Church in its profession of faith did not differ from the Orthodox Church.[5]

The third view, proceeding from fresh investigations of old sources, both Latin and domestic, disputes the Bogomil origin of the Bosnian Church while questioning that it was the Orthodox Church. As we look further into these arguments, a few words about the Bogomil heresy are in order.

The Bogomils, named after their Bulgarian priest Bogomil, appeared in the Balkans around the tenth century. They were an offshoot of dualistic movements appearing from the East and spreading westward. They rejected the Incarnation, because they considered spirit and matter irreconcilable. Striving for a spiritual life, they rejected sacraments, church organization,

4. This is the view forcefully argued by Franjo Rački in *Bogomili i Patareni* (1871). The book was reissued in Belgrade in 1931 to honor the centenary of Rački's birth.

5. Vaso Glušac, "Srednjovekovna 'bosanska crkva,'" *Prilozi* 4 (1924), pp. 1-55, and "Problem Bogomilstva," *Godisnjak Društva istoričara Bosne i Hercegovine* (Sarajevo) V, pp. 105-38. While some have accused Glušac of using his sources too selectively to support his point of view, he stimulated discussions that are continuing today.

and civil order. Their dualistic principle was reflected in their interpretation of the Genesis creation story: They ascribed to Satan the role of the creator of the material world, but out of matter already created by God. Scholars characterize this as "mitigated dualism." Satan in the teaching of Bogomils remains the ruler of the material world.

Due to the close relationship of Church and state in the post-Constantinian era, these dualists were perceived as a dangerous revolutionary threat to both Church and state. They were vigorously persecuted within the Byzantine Empire and later by the Roman Catholics. The traditional view has been that the Bogomils, expelled from Serbia by Stefan Nemanja, founder of the Serbian medieval state in the twelfth century, encountered a more tolerant atmosphere under Ban Kulin in Bosnia, where they established their community. A more recent interpretation traces the entry of the dualistic heretical group into Bosnia from the Dalmatian *ecclesia Slavonia,* members of whom were pressed into Kulin's Bosnia.[6] The Catholic Fra Anselmo (ca. 1270) attributes the rise of this Church to merchants and traders who spread it from Constantinople throughout the eastern Roman Empire.

In recent years, rejecting the identity between the Bosnian Church and the Bogomils, certain historians trace the origins of the Church to monasticism, either Eastern or Western. Due to its historical circumstances, this Church became isolated from both the Eastern and the Western Churches, and in time was called the Bosnian Church.[7]

Fine locates the specific character of the Bosnian Church in the thirteenth century, when it broke with Rome. Agents of the papacy at this time attempted to reform the Bosnian diocese, which was in the hands of what they regarded as an undeveloped monastic organization. He assumes that the Church had developed out of the Slavic rite Catholic Church in Bosnia. When the connection with the universal Catholic Church was broken, they became schismatics, but not dualistic. Fine does not exclude the possibility that Bosnian Christians, when hierarchical controls slackened, incorporated some practices that the Catholic Church considered dualistic, but that it

---

6. Sima Čirković, *Istorija srednovekovne bosanske države* (Beograd, 1964), pp. 55f.

7. We are drawing on the work primarily of two scholars who have summarized the prevailing research in this area: Fine, *The Bosnian Church,* and Dragoljub Dragojlević, *Krstiani i jeretička crkva Bosanska* (Beograd, 1987). Both authors take into account the research of preceding investigators and, reevaluating the primary sources both foreign and domestic, argue convincingly for a new interpretation of this very old problem.

was in error in identifying them with the Bogomils. Rome apparently made no distinction between the dualistic heresy and the Bosnian Church. While fighting the Manichees, the Catholics organized persecutions of the Bosnian Church as well. Although Bosnians may have acquired some practices from dualists, Fine concludes that the Bosnian Church remained fundamentally nondualistic. Rome's only interest was a Roman Catholic Bosnia, dependent upon and loyal to the Holy See, which would be ready to take part in "a Crusade against the Turks."

D. Dragojlević, a Serbian scholar, assumes that the origin of the Bosnian Church lay in Eastern monasticism. According to his view, the Bosnian Church was neither heretical nor dualistic; it was not composed of Bogomils expelled from Serbia. Nor were they Patareni, a term used for Italian dualists expelled from Split and Trogir in Dalmatia, who had much in common with the Cathari or Albegenses in France and Italy. Dragojlević defends the theory that the Bosnian Church originated in Eastern unreformed anchorite monastic practice and spirituality. There is some evidence that at certain times the Orthodox Church also regarded the Bosnian Christians as heretical, because they did not conform to the hierarchical organization of the Orthodox Church. One source of the Orthodox view of the Bosnian Church noted by historians are anathemas compiled in the *Sinodiks*, the confession of Orthodoxy, in the fourteenth century and listing certain members of the Bosnian Church along with ancient heretics who "separated" from the Church. However, we have examples of the leaders of the Bosnian Church appearing alongside Orthodox bishops and the Metropolitan of Mileševo in official ceremonies. On the whole, however, the Bosnian Church was not regarded favorably by the Orthodox side.

In addition to the large number of Latin sources, our knowledge comes from documents from the Bosnian Church itself: charters, letters, Gospel manuscripts, illustrations in books, gravestone inscriptions, etc. These sources warrant special attention, because they are of greatest value in defining the nature of the Bosnian Church from within. Scholars such as Fine and Dragojlević are paying growing attention to them.

The Bosnian Christians saw their Church as the "Church of God," and themselves as the guardians of "the true apostolic faith." They regarded the Apostle Peter as the chief apostle, in accordance with early Christian tradition.[8] The Church was hierarchically organized under its own bishop,

8. For a discussion of Peter's role, see John Meyendorff, "St. Peter in Byzantine

who was called "djed." During the persecution of the Bosnian Church under King Tomas the djed fled to Herzegovina in 1453; there is evidence that many followed him in 1459. Herceg ("duke") Stevan Vukčić, a member of the Bosnian Church, offered them refuge. He venerated the Serbian Saint Sava, and the name of the province of Herzegovina was derived from his title. Probably the djed was consecrated by the Orthodox Metropolitan of Mileševo upon his arrival. A Greek source attests to his Orthodoxy. The monks of Mount Sinai asked Patriarch Gennadii whether they could remember in their prayers as Orthodox "the bishop of Bosnia" and Herceg Stevan, who had sent them alms. The patriarch assured them that "the bishop of Bosnia is Orthodox and Serb, and that the Herceg became inwardly Christian a short time ago; if he were not he would not have distributed his property in vain."[9]

Under the bishop *(jepiskop)* was the clerical rank of *"gost."* There is no equivalent rank in other Christian Churches. Some sources from Bosnia and Dubrovnik indicate that the *gost* was in charge of a monastic brotherhood. He may have corresponded to the *iguman.* The third degree of hierarchy was *starac,* a term probably taken from Eastern monasticism.[10] The Bosnian Church is composed of *krstjani* (ordained) and *mirski ljudi* (laymen).

In contrast to the Bogomil dualists, the Bosnian Church did not reject the Old Testament. They accepted the Ten Commandments. They drew on the New Testament in its entirety. They illustrated their books with the cross, saints, and biblical figures. Several of these illustrated biblical texts were "actually used later in Orthodox Churches."[11] Unlike the practices of the dualists, the Bosnians did not avoid marriage or the material world.

A source of evidence used to prove that the Bosnian and Bogomil Churches were one and the same were "Bogomil" gravestones discovered in Bosnia. Their Bogomil origin is now seriously disputed and rejected by many scholars, who point out that the carved inscriptions and illustrations

---

Theology," and Veselin Kesich, "Peter's Primacy in the New Testament and the Early Tradition," in *The Primacy of Peter* (Crestwood, NY: St. Vladimir's Seminary Press, 1992), pp. 35-91.

9. Letter written between 1454 and 1456; see Dragojlović, p. 52.

10. For the hierarchy see S. Ćirković, *Istorija srednevekovne bosanske države* (Beograd, 1964), p. 105; Dragojlović, p. 149.

11. Fine, pp. 81-82. See also Dragojlović, pp. 166ff.

found on these stones actually contradict what we know of Bogomil beliefs. No inscription or motif clearly refers to Bogomil beliefs.[12] Many of the stones actually lack all carving or illustrations; this can hardly be used as evidence of their Bogomil origins. Moreover, these stones are spread far beyond areas associated with the Bogomils. They were put in place during Bosnia's period of relative economic prosperity in the Kotromanić dynasty. We may presume that the richer people errected elaborate carved stones, whereas the poor had plain monuments, possibly with painted inscriptions that have washed away.[13]

What is known about the symbols and the social role of the Bosnian Church also calls into question the identity of the Bosnian Church and the Bogomils. We have already noted that the cross, which was rejected by Bogomils in Bulgaria and Serbia, has been found in written and illustrative material of the Bosnian Church. In contrast to the revolutionary spirit of the Bogomils, who were destructive of existing social and political institutions, the Bosnian Church represented a moral force for cohesion and stability. Its history is most noted for its resistance against foreign influences and foreign invasions.

Clearly the Bosnian Church did not share the "mitigated dualism" of the Bogomils. They had even less in common with the "radical dualistic" opposition between the eternally coexisting principles of good and evil.[14] The "dualism" we find in the Bosnian Church resembles that in traditional Christianity in general, the product of monastic spirituality. We could call it "disciplinary" or "ethical" dualism. In ascetic practices, the spirit tries to have control over the body, and the human soul is the battleground between God and Satan.

We have noted a difference of opinion among commentators as to the origins of the Bosnian Church. Was it derived from Eastern or Western monasticism? These two sources, however, are not mutually exclusive, as early Eastern and Western monasticism possessed many common roots. Both grew out of the influence of the Egyptian hermits (anchorites), and the first communities founded in Egypt. *The Life of St Anthony* by

12. Fine, pp. 89f.

13. See Fine, pp. 92f., also Todor Pišteljić, "Srednjevekovna bosanska crkva i stećci," *Glasnik* (Beograd) 1:3 (March 1969), pp. 69-70.

14. For a clear distinction between these two dualisms, see Gordon Leff, "Cathari," in Mircea Eliade, ed., *The Encyclopedia of Religion* (New York: Macmillan, 1987) III, pp. 115-17.

Athanasius was addressed to the monks both in the East and the West, to "the monks in foreign parts." St. Jerome, a Western Father who lived in Jerusalem (374-382), kept contact alive and profitable between East and West. One of the sources of St. Benedict was St. Basil. Monastic contacts persisted long after the schism of 1054.[15] What created dissension and confusion in Bosnia is not what happened in 1054 but later manipulation of the past by forces outside Bosnia that were attempting to subjugate it to a different ecclesiastical authority. Up to the middle of the twelfth century, Bosnia was under Byzantine influence. With the rise of Serbia and Ban Kulin's struggle against Byzantium for independence, Bosnia was left isolated from the East and exposed more to Western influence and armed interference. The Bosnian Church was the local national Church; it had similarities to both the Roman Catholic Church and the Orthodox Churches, yet differed from both of them.

III. Bosnia Under Turkish Rule (1463-1878)

The conquerors from the East entered Bosnia without serious resistance. The question has been raised as to who was responsible for its easy conquest. Traditionally historians have pointed to the betrayal of the "Bogomils," who allegedly preferred the Sultan to the Pope. They of course assumed that the Bosnian Church was Bogomil. While there were individual "traitors," there is no factual support for the supposition that any Bosnian religious body invited and helped the invading army in 1463. The easy conquest of Bosnia was at least in part a direct result of the religious persecution of its inhabitants carried out by Roman Catholic authorities. These "religious cleansings," which had lasted with few interruptions for more than two hundred years, destroyed the people's strength and sapped their moral energy for resisting the Turks. The only record we have of organized resistance to the Turks in Bosnia was the Hungarian defense of Jajce in northwest Bosnia, which fell only in 1528.

Soon after the conquest, representatives of the Catholic and Orthodox Churches asked the Turkish authorities for permission to practice their

---

15. For a recent discussion of the unifying role of ancient monastics, see Theodore Nikolaou, "Between the Eastern and Western Churches: Monasticism as a Bridge," *St. Vladimir's Theological Quarterly* 37:1 (1993), pp. 23-37.

religion. Angelo Zvjezdović, the Catholic delegate, who had been born to an Orthodox family in Vrhbosna,[16] was given the privileges for his Church from the Sultan in 1463. We do not have a record of the name of an Orthodox who made the same appeal, but the same privileges were granted them. These rights were contingent upon their loyalty to the Turkish sovereign. No representative of the Bosnian Church asked for these rights, as by this time the Bosnian Church simply did not exist as a viable organized body, having been virtually destroyed by the final decade of ruthless persecutions, leading to forced conversions, the expulsion of its members, removal of its clerics, and the destruction of the monastic houses. Many, led by members of the nobility who had been associated with the Bosnian Church, converted to Catholicism in the last years of King Tomas's rule and persecution. Others, as we have already mentioned, left the country and settled in Herzegovina, joining the Orthodox Church. Some isolated leaderless groups of Bosnian Christians, to avoid the horrors of persecution, withdrew into less accessible parts of Bosnia. Presumably one such group attacked the Franciscan monastery of Visoko in 1465, killing five Franciscans in revenge.[17]

While our sources from the Bosnian kingdom speak more about the Bosnian Church than the Orthodox Church, after 1463 we find references to the Orthodox Church almost exclusively. Actually we know that the Church of Byzantium was a continuous presence in Bosnia. An Orthodox diocese under Bishop Vladimir is first recorded in the twelfth century. At the time of Ban Kulin, the see of the Serbian Church in Bosnia was in Kreševo, located in the center of Kulin's state. With the expansion of the Bosnian state into Hum in 1326, the Orthodox diocese founded there by St. Sava in ca. 1219 came under the jurisdiction of the Orthodox Church in Bosnia. As Turkish pressure on Serbia increased starting in the fourteenth century, large groups of Orthodox migrated westward into Bosnia. After the conquest and the collapse of Bosnian Church institutions, many Bosnian Church members may have simply counted themselves Orthodox or converted to Orthodoxy. All this increased the Orthodox presence in Bosnia by the time of the conquest.

Contrary to the prevailing assumption, the Bosnian Christians did

---

16. See Fine, p. 379; also Ivo Andrić, *The Development of Spiritual Life in Bosnia Under the Influence of Turkish Rule* (Durham, NC: Duke University Press, 1990), pp. 18f.
17. Fine, pp. 342f.

not convert en masse to Islam after the conquest. The pace of conversion remained slow in the fifteenth century. The Moslem rulers considered Christians as well as Jews "people of the book" and allowed them to continue their religious practices relatively undisturbed. The coexistence of these different religions actually worked to the advantage of the conqueror. The Turks were for the moment more interested in collecting special taxes imposed upon the Christian population than in their islamization, as more converts to Islam meant fewer taxes to collect.

With the restoration of the Serbian Patriarchate at Peć in 1557, the relation between the Orthodox and Muslim authorities in all conquered territories considerably improved, including Bosnia and Herzegovina. The Orthodox Church in Bosnia, as well as in other Serbian communities outside Turkish control, in the Austro-Hungarian monarchy and Venetian Dalmatia, found themselves under the national and religious leadership of the Serbian Patriarch. Under the Turks, the patriarchate was a kind of state within the state (the Ottoman millet system) and the patriarch became *miletbasha,* ethnarch. The first patriarch, Makarije, was cousin to the Serbian Janissary Mehmed Pasha Sokolović,[18] and those who came immediately after him did not oppose Ottoman power. At first they found this new arrangement beneficial for all those nations, including Bosnia, which had lost their independence and were in danger of losing their identity and faith. The millet system gave them freedom to confess their faith and to conduct marriages and civil cases. Disputes were dealt with according to the Law Code of Czar Stefan Dušan (1349, supplemented in 1354).

But this period of "balance" between the Church in captivity and its captors did not last for too long. By the late sixteenth century and throughout the seventeenth, Serbian Church leaders found the imperial restrictions intolerable and started to appeal to the West and to Russia for help. But the western powers under the leadership of the papacy were primaraily interested in *unia* (union with the papacy). The Serbs resisted *unia* while at the same time supporting the military efforts of the Austrians against the Turks. By 1573 the Austrians had established the Military Frontier around their southern border with the Turkish Empire. Here they

---

18. According to the janissary system, boys of eight or nine would be conscripted from their homes to serve in the elite guard of the sultan; see Andrić's heartrending description of this conscription in *The Bridge on the Drina,* tr. L. F. Edwards (New York, 1959), pp. 24-26.

settled Serbs from Bosnia and elsewhere, enticing them with special privileges to occupy the unpopulated, abandoned regions in the present Krajina in Croatia, which formed the line of defense against the Turkish advances. This Serbian defiance understandably enraged the Turks, ending with disastrous consequences for the Serbs left within the empire and leading to problems in Croatian Krajina, resolved only with their expulsion in 1995.

The islamization of the Bosnian population quickened its pace in the sixteenth century. Among the first converts to Islam were the Bosnian nobles, those who had belonged to the landowning classes. To keep their land, property, and status, they accepted Islam. As former adherents of the disbanded and persecuted Bosnian Church, we may suppose that they surrendered their Christian allegiance relatively easily. The Bosnian nobles became the Bosnian Muslim *begs* and as such members of the ruling class. The Bosnian Christians were now the Christian *rayah* (*kmets* or serfs). They tilled the soil and paid taxes to their masters, the Bosnian Muslim rulers. Far more than in the medieval kingdom, they were economically dependent on their lords. Ninety-five percent of the *kmets* were Christian.[19]

The *begs* offered significant advantages to chosen converts, as is reflected in this folksong of Bosnian Muslim origin:

> The *beg* did a pretty good job of making Rado a Turk.
> He married him off to pretty Anna,
> Gave him ten households of *kmets*.
> Now he is no longer called Radojica,
> Now he is called Ibro Pilipović.[20]

Special taxes were imposed on the Christian *rayah*. All male members over fourteen had to pay the *harach*. To detect a boy's age and tax status, the tax collector would measure his head and his neck. The most difficult tax for the Christian parents was the "boy-tribute" or "tribute in blood." This special conscription started soon after the Turkish conquest and lasted for more than a hundred years. The brightest and strongest boys of eight or nine were selected to serve all their lives in the Sultan's elite guard, the janissaries. Throughout the Turkish rule, *kmet* were subject to conscript labor. In 1860 the Turks decided to make two roads, one from Mostar to

19. Sabrina P. Ramet, "Primordial Ethnicity or Modern Nationalism: The Case of Yugoslavia's Muslims Reconsidered," *The South Slav Journal* 13:1-2 (1990), pp. 1-20.
20. See Andrić, *Development of Spiritual Life*, p. 20.

Sarajevo and another from Sarajevo to Brod. The *rayah* were forced to work without pay. Neither road was completed before the Austrian occupation of Bosnia in 1878. Actually the Bosnian ruling class resisted the construction of the second road, which they feared "would bring the Germans to Bosnia."[21] Under these harsh conditions of taxes, conscription, and forced labor, the Christians often voluntarily abandoned their houses and any property they might have and took refuge in the mountain regions. In addition to this "ethnic self-cleansing," there were also forced transfers of population in Bosnia, known in Turkish as *surgun*. A recent article shows that "ethnic cleansing" has a long history in Bosnia, and that the Christians were overwhelmingly its first victims.

> [*Surgun*] took the form of clearing the land of its Christian populations and replacing them with Turkish Muslim peasants and nomads. The policy was implemented by ruthless massacres and the razing of villages. Cities and towns that resisted the Ottoman advance suffered the same massacres of Christian population and their replacement by Muslim Turks, or sometimes Slav renegades to Islam. The Muslim population of Sarajevo, Skopje and other Balkan cities originated in this way. *Surgun* continued on and off throughout the middle ages and only diminished with the slow decline of the Ottoman Empire from the seventeenth century onwards.[22]

Although conversion was not forced as a rule, circumstances often favored it.

It is clear that under the Turkish Empire the position of the Christian *rayah* became progressively worse. True, they were able to practice their religion, but they could not freely repair their Churches, many of which had been destroyed or damaged. The use of church bells was forbidden until the middle of the nineteenth century. Singing inside their homes had to be muted, and mourning for the dead in the cemetery had to be done in silence. Both joy and grief had to be expressed silently. Even their appearance outside their houses was clearly defined and regulated. Their clothes had to be of a different color from Muslim attire. The *rayah* could not wear green, the color of their conquerors. His shoes had to be black, while his master could wear yellow or red. This restriction shows why Marko

---

21. Ibid., p. 31.
22. Mervin Hiskett, "Islam and Bosnia," *Salisbury Review* (June 1993), p. 6.

Kraljević, in Serbian epic poetry of the Ottoman era, wears a long green robe: the listener takes it as an act of defiance and of hope that one day he, too, will be free to wear what he wants.

Johann Roskiewicz, a traveler passing through Bosnia in 1863, just fifteen years before Ottoman rule ended, observed a "downright degrading" custom still in force in some parts of the country. When a Christian encountered a Muslim, he had to jump down from his horse, wait on the side of the road for the Muslim to pass, and then only was he free to remount his horse and proceed toward his destination.[23]

Of course there were exceptions to these laws. Some non-Muslims bribed the authorities to acquire the privileges of the ruling class. Bribes and corruption were the hallmark of Turkish rule in Bosnia. The judicial system, based on bribery and arbitrary fines, was thoroughly corrupt, as is demonstrated in the Bosnian saying *kadija te tuži, kadija te sudi* (*kadi* accuses you, and *kadi* judges you). The *kadi*, the judicial official, operated only on the basis of bribes, and a *kadi* who would not take a bribe was not to be trusted. Clearly the impoverished *rayah* was powerless in the Turkish courts. It is no wonder that such a system, which lasted for four long centuries, nurtured in the people a deep distrust of the rulers and their institutions. The English historian Sir Robert Ensor in the late nineteenth century characterized Turkish rule in the Balkans as "hideous misgovernment."[24]

For centuries the two communities, the Bosnian Muslims and the Christian *rayah*, lived not together but alongside each other. The ruling class, the Bosnian *begs*, did not feel any responsibity for the miserable plight of their fellow countrymen who had not converted to Islam. They consistently opposed reforms promulgated in Istanbul that would have lightened the *rayah*'s burden.

Turkish rule had negative consequences for the life and behavior of the Orthodox Christian people in Bosnia. The distrust of authority, lack of interest in the public good, and the conviction that there was no justice for them in the land contributed to their isolation and hopelessness. To survive and to live as far as possible from the master's harassment and humiliation, the oppressed isolated themselves also physically by withdrawing into the mountains and settling there to cultivate any ground they could. This is

23. Reported in Andrić, *Development of Spiritual Life*, p. 27.
24. Quoted in Hiskett, "Islam and Bosnia," p. 7.

why the Serbs are spread throughout the large and inhospitable mountain regions of Bosnia, native regions which they fiercely defend.

IV. Bosnia under Austria (1878-1918)

1. The Fall of Turkish Power

Throughout the nineteenth century, Ottoman power was waning in this outskirts of the empire. Serbia had succeeded in wresting its independence early in the century. As the European powers sensed Turkey's declining strength and a fundamental shift in the balance of power, they exerted pressure on the Porte to introduce reforms. In Bosnia itself the Christian population conducted a series of uprisings, culminating in the successful rebellion of 1875.

The European powers dealt with the problem of Bosnia and Herzegovina at the Treaty of Berlin in 1878, making it a protectorate of the Austro-Hungarian Empire. An agreement between the Dual Monarchy and Turkey the next year recognized that Bosnia was juridically still under Turkey. Austria protected the property rights of the Bosnian *begs,* while introducing fundamental political economic and administrative reforms that eventually undermined the privileges they had previously enjoyed.

Ivo Andrić tells us in his "Story about *Kmet* Siman" about an *aga* after the Austrian occupation who comes to take the usual tribute from his *kmet.* He finds Siman lying on the grass with his hands under his head. Without getting up to greet his master, Siman refuses to fulfill his obligation because Turkish power is now overthrown. The *aga* brings him to court, where he is dismayed to see that one of the judges is a Muslim. Here they read to Siman the decree of 1878, confirming the Turkish regulations regarding the responsibility of a *kmet* to his master. They clap Siman into jail for eight days and load him with penalties. When he gets out, Siman takes to drink, loses all he has, and becomes a beggar.[25]

25. From Ivo Andrić, *Izabrana Dela,* vol. 1 (Beograd, 1958), pp. 146-76.

2. Austrian Policy

The reforms were promoted by the Austrian governor and "strong man," Benjamin Kallay, who ruled Bosnia and Herzegovina from 1882 to 1903. A Hungarian aristocrat and distinguished scholar, Kallay spoke Serbo-Croatian and had written a *History of the Serbs,* in which he surmised that the population of Bosnia and Herzegovina was Serbian, although they may now belong to different confessions. When he became administrator of the provinces, however, he forbade the circulation of the already prepared translation of his book into Serbo-Croatian, fearing that his historical contribution might encourage Serbs in their claims on the province.

Six years before assuming his post as governor, in a letter to Julius Andrassy, Minister of Foreign Affairs of the empire, Kallay had written a revealing analysis of the "plunge into bloody struggle" that would ensue if Serbs and Croats pursued their mutually exclusive dreams. "In Serbia they dream about a great Serbia, . . . in Croatia they dream about a great Croatia," and both "include Bosnia and Herzegovina in their dreams." But worst of all from the Austrian point of view would be an alliance between these two nations against the Dual Monarchy. Cooperation between them must be prevented at all costs, he warned. They might retreat from their natural antagonism to each other, especially if they realized that the main danger to both of them came from the Austrian side. Then they might work for a united front opposing the monarchy. "But their even temporary unity would undoubtedly weaken us, particularly if we were to go to war with Russia." He urged sponsorship of the Croats in order to increase Austrian influence of the Balkans after Turkey bowed out. "Croatian expansion would only be for our benefit," Kallay noted. "In our relations with Croatia is the key of the south Slavic question," he concluded.[26]

When Kallay became governor of Bosnia and Herzegovina, he began implementing this policy. Endeavoring in every way to separate Bosnia from Serbia across the border, he called the native language of the people "Croatian with the Latin alphabet," and decreed that it was to be promulgated in all schools. A few months later the language was renamed "Bosnian." Kallay tried to develop "Bosnian" patriotism to counteract the growing Serbian nationalism. Only in 1907, after his departure, was the

26. Letter to Julius Andrassy, cited in Vasilije Krestić, *Storija Srba u Hrvatskoj i Slavoniji (1848-1914)* (Beograd: Politika, 1991), pp. 165ff.

language finally given the more correct name of "Serbo-Croatian" or "Croato-Serbian."

Kallay tried to dissipate the Serbian Orthodox predominance by resettlement. About two hundred thousand Germans, Czechs, Poles, and other mostly Catholic farmers and entrepreneurs were settled in predominantly Serbian areas. The diligent and relatively well-off settlers were resented by the natives as intruders. This resettlement hardly changed the proportions of the population in these areas. In the provincial region of Banja Luka, for example, where many settlers came, the 1910 census showed that the Serbs still had a 57 percent majority.

To promote "Bosnian patriotism" the Austro-Hungarian administration introduced many features of a modern European state: roads and railroads, industry, trade, and commerce, schools and hospitals, civil service and judiciary reform. With a generally rising prosperity, expanded opportunities, and the attraction of Catholic European culture, the governor vigorously encouraged a new Bosnia, according to the model he had set.

School reform was a particularly important aspect of the new policy. At their arrival, the Austrians found 535 small Muslim confessional schools, 54 schools for Roman Catholics, and the same number for the Orthodox. There were one lower level gymnasium in Sarajevo and two schools for girls.

The new administration started opening elementary and high schools and various technical and practical schools on the pattern already established in the monarchy. In contrast to the small confessional schools under the Turks, the newly introduced Austrian schools were for all faiths. The occupation power instituted and controlled these schools, and teachers were appointed and paid by the government. Boy's high schools (gymnasia) were opened in Sarajevo, Mostar, Tuzla, Bihac, and Banja Luka. The Austrians built a pedagogical school to prepare girls to teach in elementary schools. Stipends were available for able students. After completing high school, some attended universities in Vienna, Prague, Zagreb, or Belgrade. A primary purpose of the schools in the empire was to prepare the native populations to perform civic functions in the administrative system. But this education also aimed to make them loyal citizens of the monarchy.[27]

---

27. See Mato Dzaja, *Banjalučka Realka* (Banja Luka, 1980), pp. 9ff.

3. Bosnian Muslims

The Muslim population was apprehensive about the arrival of the Catholic Austrian authorities. At first relieved by the 1879 agreement between Vienna and the Porte, they felt their authority ebbing and assumptions challenged. Their worst fears were realized in 1908 when the provinces were annexed to Austria outright. Prior to Austrian occupation, the Bosnian Muslims lived a "politically unconscious life." Their only politics was to oppose any reforms coming from Istanbul that might threaten their comfortable way of life, their right "to own land, to serve in the Ottoman state apparatus, to wear green and to ride horses."[28] They emphasized the distinctions between themselves and the Christian population. Actually all Bosnians spoke the same language and used the Cyrillic alphabet until the late eighteenth century, when Franciscans moving in from Dalmatia promulgated the Latin alphabet, which made considerable inroads in the nineteenth century.[29]

As they found their prosperity and way of life threatened, substantial numbers of Muslims began moving out to the Turkish "homeland" and to other sections of the Ottoman Empire. We might call them "psychological refugees." They left because they could not reconcile themselves to being excluded from the ruling class. They could not live where Islam was not the dominant faith. They had no feeling of unity with the Christian Bosnians; they only expressed hatred of the Austrians, who had taken their country.

In 1905 Jovan Cvijić, a Serbian ethnographer, talked with these "Boshniak" settlers scattered through Turkey. He found them profoundly homesick for Bosnia's climate, fertile valleys, and their easy life there. They had not learned the new language, and their children no longer spoke the language of their parents. In conversation with Cvijić they expressed their sorrow that they had left Bosnia or Herzegovina, but insisted that they could not live under the Austrians. Now they were strangers in their new land; they had only Islam in common with the Turks.[30]

Of course the great majority of Muslims remained in their native

---

28. Ramet, "Primordial Ethnicity or Modern Nationalism," pp. 8f.

29. Vladimir Corović, *Bosna i Hercegovina* (Beograd, 1925), p. 95.

30. Jovan Cvijić, "O iseljavanju bosanskih Muhamedaca," *Cvijićeva knjiga* (Beograd, 1927), pp. 84-93.

Bosnia. In 1910 the population of Sarajevo was 44 percent Muslim. The new educated generation became more active politically, seeking to improve its position in the province. Pressure from the Muslims and Serbs finally led to a representative assembly, which could recommend to the governor and the imperial authorities policies affecting the local population. However limited in scope, it gave the first experience in self-government.

4. Croats in Bosnia

Before the Austrian arrival in 1878, Croats had shared with Serbs the fate of the Christian *rayah* in the Ottoman Empire. Largely rural tenant farmers, Serbs and Croats had relied upon one another. Better off Serbs had helped Croats repair their churches and offered other material assistance.[31]

The new Austrian policy gave the Croats a central place. Their religion was the established Church of the Empire. Franciscan missionaries pursued evangelization unhampered and with new vigor, driving rifts between the Croats and their Serb neighbors. Kallay's policy foresaw that the Croats would be the spearhead to increase Austrian control in the area and might even attract some Muslims. As a result of economic and political reforms, the position of the Croats notably improved, even while they remained overwhelmingly a peasant nation. The Croats soon learned to look to Vienna as their benefactor.

Croatian intellectual currents swept into Bosnia from neighboring Croatia. The "Yugoslav" idea, the union of all south Slavic people in a common state, attracted some outstanding Croatian intellectuals and leaders. The Roman Catholic bishop of Djakovo, Strossmayer (1815-1905), was the most prominent advocate of union between Orthodox and Catholics. He pragmatically pursued a nonviolent union for south Slavs, either within the empire or even under Serbian sponsorship. He ascribed the hostility between the Orthodox and the Catholics to their inadequate education. His point of view was contrary to that of Governor Kallay and the Austrian imperial authorities.

His enemy, Ante Starčević (1823-1896), the father of Croatian nationalism, whose mother was a Serb, stated that the Serbs of Croatia were not actually Serbs but Croats who had been converted to the Orthodox faith.

---

31. Djoko Slijepčević, *Istorija srpske pravoslavne crkve* (Munich, 1966) II, p. 546.

He regarded Bosnian Muslims as Croats of the Muslim faith. Starcević's nationalism was also inspired by his anticlericalism. He sharply criticized the Roman Catholic Church and Austrian influence on Croatian life. Deploring the low level of education of the clergy, he attacked them for enslaving instead of liberating the people. Therefore, while claiming that all Serbs were Croats, he did not demand that they convert to Roman Catholicism.

Joseph Frank, Starcević's son-in-law and successor, a convert to Catholicism from Judaism, differed from his father-in-law by stressing the importance of the religious factor. He emphasized the religious differences between Serbs and Croats and advocated a proclerical nationalism. He fully supported Austrian policy toward the south Slavs. His spiritual successor was Ante Pavelić, the leader of the Ustashe movement during World War II.

5. Serbs of Bosnia

When the Austrian administration arrived in 1878, the Serbs were relatively the largest nationality in the province. The Austro-Hungarian census of 1910 furnishes us with the following statistics for the province:

	Population	%	% of servile tenure
Serbs	825,418	43.5	74
Muslims	612,137	32.4	4.6
Croats	434,061	22.8	21.4[32]

The Serbs were influenced by the movements of other Orthodox nations in the Balkans toward independence from Turkey; they were especially inspired by Serbia's successful rebellion. Scattered widely through the mountainous regions of the country, overwhelmingly *kmets* or tenant farmers dependent upon the *begs*, the Serbs formed the backbone of the rebellions that culminated in the successful revolt of 1875. While some, particularly in the towns, had managed to achieve a comfortable prosperity under the Ottoman system, on the whole they "lived in misery," as Governor Kallay noted in his letter.

32. From H. C. Darby, "Bosnia," in Darby, et al., *A Short History of Yugoslavia* (Cambridge, 1968), p. 71.

At first the Serbs in Bosnia welcomed the Austro-Hungarians as fellow Christians and hoped they would relieve them of the oppressive Ottoman regime. But they soon found that the Austrian administration worked consistently against their interests. Roads and schools were, in their view, constructed primarily to benefit the empire as a whole, not the province of Bosnia. Few roads were built to bring goods directly from Bosnian provincial capitals to the Adriatic ports, for example. The new settlers, who expanded mining and manufacturing, were resented for despoiling the countryside and cutting down the forests with no perceived benefit to the Serbian peasants around them. These newcomers were perceived as interlopers who watered down the unity of the Serbian communities they settled among.

The chief instrument of the Austrian policy of "divide and rule" was Roman Catholic literature. After the relative tolerance of diverse religions under the Ottoman Empire, the energetic proselytism of the Franciscans exacerbated and enflamed relations between Catholics and Orthodox.

Austrian policy toward the Orthodox Church reflected the changed situation of the new regime. After the Peć Patriarchate had been abolished in 1776, the Church in Bosnia had come under the jurisdiction of the patriarchate in Constantinople, and from then on its bishops were Greeks from Constantinople, who were indifferent to the particular needs of their flock. Austria arranged with the ecumenical patriarchate for the Serbian Church to become autonomous, with its own hierarchy, under the patriarch in Constantinople. Serbian Orthodox bishops began the restoration of the Church and the education of its clergy.

At first the autonomy of the Church was beneficial to the Serbs. But inevitably Serbian national interests came into conflict with the Austrian design. Church-school books with images of Serbian saints and heroes were confiscated. This was all the more startling because the Ottomans had objected only to one hero from epic poetry who had killed the Turkish leader in the battle of Kosovo. Now all national material was suspect. The authorities forbade the free election of priests by parishes, realizing that these priests were enflaming national consciousness. After a prolonged struggle, the people retained the right to elect their own priests, but the Austrian authorities selected the bishops. The younger educated generation kept pressing for national goals. While the bishops were trying to preserve what had been achieved, the priests were asking for a little more, and the younger nationalist generation were revolutionaries, asking for all or nothing.[33] Due to the anti-Serbian policy and discontent with their economic position, early in this century around 40,000 Serbs left Bosnia and settled in western Serbia. Major population shifts, century by century, have been an unfortunate feature of Bosnian history for all its people.

Austrian policy, contrary to its aim, actually strengthened Serbian national consciousness. The Austrian annexation in 1908 strengthened the Serbian conviction that the Serbs would have to unite with their fellow countrymen across the border. At this period animosity was directed against the Dual Monarchy and not against the Croats.

Austrian policy did not succeed in preventing the "Yugoslav" idea of union of the south Slavic peoples from spreading among the younger intellectuals of Bosnia, both Croats and Serbs. The problems of Bosnia and Herzegovina, they saw clearly, could not be solved by the predominance of any one national group over the other. Cooperation was the only possible salvation for this area. This idea began as well to attract Muslim intellectuals, who saw that they could continue to exist only as part of a larger Slavic state. After the downfall of the Austro-Hungarian Empire in 1918, this idea came to fruition with the support of the victorious powers.

Fruits and Tares of History

If the history of Bosnia does not furnish answers for the ongoing civil war there, it provides a historical context for the conflict and throws light upon it. Certain salient developments in the twentieth century interact with the past and may help our understanding of the present.

With the downfall of the two empires, Austrian and Ottoman, the southern Slavs drew together in 1918 into one state, for many the fruit of their historical yearning. For the first time since their settlement in Illyricum, Serbs, Croats, and Slovenes, so closely related in their origins but now of three religious faiths, Catholic, Orthodox and Muslim, found themselves together. According to the census of 1921, the new kingdom of south Slavs had a population of almost twelve million. There were around 5,593,000 Orthodox Christians, 4,708,000 Roman Catholics, and 1,345,000 Muslims.

The "first Yugoslavia" was based upon the unitary principle: the three distinct groups were regarded as one nation. From the start, the kingdom

33. Slijepčević, II, pp. 555-59.

was confronted with many problems and a great number of opponents inside and outside the country. Most ruthless were the Communist Party and the extreme national terrorist groups. The major challenge from without came from the two totalitarian movements that swept into Yugoslavia. With the invasion of Nazi Germany in April 1941, the country was cut to pieces. Hitler bestowed Bosnia and Herzegovina on Ante Pavelić, the leader of the Croatian fascist *Ustashi* movement and head of the "independent State of Croatia." He immediately instituted a policy of religious "ethnic cleansing" of the Orthodox population. He was helped by some Muslims, although others protested. In the "Independent State," about half a million Serbs in Krajina and Bosnia-Herzegovina were murdered, along with thousands of Jews, Gypsies, and Yugoslav-oriented Croats. About 300,000 Orthodox were forcibly converted to Catholicism, while 400,000 were expelled into Serbia. Bosnia and Herzegovina together with Krajina became a fertile recruiting ground for Tito's Partisans and Mihailović's Chetniks, all of whom conducted guerilla warfare against the Germans and their puppets and against each other.

Out of the turmoil and atrocities of the civil war, with the collapse of Germany and the entry of the Red Army into Central Europe and Yugoslavia, the Communist Party seized power and ruled for forty-six years (1945-91).

Before the war the party for tactical reasons had enflamed nationalist passions and supported all secessionist movements. But once it had come to power, it ruthlessly suppressed any national disputes and opposition of any kind. In the name of "brotherhood and unity" all responsibility for war crimes was buried and put into cold storage. Hundreds of thousands were executed as political enemies of the state, but there was no real investigation of the war atrocities. It was hoped that they would be forgotten.

Dr. Oliver Sacks tells us a story, "Cold Storage," which may serve as a metaphor for the post–cold war period in Yugoslavia. A doctor visited a family and noticed a motionless figure lying in the corner. They told him that it was Uncle Toby, who had not moved or talked for seven years. Because of a thyroid malfunction his body temperature had dropped and "he was alive, but not alive, in abeyance, in cold storage." In the hospital the doctors raised his temperature, and finally Uncle Toby awoke, started to talk, and even to walk. The "dead" man had come to life. But the cure was not complete. The patient had had a deadly disease before his thyroid malfunction. This disease also came back, erupting in fury. Uncle Toby "expired in a fit of coughing, a matter of days later." So with the fall of the Yugoslav totalitarian system, all national groups came out of the cold storage in which they had been kept for almost fifty years, but with open wounds, many grievances, and with an outburst of nationalistic passions. Each one of them spoke bitterly about its humiliation under the Communist system, which had touched and distorted every aspect of human relationships. With pain and bitterness they pointed to the great injustices done to them. The wounded people's spirit appears to be, in the words of Isaiah Berlin, "like a bent twig, forced down so severely that when released, it lashes back with fury."[34]

With the failure to institute a civil society and democratic institutions based on freedom and responsibility, the Communist system frustrated all channels that might resolve conflicts and grievances. In Tito's Constitution of 1974, the Muslims of Bosnia and Herzegovina were recognized juridically as a separate constituent nation for the first time. Hitherto they had been regarded as Muslims of Serb or Croat nationality. Along with Serbs and Croats, the Muslims now formed one of the "constituent nations" whose consent would have to be obtained if the province was to separate from Yugoslavia. Of course Tito, like Stalin, never foresaw that these "republics" would actually secede. Bosnia had never existed as an independent sovereign state since the medieval Bosnian kingdom, before the Turkish conquest. With its multinational and complex religious makeup, it could endure only as part of a larger framework. Nevertheless, through a plebiscite, the Bosnian Muslims, allied with the Bosnian Croats, demanded an independent and sovereign state, without obtaining the consent of the third "constituent nation," the Serbs. The hasty recognition of the new state by the Western powers in 1992 ignited the layers of explosives that had been stored up throughout the centuries. All these players, domestic and foreign, contributed to the fury that has erupted in the "historical fault line," to the tragedy of the people of Bosnia and Herzegovina.

But how are we to come out of the present catastrophic, appalling crisis? Adam Michnik, the Polish dissident, tells us of the ironic comment of a French friend during the seemingly hopeless turmoil in Poland in the 1980s. There are two ways to save Poland, he said: through "common sense" — the heavenly powers would descend to free the country from its oppressors — or by "miracle": the Poles, all Poles, those who held power as well

34. *New York Review*, November 21, 1991, p. 19.

as those who had opposed them, would come to an understanding and build the foundation for a new free Poland. The situation in Bosnia is at least as desperate.

Without the miracle of reconciliation, there will be no peace in Bosnia. It is true, and it has often been said, that "past history is never entirely past." But still, future historical development is open; it is not determined. The basic dilemma remains: Will the past of Bosnia destroy its future, or will its future overcome the fears and hatreds accumulated in the past?

Looking for Home:
Evangelical Orthodoxy and the
Search for the Original Church

TIMOTHY P. WEBER

In 1987 about two thousand members, both lay and clergy, from seventeen parishes of the Evangelical Orthodox Church entered the Antiochian Orthodox Church amid much fanfare and public notice. Metropolitan Philip Saliba, head of the Antiochian Church's North American archdiocese, hailed their coming as an event of historic significance. The religious and secular press took notice too, declaring that it was the first time since the founding of the Church in the ancient city of Antioch that an already-existing denomination had entered it. Both received and receiving called the event a "coming home."[1]

Despite the obvious importance to those directly involved, within the large and complex world of American evangelicalism, which is commonly numbered at about 40 million adherents, the departure of two thousand pilgrims to Orthodoxy hardly seemed earthshaking. After all, the sanctuary of a single evangelical megachurch could easily accommodate the total number of converts with room to spare; and Southern Baptists on an average Sunday baptize over three times as many converts. Nevertheless, this modest and still-growing transference of religious allegiance is both curious and revealing. Many of the converts claimed that being evangelical had actually contributed to their becoming Orthodox. In ways that seemed

---

1. An insider's version of this story is found in Peter Gillquist, *Becoming Orthodox: A Journey to the Ancient Christian Faith* (revised and updated, Ben Lomond, CA: Conciliar Press, 1992).

surprising even to themselves, the road to Orthodoxy had been paved with evangelical beliefs and religious experience. What is even more curious is that the children of evangelicalism, who have been so thoroughly shaped by their American context, should be attracted to Orthodoxy, the least Americanized form of Christianity in the United States.

This essay will seek to do three things: (1) it will show that this turn toward Orthodoxy occurred at a time of widespread crisis over identity among evangelicals; (2) it will argue that while the reasons for "becoming Orthodox" were complex, at their root was the long-standing evangelical desire to be identified with the original New Testament Church; and (3) it will demonstrate some of the ironies involved in the attempts of the evangelical converts to make Orthodoxy something that it has never been before — a Church that is at home in America.

The Evangelical Search for Identity

The process that led two thousand evangelicals to enter the Antiochian Orthodox Church must be seen as part of a much larger crisis over evangelical identity. The 1970s were a monumental turning time for American religion, evangelicalism included. While the Protestant mainline Churches were showing early signs of declining numbers and cultural influence, the evangelical movement experienced what some people called a "renaissance." Thanks in large part to the election of Jimmy Carter in 1976, the evangelical subculture suddenly came into view. *Time* and *Newsweek* devoted feature articles to the movement;[2] and Martin Marty declared that no one could do justice to contemporary American religion without giving evangelicalism its due.[3]

After years of being ignored by nearly everyone else, evangelicals hurried to explain their movement to outsiders and to each other.[4] Such

2. Kenneth Woodward, "Born Again!" *Newsweek*, October 25, 1976, pp. 68-78; "Back to that Oldtime Religion," *Time*, December 26, 1977, pp. 52-58.

3. Martin E. Marty, *A Nation of Behavers* (Chicago: University of Chicago Press, 1976), p. 80.

4. Donald G. Bloesch, *The Evangelical Renaissance* (Grand Rapids: Eerdmans, 1973); Bernard Ramm, *The Evangelical Heritage* (Waco: Word, 1973); Richard Quebedeaux, *The Young Evangelicals* (New York: Harper and Row, 1974); David Wells and John Woodbridge, eds., *The Evangelicals* (Nashville: Abingdon, 1975); Donald Dayton, *Discovering an Evangelical Heritage* (New York: Harper and Row, 1976).

efforts demonstrated that it was not easy to find the institutional limits of evangelicalism or to define the movement in precise theological terms.[5] If one stepped back far enough, one could see a vibrant subculture unified around a complex network of institutions and some core convictions: that salvation comes through faith in Jesus Christ (not human works), which each person needs to experience through an act of personal conversion; that the Bible (not church tradition) is divinely inspired and authoritative in all matters of living and believing; and that those who have personally experienced the grace of God need to share it actively with others. But if one moved closer, one could see complexities and even deep cleavages based on different histories, theological orientations, and styles. Even those who wanted to affirm that there was an evangelical "whole" had to admit that it contained many parts.[6]

It was only natural, then, that when evangelicals began to explain themselves to outsiders during the 1970s, a war over definitions broke out. Long-standing differences, deeply rooted in nineteenth-century evangelical life, resurfaced with new urgency. As in all "we're-truer-than-you" arguments, ultimately at stake were matters of identity, authenticity, and the power to control institutions.

No one was more concerned about evangelical identity than Harold Lindsell, whose *The Battle for the Bible* argued that some evangelicals were abandoning what he considered the *sine qua non* of historic evangelicalism — the doctrine of biblical inerrancy.[7] Lindsell believed that without inerrancy, evangelicals were sure to reject additional theological commitments; so he named names and warned that unless inerrantists took decisive action, evangelicalism would lose its distinctiveness and historic identity.[8] Sup-

5. Donald W. Dayton and Robert K. Johnston, eds., *The Variety of American Evangelicals* (Downers Grove, IL: InterVarsity Press, 1991).

6. George Marsden, "The Evangelical Denomination," in *Evangelicalism in Modern America*, ed. Marsden (Grand Rapids: Eerdmans, 1984), pp. vii-xvi.

7. Harold Lindsell, *The Battle for the Bible* (Grand Rapids: Zondervan, 1976); *The Bible in the Balance* (Grand Rapids: Zondervan, 1978).

8. Lindsell did not start the battle for the Bible. For over a decade evangelical scholars had been debating the relationship between inerrancy and biblical scholarship. See, for example, Dewey Beegle, *The Inspiration of Scripture* (Philadelphia: Westminster, 1963), and *Scripture, Tradition, and Infallibility* (Grand Rapids: Eerdmans, 1973). For an overview of evangelical biblical scholarship, see Mark A. Noll, *Between Faith and Criticism* (2nd ed., Grand Rapids: Baker Book House, 1991).

porters of inerrancy organized themselves into the interdenominational International Council on Biblical Inerrancy and into purposive groups in various denominations in order to protect the doctrine from its detractors and eliminate noninerrantists from leadership positions within evangelical organizations.[9]

Though it was difficult to ignore the inerrancy crusade, a few evangelical leaders understood that other things contributed to the identity crisis. Carl F. H. Henry claimed that evangelicals were at odds on a number of fronts. "While he is still on the loose, and still sounding his roar, the evangelical lion is nonetheless slowly succumbing to an identity crisis. The noteworthy cohesion that American evangelicals gained in the sixties has been fading in the seventies through multiplied internal disagreements and emerging counterforces."[10]

In addition to the conflict over biblical inerrancy, Henry cited the disagreements over the relationship between evangelism and political action and the place of charismatic religious experience in modern church life. He lamented the fact that "Evangelicalism has shown itself painfully weak in shaping American national conscience, despite the massive impact of the Graham crusades and the personal popularity of the evangelist."[11] He noted that many young evangelical scholars who had not personally experienced the fundamentalist war with modernism were less inclined to contend for the faith than the older leadership had been. With rare insight, he predicted that "the evangelical far right is regathering for a massive initiative all its own"[12] and counseled special care as evangelicals explored the latest "media frontiers" in television and mass communications. Though Henry himself did not see the positive side of the identity crisis, there was one: evangelicalism's "coming of age" meant that it had to reassess its core commitments, its varied histories, and its connections to other movements.

Unnoticed by either Lindsell or Henry was the growing interest in evangelicalism's relationship to historic, catholic traditions. Evangelicals had always considered themselves *orthodox* — either because they affirmed

9. The International Council on Biblical Inerrancy was founded in Chicago in 1978; and in 1979, inerrantists within the Southern Baptist Convention started a movement to establish their control of the denomination.

10. Carl F. H. Henry, *Evangelicals in Search of Identity* (Waco: Word Books, 1976), p. 22.

11. Ibid., p. 42.

12. Ibid., p. 22.

more-or-less historic Christian dogma (as interpreted through the Protestant Reformation) or because they adhered to the teachings of the Bible — but rarely had they described themselves in *catholic* terms.[13] For most of their history in America, evangelicals had defined themselves over against catholicism, by which they meant Rome.[14] From the evangelical perspective, Roman Catholicism was wholly other and therefore defective: Papal infallibility, the veneration of Mary and the saints, the mysterious (and probably superstitious) sacramental system, and its strange pieties were considered nonbiblical and completely outside evangelical parameters.

At the beginning of the 1970s, most rank-and-file evangelicals probably still viewed catholicism in such negative terms; but a growing number was ready to reconsider. The reasons for this more open attitude were many. For some, the charismatic movement had broken down old barriers between evangelicals and Catholics. For others, formal study of early church history or deep dissatisfaction with evangelical low-church and often anti-sacramental worship styles raised new questions. Still others realized that assertions of evangelicalism's orthodoxy were meaningless apart from some connection to historic Christian Churches. Finding one's identity within the one, holy, catholic, and apostolic Church meant examining the differences that still divided evangelicals and catholics of various kinds.

A relatively easy way for some evangelicals to "go catholic" was to become Episcopalian. After all, American evangelicalism had always been big enough to include Episcopalians;[15] and a number of British Anglicans (J. I. Packer, John R. Stott, and, of course, C. S. Lewis) were well known and admired by American evangelicals. Because Anglicanism on both sides of the Atlantic included an "evangelical party," a niche already existed for evangelicals who wanted to join. Robert Webber was one of the early and most vocal converts to Episcopalianism. His scholarly and popular studies of the history

13. The big exception to this statement in the nineteenth century was the "evangelical catholicism" of Philip Schaff in the Mercersburg Theology. See James Hastings Nichols, *Romanticism in American Theology: Nevin and Schaff at Mercersburg* (Chicago: University of Chicago Press, 1961).

14. To understand how Catholics used their outsider status to fashion their own identity in America, see R. Laurence Moore, *Outsiders and the Making of Americans* (New York: Oxford University Press, 1986), pp. 48-71.

15. Alan Guelzo, *For the Union of Evangelical Christendom: The Irony of the Reformed Episcopalians* (University Park, Pennsylvania: Pennsylvania State University Press, 1994).

and theology of worship[16] were important in leading numerous others (including many of his students from Wheaton College) down "the Canterbury trail."[17] Those converts who explained their reasons for becoming Episcopalian all said much the same thing: they desired a sense of mystery, which was absent in "propositional" evangelicalism; they longed for meaningful worship experiences, including a more profound appreciation of the sacraments; they felt cut off from the long memories and practices of historic Christianity; and they lacked a sense of belonging to the whole Church.[18] In the words of Thomas Howard, whose own walk down the Canterbury trail finally ended up in Rome, being "evangelical is not enough."[19]

But one did not have to become an Episcopalian to explore evangelicalism's catholic connections. In May, 1977, at the urging of Robert Webber, Donald Bloesch, and Thomas Howard, forty-five evangelical professors, pastors, editors, authors, and graduate students from a variety of denominations gathered in Chicago.[20] The result was "The Chicago Call: An Appeal to Evangelicals."[21] In his personal account of the events leading up to the Chicago meeting, Webber described how he and other conferees "have been growing beyond the borders of what has, until now, been regarded as the limits of evangelicalism." Just as evangelical leaders like Billy Graham, Harold John Ockenga, Harold Lindsell, and C. F. H. Henry had moved beyond the borders of fundamentalism in the forties and fifties, so other "orthodox evangelicals" have "continued to look beyond present limitations toward a more inclusive and ultimately more historic Christianity."[22]

16. Robert E. Webber, *Common Roots: A Call to Evangelical Maturity* (Grand Rapids: Zondervan, 1978); *Worship Old and New* (Grand Rapids: Zondervan, 1982); *The Biblical Foundations of Christian Worship* (*The Complete Library of Christian Worship*, vol. 1, Nashville: Star Song, 1993). *Twenty Centuries of Christian Worship* (*The Complete Library of Christian Worship*, vol. 2, Nashville: Star Song, 1994); *The Renewal of Sunday Worship* (*The Complete Library of Christian Worship*, vol. 3, Nashville: Star Song, 1993).

17. Robert E. Webber, *Evangelicals on the Canterbury Trail: Why Evangelicals Are Attracted to the Liturgical Church* (Waco: Word Books, 1985).

18. Ibid., pp. 19-161.

19. Thomas Howard, *Evangelical Is Not Enough* (Nashville: Thomas Nelson, 1984).

20. For media accounts of the meeting, see *Newsweek*, May 23, 1977, p. 76; *Christian Century*, June 1, 1977, p. 527; *Christianity Today*, June 17, 1977, p. 27, and July 29, 1977, p. 8.

21. Robert E. Webber and Donald Bloesch, eds., *The Orthodox Evangelicals: Who They Are and What They Are Saying* (Nashville: Thomas Nelson, 1978).

22. Ibid., p. 19.

The Chicago Call was an amazing document in many ways. In its Prologue, it declared that evangelicals had "a pressing need to reflect upon the substance of the biblical and historic faith and to recover the fullness of this heritage."[23] The main body of the document consisted of eight "calls" to historic roots and continuity, biblical fidelity, creedal identity, holistic salvation, sacramental integrity, spirituality, church authority, and church unity. Each of the eight statements posed a problem and then proposed a solution.[24]

Even a casual reading of the Chicago Call reveals that its signers had a much broader definition of evangelicalism than did most people who applied the label to themselves. The Call recognized that throughout church history there has been an "evangelical impulse to proclaim the saving, unmerited grace of Christ, and to reform the church according to the Scriptures." This evangelical emphasis could be seen not only in the work of the Protestant Reformers and their heirs, but in the theology of the ecumenical councils, the piety of the early Church Fathers, Augustine's theology of grace, the reforming work of monastics and mystics, and the theology of the Christian humanists. In fact, the Call went on to say, the evangelical impulse is evident whenever "the Gospel has come to expression through the operation of the Holy Spirit," including renewal movements within Eastern Orthodoxy, Roman Catholicism, and ecumenical Protestantism. "We dare not move beyond the biblical limits of the Gospel; but we cannot be fully evangelical without recognizing our need to learn from other times and movements concerning the whole meaning of the Gospel."[25]

The Call was long on critique but rather short on concrete, specific proposals for action. It rejected evangelicalism's tendency toward individualistic interpretation of the Bible in favor of an approach that was both scholarly and in touch with "the historic understanding of the church." The authors stated that historic confessions should serve as "a guide for the interpretation of Scriptures," but they did not specify which confessions or exactly how their guidance would work.[26]

Likewise, the Call decried the "poverty of sacramental understanding"

23. Ibid., p. 11.
24. The entire Chicago Call can be found in ibid., pp. 11-18.
25. Ibid., p. 12.
26. Ibid., pp. 12-13.

among American evangelicals, who did not recognize that "the grace of God is mediated through faith by the operation of the Holy Spirit in a notable way in the sacraments of baptism and the Lord's Supper."[27] But the authors did not define how the Spirit worked in the sacraments or how the sacraments should be observed. Furthermore, the Call criticized evangelicals' "disobedience to the Lordship of Christ as expressed through authority in his church," which resulted in a spirit of autonomy and even anarchy. All Christians should be in practical submission to each other and "to designated leaders in a church under the Lordship of Christ." But the Call took no position on the form of such leadership or how submission should take place. The Call also deplored the "scandalous isolation and separation of Christians from one another" and evangelicalism's "ahistorical, sectarian mentality," which failed "to appropriate the catholicity of historic Christianity, as well as the breadth of the biblical revelation." Accordingly, evangelicals must "recognize that God works within diverse historical streams." While the Call rejected "church union-at-any-cost," it did advocate "encounter and cooperation within Christ's church" by "earnestly seeking common areas of agreement and understanding."[28]

In retrospect, the Call bore witness to a growing catholic awareness among certain evangelicals and their inability to decide what in particular to do about it. Robert Webber and Donald Bloesch both admitted that the "orthodox evangelicals" at Chicago were deeply divided over what to do with the Reformation: were the Protestant Reformers in continuity or discontinuity with the early Church? To be authentically orthodox did one have to disavow the Protestant revolt against catholicism or should one embrace Reformation concerns as a needed corrective to earlier catholic corruptions?[29] A Roman Catholic participant-signer noted that the Call was a "consensus statement drafted and signed by people who were coming from very different theological places" and that those differences often grew out of the "old Reformation problem of Scripture and tradition."[30] That basic disagreement in perspective accounted for the Call's ambiguity and

27. Ibid., p. 14.

28. Ibid., pp. 14-16.

29. Ibid., pp. 25-27; Donald Bloesch, The Future of Evangelical Christianity (Garden City, New York: Doubleday, 1983), pp. 48-52.

30. See Webber and Bloesch, The Orthodox Evangelicals, pp. 225-33, for Benedict Viviano's reflections on the conference and pp. 16-17 for a list of the signers.

was the primary reason that a few conference participants refused to sign it.[31]

The Search for the Original Church

A few of the "orthodox evangelicals" at Chicago were already well down the road to "Evangelical Orthodoxy." Of the forty-five who drew up the Chicago Call, five were identified with the New Covenant Apostolic Order,[32] a group of evangelicals who were essentially "storming orthodoxy by the back door,"[33] or rather making up Orthodoxy as they went along.

The road that led this group into the Antiochian Orthodox Church in 1987 started in the 1960s at Arrowhead Springs, California, the headquarters of Campus Crusade for Christ.[34] Founded in the early 1950s by Bill Bright, Crusade had become one of the most successful parachurch organizations to grow out of the "new evangelical" movement after World War II. By the late 1960s hundreds of staff members were conducting Bible studies in dormitories and in fraternity and sorority houses and leading students to Christ by means of the "Four Spiritual Laws."[35] As a parachurch organization, one of those "voluntary associations" that evangelicals have used to accomplish specialized ministries outside of churchly structures, Crusade had problems turning college-age converts into church-going Christians. During the sixties, campus ministries often took on the counter-cultural ethos of the campuses. Many new converts recoiled at the stodgy "establishment" evangelical congregations to which their Crusade leaders directed them. Radically committed to Christ, many students felt alienated from the Church.

Many Crusade leaders agreed with these anti-Church sentiments; but they also believed that their converts needed what only churches could

31. David Wells did not sign the Call. For his reasons, see ibid., pp. 213-24.
32. Jon Braun, Peter Gillquist, Kenneth Jensen, Ray Nethery, and Gordon Walker. See Webber and Bloesch, *The Orthodox Evangelicals*, pp. 16-17.
33. With apologies to Nathan Hatch, whose wonderful phrase "storming heaven by the back door" I am adapting here. See Hatch, *The Democratization of American Christianity* (New Haven: Yale University Press, 1989).
34. The outlines of the story are taken from Gillquist, *Becoming Orthodox*.
35. Richard Quebedeaux, *I Found It! The Story of Bill Bright and Campus Crusade* (San Francisco: Harper and Row, 1979).

provide, a nurturing *community* of faith that could sustain them through all the stages of their life. Without such community connections, most converts soon fell by the wayside. According to Peter Gillquist, one of the "stars" of Crusade's staff, "we didn't like the institutional Church and we didn't like the world system, and we were out to change them both."[36]

By the middle of the sixties, many Crusade campus leaders had concluded that a parachurch organization could not reform either world or Church. During the annual training session at Arrowhead Springs in the summer of 1966, a number of Crusade's area directors decided that Campus Crusade needed to move from parachurch to Church. "We sensed a lack of freedom. We wanted to pull out all the stops and do 'everything they did in the first century' — baptize our converts, serve communion, take more vocal stands against evil. In short, we wanted above all else to be the New Testament Church."[37]

That program was completely out of step with the founding vision of Bill Bright, so by 1968 a group of extremely frustrated Crusade leaders left the organization. By then most of them were thoroughly disillusioned with the institutional Church. They knew what they wanted but had not found it in any of the existing denominations. "The Church was the answer, but not any Church we had ever seen. It was the New Testament Church that we sought. And we were soon to find that countless others were looking for the same things. We were beginning what we soon began to call *The Phantom Search for the Perfect Church*."[38]

For the next five years, the former Crusaders pursued other occupations, but kept alive their dream of the True Church by founding "house churches" in the Midwest, South, and West Coast. These house churches took the New Testament as their only guide and tried to reproduce not only the form but also the power and commitment of the original Church.

This pursuit of original New Testament Christianity is common in American religion. Historians have noted the strong strains of *primitivism* and *restorationism* in American history.[39] Though the two concepts are

36. Gilquist, *Becoming Orthodox*, p. 5.
37. Ibid., p. 17.
38. Ibid., p. 19.
39. Richard T. Hughes and C. Leonard Allen, *Illusions of Innocence: Protestant Primitivism in America, 1630-1875* (Chicago: University of Chicago Press, 1988); Richard T. Hughes, ed., *The American Quest for the Primitive Church* (Urbana and Chicago: University of Illinois Press, 1988).

sometimes difficult to distinguish, their adherents agree that some time shortly after the apostolic age, the Church "fell" on account of its own corruptions and superstitious practices. Often the Church's fall was located in the rise of Constantine, through whom the Catholic Church and the Roman state became unholy allies. Thus the story of postapostolic Christianity was mainly one of decline and defection from the pure forms and beliefs of the New Testament period.

Accordingly, the reform of the Church consisted of putting it back into its pre-fall condition. In America such sentiments have produced powerful "back to the Bible" or "no creed but Christ" movements. Some reformers were "restorationists" who believed that since the Church's fall no true Church existed in the world — until it was finally restored in their own movements.[40] "Primitivists" believed that New Testament Christianity was reproducible whenever people faithfully followed the Bible, not ecclesiastical traditions.[41] Both groups were convinced that the best Church was the first Church, which was completely recoverable.

Twentieth-century evangelicals and fundamentalists often sounded like restorationists and primitivists. They claimed to put the Bible above all other authorities and often called themselves simple, New Testament Christians. But in most cases their primitivism was not pure. Parts of the historic Christian tradition they fully embraced. Though most probably believed that the Church fell sometime after the apostles, they also believed that the original gospel was more or less restored by the Reformation. Consequently, to them "that old time religion" meant more than the New Testament Church; it also referred to the legacy of the Reformation.[42]

It was this primitivistic search for the original New Testament Church that drove the former Campus Crusaders in new directions. By the end of 1973, the old Crusade network reconnected to lend support for the common experiment with house churches. Seven men over forty were designated "elders" and agreed to meet together once a quarter to study and

40. Committed to this perspective were Alexander Campbell's Disciples, Barton W. Stone's Christians, Joseph Smith's Church of Jesus Christ of Latter Day Saints, and the pentecostals of the early twentieth century.

41. See Hatch, *The Democratization of American Christianity* for a study of how such notions produced powerful populist movements in the early nineteenth century.

42. Joel A. Carpenter, "Contending for the Faith Once Delivered: Primitivist Impulses in American Fundamentalism," in Hughes, ed., *The American Quest for the Primitive Church,* pp. 99-119.

strategize. According to Peter Gillquist, one of the newly-designated elders, at one of the group's first meetings the discussion took an unexpected turn. Jack Sparks, who had the advantage (according to Gillquist) of not having had any formal theological education, raised a new issue: "As Protestants, we know our way back to A.D. 1517 and the Reformation. As evangelicals — Bible people — we know our way up to A.D. 95 or so, when the Apostle John finished writing the Revelation. It's time to fill the gap in between."[43] What happened to the New Testament Church between its fall in the second century and its restoration in the Reformation?

None of the assembled elders claimed to know *where* the New Testament Church had gone. Jon Braun said, "In all honesty, I was taught that the minute the Apostle John drew his last breath, the Church began to head downhill. Is that really right? And if it isn't, then where and when did the Church go wrong? How could the Reformation have been avoided, anyway?"[44] The elders then assigned topics: Sparks took worship, Braun early church history, Richard Ballew doctrine, Ken Berven the pre-Reformation period, and Ray Nethery the post-Reformation era. Gordon Walker was assigned to check all conclusions by the Bible, and Peter Gillquist acted as administrator for the project. "Our basic question was, whatever happened to that Church we read about in the pages of the New Testament? Was it still around? If so, where? We wanted to be a part of it."[45]

The group reconvened in February, 1975 and shared findings. Much to everyone's surprise, they discovered that the Church of New Testament period kept on going into the second, third, and fourth centuries and was liturgical, sacramental, hierarchical, and conciliar. Thus, they concluded, the New Testament Church had been "catholic" from the beginning. Here were some rather uncritical assumptions and untested conclusions about the nature of both the Church and history. That the apostolic Church continued after the apostles comes as no surprise to any beginning student of church history; but the former Crusaders evidently assumed that continuation meant changeless continuity.

On the basis of this discovery, the elders decided that their house churches needed to change. They organized the New Covenant Apostolic Order (NCAO), which adopted a hierarchical structure (one bishop pre-

43. Gillquist, *Becoming Orthodox*, p. 24.
44. Ibid., pp. 24-25.
45. Ibid., p. 28.

siding over each congregation) and a more liturgical worship style.[46] Such changes reflected a deeper shift in the group's evangelical identity. Instead of defining themselves primarily in terms of the Bible and the Protestant Reformation, the people in NCAO began to identify more with the historic, pre-Protestant Church and its practices. They set out on the difficult task of tracing the pure, unaltered New Testament Church through time.

Such an enterprise is filled with hazards. The history of Christianity is complicated, to say the least. Even for those with deep loyalties to the historic Christian tradition, unraveling the relationship between continuity and change can be daunting. Students of early Christianity must face up to certain difficult issues. For example, what difference did the Gentile mission make in the early Church's identity? What impact did adopting Greek philosophical categories have in the development of Christian theology? How did living under an imperial political structure influence the Church's approach to hierarchical leadership? And how did the Church's expansion into "barbarian" territories effect its piety and liturgy? It is important to emphasize that leading Orthodox scholars do understand these issues and are careful to nuance their discussions about the Church's continuity with the apostolic Church.[47] In contrast, the leaders of the NCAO took a naive and unsophisticated approach that failed to take the Church's complex passage through time seriously.

As Grant Wacker has pointed out, from the late nineteenth century on, evangelicals have been deeply troubled by what he calls "historical consciousness," the realization that movements are unavoidably shaped by

---

46. The NCAO's views of episcopal authority were roundly criticized in some evangelical circles as authoritarian and abusive. Bill Counts, *The Evangelical Orthodox Church and the New Covenant Apostolic Order* (Berkeley: The Spiritual Counterfeits Project, 1979).

47. See, for example, Georges Florovsky, *Bible, Church, Tradition: An Eastern Orthodox View* (Belmont, MA: Nordland Publishing, 1972); idem, "The Predicament of the Christian Historian," reprinted in *God, History, and Historians*, ed. C. T. McIntire (New York: Oxford, 1977), pp. 406-42; idem, "The Limits of the Church," *Church History Review* 117 (1933), pp. 129ff.; Alexander Schmemann, *The Historical Road of Eastern Orthodoxy* (Crestwood, NY: St. Vladimir's Seminary Press, 1992); John Meyendorff, *Living Tradition: Orthodox Witness in the Contemporary World* (Crestwood, NY: St. Vladimir's Seminary Press, 1978); idem, *Catholicity and the Church* (Crestwood, NY: St. Vladimir's Seminary Press, 1983); S. Breck, J. Meyendorff, and E. Silk, *The Legacy of St. Vladimir* (Crestwood, NY: St. Vladimir's Seminary Press, 1990), pp. 14-20; Bradley Nassif's chapter in *New Dimensions in Evangelical Theology* (Grand Rapids: Baker Book House, forthcoming).

their contexts, that nothing in history is free from forces that both expand and limit.[48] Large segments of American evangelicalism have never come to terms with this perspective, preferring to stress the supernatural over the natural or to separate the two until the supernatural operates apart from the natural. Consequently, by this perspective, a church is either pure or impure, apostolic or nonapostolic, "New Testament" or some corrupt defection. At their base, then, such a view attempts to keep the Church free from historical contingencies and corrupting influences. The real Church is *in* history, but it is not *of* history.

In their search for the original Church, the NCAO adopted such an approach. For them, the history of the New Testament Church through time looked remarkably straightforward and uncomplicated. For a millennium, the Church carried on virtually unscathed, able to ward off anything that might compromise its essential purity and its continuity with the original Church. But then, in 1054, the unity of the New Testament Church was broken by the Great Schism, in which papal pretensions and the Western Church's addition of *filioque* to the Creed drove a wedge between the Eastern and Western Churches. Not even the Protestant Reformation could overcome the schism and reestablish unified New Testament Christianity. In their zeal to correct the abuses of Roman Catholicism, many Protestants rejected crucial elements of the original Church, such as hierarchy, liturgy, the sacraments, and the like.

> Thus, while retaining in varying degrees portions of foundational Christianity, neither Protestantism nor Catholicism can lay historic claim to being the true New Testament Church. In dividing from the Orthodox Church, Rome forfeited its place in the Church of the New Testament. In the divisions of the Reformation, the Protestants — as well meaning as they might have been — failed to return to the New Testament Church.[49]

This view of church history can be clearly seen in "A Time Line of Church History."[50] It shows the "one holy catholic and apostolic church"

---

48. Grant Wacker, *Augustus H. Strong and the Dilemma of Historical Consciousness* (Macon, GA: Mercer University Press, 1985).

49. Jon Braun, *Finding the New Testament Church* (Ben Lomond, CA: Conciliar Press, 1992), pp. 16-17.

50. The time line can be found in Gillquist, *Becoming Orthodox,* pp. 48-49, or in a pamphlet entitled *A Time Line of Church History,* available separately from Conciliar Press.

stretching out in a straight line from Pentecost to the Great Schism in 1054, where a branch labeled the Roman Catholic Church splits off. From that branch other splits emerge, including those of the Reformation. While the Roman Catholic Church and Protestant Churches head off in other directions, the one holy catholic and apostolic Church continues in its straight line, which after 1054 is labeled "the Orthodox Church."

Historians of American religious history will recognize this plot line as a kind of "successionism." Unlike restorationists who teach that the Church fell early on and had to be restored in more recent times, successionists hold that the true Church never ceased to exist. While the rest of "Christendom" degenerated, a remnant of the New Testament Church continued on, alive, pure, and uncompromising. Landmarkist Baptists, for example, trace a pure "trail of blood" through the history of corrupt Christianity into the present day, thereby proving that only Baptists have New Testament legitimacy.[51] Of course, to arrive at such conclusions, successionists must be highly selective and ignore all evidence to the contrary. They must also maintain an idealized and naive view of the past. In the end, successionism is based on one's theology or ideology, not on any critical historical analysis.[52]

This orientation to the past is common among the Evangelical Orthodox. A number of evangelical clergy who converted to Orthodoxy told their stories in *Coming Home*.[53] According to the book's editor, "Almost every author shares his fervent desire for the New Testament Church, the Faith of the Apostles, the Pearl of Great Price, authentic worship in spirit and in truth — in short, original Christianity."[54] A former Presbyterian and graduate of Westminster Theological Seminary claimed that "I am now serving Him in the very Church of Antioch which Saint Luke describes so

51. Because successionist groups consider themselves to be in the unbroken line of New Testament churches, they do not consider themselves Protestants: if one's Church has never been corrupted, there is no need to reform it. On Baptist successionism, see James Edward McGoldrick, *Baptist Successionism: A Crucial Question in Baptist History* (ATLA Monograph Series 32; Metuchen, NJ: American Theological Library Association/Scarecrow Press, 1994).

52. Of course, the Evangelical Orthodox successionist claims have much more warrant than those of Landmarkist Baptists; but both groups view the past in remarkably similar terms and build their cases in selective and uncritical ways.

53. Peter E. Gillquist, ed., *Coming Home: Why Protestant Clergy Are Becoming Orthodox* (Ben Lomond, CA: Conciliar Press, 1992).

54. Ibid., p. 14.

vividly in Acts, and which has continued on unabated for almost two thousand years."[55] A former Baptist minister exclaimed, "I had found the Church which our Lord said would stand the test of time and assault the very gates of hell."[56] According to a former Lutheran, "The Church of the New Testament, the Church of Peter and Paul and the Apostles, the Orthodox Church — despite persecution, political oppression, and desertion on certain of its flanks — miraculously carries on today the same faith and life of the Church of the New Testament."[57]

Fashioning an Orthodox Church for America

By the mid-1970s, then, the NCAO's search was clearly leading in the direction of Orthodoxy. But none of the Church's leaders knew anything about Orthodoxy in the modern world. "Where was this Orthodox Church today? Was it still around? Or had it quietly died away sometime in the late Middle Ages? The truth is, *none* of us had ever to our knowledge been inside an Orthodox Church. Most of us did not know it existed. For that reason, I am chagrined to report that we decided to try to start it over again!"[58]

The year 1977 was a turning point for the NCAO. First, it founded a school of its own, the Academy of Orthodox Theology (later renamed after St. Athanasius) in Santa Barbara, under the leadership of Jack Sparks.[59] Second, it started its own publishing house, Conciliar Press, which issued *Again* magazine.[60] Third, it made its first contacts with contemporary Orthodoxy. Alexander Schmemann of St. Vladimir's Seminary in New York heard about the group in Santa Barbara, then informed Bishop Dmitri of the Orthodox Church of America, who asked Ted Wojcik, pastor of the Saint Innocent Orthodox Church in a Los Angeles suburb, to call on the Academy.

That single visit opened many other doors. During the next year (1978), the contacts with Orthodoxy dramatically increased. A group of

---

55. Ibid., p. 42.

56. Ibid., pp. 99-100.

57. Gillquist, in *Becoming Orthodox,* p. 57.

58. Ibid., p. 54.

59. After the Evangelical Orthodox joined the Antiochian Church, the Academy became a correspondence school.

60. The magazine is still published quarterly, with about five thousand copies of each issue printed.

NCAO leaders visited Fr. Wojcik's parish in Los Angeles and saw for the first time an Orthodox liturgy. Then a delegation visited St. Vladimir's Seminary to consult with professors there, including Alexander Schmemann, Thomas Hopko, and John Meyendorff. Schmemann took a special interest in the group and traveled to Santa Barbara to advise NCAO leaders. Bishop Dmitri, who had grown up a Texas Southern Baptist, also visited the Academy during 1978 and lent his support.

By 1979, their minds were made up: Orthodoxy was the New Testament Church; and they must be a part of it. Accordingly, the NCAO, which had been a rather informal network of congregations, became the Evangelical Orthodox Church (EOC), "a Denomination within the One Holy Catholic and Apostolic Church."[61] Doctrinally, the EOC affirmed the Apostles', Nicene, and Chalcedonian Creeds. It declared itself against abortion, divorce, homosexuality, and women serving as spiritual leaders. It also rejected "as a mark of apostasy [sic] the spread of parachurch movements as a substitute means of accomplishing the great commission of the Church."[62] The EOC's highest governing authority was the Council of Bishops, on which nineteen bishops served, including Peter Gillquist, who was appointed presiding bishop.[63]

If these evangelicals wanted to become Orthodox, why did they not simply join existing Orthodox parishes?[64] The answer is not difficult. First,

61. George Vecsey, "New Group Combines Evangelism and Orthodoxy," *New York Times,* May 11, 1979, p. 25. The quotation is from a promotional brochure distributed by the EOC. The brochure is hereafter referred to as *The Evangelical Orthodox Church.*

62. *The Evangelical Orthodox Church.*

63. The brochure listed the books published by its bishops: J. Richard Ballew, *The Place Where God Lives* (Seattle: Conciliar Press, 1976); idem, *Coming in Out of the Cold* (Seattle: Conciliar Press, 1976); Kenneth A. Berven, *Blest Be the Tie That Frees* (Minneapolis: Augsburg, 1973); idem, *I Love Being Married to a Grandma* (Nashville: Thomas Nelson, 1978); Jon E. Braun, *It Ain't Gonna Reign No More* (Nashville: Thomas Nelson, 1978); idem, *Whatever Happened to Hell?* (Nashville: Thomas Nelson, 1979); Peter E. Gillquist, *Love Is Now* (rev. ed., Grand Rapids: Zondervan, 1978); idem, *The Physical Side of Being Spiritual* (Grand Rapids: Zondervan, 1979); Jack N. Sparks, *The Mindbenders* (Nashville: Thomas Nelson, 1977); idem, *The Apostolic Fathers* (Nashville: Thomas Nelson, 1978); idem, *Going Back Home* (Seattle: Conciliar Press, 1979); *idem, The Resurrection Letters* (Nashville: Thomas Nelson, 1980); Gordon T. Walker, *Twentieth Century Apostleship* (Seattle: Conciliar Press, 1976).

64. It must be remembered that numerous evangelical Protestants had converted to Orthodoxy before the dramatic entry of the Evangelical Orthodox in 1987. For them, there had been no other alternative but to join existing congregations.

by the time the leaders decided to become Eastern Orthodox, they were presiding over congregations with histories of their own and a strong sense of their own identity. To join existing Orthodox parishes would mean breaking up closely-knit religious communities with established authority structures.

Second, they discovered that the road to Orthodoxy was strewn with perils of various kinds. To be in love with Orthodoxy as a historical abstraction was one thing, but to come in contact with it as a contemporary reality was something else again. When the Evangelical Orthodox finally started to visit Orthodox parishes, their first impressions were often negative and disillusioning. The liturgies were not in English; the congregations were ethnic and apparently uncommitted; and the worship practices were exotic.[65] The search for the original Church had led these unsuspecting American evangelicals into a world of strange sights, sounds, and smells: clouds of incense, elaborate vestments, prayers to the saints and for the dead, and veneration of the Mother of God and the holy icons, some of which even wept occasionally. Historically, evangelicals had considered such practices as clear evidence of Orthodoxy's *fallenness*. Where were such things found in the New Testament? But if the evangelicals were going to complete their pilgrimage, they had to find a way of embracing them. "Becoming Orthodox" in the full sense meant accepting the Tradition whole: the faithful were not allowed to pick and choose what they liked.

That took some time. In 1981, for example, Gillquist reflected on where the EOC stood on a number of issues. "From what I can tell of the relationship in Orthodoxy between Holy Scripture and tradition, we have no problems. We have read Timothy Ware's *The Orthodox Church* and concur with its stance." Concerning the saints, Gillquist affirmed that "the righteous dead are far from dormant. If they can intercede for us as earthly saints, they can certainly pray for us as saints in their heavenly state as well." He struggled a bit more with Orthodoxy's teachings about Mary. While he could affirm Mary as *theotokos* against the Nestorian heresy, the matter of her "ever-virginity" was more of a problem: "We would give our eye-teeth, however, for a verse or two in Scripture to back this up — that would certainly make it much easier for us to communicate orthodoxy with our

---

65. Gillquist, *Coming Home*, pp. 87, 117, 123-24, 156; Frank Schaeffer, *Dancing Alone: The Quest for Orthodox Faith in the Age of False Religions* (Brookline, MA: Holy Cross Orthodox Press, 1994), pp. 297-315.

Protestant assailants." On icons Gillquist said, "We feel that in the West, it would be helpful if the iconography were *a bit more* in keeping with our culture, rather than with 9th Century Byzantium. But we are certainly flexible on that particular issue."[66]

The EOC bishops forged ahead in their attempt to reconnect with historic Orthodoxy. They consulted with Orthodox leaders from the three jurisdictions in North America, they asked questions, and they set up altars and icons in their parishes. They worked hard to develop an Orthodox *phronema* (mindset). By 1985 the EOC decided to seek formal entry into the Orthodox Church; but they quickly discovered that the leaders of the Greek and Russian jurisdictions were reluctant to receive them. Discouraged by the poor reception in America, the EOC decided to seek the approval of the Ecumenical Partriarch and his advice about the best way to enter the Church. After considerable planning, in June 1985 a contingent of EOC bishops traveled to Constantinople (Istanbul); but before they arrived, a number of Greek Orthodox clergy had persuaded the Patriarch not to meet with the EOC group because they feared that evangelicals would subvert the Hellenic culture of parishes in America. Disillusioned and angry, the EOC bishops returned home empty-handed.[67]

A few days after their return, Peter Gillquist, Jon Braun, and Richard Ballew met in Los Angeles with Metropolitan Philip Saliba and Patriarch Ignatius, who were enthusiastic about the possibility of receiving the EOC into the Antiochian Archdiocese of North America. Over the next year and a half, the details unfolded. Both sides agreed on a proposal for how the EOC should be received, the EOC's liturgical practices were reviewed and adjusted, and final arrangements were made for early 1987. From February through March, Antiochian bishops received clergy and lay people from the EOC into the Church. Because Orthodox tradition does not allow married bishops, the EOC bishops could not maintain their episcopal rank. They were ordained first as deacons, then as priests of the Antiochian Church. Seventeen of the EOC parishes were received and allowed to remain

66. Peter Gillquist, "The Evangelical Orthodox Church," *Theosis* (February 1981), pp. 3-6. Later on, Gillquist was less tentative. He vigorously defended the perpetual virginity of Mary, along with her assumption and her heavenly intercession for sinners. Peter Gillquist, *Facing Up to Mary* (Ben Lomond, CA: Conciliar Press, n.d.), pp. 9-10, 13-14.

67. I am following the account in Gillquist, *Becoming Orthodox*.

intact. The movement that had begun with Campus Crusade for Christ had now become the Antiochian Evangelical Orthodox Mission (AEOM), a full-fledged part of Orthodoxy.[68]

When Metropolitan Philip Saliba welcomed the evangelicals, he expressed hope that they would spearhead an Orthodox evangelistic outreach into American culture.

> In America, our various Orthodox jurisdictions have been ministering to ethnic communities. We have lost some of the Church's missionary spirit, and so far have not made any breakthrough in American society.
>
> I think the main task of the EOM is to preach the gospel to America. I don't want them to lose their identity as an evangelical missionary group. I feel strongly that our best gift to America will be a stable Christianity that is rooted in the Bible, holy tradition, and the fathers of the Church.[69]

The AEOM took this mandate seriously. The year after entering the Church, they sponsored a Conference on Missions and Evangelism; but no one outside the Antiochian Archdiocese came. In 1990 representatives of the Orthodox Church of America (the Russian Orthodox jurisdiction) attended and offered to join forces with the AEOM. In 1991, an observer from the Greek Orthodox Church came and almost immediately got permission from Archbishop Iakavos to align the Greek Church with the annual conferences. By 1992, the gathering was renamed the "Pan-Orthodox Conference on Missions and Evangelism," and marked a new level of cooperation among the three Orthodox jurisdictions. This kind of networking around mission concerns is historically what American evangelicals do best and indicates something of the zeal and contagious enthusiasm of the evangelical converts.[70]

---

68. Not everyone in the EOC went along. Five of the nineteen bishops and about 1,200 lay people declined the invitation to join. The main problem seemed to be ecclesiological: some did not want to put themselves under the control of "foreign" jurisdictions; and others resisted having to submit to an outdated canon law that forbade married bishops when the Bible allowed the practice (1 Tim. 3:2). See James Mark Kushiner, "The Evangelical Orthodox," *Touchstone* (Fall 1987), pp. 20-21, 24. Kenneth Samuel Jensen, "The Case for a Living Orthodoxy," *Touchstone* (Winter 1989), pp. 14-18.

69. Quoted in Bradley Nassif, "Evangelical Denomination Gains Official Acceptance into the Orthodox Church," *Christianity Today* 31 (February 6, 1987), p. 40.

70. Telephone interview with Peter Gillquist, August 16, 1994.

Another significant accomplishment of the AEOM is the *Orthodox Study Bible: New Testament and Psalms,* which was published in 1993.[71] The *Study Bible*'s purpose is obvious: to encourage Bible study among the Orthodox and to demonstrate that Orthodoxy is rooted in biblical teaching. Thus the notes at the bottom of each page often quote from Orthodox sources or explain how the text relates to Orthodox teaching or practice. Following the basic format of other evangelical study Bibles (e.g., the *Scofield Reference Bible* and the *Ryrie Study Bible*), the *Orthodox Study Bible* also includes brief introductions and outlines for each biblical book, cross references, a concordance, a glossary, a harmony of the Gospels, articles on various themes, a lectionary, a collection of morning and evening prayers, maps, and numerous icons to illustrate the text. Peter Gillquist served as project director, and first drafts of the textual notes were prepared by people at the AEOM's St. Athanasius Academy. Their work was then reviewed by other Orthodox biblical scholars and hierarchs. In its first year, the *Orthodox Study Bible* sold 75,000 copies and is the first Bible of its kind produced by and for the Orthodox in America.

No activities are more typically evangelical than strategizing for evangelism and putting the Bible into the hands of lay people — and no activities have more potential for disturbing established ecclesiastical hierarchies. In the history of American religion, evangelism — especially the kind that works — has tended to challenge traditional structures and the theologies behind them. Likewise, putting the Bible into the hands of common people — especially those who like to read it on their own — has sometimes had revolutionary and unintended consequences. Bible-reading by lay people, some creedal churches have learned to their cost, can cause more trouble than it is worth. Furthermore, ethnic churches that try to evangelize the broader American culture often end up being Americanized themselves.

As sincere as Evangelical Orthodox mission to America is, many questions remain. What if the AEOM succeeds? What if Americans begin to respond to the evangelistic program in significant numbers? Will they be welcomed in non-AEOM, ethnic Orthodox parishes? What kinds of cultural and religious identity crises will result from a successful mission to America? What if American Orthodox laity read their Bibles and come to conclusions different from those of their bishops? How long will it be before those in

---

71. *The Orthodox Study Bible: New Testament and Psalms* (Nashville: Thomas Nelson, 1993). The translation is the New King James Version.

charge stop dreaming of turning America Orthodox and start worrying about Orthodoxy becoming too American? Before 1987, evangelical Protestant converts to Orthodoxy joined existing congregations and had to cope with ethnic realities: but what will happen now that the evangelicals have their own parishes, where a distinctly American style can develop?

Of course, it is much too early to answer such questions. As things now stand, the AEOM seems to be no threat to the Orthodox establishment. Their parishes are growing, but not explosively. As recent converts, the evangelicals are enthusiastic, loyal, and obedient. Though their style is sometimes not what most Orthodox are accustomed to — an Orthodox *phronema* is not achieved overnight — their theology is unabashedly Orthodox.[72] In fact, on some crucial doctrines, they no longer sound like Protestant evangelicals at all.

For example, no issue is more important to evangelicals than the doctrine of salvation. At the heart of evangelicalism is the conviction that salvation is a gift of God's grace that comes to sinners through their faith in Christ. Salvation cannot be earned or merited; it must be received by faith, apart from human works. Evangelicals believe that being baptized or holding church membership or even believing the right things is not enough. Each person needs to repent and trust in Christ. This is what evangelicals mean by being "saved" or "born again," and why they invite others to receive Christ and experience conversion by the power of the Holy Spirit.[73]

The leaders of the AEOM no longer teach this doctrine. In fact, they are quite critical of it. Frank Schaeffer, a former evangelical whose pilgrimage did not follow the Campus Crusade-NCAO-EOC-AEOM route, calls the standard evangelical doctrine a "false bill of goods." "The simplistic 'born-again' formula for instant painless 'salvation' is not only a misunderstanding, I believe it is a heresy. It contradicts the teaching of Christ in

---

72. Conciliar Press, the AEOM's publishing arm, publishes a series of booklets that explain Orthodox doctrine to outsiders, especially Protestant evangelicals. Titles include: *Finding the New Testament Church; No Graven Image; Which Came First: The Church or the New Testament; Entering God's Kingdom; Facing Up to Mary;* and *Scripture and Tradition.*

73. For two typical Protestant evangelical theologies of conversion, see Donald Bloesch, *Essentials of Evangelical Theology: God, Authority, and Salvation,* vol. 1 (New York: Harper and Row, 1978), pp. 181-252; Stanley J. Grenz, *Theology for the Community of God* (Nashville: Broadman and Holman, 1994), pp. 528-99.

regard to the narrow, hard, ascetic, difficult way of salvation." Real salvation "is not found in simplistic formulas but in choosing to grow into the people God created us to be and by a life-long ascetic, sacramental struggle for holiness.[74]

In his booklet on "Entering God's Kingdom," Pete Gillquist sounds like the old Campus Crusade evangelist when affirming that salvation is God's gift, impossible to earn by our own merit; but then he adds a distinctly Orthodox perspective: "through Christ, we are born from above through Holy Baptism into newness of life." For salvation to be authentic, it must be lived out within the Orthodox Church: "For one must live within the body of Christ, be fed by her sacraments, be instructed in her true faith, and worship at her altar to attain the godliness and righteousness that lead to the Kingdom's open doors."

> Let me ask you a sincere question. Are you willing to flee to Jesus Christ for protection in His Holy Church, to learn to know Him, to be cleansed and changed? If so, a new life in Christ lies ahead for you. Your next step is to get to know an Orthodox priest in your area who can guide you through a time of preparation and instruction in the Christian faith, and then union with Christ in Holy Baptism.[75]

In the *Orthodox Study Bible* the Protestant evangelical doctrine of salvation is often used as a foil for Orthodox teaching. Even common evangelical phraseology is criticized: "Becoming a Christian is not so much inviting Christ into one's life as getting oneself into Christ's life."[76] Justification is *not* by faith *alone*, since from apostolic times Orthodox have believed that "salvation was granted by the mercy of God to righteous men and women."

> This is why the modern evangelical Protestant question, "Are you saved?" gives pause to an Orthodox believer. As the subject of salvation is addressed in Scripture, the Orthodox Christian would see it in at least three aspects: (a) I have been saved, being joined to Christ in baptism;

74. Schaeffer, *Dancing Alone*, pp. 256-57. Frank Schaeffer and his father Francis Schaeffer were well-known evangelical apologists and social critics during the seventies and eighties.

75. Peter Gillquist, *Entering God's Kingdom* (Ben Lomond, CA: Conciliar Press, 1987), pp. 7, 13-14.

76. *Orthodox Study Bible*, p. 439.

(b) I am being saved, growing in Christ through the sacramental life of the Church; and (c) I will be saved, by the mercy of God at the Last Judgment.[77]

Such statements make it obvious that the Evangelical Orthodox have left their former views of evangelism far behind. Whereas some evangelicals in sacramental traditions (e.g., the Lutherans and Episcopalians) might view the relationship between conversion and the sacraments in similar ways, most evangelicals would not. In an effort to correct what they believe was their earlier error — of leading people to Christ without adequately stressing the importance of the Church or the need for obedience to Christ's commands — the Evangelical Orthodox now affirm a doctrine of salvation that most evangelicals cannot accept. From an evangelical perspective, their teaching does not make distinct *enough* the absolute importance of personally receiving by faith the gracious gift of God in Christ, apart from all human works — even good religious ones. Such a "Catholic" view of faith and works dangerously confuses the closely connected but still distinct doctrines of justification and sanctification: once justified, the redeemed are able to do works of righteousness (Eph. 2:8-10); but good works play no role in the sinner's justification before God. Sanctification (becoming holy) follows justification; it is not the basis for justification. One thing seems clear: in their mission to America, the Evangelical Orthodox will not preach the same message that they used to preach.

What about the AEOM's relationship to the Orthodox "system"? Many of the evangelicals are bewildered by the three Orthodox jurisdictions in America and a bit put-off by the Church's ethnic identity. But their successful bridge-building between the jurisdictions through the Pan-Orthodox Conferences on Missions and Evangelism and their ability to fashion their own nonethnic congregations have mitigated those concerns to some extent. Likewise, the Evangelical Orthodox seem to be on the best of terms with the bishops. In fact, some reform-minded "cradle Orthodox" have accused the AEOM of being too compliant. Archimandrite Fr. Eusebius Stephanou, whose Orthodox Brotherhood of St. Symeon the New Theologian promotes charismatic renewal within the Church, has criticized the AEOM for preaching Orthodoxy rather than Christ and viewing "everything in the Orthodox Church through rose-colored glasses." So concerned

---

77. From an article on "Justification by Faith" in *The Orthodox Study Bible*, p. 348.

to appear loyal to the bishops and the Tradition, the evangelicals are, he says, unrealistic about the real state of the Church, blind to its desperate need for renewal, and too uncritically obedient to the hierarchy.[78]

Nevertheless, there are already signs that the evangelicals are willing to address some problems. In addition to saving souls, evangelicals have historically also been interested in the renewal of churches, which requires a willingness to engage in prophetic critique. As delighted as they were to finally be part of the New Testament Church, the evangelicals were shocked to discover that many Orthodox did not appreciate the "Pearl of Great Price" that they already possessed. The Orthodox Church was true, but it was not perfect.

No one has been more outspoken on such matters than Frank Schaeffer, who was an often abrasive critic within and against evangelicalism before his conversion to Greek Orthodoxy in 1990. Now a frequent speaker in Orthodox circles, Schaeffer has turned his critical eye on his new spiritual home.[79] Like the other evangelical converts, Schaeffer is convinced that he has finally found the New Testament Church: "Our altars are clean, our liturgies are pure, the Spirit dwells within our sanctuaries. We have not changed."[80] Yet Schaeffer sees two Orthodox Churches in the United States. One is the historic Church, unchanging and undefiled; the other is "a sort of social-ethnic club" infected with nominalism, materialism, ethnic pride and exclusivism, indifference to the sacraments, and "the Protestant disease of individualism and democracy." Many recent converts, eager to experience New Testament Christianity in the modern world, have felt unwelcome in Russian, Greek, or Middle Eastern congregations. Schaeffer calls this division of Orthodoxy into ethnic jurisdictions the "Protestantizing" of Orthodoxy in America.

"Becoming Protestant" is a great temptation for Orthodoxy in America, according to Schaeffer. This tendency can be clearly seen in the way parish councils quarrel with their dioceses over financial matters and show disrespect to local priests who stand "in the place of the bishop, and ultimately of Christ."[81] It can also be seen in Orthodoxy's participation in the

---

78. Eusebius Stephanou, "Converts to Orthodoxy: A Grave Concern," *The Logos* 25 (November-December 1992), pp. 1-2, 4.

79. Schaeffer, *Dancing Alone*, pp. 297-315.

80. Ibid., p. 311.

81. Ibid., pp. 298-99. The use of parish councils in local Orthodox parishes grew out of the legal requirements of incorporation. As other episcopal churches (e.g., Roman Catholic and Episcopalian) in America have discovered, local lay control is difficult to avoid.

ecumenical movement, desiring to fit into the broader Christian community in America. This is a serious mistake, says Schaeffer, who calls Orthodox ecumenist Fr. Georges Florovsky "misguided" and "blinded by his own innocent good will."[82]

Though Schaeffer does not speak for all of the evangelical converts to Orthodoxy, his analysis of the Church and his hopes and fears for Orthodoxy's future in the United States are probably widespread. While he urges Orthodoxy to mount a crusade to win America to Christ, he also wants the Church to remain free of corrupting American and Protestant values, unchanged in its ancient theology, and firmly under the authority of its bishops and to become less ethnic at the local level and more aggressive in making its case against other Christian groups.[83]

As the history of the Orthodox Church demonstrates, it is not easy to contextualize the faith in a given culture without accommodating to its values. From Constantine on, in the many places where Orthodoxy aligned with state powers, the Church became identified with the surrounding culture. During subsequent centuries of persecution and marginalization, the Church's isolation only deepened its ethnic identities. Thus the differences within the Orthodox family of churches are cultural, linguistic, and social, not essentially theological. Such "ethnic" differences have undercut attempts to evangelize the American people in any effective way. Will the coming of the Evangelical Orthodox provide this entree into American life? And is the Church ready for the changes that contextualizing its message in America will bring?

No one can say, but therein lies the irony. The hierarchy welcomed the evangelicals in hopes that they might help Orthodoxy become something it has never been: a church that is at home in America. But the evangelicals converted in large part because Orthodoxy was *not* identified with American culture: it was the New Testament Church, unstained by history and modernity, not just another watered-down and Americanized version of the original church. Maybe the most important question is whether the Evangelical Orthodox still have what it takes to mount a popular mission to post-Christian America. For the AEOM to succeed, it will have to preach Christ more than Orthodoxy — at least as it presently exists.

82. Ibid., pp. 307-9.
83. Ibid., pp. 310-15.

One other irony needs to be mentioned. In the 1990s, the growing edge within otherwise declining mainline churches is found in vibrant ethnic congregations, in which African-American, Latino, Korean, and Chinese people create their own distinctive kinds of Christianity. In Orthodoxy, the best chance for future growth lies in creating new "American ethnic" congregations which have their own distinctive style. Whether or not this mission to America can be embraced and affirmed by the other ethnic Orthodox is uncertain.

Still, the hierarchy's hopes for the AEOM might be realized. After all, according to some experts the current big winners in the American free-market religious economy are those groups that build high walls, make high demands, and never waiver from their convictions.[84] Because of their successful search for the New Testament Church, the Evangelical Orthodox believe they can make the most exclusive claims of them all.

---

84. Roger Finke and Rodney Stark, *The Churching of America, 1776-1990: Winners and Losers in Our Religious Economy* (New Brunswick, NJ: Rutgers University Press, 1992).

THEOLOGY

The Church as Communion

AVERY DULLES, S.J.

I gratefully dedicate this essay to the memory of Father John Meyendorff, one of the outstanding ecumenists of our time. On March 16, 1989, in responding to one of my lectures at Fordham University, he made very impressively the point that in spite of our differences, and perhaps partly because of them, we Roman Catholics and Orthodox need each other. I have greatly profited from reading some of Father Meyendorff's observations relating to the theme of the present article, "The Church as Communion." In an important paper that I heard him deliver at Louvain in 1971, he raised the question: "What is the *koinōnia* and the 'unity' of the Church?" He promptly replied: "Obviously and primarily a unity of man *with God*, and only secondarily a unity of men with each other."[1] He went on to speak of the eucharistic, ecclesial, cosmic, anthropological, and eschatological implications of *koinōnia*.

In the pages that follow I propose to examine the use of the concept of communion *(koinōnia, communio)* as a description of the Church in Roman Catholic theology. In Part I I shall deal with the biblical and patristic roots of the idea, the decline of *communio* theology in the Middle Ages and early modern times, the recent revival of that theology, and its influence at Vatican II. In Part II I shall take up some questions that continue to be

---

1. "The Unity of the Church and the Unity of Mankind," reprinted in John Meyendorff, *Living Tradition: Orthodox Witness in the Contemporary World* (Crestwood, NY: St. Vladimir's Seminary Press, 1978), pp. 129-48, here p. 135.

debated among Catholic theologians who accept an ecclesiology of communion. I shall make no effort to deal with the distinctive positions of the Orthodox or other Christian churches, since an excursion into comparative ecclesiology would take me far beyond the limits of a single essay. The inner-Catholic discussion is more than sufficiently complex to be handled in these few pages.

I

As a mere term, "communion" does not say a great deal. It is an abstract word, generally signifying a relation of fellowship, even intimacy. In Christian usage, the term connotes participation in the sacraments. The term *communio sanctorum* (or *koinōnia ton hagion*) in the Apostles' Creed seems to have meant, originally, not the "communion of saints" but rather "participation in holy things."[2] Even today, the term commonly suggests Holy Communion, the reception of the Body and Blood of Christ. Not only through the Eucharist but through its other sacraments and ministrations the Church puts its members in communion with God and with one another. To affirm that its members are brought into this kind of relationship, however, is not the same as to call the Church itself, substantively, a communion. Acknowledging the vagueness of the term, the Congregation for Doctrine, in a letter of May 28, 1992, insisted that "communion," in its specifically ecclesial usage, must be integrated with the great images used in Scripture and tradition, such as People of God, Body of Christ, and sacrament.[3] Thus the concept of communion cannot serve as a simple replacement for these other terms.

Notwithstanding the reservation just expressed, it is broadly agreed today that the Church is a communion *(koinōnia, communio)*. The Extraordinary Synod of Bishops, which was convened at Rome in 1985 to reflect on the significance of Vatican II, asserted in its Final Report: "The ecclesiology of communion is the central and fundamental idea in the council's

---

2. Werner Elert gives an impressive argument for this position in his *Eucharist and Church Fellowship in the First Four Centuries* (St. Louis: Concordia, 1966), chapter 1 and excurses 1, 2, and 3.

3. "Some Aspects of the Church Understood as Communion" no. 1, *Origins* 22 (June 25, 1992), pp. 108-12, here p. 108.

documents."[4] The Congregation for the Doctrine of the Faith, in the letter already referred to, added that the concept of communion "is very suitable for expressing the core of the mystery of the Church and can certainly be a key for the renewal of Catholic ecclesiology."[5]

The category of communion is ecumenically fruitful since it is widely accepted not only among Roman Catholics but also among Orthodox, Anglicans, and Lutherans.[6] The World Council of Churches, especially in its Faith and Order Commission, has favored this category. The theme "Towards *koinōnia* in Faith, Life, and Witness" was selected for the Fifth World Conference on Faith and Order, meeting at Santiago de Compostela, Spain, in August 1993.

In some ways this gravitation to the concept of communion is surprising since the Church is never called a communion in Scripture, nor is it so called in the documents of any ecumenical council of the Catholic Church, including, I believe, Vatican II. Vatican II spoke of the Church as a sacrament of unity, as the Body of Christ, as Bride, and especially as People of God. It declared that Christ had founded the Church to bring people into communion, and repeatedly described communion as one of the bonds that unites the members of the Church to one another and to Christ the head. But the Council nowhere declared that the Church itself is a communion.[7] Most of

4. "The Final Report," IIC, 1; text in *Origins* 15 (December 19, 1985), pp. 444-50, here p. 448.

5. "Some Aspects" no. 1, p. 108.

6. See the booklet *Communio/Koinonia: A Study by the Institute for Ecumenical Research* (Strasbourg: Lutheran World Federation, 1990); also Avery Dulles, "Communion," *Dictionary of the Ecumenical Movement* (Geneva: World Council of Churches/Grand Rapids: Eerdmans, 1991), pp. 206-9.

7. Oskar Saier in his thorough study *"Communio" in der Lehre des Zweiten Vatikanischen Konzils* (Munich: Max Huebner, 1973), p. 35, says that "It is true that with one sole exception 'communio' is not used as a synonym for 'Ecclesia.'" The exception, he thinks, is UR 2, but I believe that even in this text "communio" can easily be understood as the intimate union of the faithful in Christ that comes about in the Church rather than as a synonym for the Church itself. Among the many texts in which "communio" is used with strong ecclesial connotations LG 9, LG 14, and GS 32 should be examined. Some of the translations are misleading; for instance, LG 9 is translated as stating that Christ founded the Church "as a communion," although Latin texts says "for the sake of communion" *(in communionem)*. A similar error occurs in some translations of GS 32.

Documents of Vatican II are cited in this essay according to the initials of the Latin titles, thus:

AA   *Apostolicam actuositatem* (Decree on the Apostolate of the Laity)

the commentaries took "People of God" to be the dominant idea of the Council's ecclesiology.

The Synod of 1985 seems to have made a deliberate effort to oust "People of God" from its position of primacy. Many of the bishops at the Synod, together with Cardinal Ratzinger, objected that that concept had been abused in a political and populist sense, thus tending to divide the Church into contesting classes and parties. Some theologians of a Marxist tendency had proposed a "people's Church" in opposition to the "hierarchical Church." The Synod preferred the concept of communion because it was not amenable to sociological reduction and seemed conducive to internal unity and peace.

The modern concept of the Church as communion is heavily indebted to the historical development of the first few centuries. In Holy Scripture *koinōnia* is a very flexible term that extends to practically every facet of the Christian life.[8] Depending on the context it can be translated by words such as "participation," "association," and "contribution." According to Paul Christians are called into *koinōnia* with Christ and one another through faith (Phlm. 6) and baptism (1 Cor. 1:9). He describes the Eucharist as a *koinōnia* in the body and the blood of Christ (1 Cor. 10:16-17). The ministers of the gospel are joined to one another in *koinōnia,* inasmuch as they are associated in their apostolic labors (Gal. 2:9; 2 Cor. 8:23). In sharing their material goods (Acts 2:42) and contributing financially to the relief of the poor (2 Cor. 8:4; 9:13, etc.) Christians engage in *koinōnia.* Their joys and sufferings are transformed through *koinōnia* with Christ (Phil. 3:10-11; 2 Cor. 1:7; cf. 1 Pet. 4:13). The faithful have *koinōnia* with the Son (1 Cor. 1:9), with the Holy Spirit (2 Cor. 13:13), and with the Father himself (1 John 1:3). The *koinōnia* that they already experience on earth is a foretaste of the perfect unity to be enjoyed in heaven (1 Cor. 1:7-9).

CD   *Christus Dominus* (Decree on the Pastoral Ministry of Bishops)
GS   *Gaudium et spes* (Pastoral Constitution on the Church in the Modern World)
LG   *Lumen gentium* (Dogmatic Constitution on the Church)
SC   Sacrosanctum concilium (Constitution on the Sacred Liturgy)
UR   *Unitatis redintegratio* (Decree on Ecumenism)

8. Among the many biblical studies of this theme one may still warmly recommend John Michael McDermott, "Biblical Doctrine of Koinonia," *Biblische Zeitschrift* 19 (1975), pp. 64-77, 219-33.

The Church in the postapostolic era did not exist in the form of a single social organization, but rather in the form of local churches under their bishops. The faithful belonged to the Church insofar as they were admitted to communion by their own bishop. Travelers who were in good standing in their local churches were commonly provided with letters of communion from their bishops that would entitle them to hospitality and admission to the sacraments in other dioceses. The bishops recognized other bishops as being in communion with themselves and with the universal Church. Certain serious offenses such as schism and heresy were seen as excluding their perpetrators from the Catholic communion.

In effect, then, the Church was a vast network of local churches under bishops who mutually recognized one another. The body of churches that were in communion could be called, in a certain sense, a communion. The communion was visible; it was established by the actions of the bishops issuing the appropriate letters and documents and was sealed by their liturgical actions, such as eucharistic concelebration and admission to the sacraments. To partake of the sacrament from a bishop was to enter into communion not only with the Lord but also with the bishop and with all who received the sacraments from him.

In theory all bishops had the power to enter into, or break off, communion with one another. For reasons of prudence, they usually saw to it that they acted in concert with the more venerable metropolitan sees, especially those that could trace their foundation to apostles. The Church of Rome, by reason of its historical links with Peter and Paul, who had been martyred there, and perhaps also by reason of the political prestige of the city, its wealth, and its strategic importance as a center of communications, gradually came to be recognized as having a universal primacy, the exact nature of which was as yet somewhat undefined. For many Christians, to be a catholic Christian meant to be in communion with Rome. In situations of controversy, authors such as Ambrose, Jerome, and Augustine made it clear that they chose to be in communion with the Church of Rome.

The authority granted to preeminent sees, and especially to Rome, progressively undermined the communion concept of the Church.[9] By the

---

9. The decay of the "communion" concept of the Church in the Middle Ages has been traced by many authors. The classic essay on the subject is still Yves Congar, "De la communion des églises à une ecclésiologie de l'Église universelle," in *L'Épiscopat et l'Église universelle* (Paris: Cerf, 1962), pp. 227-60. A recent treatment may be found in

end of the first millennium all the churches in the West were subject to the jurisdiction of Rome, whereas in the East, Constantinople was clearly the dominant church, since the other patriarchal churches (Alexandria, Antioch, and Jerusalem) had lapsed into schism or insignificance. With the revival of Roman law in the West, reciprocity among equals was outweighed by jurisdiction from above. The vertical lines of authority from Rome to the bishops replaced the horizontal lines of communion among bishops and among churches. The pope came to be viewed as the supreme and universal bishop — the sovereign bishop of the Catholic Church.

The decline of communion theology in the West was accelerated by the rise of Scholastic theology which, under the influence of Augustine, interiorized and spiritualized the concept of communion. For the great theologians of the thirteenth century, communion was the final spiritual effect of the devout reception of the sacraments. Communion, in this view, was a mysterious grace-relationship of the individual with God. Sacraments such as baptism and the Eucharist were no longer seen as bringing one into communion with the local church and its bishop, but rather into a universal, undifferentiated communion of grace. All who were living in the grace of God were members of the body of Christ, a body now conceived as being mystical and invisible. Although the medieval concept of the Church included visible structures, communion was considered to be primarily interior. The seeds were being planted for the doctrine of the invisible Church, which flowered in some of the Protestant Reformers.

Reacting against the Reformers, the theologians of the Counter-Reformation gave greater emphasis to the institution, considered in juridical terms. They depicted the Church as a centralized body in which all the members, including bishops, were subjects of the pope, the vicar of Christ. The local church came to be seen almost as an administrative unit under the pope, who wielded the fullness of power. Even ecumenical councils could not restrict the authority of the pope, since it was his prerogative to summon councils and to approve their decrees under pain of invalidity.

On the eve of Vatican II a number of authors, dissatisfied with the prevailing institutionalism, sought to revitalize the Church by a return to patristic models. This process led to a vision of the Church as an interper-

---

Medard Kehl, *Die Kirche: Eine katholische Ekklesiologie* (Würzburg: Echter Verlag, 1992), esp. pp. 346-54.

sonal communion, patterned on the mutual relations of the divine persons in the Trinity. In this vision the ecclesial significance of the sacraments took on new meaning. The local church celebrating the Eucharist under the presidency of its bishop came to be viewed as the paradigmatic realization of the Church. The bishops were regarded as representative heads of particular churches, receiving their basic powers directly from Christ himself through the sacrament of ordination. The bishops, as pastors of particular churches, were held to constitute a college, in which all were coresponsible for the supreme direction of the universal Church.[10]

This revived communion theology had a major impact on Vatican II (1962-1965), which envisaged the Church as a kind of sacrament (LG 1), signifying and effecting a communion of charity among its local realizations and individual members (LG 9), all of whom were held together by the gifts and charisms of the Holy Spirit (LG 7), who is the principle of unity in the Church (UR 2).[11] Within this communion each local church was seen as called to share its gifts with the others (LG 13). This theological vision served as the basis of a revitalization of the particular church at worship. According to the Constitution on the Liturgy, "the Church reveals itself most clearly when a full complement of God's holy people, united in prayer and in a common liturgical service (especially the Eucharist), exercise a thorough and active participation at the very altar where the bishop presides in the company of his priests and other assistants" (SC 41). This principle was repeated in the Constitution on the Church to emphasize the theological importance of the particular church (LG 26) and in the Decree on the Bishops' Pastoral Office to bring out the dignity of the diocesan bishop (CD 11).

All the bishops, according to Vatican II, are linked to one another in

10. This type of ecclesiology, which owes a great deal to the historical research of Bernard Botte, Joseph Lécuyer, Henri de Lubac, Yves Congar, and others, is exemplified in several volumes growing out of conferences held at Chevetogne in Belgium on the eve of Vatican II: *Le Concile et les conciles* (Chevetogne: Chevetogne, 1960); *L'Église et l'Épiscopat universelle,* cited above; and *La collégialité épiscopale* (Paris: Cerf, 1965).

11. On Vatican II's communion ecclesiology see, in addition to the study of Saier mentioned above, Walter Kasper, "The Church as Communion: Reflections on the Guiding Ecclesiological Idea of the Second Vatican Council," in his *Theology and Church* (New York: Crossroad, 1989), pp. 148-65; also Joseph Ratzinger, "The Ecclesiology of the Second Vatican Council," in his *Church, Ecumenism and Politics* (New York: Crossroad, 1988), pp. 3-28.

hierarchical communion. Each of them makes the supreme authority of the Church present in a given locality. Since they are fellow bishops with the bishop of Rome, they cannot be regarded as mere delegates of the pope (LG 27). The pope is depicted not as an absolute monarch but as a moderator "presiding over the assembly of charity" (LG 13).

The Council fathers were convinced that this communion-centered vision could be successfully integrated with the teaching of Vatican I about the universal primacy of the pope as successor of Peter. The papacy, they maintained, was needed both to protect legitimate diversity and to prevent diversity from impairing unity. Using communion theology to correct the excessive centralism and clericalism of recent centuries, the Council encouraged different local and regional churches to take on their own distinctive character within the Catholic fellowship. "Through the common sharing of gifts and through the common effort to attain fullness in unity," said the Constitution on the Church, "the whole and each of the parts receive increase" (LG 13). And again: "The variety of local churches with one common aspiration is particularly splendid evidence of the catholicity of the undivided church" (LG 23). Since Vatican II bishops' conferences have developed in the various nations and continents, giving the Catholic Church an inner diversity that it previously lacked. The vernacular in the liturgy is only one element of this adaptation.

The idea of communion was also used at Vatican II to revitalize the theology of the laity. Lay people, according to the Council, are not just docile subjects executing the orders of the hierarchy. Through baptism and confirmation each individual has an active share in the threefold office of Christ as prophet, priest, and king (LG 31; AA 3; SC 14). All Christians participate actively in the life and mission of the Church. Anointed by the Holy Spirit, they have a supernatural sense of the faith, equipping them to recognize what doctrines are in accordance with, or opposed to, the new life given in Christ (LG 12; cf. 25).

As is evident from what I have said, Vatican II blended earlier forms of communion ecclesiology with elements from the Scholastic and juridical heritage of the past few centuries. The result was an original synthesis that did not fully satisfy theologians exclusively committed to certain interpretations. Content to lay down the basic doctrinal principles, the Council did not attempt to settle debated theological questions.

II

The debates at the Council and in the subsequent literature have made it clear that within the broad category of Vatican II ecclesiology there are at least two major tendencies — a personalist approach that builds on early patristic models and a juridico-mystical approach that owes more to medieval Scholastic theology and to canon law. These approaches do not lend themselves to easy labeling. Some authors contrast them as "ascending" and "descending" ecclesiologies, ecclesiologies "from below" and "from above."[12] The approach that starts from the local community may in a certain sense be called particularist; the other, which starts from the global community, may be called universalist. Acknowledging the limited value of all these labels, I shall here speak of the universalist and particularist tendencies.

While few if any theologians conform perfectly to type, it might be permissible to think of Henri de Lubac as a universalist and of Leonardo Boff as a particularist within the communion genre. Joseph Ratzinger in his recent work might be called be a moderate universalist and Jean-Marie Tillard a moderate particularist. Most theologians combine some elements of each approach. My present concern is not with labeling individuals but with sketching two tendencies, both of which accept the ecclesiology of Vatican II, even though they focus on different phrases and texts from the council documents.

The two theologies differ in their very interpretation of the term *communio*. The universalists are inclined to understand it as meaning participation in the divine life, achieved through the objective means of grace, notably the sacraments. In this view the Christian's communion is (as we have heard from Meyendorff) in the first instance with God, and secondarily with all who share in the same divine life. Contemporary particularists, under the influence of modern personalism, are inclined to understand the term "communion" as directly signifying a fellowship of love and intimacy achieved in a local community. The two approaches are not sharply opposed. Membership in a small association, in which the members know

---

12. Joseph Komonchak prefers an ecclesiology "that begins with the local church (an ecclesiology 'from below')." See his "The Church Universal as the Communion of Local Churches," in *Where Does the Church Stand?* (Concilium 146; Edinburgh: T. and T. Clark, 1981) pp. 30-35, here p. 31.

one another and interact, can prepare one for communion with God and with all other human beings. The universal communion grounded in God, conversely, can dispose its members to enter into cordial relations with their neighbors.

The two points of view have consequences all along the line, beginning with baptism. Does the sacrament of baptism incorporate a person into the local church, the universal Church, or both? Baptism is celebrated in a particular community, into which the candidate is received, but at the same time it makes its recipient a member of the universal Church. It is important for the full meaning of baptism that the baptized be welcomed into a living community of faith. But the universal membership is perhaps more fundamental, since baptism can be validly administered where no community is present and since some baptized Christians, while lacking any stable relationship to a particular parish or diocese, are entitled to receive the sacraments wherever they go.

Similar questions arise concerning the Eucharist. Granted that the particular church has the power to offer the Eucharist, it may be asked whether that power makes the particular church self-sufficient or whether, on the contrary, the Eucharist is precisely what excludes all self-sufficiency on the part of the particular church.[13] In the particularist approach, the Eucharist appears as the sacrament that builds the individual congregation, bringing about fellowship among all who partake at the same altar. Universalists make the point that the Eucharist is essentially ordered toward the whole Church, in the name of which the sacrifice is offered. Indicating the universality of the communion, the celebrant mentions by name the bishops of other dioceses, or at least the pope. Holy Communion, say the universalists, unites the communicant first of all with God and, as a result, with all other Christians who are living in the grace of God.

How is the local church formed? According to universalists the Church was orginally founded on Peter and the apostles as a universal society, and only subsequently came to be divided into particular regional or local realizations. The particularist view tends to see groups as being spontaneously formed under the impulse of the Holy Spirit and as consti-

---

13. The latter alternative is asserted by the Congregation for the Doctrine of the Faith in "Some Aspects" no. 11, p. 110. The "Catholic" dimension of the Eucharist is discussed in Joseph Ratzinger, "Catholicity as the Formal Principle of Christianity," in his *Principles of Catholic Theology* (San Francisco: Ignatius, 1987), pp. 285-311, esp. 293f.

tuting themselves, even to the extent of appointing their own leadership. Some speak of the basic ecclesial community as the locus where "ecclesiogenesis" occurs.[14] The universal Church, from the particularist perspective, is formed through the mutual recognition and fellowship of churches that were originally local. A mediating position holds that the apostolic heritage is preserved in particular churches and groups of churches to the extent that they stand in the historical succession, even though they may be estranged from other apostolic churches.

On the respective priorities between the particular and the universal Church, each party can find passages in Vatican II that, taken in isolation, seem to support its point of view. The particularists can quote from the Constitution on the Church (LG 23) the assertion that "the one and only Catholic church" exists "in and from" the particular churches.[15] The universalists, however, call attention to the previous clause, in which the particular churches are declared to be formed according to the pattern of the universal Church, which, according to the Council, is present and operative in them (CD 11).[16] The particularists are on solid ground when they argue that the Holy Spirit can inspire ecclesial initiatives that are not directly dependent on the hierarchy of the great Church. Local churches can greatly enrich the universal Church by their distinctive contributions (LG 13). But the universalists would seem to be correct in insisting that the Church was originally founded as a single society and only gradually came to be articulated as a plurality of particular churches. The universal Church is not, as some particularists allege, an abstraction; it is a concretely existing whole apart from which particular churches have no rightful existence.

The question just discussed would seem to lie at the heart of the current dispute in Catholic ecclesiology about whether the principle of

14. According to Leonardo Boff the term "ecclesiogenesis" was coined at the First Inter-Church Meeting of the Basic Communities of Brazil at Vitória, Brazil in 1975. See his *Ecclesiogenesis: The Base Communities Reinvent the Church* (Maryknoll, NY: Orbis, 1986), pp. 34f. According to him, "The hierarchy has the sacramental function of organizing and serving a reality that it has not created but discovered, and within which it finds itself" (p. 26).

15. ". . . *in quibus et ex quibus una et unica ecclesia catholica exsistit.*"

16. ". . . *ad imaginem ecclesiae universalis formatis*" (LG 23). CD 11 speaks of the particular church, "*in qua vere inest et operatur una sancta catholica et apostolica Christi ecclesia.*"

subsidiarity applies to the Church.[17] The particularists, holding that the local community has all the essentials required to constitute a church, tend to regard the machinery of universal government as a merely "subsidiary" structure to take care of exceptional cases that the local churches are unable to resolve through their own resources. Universalists, by contrast, hold that the responsibilities of the universal leadership are constitutive of the Church itself and not simply subsidiary. Unless a parish or diocese is visibly joined to the universal body, its own integrity as a church is deficient. On this last point the universalists would seem to have Vatican II in their favor. Without integration into the universal society over which the successor of Peter and the bishops in communion with him preside, there can be no full incorporation into the one Church of Christ (LG 8, 14; UR 3).

The two tendencies within contemporary Catholicism both accept the episcopal form of government, but with different views of what it means to be a bishop. The universalists hold that the episcopate is collegial by its very nature: by sacramental ordination the new bishop is received by other bishops into the body corporately charged with the supreme direction of the universal Church. It is very fitting, universalists assert, for bishops to be appointed as pastors of dioceses, but members of the hierarchy who receive no such appointment can still be bishops in the true sense of the term. For the particularists, on the contrary, a bishop is primarily the pastor of a diocese, and only for that reason is he entitled to have a voice in the episcopal college. In principle, then, the college should be made up of the responsible heads of particular churches. The universalist view of the episcopacy, I believe, has better support from Vatican I (*Pastor aeternus*, Prologue) and Vatican II (LG 21-22), but the particularist view has stronger roots in history. The universalist approach takes the functions of Peter and the apostles as its model; the particularists rely more on what bishops did in the early centuries. The resolution of the dispute will probably depend on what one thinks about the permanent value of the patristic precedents and about the possibilities for dogmatic development.

17. The universalist perspective on the question of subsidiarity is reflected in Jean Baptiste Beyer, "Principe de subsidiarité ou 'juste autonomie'?" *Nouvelle revue théologique* 108 (1986), pp. 801-22. For the particularist perspective see Peter Huizing, "Subsidiarity," in *Synod 1985 — An Evaluation*, ed. G. Alberigo and J. Provost (Concilium 188; Edinburgh: T. and T. Clark, 1986), pp. 118-23. Further discussion is given in Avery Dulles, *The Reshaping of Catholicism* (San Francisco: Harper and Row, 1988), pp. 204f., 262f.

In both its expressions, Catholic communion theology accepts the primacy of the pope. The universalists look upon the pope as the successor of Peter and as visible head of the whole flock of Christ. For them it is a secondary matter that he is bishop of Rome. Some even speculate that the primacy could be transferred from Rome to another see.[18]

The particularist view holds that the primacy belongs in the first instance not to the pope but rather to the local church of Rome. In their view, the pope never acts as pope except when he acts as bishop of Rome. As a bishop he is a kind of elder brother, a senior colleague, but not more than a bishop. Whatever primacy he enjoys comes from the fact that his church, that of Rome, is heir to a preeminent apostolic heritage.[19] This opinion has excellent support in early church writers but is more difficult to reconcile with the two Vatican councils, both of which emphasize the unique status of the pope as Peter's successor.

Neither group favors a monolithic Church. Both accept diversity, but they have different attitudes toward it. The universalists see unity as the given and diversity as a matter of accommodation, inasmuch as it may be necessary for the Church to adapt itself to various cultures. Particularist theologians look on diversity as original and on unity as a subsequent achievement. Unity, according to them, is to be required only in necessary matters. As far as possible, they would say, diversity should be allowed. The different opinions on this point are linked to different understandings of the relationship between faith and culture. To what extent does the Church value and borrow from existing cultures (which are various), and to what extent does it seek to transform them through the gospel (which is one)?

Ecumenism, finally, is differently understood in the two perspectives.[20] For the universalists it is a matter of reconstituting the unity of

---

18. Hans Urs von Balthasar, *The Office of Peter and the Structure of the Church* (San Francisco: Ignatius, 1986), holds that the primacy of the bishop of Rome follows from Peter's primacy, but questions whether Rome must necessarily be the seat of the papacy (p. 52, n. 52).

19. This particularist perspective is illustrated by Jean-Marie R. Tillard, *The Bishop of Rome* (Wilmington, DE: Michael Glazier, 1986). See also the same author's *Church of Churches* (Collegeville, MN: Liturgical, 1992), 284-307.

20. Several authors of great authority have recently presented Catholic ecumenism in the light of the ecclesiology of communion; for example, Johannes Willebrands, "Vatican II's Ecclesiology of Communion," *Origins* 17 (May 28, 1987), pp. 27-33; Pierre Duprey, "A Catholic Perspective on Ecclesial Communion," in *Christian Authority:*

Christians by inducing all to accept the fullness of the apostolic heritage, indefectibly present in the Roman Catholic communion. They quote from Vatican II's Decree on Ecumenism that unity "subsists in the Catholic Church as something she can never lose" (UR 4). Following this line of thought, in 1992 the Congregation for the Doctrine of the Faith called upon the other churches to undergo a "new conversion to the Lord" so that they might "recognize the continuity of the primacy of Peter in his successors, the bishops of Rome."[21] This view puts special burdens on churches that are not Roman Catholic to acquire elements of the Christian patrimony that are still lacking to them.

No Catholic theologian will deny the desirability of all Christians coming to accept the Petrine office as exercised by the bishop of Rome. But surely the Congregation for Doctrine had no intention of reducing ecumenism to this one objective. The Catholic Church recognizes that the Petrine office is only one of many bonds constitutive of communion. Scripture and tradition call attention to many others, including the word of God, faith, baptism, the Eucharist, prayer, hospitality, and service toward the poor. All of these elements, moreover, must be seen as instruments in the hands of the Holy Spirit, who bestows the grace of fellowship with God. Churches that from a Catholic perspective lack certain elements of the apostolic heritage may still possess many bonds of communion and may live in deep fellowship with the Father, the Son, and the Holy Spirit. The Roman Catholic Church, while retaining the full institutional heritage, may be deficient in its actual fidelity to the gospel. It may fall short of other communities in its life of faith, of prayer, and of practical charity.

The goal of ecumenism, as proposed by Vatican II and reaffirmed by the Synod of 1985, is to build on the incomplete communion that now exists among Christian churches and to progress, with God's grace, toward full communion. This vision of ecumenism is particularly pertinent to relations between Rome and the Eastern churches, which Rome recognizes as possessing "true sacraments and especially, through apostolic succession, the priesthood and the Eucharist, whereby they are still linked with us in closest intimacy" (UR 15). The traditions of the Eastern churches are such

---

Essays in Honour of Henry Chadwick, ed. G. R. Evans (Oxford: Clarendon, 1988), pp. 7-19.

    21. "Some Aspects" no. 18, p. 111.

that, in the words of the Decree on Ecumenism, "it is not surprising . . . if from time to time one tradition has come nearer than the other to a full appreciation of certain aspects of a revealed mystery, or has expressed them to better advantage" (UR 17). The authentic theological, spiritual, and liturgical traditions of the Eastern churches, according to the same Decree, "promote the right ordering of life and, indeed, pave the way to the full contemplation of Christian truth" (UR 17).

Yves Congar, in the spirit of Vatican II, calls for "a unity not of uniformity and imperialism, but of communion through the one who, distributing his charisms of every kind, wants to lead everything back to the Father through the Son."[22] He saw very clearly, as did Father Meyendorff, that communion derives from the triune life of God and involves a fruitful association of parties that retain their distinct identities. In the universal Church there must be bonds that are universal and bonds that are regional and local. The ancient Christian writers were accustomed to compare the universal Church to a chorus of many voices. Some universal authority is needed to assure harmony, but a measure of autonomy is desirable to prevent monotonous uniformity. Through diverse but concordant liturgies, spiritualities, and systems of law and doctrine, the Church can best reflect the inexhaustible mystery of the triune God, who invites us to share in his life in ways that lie always open to deeper exploration.

22. Yves Congar, *I Believe in the Holy Spirit*, vol. 3 (New York: Seabury, 1983), p. 272.

Chalcedon Revisited:
A Historical and Theological Reflection

RICHARD NORRIS, JR.

The *Definition* of the Council of Chalcedon — a relatively brief paragraph appended to the conciliar decree as its conclusion — has always been a focus for controversy. Historically speaking, it perches, placidly and perhaps rather quizzically, at the center of a storm. Penned under the pressure of a passionate doctrinal debate to which was wedded an equally passionate power-struggle, it was no sooner promulgated than it gave rise to a new series of controversies, which for two centuries and more disturbed the peace of the early Byzantine Empire, frustrated the hopes and policies of a whole series of emperors, and in the end left the churches of the East divided by schisms that have endured to the present day. And as if that were not enough, it has now once again become a focus of criticism and debate, this time in the theological academy. After centuries during which, at least in the West, it enjoyed the obscurity that comes of success and served as the unexamined basis of an elaborate tradition of discourse on the person of Christ, the Chalcedonian *Definition* is at length paying the price of that success. It is now being called to account for that entire tradition, in the light of more recent readings both of the New Testament and of the philosophical heritage of the past.

The Chalcedonian *Definition's* language and thought, then, are closely and intricately woven into the tradition of Christian teaching and speculation about the person of Christ, and for that reason there is no way of isolating it either from the debates that led up to it or from the criticisms and interpretations it has evoked: like some other focal texts of Christian history, it belongs to more than one place and time. Nevertheless one is bound to inquire what the original burden of the *Definition* was and what, in the light of an answer to that question, it may have to say about the very controversies to which it has given rise. In the end, one might hope to allow the *Definition* to comment on its commentators, and thus to bring it back into dialogue both with its critics and with its admirers.

I

The bishops assembled at Chalcedon were not, as modern interpreters have tended to make them out, professional philosophers or even, in the contemporary sense, professional theologians. In their day, academic theology did not exist (there appear to have been no *periti* in attendance at the Council), and the only "schools" with which they were concerned were those in which catechesis occurred. They would have been startled, then, to know that their statements have latterly been read as propounding some particular, theoretically devised "christology" (a useful modern term with which they were not familiar). In their view, after all, it was even questionable whether they had any business to go beyond the statements made in what, by their time, was the normal basis of doctrinal catechesis, namely, the Nicene faith in its several versions.[1] "This wise and saving symbol of the divine grace," they said,

> should have been sufficient for the knowledge and support of true religion, for it gives the complete teaching about the Father and the Son and the Holy Spirit, and to those who receive it faithfully it interprets the Lord's becoming human.[2]

Hence they understood their *Definition*, as its opening phrase "Following the holy Fathers" indicates clearly enough, to be little more than an exegetical note calculated to render the teaching of the Nicene faith on "the Lord's becoming human" explicit.

---

1. The principle of the sufficiency of the Nicene "creed," which seems to have been assumed in the controversy between Cyril of Alexandria and Nestorius, was explicitly enjoined by the Council of Ephesus in 431.

2. For the translation, see R. A. Norris, *The Christological Controversy* (Philadelphia, 1980), p. 157.

What is more, the exegetical note itself is essentially a pastiche of allusions and quotations. It drew its language from writers as far back as Irenaeus and Tertullian, but the immediate sources of the formulas it employs were texts whose phraseology was shaped in the course of the Nestorian and Eutychian controversies. It echoed Leo the Great's *Tome* and certain of Cyril of Alexandria's letters. It repeated the language of the Formulary of Reunion, which Cyril had applauded in his letter *Laetentur caeli* to John of Antioch, and of Flavian's profession of faith before the Home Synod at Constantinople.[3] For the use of "one hypostasis" in conjunction with "in two natures," it seems to have drawn on the usage of Proclus of Constantinople.[4]

Thus the *Definition* presents itself tacitly both as a consensus document and as a reiteration of tradition. It aims to exhibit an underlying and substantive agreement among the great sees of Rome, Constantinople, Alexandria, and Antioch and therefore among the traditions they represent — even though certain of their prominent representatives, like Nestorius and Eutyches, might in the past have departed from this broad consensus and even if certain ways of speaking about Christ that one or more of these traditions had found acceptable in the past needed to be set quietly aside as inconsistent with the wider consensus.

By their very attempt to put this consensus — this *traditional* consensus, as they saw it — into words, however, the bishops at Chalcedon were condemned to at least a modest originality. Even though their language was deliberately and systematically unoriginal, even though their grasp of its sense was merely "intuitive," and "none of them could have given a definition of the concepts"[5] that they were using, they were bound, not only because of the issues immediately before them but also because of the very language of the Nicene faith, to tackle one central problem.

That problem was to explicate the Nicene symbol's statement that there is "one Lord Jesus Christ," identified as "true God from true God" who "became incarnate" *(sarkōthenta)* and "became human" *(enan-*

---

3. On this point see A. Grillmeier, *Christ in Christian Tradition*, vol. I (2nd ed., Atlanta, 1975), p. 544; and R. V. Sellers, *The Council of Chalcedon: A Historical and Doctrinal Survey* (London, 1953), pp. 210ff.

4. See Jean Galot, "'Une seule personne, une seule hypostase,'" in *Gregorianum* 70 (1989), esp. pp. 257-65.

5. Grillmeier, *Christ in Christian Tradition* I, p. 545.

thrōpēsanta), and indeed "was crucified for us . . . and suffered . . . and rose on the third day." These words of the creed take the form of a brisk narrative account whose subject is the "Lord Jesus Christ"; and they speak of this Christ first as God and then as a human being, while conveying the unmistakable impression that he retains his fundamental identity throughout, since there is only one *subject* to whom the narrative attributes both sets of epithets, divine and human.[6] The bishops' problem, then, was to find a way of making sense of the basic assumption of this narrative: the assumption, namely, that an individual identified as "God from God" can also — and truly — be a human being without ceasing to be one and the same individual. And this of course was precisely the problem that had been raised in an acute form by both Nestorius and Eutyches and that had taken the form of a political confrontation that embroiled all the great sees of the Church.

In the text of their *Definition,* the bishops begin, therefore, with what they are confident everyone is prepared to agree on. They present what amounts to a transposition of the creedal narrative into a new form. Where the symbol of faith tells what happens to its subject, the *Definition* gives an account of how, in the light of that narrative, its subject is to be characterized. The result, naturally enough, is a resounding affirmation of the *oneness* of the Christ, a statement that can be read simply as a rhetorically enhanced analysis of what the creedal account of the incarnation directly implies about Christ's person. The bishops speak of "one and the same Son, who is our Lord Jesus Christ"; and they then proceed to reiterate the phrase *ho autos* ("the very same") five times, in each case predicating of this one subject, the Christ, a double set of attributes. He is "complete *(teleios)* in his deity and . . . complete in his humanity," "coessential *(homo-ousios)* with the Father . . . and coessential with us." Here, then, there is stated — no doubt in a form calculated in principle to frustrate the errors of Nestorius and Eutyches alike — what the bishops took to be the heart of God's *oikonomia* of salvation, the Incarnation.

This paraphrase, however, for all its illumination of the unity-in-duality of Christ, did not directly address the burning issue of the time, which turned on the mode — or at any rate on the proper mode of expres-

6. Compare Leo's *Tome* 2 (Norris, *Christological Controversy,* p. 146), where Leo appeals in a similar fashion, and to the same end, to the language of the traditional Roman baptismal symbol.

sion — of Christ's unity. Accordingly, in the second part of the *Definition*, which also opens with a ringing affirmation of "one and the same Christ," the bishops offer what amounts to a tacit criticism of the ways in which the terms "subject" *(hypostasis)* and "nature" *(physis)* had been employed in the controversies evoked by the teaching of Nestorius and, later, Eutyches. On both sides of that debate, "subject" and "nature" had been used, if not as synonymous in their connotation, then at any rate as synonymous in their reference. The affirmation of two natures was taken, in the tradition of the school of Antioch, to entail that of two hypostases, presumably on the assumption that there can be no real nature save in the form of a complete and concrete existent;[7] and similarly, in Alexandrian circles, "one hypostasis" was widely taken to imply "one nature," even if Cyril of Alexandria had, though subtly and seldom, intimated the contrary.[8]

The *Definition*, however, drew on the language of Proclus of Constantinople and Basil of Seleucia[9] to make a distinction between hypostasis and nature. If it were granted that this "one and the same Son" is at once complete in deity and complete in humanity (a proposition to which all would presumably subscribe), sharing the *ousia* of God on the one hand and of human beings on the other — and if, as was generally understood, *ousia* ("essence") and *physis* ("nature") meant roughly the same thing, then it made perfect sense to summarize the teaching of the opening section of the *Definition* in the words "one and the same Christ, Son, Lord, Only-begotten, acknowledged [to be] . . . *in two natures*." This crucial and controverted phrase, then, appears in the text of the *Definition* as nothing more than a summary transcription of what had already been said in its first section, as, that is, a reasonable and indeed almost inevitable way of putting what everyone was already agreed about. To be sure, one had to remember that each nature was "complete" (or "perfect": *teleios*) and thus continued, even in the incarnation, to be itself, distinct from the other, even though it did not exist apart from the other. Hence the bishops added to this phrase their four famous adverbs — "unconfusedly, unalterably, undividedly, inseparably" — to guarantee just these points.

---

7. See, e.g., L. Scipioni, *Richerche sulla cristologia del 'Libro di Eraclide' di Nestorio* (Fribourg, 1956), pp. 45ff.

8. On this point see the complex discussion of Grillmeier, *Christ in Christian Tradition* I, pp. 480ff.

9. See Galot, " 'Une seule personne, une seule hypostase,' " n. 4; Grillmeier, *Christ in Christian Tradition* I, p. 548.

And having thus — as they thought — reiterated in different terms the affirmations of the opening section of the text, they proceeded to do so once more, but with a different emphasis. Their first transcription had started with the "one and the same" Son and gone on to affirm that he is "acknowledged" (or perhaps "recognized") "in two natures." The second transcription, intended further to clarify the first, starts out with the two natures and moves thence to the ground of their unity.

> . . . the difference of the natures is not destroyed because of the union, but on the contrary, the character of each nature is preserved and comes together in one person *(prosōpon)* and one hypostasis.[10]

The interesting circumstance here is the substitution of "one person and one hypostasis" for "one and the same Christ." Once again, the *Definition* works by rephrasing, or paraphrasing, its basic affirmations. Just as one can use "nature" as a convenient and plausible term to refer summarily to the respects in which Christ is twofold (as being "complete" both in deity and in humanity), so one can employ "person" or "hypostasis" to denote that "one and the same" to whom these "natures" are attributed. This legitimizes the traditional Antiochene use of *prosōpon* to refer to the one Christ, but at the same time insists that the term be regarded as an equivalent for *hypostasis* — which was by no means an outrageous demand, since the two words had been employed in this way in discourse about the Trinity since the last quarter of the previous century.

The Chalcedonian *Definition*, then, though not without some precedent, intimates a distinction of meaning as between "nature" and "hypostasis" — a distinction that would allow one to speak of Christ as *one hypostasis in two natures*. It must be noticed, however, that the Council never uses this expression nor, what is more important, defines these terms. They had been delivered to it, to be sure, as part of the idiom in which a burning theological and political controversy was being conducted. In the *Definition*, however, the terms in question derive their sense not from any explicit delimitation of meaning that might elevate them to status as technical terms, nor even from the ways in which they had been used in earlier stages of the controversy,[11] but strictly from the way they

---

10. Norris, *The Christological Controversy,* p. 159.

11. While the Council employs the terms "nature," "person," and "hypostasis," it is a point insufficiently stressed that it uses them in a way that does not appear to

are employed *in this text,* that is, from the fact that they transcribe, in a generalizing and abstract fashion, what had been directly said in the opening section of the *Definition.* "Hypostasis" is short for "one and the same Christ, Son, Lord, Only begotten," and "two natures" transcribes, with useful brevity, the fact that this hypostasis is regularly characterized — not only in the *Definition* itself, but in the Nicene symbol — by two different *sets* of predications, distinguishable because one set contains the sorts of things one normally says about God, and the other, the sorts of things one normally says about human beings. The formula affirms, then, that there is a case, the case of Jesus Christ, in which "one and the same" reality *(hypostasis)* is properly characterized at once as a divine reality *(physis)* and as a human reality *(physis).*

Now it is arguable that a formula like this, apart from any clear specification of the meanings of the terms it employs, represents not so much a solution of the problem as it does a mere statement of it. Such a judgment, moreover, is entirely consonant with the real, if commonly un-acknowledged, modesty of the Fathers of Chalcedon. Nevertheless, the judgment needs some qualification, for the *Definition*'s "statement of the problem" accomplished precisely what it set out to accomplish and thus did not leave the christological state of affairs unaltered. First, it clearly excluded, on the one hand, the Nestorian doctrine of "two sons" and, on the other, the view — intimated in the public testimony of Eutyches at his trial — that the human "nature" of Christ is somehow fused into, or ab-sorbed by, his divine "nature." But second, it accomplished these ends not by writing a new and freshly inspired "christology," but by teasing out certain assumptions that it saw underlying the Nicene symbol's account of the divine *oikonomia* of salvation and by phrasing them in the established idiom of the disputes about the person of Christ that had been rumbling since the days of Apollinaris of Laodicea. Hence the bishops' "statement of the problem" was also a bit more than just that. It was also a ruling that

---

correspond with the usages of Apollinaris, Theodore of Mopsuestia, and Nestorius, or even of Cyril of Alexandria (as Severus of Antioch was quick to insist). "Nature" in particular was a term of plastic sense. Leo I's use of it, for example, seems to involve a reminiscence of Tertullian's *substantia* (see Tertullian, *Adversus Praxean* 27). On Cyril's understanding of Christ's humanity (which he did not like to call a nature), see the learned and helpful article of Ruth M. Siddals, "Logic and Christology in Cyril of Alexandria," *Journal of Theological Studies* n.s. 38 (1987), pp. 341-67.

excluded certain teachings and at the same time a definition of what one might call the agenda of christological inquiry: an agenda determined by the grammatical and logical structure of the narrative of the second article of the Nicene symbol. Thus the bishops at Chalcedon did not, even in the end, fail to keep faith with the Ephesian Council of 431, nor did they waver in their conviction that the *Definition* ought to be, even if it was not, superfluous.

II

How wrong they were in this conviction was to be demonstrated by the two great spates of criticism that their *Definition* evoked in the course of the later history of the Christian movement. The first of these, of course, was the critique mounted by the Monophysites, who, out of loyalty to Cyril of Alexandria, and also eventually no doubt out of distaste for Byzantine hegemony, sought to maintain, in opposition to the language of two natures, the formula *One incarnate nature of the divine Word.*[12] The second is a debate that is still going on — a debate stimulated in part by modern critical interest in the figure of "the historical Jesus," with its concomitant delight in "christology from below," but also by severe doubts about the utility and coherence of the traditional discourse about natures and hypostases. In what follows, I will hope to indicate that there is a connection between these criticisms of the Chalcedonian *Definition,* a connection that brings into bold relief the virtues of the modesty with which the Council did its business.

The struggle between defenders of Cyril of Alexandria's formula, "One incarnate nature of the divine Word," and later proponents of the Chalcedonian "in two natures" turned essentially on the issue of the sense in which the humanity of Christ represented an independent or self-standing factor in the economy of salvation. To be sure, there were Monophysites and

12. Here one ought of course to mention also the ill-fated attempt at compromise with Monophysitism that goes under the name of Monothelitism. The controversy over the issue of "one will" or "one energy" in Christ touched on a central issue in the debate between Chalcedonians and Monophysites; but the formula cannot be described with strict accuracy as a product of the Monophysite camp and was in fact inspired by a desire to evade use of the expression "one nature."

Monophysites, just as there were Chalcedonians and Chalcedonians. A Monophysite thinker and leader like Severus of Antioch objected strongly to the Eutychianism or "synousianism" of those who interpreted "one nature" to mean that Christ was some sort of unprecedented "cross" between humanity and divinity. But he objected just as strenuously to the Nestorian hypothesis of two hypostases or subjects in Christ; and it was Nestorianism that he discerned in the language of Leo the Great's *Tome*, with its assertion that

> Each "form" [cf. Phil. 2:6-7] carries on its proper activities in communion with the other. The Word does what belongs to it, and the flesh carries out what belongs to it. The one shimmers with wondrous deeds, the other succumbs to injury and insult.[13]

To Severus and those who thought like him, this suggestion that "the flesh" of Christ "carries on its own proper activities" implied that it belonged ultimately to itself and not to the divine Word; and this contention they took to constitute the heart of the Nestorian error. Yet the Council of Chalcedon had not merely used the phrase "in two natures;" it had canonized this *Tome* of Leo's and thus indicated that Leo's views were consistent with its *Definition*. To be sure, it had also, to use its own words,

> received . . . the synodical letters of the blessed Cyril . . . to Nestorius and the Orientals, for the sake of refuting the follies of Nestorius and for the instruction of those who, in religious zeal, seek understanding of the saving Symbol.[14]

But the contention, thus embodied in conciliar action, that "Leo agrees with Cyril" (as the Council Fathers had even shouted at one point) was at the very least difficult to sustain; and this was precisely the point of the Monophysite polemic. The conciliar *Definition*, it argued, was for all practical purposes a Nestorian document.

At the base of this Monophysite polemic, then, there lay a straightforward loyalty to the views and insights of Cyril of Alexandria. Monophysitism arose out of a belief that the Council of Chalcedon had betrayed both Cyril and the Ephesian Council of 431, which was associated with

---

13. *Tome* 4, in Norris, *The Christological Controversy*, p. 150.
14. Ibid., p. 158.

Cyril's name. Essential to this belief, however, was a further conviction, quite correctly noted by John of Damascus, that the words "hypostasis" and "nature" (to which list "person" might also be added) "mean the same thing";[15] for given this conviction, it was impossible for a teacher like Severus of Antioch not to descry Nestorianism in any assertion of two natures. On the other hand, this Cyrillian Monophysitism was just as resolutely opposed to any notion that the humanity of Christ ceased to be humanity or the divinity, divinity. The "union" *(henōsis)* or "composition" *(synthesis)* through which the Word became flesh created a single individual subject, just as the union or composition of soul and body in a human person creates a single individual subject. Nevertheless the defining "what" of these elements is not altered: there is no confusion of divinity and humanity in Christ, any more than soul ceases to be soul or body ceases to be body in the human individual.[16] The important point for someone like Severus of Antioch is by no means that the humanity should cease to be human, but that it should be a humanity that *belongs to* the Word (even as a body is said to belong to its soul) and in that sense is completely at one with the Word and expressive of the divine and salvific purpose that the incarnation enacts.[17]

The odd thing is, then, that a Monophysite like Severus of Antioch in the end constructed an account of the person of Christ that, in spite of its refusal of the language of "two natures," *says* more or less exactly what the Council of Chalcedon had insisted upon. Like the bishops of the Council, Severus sees himself beset on the one hand by a Nestorian dualism and on the other by a synousianism that cannot tell, or refuses to maintain, the difference between humanity and divinity in Christ. Like the bishops of the Council again, Severus responds by insisting upon "one and the same Christ" in whom deity and humanity are united in one reality while remaining distinct in the "what" that each is. If one were to institute a search for the real difference between them, it would be hard to identify, apart from Severus's refusal to employ the term *physis* to denote the "what" of

15. *To auto legein: De fide orthodoxa* 3.3 (*Patrologia Graeco-Latina* [hereafter *PG*] 94:992A). See also the remarks of J. Lebon, "La christologie du monophysisme syrien," in A. Grillmeier and H. Bacht, eds., *Das Konzil von Chalkedon* (Würzburg, 1951) I, pp. 461-67, with the references there.

16. See Lebon, "La christologie du monophysisme syrien," 472-77.

17. For this point, see the important discussion in I. R. Torrance, *Christology after Chalcedon* (Norwich, 1988), pp. 82ff.

divinity on the one hand and of humanity on the other; and this difference, it seems, is not substantive but turns merely on the matter of how each party stipulated the sense of a particular term.

But is this conclusion justified? Surely in the end there *is* a significant difference between the two parties — a difference apparent on the one hand in Severus's early polemic against Leo's *Tome* and on the other in the orthodox view, represented much later by Maximus the Confessor and John of Damascus, of the relation between nature and will *(thelēma)* or energy *(energeia)*. In the words of the Damascene:

> Since . . . Christ has two natures, he also has two natural wills and two natural energies. But since there is one hypostasis of his two natures, we say that it is "one and the same" who wills and energizes naturally in accordance with both of the natures out of which, and in which, and which Christ our God is; and [we say] that he wills and energizes not dividedly but in a unified manner. For he wills and energizes in each "form" [cf. Phil. 2:6-7] in union [*koinônia*] with the other. For things that have the same essence have the same will and energy; but things whose essence is different have a different will and energy.[18]

Here John is asserting the principle, long established in trinitarian discourse, that activity *(energeia)* is a function of essence *(ousia)* or of nature, not of subject. That is, the way something acts depends on its "what" and not on its "who." Therefore the humanity of Christ, if it is real and distinct from his divinity, will retain its own ways of acting (and hence its own will, since humanity is rational) in the incarnation. This statement of John's, though, is a reiteration of the very idea, and indeed embodies a reminiscence of the very passage, in Leo's *Tome* that had most offended Severus; and it seems to justify entirely his belief that Chalcedonians were wedded to some idea of the *independence* of Christ's human nature. For to speak of a human will in Christ is, surely, to repeat the error of Nestorius, since it inevitably makes the Lord's humanity a free-standing agent and reduces the unity of God and humanity in Christ to the level of a friendly alliance.

John of Damascus, of course, would regard such an accusation as false. He makes it perfectly plain that the *subject* of Christ's human acting and willing is the Word, and that the human nature in Christ is, as we might say, perfectly

---

18. *De fide orthodoxa* 3.14 (*PG* 94:1033BC).

in tune with the divine since it is in a natural and not a sinful state, as the Third Council of Constantinople (680) had insisted. John's "neo"-Chalcedonianism, then, intends — or at least manages — to accommodate both Leo the Great and Severus on this issue: to intimate that Leo's concern for the reality and fullness of Christ's human nature is not inconsistent with Severus's insistence that after all the work of human salvation has God, in the person of the Word, not merely as its "subject" but as its primary agent. Furthermore, if my account of the Chalcedonian *Definition*'s sense is correct, then John is right to take this line, since it accords exactly with Chalcedon's rule for discourse about the person of Christ: that "one and the same" Christ, who is in the first instance understood and spoken of as God, is also, in virtue of the incarnation, truly understood and spoken of as a human being.

III

The interesting difference to be noted, then, is not the difference of emphasis between John of Damascus and Severus, or for that matter between Leo and Cyril, but a more subtle one between Chalcedon itself and the positions of all or any of these contributors to the great christological controversy. To define this difference, moreover, is to discern the source of much modern skepticism about traditional talk of "natures" in christology — and also, at the same time, the degree to which contemporary theology perpetuates, in its own charac- teristic way, the very incoherence it criticizes in the tradition.

The Chalcedonian *Definition,* as I have indicated, offers little more than a paradigm. It does not explicitly explain or define what "nature" and "hypostasis" mean, save by tacit reference to the way in which the Nicene symbol *speaks* of Christ; and to that extent, what it provides is essentially a transcription and an account of a pattern of predication. By contrast, the contributors to the debates that surrounded Chalcedon take another course. Even when their language conforms to this paradigm, they interpret the two sets of predicates as referring to things or substances of the sort that occur in the normal world of human experience. The "natures," in short, are reified. Thus these thinkers discern an analogy to the incarnation in the wedding of soul and body in the human individual (as we have seen in the case of Severus of Antioch);[19] or they exploit the well-known image of the

---

19. John of Damascus used the same image to his own purposes (see *De fide*

"mixture" of iron and fire[20] and speak of "putting together" *(synthesis)* and "unification" *(henōsis)*, not to mention the Antiochene "indwelling." John of Damascus conceives of human intellect (or rational soul), in view of its being the image of God, as "in the border-area between God and flesh" and thus envisages it as the "medium" *(mesos)* through which the Word was united to or mingled with flesh.[21] In other words, the interpreters and critics of Chalcedon employed what one might call "physical" models to convey the virtues or limitations of the Council's paradigm.

Now each of these models depends on the plausibility of an analogy. Each amounts, for all practical purposes, to a *metaphor* for the relation between Word and flesh. So much is apparent from the very manner in which the models in question are handled. Thus the fundamental analogy of synthesis or mixture appeared, on examination, to have certain disadvantages. It seemed to presuppose the existence of two distinct and parallel "somethings" that "come together" in the incarnation. Such an image, however, might well suggest the need for a third, external factor to function as the agent or agency by which the union of the two is effected; and it certainly intimates that each of things that are united *preexist* their "coming together." All parties to these controversies, however, were instant to repudiate any such suggestions as these (for reasons I have already indicated); and so they set about the business of controlling or qualifying this particular range of metaphors by another. They turn from analysis of the constituents of Christ's person to narrative discourse about the incarnation; and by doing so they intimate that the "natures" that are brought together are not related symmetrically. Thus Leo the Great describes the incarnation by reference to Proverbs 9:1 ("Wisdom has built herself a house"), taking this text to mean that "lowliness is taken on by majesty, weakness by power, mortality by eternity."[22] It is the divine Word, then, who by a self-emptying that takes the form of an act of appropriation, *makes humanity his own* — brings into being his own particular humanity. This shift of metaphor

---

orthodoxa 3.16), as indeed Theodore of Mopsuestia had used it to his very different purposes (H. B. Swete, ed., *Theodori Episcopi Mopsuesteni in Epistolas B. Pauli Commentarii* [Cambridge, 1882] II, p. 318).

20. See, e.g., John of Damascus, *De fide orthodoxa* 3.15 (*PG* 94:1053CD).

21. Ibid., 3.18 (*PG* 94:1073A), 6 (*PG* 94:1005B). The idea is no doubt derived from Gregory of Nazianzus.

22. *Tome* 3 (in Norris, *The Christological Controversy*, p. 148).

makes it plain that the agent or agency of the "union" is not external to it, but is one of the "somethings" involved in it; and this revision changes the picture in a significant way because it implies that the "somethings" are neither parallel nor equal — are not "factors" in the same sense. The one — humanity — is real only *in* the reality of the other *(enhypostasia)*, being the "own" humanity — the ensouled body — of the divine Word.[23] The incarnation, then, is understandable only as a salvific act of God designed for the liberation and elevation of human nature "in Christ": it cannot rightly be pictured as a "convergence" of otherwise independent elements.

Now let there be no doubt that such an account of the incarnation accords admirably, as I have indicated, with the language of Chalcedon. Indeed the strategy of introducing the metaphor of "appropriation" has precisely the effect of conforming the original metaphor of "union" or "synthesis" or "mixture" to the Chalcedonian paradigm. To be sure, in doing so, it shores up the conception of christology as an analysis of the makeup of Christ's person, that is, as a kind of sacred physics; but this, after all, is no more than natural. The difficulty in this discourse lies elsewhere — namely in the fact that the sort of christological discourse pursued by Leo, Severus, and John of Damascus tends to misunderstand its own modus operandi. It resorts systematically to analogy and metaphor to convey the meaning of the incarnation — that is, to be specific, it explains the relationship of divine Word and human flesh by reference to a variety of *other* relationships, of the sort that obtain between realities *within* the created order. Nevertheless, this discourse fails in practice to acknowledge its own radically improper and metaphorical character.[24] By taking themselves quite literally, these accounts forget that the divine "nature" of which they speak is no part of the natural order — that is, that it is not of the same order as the human "nature"; and therein they run the risk of reducing themselves to incoherence.

The reason for this can best be grasped by taking a closer look at the term "nature." For commonsense purposes, "nature" meant, then as now,

---

23. See John of Damascus, *De fide orthodoxa* 3.9 (*PG* 94:1017AB), 12 (*PG* 94:1029B).

24. There is a further difficulty to be noted in the fact that many of these metaphors cease to illuminate when the relationships to which they allude are no longer recognized. The ancient Stoic theory of mixture *(krasis)*, for example, fails to provide moderns with an illuminating metaphor for much of anything, any more than does an ancient understanding of the relation of soul to body.

"what something is," or "the state of being (a) something." Thus the expression "human nature" connoted, for Christians of the fifth and following centuries, the state of being a created composite of rational soul and body; and this characterization qualified as normal, literal language. It was this state upon which the divine Word entered when he assumed the "measures," as Cyril of Alexandria might have put it, of human existence. Furthermore, such an act of incarnation, while surely not itself a "natural" occurrence, made a degree of sense if one acknowledged the truth that humanity, as the creature fashioned "after the image" of God, bears a certain analogy to the divine Word; for in that case the person of Christ would seem to embody a drawing of like together with like.

On the other hand, this happy analogy seemed to dissipate once one attempted to indicate, in similarly ordinary and literal language, the meaning of the expression "divine nature." For while it is possible to distinguish the nature of humanity from that of other sorts of beings within the created order by the enumeration of a few significant *differentiae,* the contrast between a creature — even a rational creature — and the Uncreated could in the end, it seemed, be expressed only by a systematic exclusion of all creaturely characteristics from the divine nature. Thus "divine nature" had to connote that which is non-mutable, non-temporal, non-material, non-passible — and the like; and such language, calculated as it is to stress the logical contrariety of the divine and human "natures," would appear to render the incarnation not so much implausible as inconceivable, and any statement of it an oxymoron. Classical christology thus appears to insist upon a synthesis or union of *incompatibles* — precisely because it takes its physical models too seriously.

One might of course contend that much of such negative language is, for practical purposes, little more than rhetorical in its function. It is intended to evoke the wonder, the mystery, and the exaltedness of God, much as Leo the Great does when he speaks of "lowliness . . . taken on by majesty, weakness by power. . . ."[25] But this response, while not false in what it asserts, is far too easy. The language of classical christology, which emerged precisely in the disputes of which the Chalcedonian *Definition* was the focus, was most commonly employed, as I have said, to serve as the idiom of a kind of sacred physics. Hence even if this language did serve the legitimate purposes of rhetoric — that is, the purposes of evocation and

25. See n. 22 above.

persuasion — that was not its primary intent. Its primary intent was to *explain* or to *show* how it is possible to speak consistently of the divine Word's appropriation of the human way of being: to construct, as it were, an analysis of the constituents of the Christ. It was to this end, accordingly, that the discourse about natures was shaped. And for these purposes, it seemed necessary both to *say* what one meant by "divine nature" and to take the definition that one produced with complete and literal seriousness, as though the two "natures" were entities *on the same level,* different locations, as it were, on the same map — and this even though the *relation* between the two natures could be conveyed only by a series of highly, and admittedly, improper analogies. Thus, for example, one was put in the position of using the analogy of total mutual interpenetration *(krasis)* to describe the relation of two substances one had previously defined as mutually opposed in nature.

Such a procedure is, to say the least, perplexing; and for just this reason, most modern students of the classical discourse about the person of Christ have been disposed to discount that entire earlier enterprise. This reaction, however, while understandable, has itself failed to deal with the problem that evoked it. In simply dismissing the christology that grew up in the course of the period between, roughly, 375 and 700, modern theology does not appear to have questioned or reexamined the sense of the radical inconsistency between God and humanity that informed the accepted version of the doctrine of two natures. Even if it has not attempted the same sort of sacred physics, it seems even more obsessed than the ancients with a sense of the incompatibility, not so much between human and divine "natures," as between discourses in which God is cast as an actor and those in which human beings are the agents. Moreover, it is less disposed than were the shapers of the classical style in christology to tolerate, and even sometimes to learn wisdom from, its own moments of incoherence. Consequently it struggles, in a contest of uncertain issue, with a new type of Monophysitism — a tendency, in the face of its own strong sense of the incompatibility of divine and human agencies, to reduce the Christ not to a God fitted out with the vestiges of humanity but to a human being adorned with the vestiges of divinity.

What classical and contemporary christologies have in common, then, is a tendency — to use the familiar vocabulary of the ancients — to imagine that in speaking of a divine and a human "nature" one is speaking of two *interchangeable contraries* — not unlike a Queen and a Knight which, if they sit on the same chessboard, cannot, given the rules of the game, inseparably occupy the same square at the same time. Indeed, the one that moves "takes" the other, performing even as one or the other "nature" does in a Monophysite christology. One might of course, with the problems of christology in mind, invite people to *imagine* a Queen and a Knight occupying the same square on the same board; and one might hope, in doing so, that the very oddity of the notion would, in the manner of all startling metaphors, trigger insight into the meaning of the incarnation. Indeed I venture to think that this is precisely the force of christologies like those of Leo, Severus, or John of Damascus: by the elaborate lengths to which they go in the effort to say something that is, in the end, unsayable under the tacit rules of their game, they evoke a vision of the unity of Word and flesh, God and humanity, that pierces beyond the limitations of their discourse. The trouble is that they would be bound to repudiate any such account of their enterprise, for the good enough reason that they seem, in spite of themselves, to think that the word "nature" can be used of God in the same sense that it is used of humanity.

This belief, though, which lies at the root of the picture of God and humanity as interchangeable contraries, is precisely what needs to be examined critically. Apples and oranges are interchangeable contraries — mutually inconsistent because of their differences, but interchangeable in that both can be assigned to the category of edible fruits. Creator and creature, however, are neither different in this sense nor interchangeable in this sense, since *there is no overarching category in which both can be classified.* "God," if the monotheistic hypothesis is correct, does not fall into any class, even if human beings do; and that circumstance, while it certainly marks a difference between God and *any* creature, does not mark the sort of difference that is discerned between people and trees, apples and grapes, or (in chess) Queens and Knights. And to the extent that this is true, then the sort of incompatibility that obtains between contraries cannot be thought to obtain between God and creatures. It is in failing thoroughly to explore this vertiginous thought that both classical and modern christologies have, as it were, spiked the gun of their sacred physics.

Further reflection, then, is needed on the force of the "negative" theology — that is, on the force of expressions like "non-mutable," "non-passible," "non-temporal," and "non-spatial" when they are applied to God. The general assumption, no doubt stemming from the very use of physical models for the incarnation, seems to have been that such terms actually do serve to *put God in a category* of some sort. Occasionally, however — and most notably perhaps in the case of the Cappadocian response to neo-Arianism — they have in effect been taken to intimate instead that God is *apeiros* — infinite, not capable of being categorized — and hence not capable of being grasped in human concepts. This interpretation, moreover, is commended by the consideration that a strictly negative theology, if it is, *per impossibile*, construed to classify God, can do so only by marking God off as, so to speak, not an ordinary contrary but as the *contradictory* of any creaturely reality; and this would seem to imply in turn the paradox that one can only speak of the Creator in the absence of creatures. In fact, however, as both classical and modern christological discourse testify, it is of the essence of Christian faith — and not of Christian faith alone — that one speaks of God conjointly with creatures, as, for example, "with us." Thus it would seem that a negative theology is best interpreted as saying precisely that the *difference* between God and humanity is a matter neither of contrariety nor of contradiction, that God is not related to us as an element or factor or reality that is either interchangeable with the creature as a contrary (i.e., a different thing of the same general sort) or incompatible with the creature as its utter negation.

IV

And curiously enough it is the Council of Chalcedon's *Definition* — as distinct from most of the christologies it has generated — that allows room for such a conclusion and for the rethinking to which it might lead. If, as I have suggested, the Chalcedonian discourse about natures and hypostases provides what is essentially a rule of predication, a reflective formulation of the way in which the traditional narrative about Christ speaks of him, then it is has to be construed as noncommittal with regard to the logical relation between the set of "God-befitting" predicates (which it fails in any case to enumerate) and those that construct the meaning of "human na-ture." What it insists upon is a threefold scheme.

First, it insists that there can be no reason to talk about a "Christ" (and *a fortiori* an "incarnation") save as an event which, being salvific, can only be construed as a self-manifestation of God in the Word. Whatever species of sacred physics one may happen to favor, ancient or modern, the impulse for indulging in it in the first place is faith's acknowledgment that in Christ *God* is with us — that a relation with Christ entails and is an encounter with God. The ultimate subject of christological predication is, then, a divine subject, spoken of in the way that people normally speak of God.

But in the second place it insists that to talk about Christ is to talk about one whose being humans share, and therefore one whose calling and destiny they *may* share. That is, to talk about Christ is to talk about him in straightforwardly human terms.

Finally, it insists that these ways of talking are indeed different, and not to be confused. It does not, however, define the *nature of this difference:* and it is in that sense that the *Definition* of Chalcedon can be judged merely to have stated the terms of the christological problem. If interpreters of Chalcedon, friendly and unfriendly, have tended, by reason of a misapprehension of the status and function of their sacred physics, to render this difference as a relation of logical contrariety, thus tacitly making of God and humanity differing items of the same order, that is understandable, but neither it nor the confusion it entails is requisite.

In stating the "terms of the christological problem," Chalcedon, wittingly or not, defined an agenda and thus posed a question. And the question — the challenge — was not how to fit two logical contraries together into one, as its ancient and modern interpreters have all but uniformly supposed, but how to dispense with a binary logic in figuring the relation between God and creatures. Maybe after all, suggests Chalcedon, God and humanity are not related as "yes" and "no" or "off" and "on." And this *theological* issue is the real agenda item it defines.

Tradition as Life[1]

GERARD H. ETTLINGER, S.J.

Tradition, as a concept and a reality, is crucial for the life, faith, and theology of the Orthodox and Roman Catholic churches; it is, therefore, a fitting topic for this essay in this volume, since it transcends confessional boundaries and reflects both the ecumenical attitude of John Meyendorff and the relationship that existed between him and me. Our common interest in Greek patristic life and thought brought us together on many doctoral dissertation committees in History and Theology, with one as mentor and the other as reader, depending on the subject matter. The scholars (Orthodox, Roman Catholic, and Jewish) who emerged from this collaboration are living proof of its value.

In his book *Living Tradition*,[2] Meyendorff described this understanding of tradition and applied it to a number of issues, some specific to the Orthodox faith and others with ecumenical import. He says of Orthodox theology that it is traditional, "in the sense that it is consistent not only with Scripture but also with the experience of the Fathers and the saints, as well as with the continuous celebration of Christ's death and resurrection in the liturgy of the church." This is different from a dead traditional

1. Parts of this paper were delivered at the annual conference of the North American Patristic Society held at Loyola University of Chicago in May 1988. Biblical texts are translated from the patristic texts.

2. All the quotations in this paragraph are from John Meyendorff, *Living Tradition: Orthodox Witness in the Contemporary World* (Crestwood, NY: St. Vladimir's Seminary Press, 1978), pp. 7-8.

159

theology, which identifies "traditionalism with simple repetition"; indeed mere repetition of the Fathers is a sign of infidelity "to their spirit and to the intention embodied in their theology." Being traditional, therefore, "implies an imitation of the Fathers in their creative work of discernment."

The Church's tradition, then, is an unceasing, creative, life-giving activity, connected to an ever-present point of origin in Scripture, but not a simple repetition or restatement of the past, not even of Scripture, nor a glorification of bygone moments or events. Just as the life of the human body depends on constant growth and change, which nonetheless leave personal identity intact, so too the Church, through tradition, without losing its identity, draws life from the continuous renewal that takes place as it acts in accordance with that identity and strives to clarify it. Early Christian thought and practice confirm this concept of tradition, as several crucial moments and a few concrete issues from its early historical development will illustrate and verify.

The concept of tradition appeared in the earliest New Testament documents.[3] Thus Paul referred to the traditions that he handed on and said that he handed on what he had received from the Lord,[4] but the opposition he encountered from his apostolic colleagues indicate that this was not simply a case of repetition. In early postscriptural Christian thought, "tradition" was used to describe the process of God's self-revelation to human beings, which began with the Old Testament prophets[5] and was later transmitted through Jesus Christ to the apostles; they in turn handed it on to succeeding generations of teachers, but especially to their successors, the *episkopoi*, the overseers of the local churches. The transmission of this tradition about God's self-revelation was seen as a continuous movement from the original self-revelation given to the prophets, but its content was more or less fixed and was often expressed in a form called the "rule of faith" or "rule of truth." This was a brief summary of the major points of Christian faith similar to later, more developed creeds, but appearing with variations in different authors. In his work *Against Heresies* (III.11.1) Irenaeus of Lyons, for one, said that John the Evangelist wished

---

3. The word "tradition" refers to the Greek verb *paradidōmi* and the noun *paradosis*.

4. See 1 Corinthians 11:2, 23.

5. In this context the term "prophet" also referred to such figures as Abraham, Moses, and David.

"to establish the rule of truth in the Church that there is one almighty God, who through his Word made all things visible and invisible. . . ."[6] This example shows that these brief declarations usually affirm a belief in at least the creator God, and often also in God's Word, or in Jesus Christ, who brought God's self-revelation.

The Old and New Testaments were thus considered the foundation books of Christianity because they embodied this self-revelation in a special way; in this understanding Scripture constituted tradition, but was in fact a part of it as well. Christian faith and life are, therefore, rooted in the organic unity between Scripture and the interpretation of Scripture at any and every moment in history. Like later creedal statements, the rule of faith, as just seen, proclaimed the object of faith, or more accurately, the person in whom one must believe. But neither that rule nor those creeds explained their contents, and this resulted in ambiguities that were the source of a rich variety in early Christian thought and life, not only in movements such as Gnosticism, which were eventually condemned as heretical, but also in so-called mainstream or orthodox Christianity, which pronounced those condemnations.

Heresiologists such as Tertullian and Irenaeus objected to the teachings and lifestyles of Gnosticism, not only because it was different, but because they were convinced that in principle its proponents were distorting and destroying the true identity of Christianity. Their judgments appear to be valid when applied to the Gnosticism that they described and as they presented it. Modern discoveries of original Gnostic writings, such as the Nag Hammadi library, present a different picture, however, and show that they themselves, whether deliberately or not, were guilty of some distortion.

As for so-called mainstream Christianity in the second century, one need only compare, for example, the person and role of Jesus Christ depicted in the writings of authors such as Clement of Rome, Ignatius of Antioch, Hermas, and Justin Martyr. They all began with Scripture as they sought to transmit the faith they were taught: salvation comes through Jesus Christ; but the end results were strikingly different. For Clement, God the creator was the beginning and end of salvation, and Jesus was the mediator, through whom one prays to God and comes to God.[7] Ignatius expressed

---

6. Adelin Rousseau and Louis Doutreleau, *Irénée de Lyon. Contre les Hérésies,* Livre III, Tome II (Sources Chrétiennes, 211; Paris: Cerf, 1974), p. 140, lines 18-20.

7. See the *First Epistle of Clement to the Corinthians,* in Kirsopp Lake (tr.), *The*

such a rich theology of Christ, divine and human, and the center of Christian life in all ways, that some have argued that he must have lived several hundred years later than the traditional dates ascribed to him.[8] Hermas never mentioned the historical person Jesus Christ, and in his teachings about penitence and repentance he referred to the Son, whom he appears to have identified with the Spirit as the one who became flesh.[9] Justin employed his philosophical training to develop a quasi-theological picture of the human Jesus united with the divine Logos, the Word of God; but this Word, like the Spirit, was subordinate to the one God, the creator of all.[10] Judged in the light of later development, some of these ideas would have been condemned as heretical. But at this early point in church history certain doctrinal variations were overlooked and were not considered destructive; Clement, Ignatius, and Justin were highly regarded, and the early Church actually debated (although it eventually rejected) the possible canonicity of the *Shepherd of Hermas.*

In the fourth century, the teachings of Arius were rejected by his opponents as contrary to authentic Christian tradition, and the bishops who assembled at Nicaea in 325 moved to ratify this rejection by defining the tenets of the orthodox, or official, Christian faith.[11] From the time of the council of Nicaea, then, under the influence of conciliar authority and the imperial desire for ecclesiastical peace, acceptance of diversity tended to yield to a search for uniformity. The resulting tension introduced a static quality into the understanding of tradition. In questions of doctrine, as the content of Christian tradition was reformulated or clearly expressed for the first time, new formulas were often taken to be absolutely definitive statements, although postconciliar developments showed that determining the true meaning of an apparently simple formula was more complicated than had been

---

Apostolic Fathers I (Loeb Classical Library; London and Cambridge, MA: William Heinemann and Harvard University Press, 1945), passim.

8. See the seven authentic *Epistles* of Ignatius in ibid., passim.

9. See *The Shepherd of Hermas,* Parable (or Similitude) V.5-6, in Lake, *Apostolic Fathers* II (1946), pp. 164-68.

10. *First Apology,* chapter 13; see Alexander Roberts and James Donaldson (eds.), *The Ante-Nicene Fathers* (reprint, Grand Rapids, MI: Eerdmans, 1973) I, pp. 166-67; this volume will be cited here as *ANF.* The Greek text can be found in the edition of J. C. T. Otto (3 vols., Jena, 1842-48; 3 vols. in 5, 1876-81).

11. See Norman P. Tanner, S.J. (ed.), *Decrees of the Ecumenical Councils* (London and Washington: Sheed and Ward and Georgetown University Press, 1990) I, p. 5.

thought. This tension was compounded by the reluctance of post-Nicene writers to change or add to the wording of the Nicene creed, even if they believed the council's declaration to be unclear or even inadequate.[12] But a process began during this period that led to the declaration of the Holy Spirit's divinity, and it shall be presented as an example of the living, creative force of tradition that is operative in a question of doctrine and faith.

The council of Nicaea declared the divinity of the second person of the trinity by adding to its proclamation of faith in one Lord Jesus Christ a series of phrases that said, in effect, that he was God as the Father was God. With respect to the third person the council simply stated its belief "in the Holy Spirit."[13] As the Arian controversy over the divinity of God's Word dragged on through the fourth century and finally drifted into obscurity, questions about the Spirit's divinity came to the fore, since even the so-called orthodox did not feel that the council had answered them. Basil of Caesarea, writing to Epiphanius in about 377 said that "we cannot add anything, no matter how insignificant, to the faith expressed at Nicaea, except to ascribe glory to the Holy Spirit, since our Fathers only mentioned this point in passing, because no question had arisen yet at that time about the Spirit."[14]

In his funeral oration for Basil, Gregory of Nazianzus describes, mostly with approval, how Basil was very careful on certain occasions not to proclaim the Spirit's divinity openly, even though his discretion gave heretics the upper hand; he did this because he felt that the time was not ripe for clear statements, and so he taught the truth by way of circumlocution, but through scriptural language and other terms that unequivocally taught this doctrine.[15] Gregory says that Basil obviously believed in the Spirit's divinity because he often taught it in public and confessed it eagerly in private conversations.

Eulogizing Athanasius of Alexandria in 380, Gregory praised him for his courage on this issue:

> When all the others who shared our doctrine were divided into three groups — many were weak when it came to the Son, even more were

12. See the text of the following paragraph and note 14 below.

13. Tanner, *Decrees* I, p. 5.

14. *Epistle* 258.2, in Yves Courtonne, *Saint Basile. Lettres*, III (Paris: Société d'Édition "Les Belles Lettres," 1966), pp. 101-2.

15. *Oration* 43.68, in Jean Bernardi, *Grégoire de Nazianze. Discours 42-43* (Sources Chrétiennes, 384; Paris: Cerf, 1992), pp. 274-78.

weak about the Holy Spirit *(an issue in which a minor heresy was considered orthodoxy)*, and few were healthy in both areas — he was the first and only one, alone or with the support of a few, who dared to declare clearly and openly the true teaching, when he confessed in writing the one divinity and substance of the three.[16]

Cyril of Jerusalem taught,

Let us say about the Holy Spirit nothing but what was written [in Scripture]; if something has not been written, let us not meddle with it. The Holy Spirit itself spoke the Scriptures and said about itself as much as it wished to, and as much as we could comprehend. Let its words be spoken, therefore, for what it did not say, we do not dare [to say].[17]

The problem, of course, was to determine exactly what Scripture did say, but the Church's tradition and teaching about the Holy Spirit was simply not obvious at that time. Gregory of Nazianzus summed up both the problem and the process that solved it in his discourse on the Holy Spirit where he said that the fullness of the Church's teaching about God was achieved by development through addition:

The Old Testament proclaimed the Father clearly and the Son rather obscurely. The New Testament manifested the Son and suggested the divinity of the Spirit. The Spirit now dwells among us and provides us a more clear revelation of itself. For it was not good to proclaim the Son clearly, when the Father's divinity had not yet been acknowledged, nor to add the burden (to use a bold expression) of the Holy Spirit, when the Son's divinity had not been accepted.[18]

These few quotations from a lengthy and broad discussion show living tradition at work. God's self-revelation, even through Scripture, did not take place in a single static moment of enlightenment and understanding; there was instead a process of unfolding, found in and directed by the Scripture, that took place in the life of the Jewish people prior to the

16. *Oration* 21.33, in Justin Mossay, *Grégoire de Nazianze. Discours 20-23* (Sources Chrétiennes, 270; Paris: Cerf, 1980), p. 182.

17. *Catechetical Oration* 16.2: *Patrologia Graeco-Latina* (PG) 33:920.

18. *Oration* 31.26, in Paul Gallay, *Grégoire de Nazianze. Discours 27-31 (Discours Théologiques)* (Sources Chrétiennes, 250; Paris: Cerf, 1978), p. 326.

existence of Jesus Christ and then in the life of the Christian community over a period of almost 400 years.

In the year 381 a council of bishops in Constantinople did for the Spirit what Nicaea had done for the Son, adding to the Nicene proclamation of faith in the Spirit a series of phrases that said, in effect, that the Spirit is God as the Father and Son are God.[19] If Cyril of Jerusalem's exhortation to repeat only what Scripture said had been accepted in the spirit of the traditionalism described earlier, this council could never have taken place. But because the Church's tradition was living, the creative process that Gregory of Nazianzus described in *Oration* 31.26 ended in the expression of the full, true meaning of the scriptural data. This understanding could never have been achieved simply by reading Scripture at a given point in time; it required many years of life, pre-Christian and Christian, to reach its fulfillment — tradition as life.

The problems that arise with respect to tradition took on a different form in questions concerning nondoctrinal areas of early Christian life and praxis. Here tradition was still rooted in Scripture, but was now expressed in the form of practical teachings, based on the distinction between right and wrong, that offered instruction for daily life. Such teachings, of their very nature, were formulated in directives that demanded a certain clarity and stability. In this context, tradition could easily be confused with custom, which had a legal basis that tended to be more concerned with the kind of repetition typical of traditionalism. The following examples show that in certain crucial matters such confusion did actually occur and that it threatened to stifle the true vitality of Christian tradition. Analysis of the interaction between custom and tradition will further clarify and authenticate the latter's living nature and life-giving power. The personalities involved in this question were Basil of Caesarea and his good friend, and sometime critic, Gregory of Nazianzus; the directives referred to marriage and married life.

Like all aspects of tradition, marital legislation in the early Church was based on Scripture. Thus the cases cited here employed both the New Testament, as a primary source, and the Old Testament, in a somewhat eclectic manner. The latter was quoted to support Christian practice, especially when the two Testaments seemed to coincide, but it was sometimes rejected when there appeared to be a conflict, on the grounds that it had

19. See Tanner, *Decrees* I, 24.

been superseded by the New Testament. Christian legislation and practice were also influenced by the secular laws and usages of the contemporary Roman Empire.

Basil gave an example of the force of custom[20] in a letter to a man named Diodore.[21] Basil related how someone, using Diodore's name to gain credibility, advised a man who wanted to marry his deceased wife's sister to go ahead with his plans. Basil expressed shock, not only because the forger even dared to entertain such a question, but also because he enthusiastically supported a practice that Basil considered a lewd desire. Basil explained to Diodore that he was writing to counteract the forgery, which, he felt, could easily damage those who heard of it — presumably by itself becoming the basis of a new custom. He began to explain his argument in this way:

> First of all, therefore, and most important in such cases, is our custom (ethos), which we can put forth as having the force of law, because the regulations were handed down (paradidōmi) to us by holy men. And this is that custom: If someone, through passion, should ever be overcome by impurity and fall into unlawful intercourse with two sisters, one may not consider this a marriage or allow them to participate fully in church life before they separate from one another. Even if there were nothing else to say, therefore, custom would have been enough to prevent the evil.[22]

Basil then attempted to prove his case with texts from both Testaments. He rejected the use of Leviticus 18:18 to justify this act[23] because, he said, Old Testament laws applied only to the Jewish people;[24] then he went on to quote other Old Testament passages that supported his posi-

20. For "custom" Basil utilized two Greek words: ethos and synētheia. The first word appears to be rooted in the notion of intrinsic habituation, while the latter refers more to external characteristics and/or circumstances. Basil used them interchangeably, while Gregory, in the passages discussed here, employed synētheia alone.

21. Epistle 160, in Courtonne, Saint Basile. Lettres, II (1961), pp. 88-92.

22. Epistle 160.2, in Courtonne, II, pp. 88-89.

23. This passage forbade a man to marry his wife's sister while his wife was still alive; for Basil the precise issue was not the rejection of polygamy, but his opponent's argument that this regulation implied that a man might legally marry his wife's sister after his wife's death.

24. Epistle 160.3, in Courtonne, II, p. 89.

tion. The validity of Basil's interpretation of Scripture is not the question here, for he obviously believed that the strongest argument against this practice derived from "custom," which he viewed as a form of tradition, since it was handed on by holy men. In this particular case, custom was similar to legal precedent and had the force of law. What was extraordinary was that Basil quoted Scripture to support his opinion, but at the same time used custom to contradict Scripture in order to effect a change. He saw no problem in this, moreover, since it was Old Testament practice that he rejected.

But it is even more striking to note that custom could contradict the New Testament itself in the name of what might be called a contemporary (i.e., with Basil) liberal adaptation to circumstances; as the next example will show, however, opposition to such an approach existed and functioned in what could be described as a conservative, backward-looking way. The latter methodology paradoxically proved to be more fruitful for doctrinal development, since it rested on genuine tradition and sought to return, through Scripture, to God's authentic self-revelation. In this case, then, custom, a recent phenomenon, purportedly adapted to the present the tradition on which it was based; but in fact it rejected the roots of tradition and thereby distorted it. Tradition, which looked to the past for its inspiration, seized the heart of tradition and became a force for life and development in the contemporary world. The object here is not support for either a liberal or a conservative approach in twentieth-century Christianity. At stake rather is the clarification of the paradoxical nature of tradition that can, at any historical point in time, live and give life by looking to the past, or the present, or the future, as long as it remains in touch with its roots and is faithful to its own history.

The situation was different in *Epistles* 188 and 199, the so-called canonical epistles, addressed to bishop Amphilochius, which detailed penitential practices known to Basil; in this legal context the power of custom proved to be definitive. Although these letters dealt primarily with practice and discipline, they also touched on theological questions that belonged to the essence of Christianity as a developing way of life. Major issues were Basil's conception of the relationship of Scripture, custom, tradition, and Christian life and the question of whether this relationship was a living process or a fixed and static reality.

In the first of these letters, Basil referred to church discipline on marriage and divorce derived from the familiar text of Matthew 5:32, where

Jesus forbade divorce except for reasons of unchastity. Basil described the practice he followed:

> According to the natural logic of thinking, the Lord's declaration about the impermissibility of withdrawing from a marriage except on the ground of unchastity applies equally to both men and women. Custom (*synētheia*), however, is different; we find instead that women are treated very strictly. . . . But custom commands that wives must keep husbands who commit adultery and acts of unchastity. And so I do not know if the woman who lives with a man who has been divorced can be called an adulteress; for the charge in this case falls on the woman who left her husband, depending on the reason for which she withdrew from the marriage. For if it was because she was beaten and would not put up with the blows, she should have endured rather than be separated from her spouse; if it was because she would not stand for losing her money, that too is not a legitimate excuse. But if it was because he was living in sexual sin, we do not find this condition in church custom; in fact a wife was not ordered to separate from an unbelieving husband, but to remain [with him] because the outcome was uncertain. . . .[25] This is why the woman who abandoned her husband was guilty of adultery if she went to another man. But the man who was abandoned can be pardoned, and the woman who lives with such a man is not condemned. If, however, the husband left his wife and went to another woman, he too is guilty of adultery, because he makes her [his first wife] commit adultery; and the woman who lives with him is also guilty of adultery, because she drew someone else's husband to herself.[26]

In this case Christian custom, according to Basil, directly contradicted, not the Old Testament, but the words and spirit of Jesus himself. It also went contrary to the post-Scriptural Christian practice seen in both *The Shepherd of Hermas* and Justin,[27] which gave the woman equal rights with the man in the question of divorce. The custom that Basil details became, in fact, a force against changes that developed in the New Testament and

25. Basil here quotes 1 Corinthians 7:16, which told a Christian wife not to leave her unbelieving husband because she could never know whether he might be blessed through her; Paul's case has nothing to do with Basil's custom here.

26. *Epistle* 188.9, in Courtonne II, pp. 128-29.

27. *The Shepherd of Hermas*, Mandate IV.1, in Lake, *Apostolic Fathers* II, pp. 76-80; Justin's *Second Apology*, chapter 2, in *ANF*, pp. 188-89.

in early Christian life since it supported secular Roman legislation, which subordinated the rights of women to those of men and allowed men to commit adultery with impunity.

The same is true of the ecclesiastical distinction between the sins of fornication and adultery, according to which the latter was considered a more serious sin and thus subject to harsher penalties. In practice an unfaithful married man was judged guilty of adultery only if his partner was a married free woman; if she was a slave (married or unmarried) or an unmarried free woman, his sin was fornication. An unfaithful married woman was always judged guilty of adultery, no matter who her partner was. The following passage from Basil sheds light both on this topic and on his attitude:

> In the case of a man who lives with a wife, when he is not satisfied with his marriage and falls into unchastity, we judge such a man to be guilty of fornication and prolong the time of his punishment. We do not, however, have a rule that subjects him to the charge of adultery, if the sin was committed against an unmarried woman. . . . And yet the man who has fornicated will not be excluded from cohabitation with his wife. The wife, therefore, will take her husband back when he returns from fornication, while the husband will send his defiled wife out of his house. The rationale behind this is not easy, but it is what custom has commanded.[28]

In a remarkable, though probably unwitting, example of understatement, Basil admitted that the negative effect of custom on Christian life "is not easy" to understand. As in the previous case, the subject matter here was disciplinary, but, by placing Scripture in opposition to Christ and prior Christian tradition concerning women, marriage, and sexual sin, Basil's custom, as in the previous case, touched the core of Christian life.

A final quotation from Gregory of Nazianzus appears to answer directly the situation described by Basil, if not Basil himself. Gregory was discussing the response of Jesus to the question of the Pharisees about divorce in Matthew 19:1-12, a parallel passage to Matthew 5:31-32, which was the basis of the previous discussion. According to Gregory, Jesus answered the Pharisees, despite their bad will, whenever he was asked a question deserving of a response:

28. *Epistle* 199.21, in Courtonne II, pp. 157-58.

It seems to me [Jesus says] that the question you have asked pays honor to chastity and deserves a kind response. Chastity is a subject toward which I see [Gregory now expresses his own ideas] that many people are badly disposed, and that the law itself is unjust and unfair. For why did they punish the female, but indulge the male? And why does a wife who has sinned against her husband's bed commit adultery and suffer the harsh penalties of the law for this, while a husband who is unfaithful to his wife goes unpunished? I do not accept this legislation; I do not approve of the custom (*synētheia*). The legislators were males (*andres*), and that is why the legislation is anti-female. . . . This is not God's way. . . . How can you demand chastity, when you do not give it in return? How can you ask for what you do not give? How can you pass unequal legislation, when you are a body of equal honor? If you think of lower things, the woman sinned — so too did Adam; the serpent deceived both of them. One was not found to be weaker and the other stronger. Are you thinking about higher things? Christ saves both through his sufferings. Did he become flesh for the sake of the man? He did the same for the woman. Did he die for the man? The woman too is saved by his death. He is named by his descent from David; do you think perhaps that this honors the man? Well he is also born of a virgin, and this is in the woman's favor.[29]

This was a remarkable statement for a fourth-century bishop, especially since Gregory was by no means a feminist. He shared the basic attitude of his day, which viewed the woman as the weaker sex and subordinate to the man. But because of his understanding of the tradition and life of the Church, Gregory was able to transcend the limitations of his own cultural background. The main point here, then, is his rejection of this particular custom and the laws based on it. He criticized it as sexist; but when he said "This is not God's way," he was not merely comparing divine and human legislation. He was responding to the attitude of Basil's "custom, however, is different"[30] and thus appears to have drawn a contrast between God and custom. For Gregory, therefore, custom sometimes wrongly opposed God; it should certainly never have functioned as a force in Christian life that negated the words and spirit of Christ. Such a custom, in Gregory's eyes,

29. *Oration* 37.6-7, in Paul Gallay, *Grégoire de Nazianze. Discours 32-37* (Sources Chrétiennes, 318; Paris: Cerf, 1985), pp. 282-86.

30. See above, p. 168.

did not derive from God's self-revelation and was therefore contrary to Scripture and not in harmony with true Christian tradition. Instead it followed secular marital legislation and reflected a bias for the man against the woman; it thus supported a non-Christian approach to marriage and devalued the humanity of women. One may conclude that such a custom was not part of a living process, but was rather a principle of spiritual stagnation and death.

The diverse examples given here are clear instances of tradition at work in the fourth century of Christian history. At its best, tradition was seen as a force that developed through the present into the future, but that always led the Christian back to the self-revelation of the saving God. There was always a danger that the true genius of Christian tradition could be stifled, particularly if it turned away from its source and/or lost sight of its dynamic reality. The literalist approach to Scripture espoused by Cyril of Jerusalem could have caused such a problem, but he apparently did not press his case, and the Church in any event did not embrace it.[31] Basil clearly sensed the problems raised by his teaching on custom, but he did not face their consequences and simply accepted them as part of church life. Gregory, however, rejected this approach and, by looking back to the source of Christian life for authentic tradition, he was able to voice a demand for growth and change.

In closing, one must note that the life-giving results of Gregory's words and attitude had little effect on Christian tradition itself and on the understanding of that tradition's nature in the centuries that immediately followed his own. The thrust of the type of custom promoted by Basil survived, however, and has affected the entire history of Christian tradition.

31. See above, pp. 164-65.

Dogmatic Development and *Koinonia*

J. M. R. TILLARD, O.P.

The question of so-called "dogmatic development" is certainly one of the most difficult issues that the ecumenical movement will soon have to study in depth. This is important for many reasons. Everywhere, even in the most ancient churches, strong fundamentalist movements are suddenly thriving, some with unexpected influence. They preach "reconversion to the letter of the Bible" together with the affirmation that "the teaching of the last centuries corrupted the authentic content of the gospel." In some Protestant churches, refusal of the most important results from ecumenical dialogue is quite often based on the explicit desire to "not depart from the confessional basis of the group." It is also by an implicit negation of the possibility of any momentous development in doctrine and in *praxis* that — in spite of the most balanced opinions of theologians and scholars — some groups belonging to the Eastern traditions continue to maintain a priori that "nothing which happened after the seventh ecumenical council has to be considered germane or relevant to discussions of the content of Christian faith." Within the Roman Catholic Church, much opposition to the decisions and affirmations of Vatican II have come from the opinion (constantly expressed by Msgr. Marcel Lefebvre) that "everything which changes the decisions of the Council of Trent and the declarations of the popes of the last centuries has to be rejected." It is, therefore, clear that an authentic understanding of "dogmatic development" is one of the main preconditions for a sane *reception* of what those exercising *episkopē* (episcopal office) propose as the fruit of the action by the Holy Spirit in the living Tradition of the Church.

On the other hand, many Anglicans and Roman Catholics who struggle for the ordination of women try to justify their actions by affirming the validity of any development, even costly development, as soon as a serious reading of the "signs of the times" shows that it is required by the relevance of Christian faith. In the Roman Catholic Church, it is also because one recognizes the action of the Holy Spirit in the development of church doctrine that the dogmatic definitions (ex cathedra) of the bishop of Rome are *received* as expressing truths really "revealed" by God in Jesus Christ.

All these examples illustrate the complexity of the problem. How does the theory of doctrinal development harmonize with the strong traditional conviction that divine Truth has been disclosed *ephapax* ("once for all") in Christ Jesus?

I

1. We cannot discuss in this short essay the two classical theological explications of doctrinal development. The well-known book of John Henry Newman (*An Essay on the Development of Christian Doctrine*, 1845)[1] and the long article by Vladimir Soloviev in *Pravoslanoè obozrénié* (3 [1885], pp. 727-98)[2] are certainly important. In both it is easy to discover the influence of the philosophy of evolution which flourished in their century, even if they reject its main conclusions. In my judgment, neither of these theologians is entirely convincing. The brilliant and impressive book by Newman is probably less in tune with the main insights of the first Christian centuries than the far more humble booklets of Soloviev.

1. On Newman, see J. Guitton, *La philosophie de Newman* (Paris, 1933); O. Chadwick, *From Bossuet to Newman* (Cambridge, 1957); J. H. Walgrave, *Newman, le développement du dogme* (Paris, 1957); P. Misner, *Papacy and Development: Newman and the Primacy of the Pope* (Leiden, 1976); P. Gauthier, *Newman et Blondel. Tradition et développement du dogme* (Paris, 1988); H. de Lubac, *Théologie dans l'histoire*, vol. 2 (Paris, 1990), 38-70; J. Honore, *Newman. Sa vie et sa pensée* (Paris, 1990). For a direct treatment of our theme see Nicholas Lash, *Newman on Development: The Search for an Explanation in History* (Shepherdstown, 1975). Newman's book is a fascinating piece of theological research. It is important to remember that the famous book of Charles Darwin on the origins and evolution of species was published in 1859.

2. See Vladimir Soloviev, *Le développement dogmatique de l'Église*, tr. and ed. François Rouleau et Roger Tandonnet (Paris, 1991).

After careful study of these two master works I am also concerned about whether it is absolutely right to think that progress and development are necessarily positive aspects of human history. Is it, therefore, convenient for the divine *oikonomia* ("dispensation") to follow this law of human progress and for the Holy Spirit to lead the Church toward an ever fuller understanding of the revealed Truth? At the end of our own century, described as "the century of progress," we are aware that many of the lauded advances in the development of human thought and culture have been actually steps backward that are now impossible to escape. The images of the "seed" that already contains the tree and of the "dough" that already contains the bread show, indeed, that natural and physical development are in continuity with their origins. They also illustrate how the origin is entirely related to its future development. The logical theory of the inference of one proposition from another more explicit one explains very well how in one fundamental insight or affirmation the whole of a doctrinal system may already be present. But is it equally certain, according to God's design, that at Christ's *parousia* ("second coming") the doctrine of the Church will be like a centenary chestnut tree, rich with branches and flowers, while the doctrine as it existed in the third century had to be only an acorn or a shrub, full of potentials entirely ignored? Moreover, in the realm of thought and doctrine, is any new generation necessarily the bearer of a more accurate knowledge of truth than the preceding generations? What happens in the field of positive sciences does not necessarily happen where ideas about the meaning of life, the implications of human destiny, and the unfolding of spiritual gifts are at stake. Consequently, the parallel between the laws of human history or of science and the *oikonomia* of God's disclosing of salvific Truth is not perfect. Sometimes it looks quite vague and fuzzy. Furthermore, divinely revealed Truth cannot be identified with a philosophy, a system of thought, an ideology. Christ Jesus, the divine Logos, is the *alētheia* ("truth"). But in the Old and New Testaments, 'emet̠ and *alētheia* are never related only to the mind. They are also associated with the *lēb*, that is the heart, the place where decisions are made, the source of the dynamism that makes actions possible. The so-called logical explication of Christian doctrinal development does not seem, therefore, entirely consistent with the nature of Truth revealed in Christ Jesus.

2. The ecclesiology of *communion* — according to which the Church of God is a *koinōnia* ("communion") of local churches — may help theologians find another way to understand the authentic nature of doctrinal

or even dogmatic development. This way seems more in harmony with the whole of the patristic tradition than the other two. Moreover it shows better why, because of the nature of the gospel of God *(euangelion tou theou)*, Christian truth may be from age to age and place to place expressed more distinctly or in a new form, but nevertheless remain essentially unchanged, *semper ipsa nunquam eadem*. This ecclesiological understanding of development is based on what I have called in some of my writings the constant *re-reception* of divine revelation in the multiplicity of times and places.

II

1. It is evident that the idea of a constant *re-reception* is entirely foreign to the notion of a linear development in which each generation adds its own contribution to the accomplishments of the preceding. It is foreign to the analogy of the seed growing to its full size or the logical deduction explicating the full content of a proposition.

According to this ecclesiological explanation, development does not rest on an addition of truths and a sum of doctrinal propositions deduced from the gospel. It comes from the inner catholicity (the *katholou*) of Christian truth. This truth is one and for all since it is identified with Christ who came from the Father, preached the gospel, died on the cross, and was raised from the dead in order to make real the content of the *euangelion tou theou*. The content of that is clear: the Father offers to all people of all times and in all places the whole of salvation through *communion* with the only one in whom he reveals the *truth* of his design and gives the *true* means that is required to live *truly* in this *communion*. This is the gospel of God. The salvation it proclaims implies that in Christ Jesus, through communion with God, humanity will be rescued from the main sources of its distress. Sharing the same divine gifts, belonging to the same body of Christ, there will be "neither Jew nor Greek, slave nor free, male nor female" for all will be one (Gal. 3:28). Division will be supplanted by *koinōnia* since all people of all places, all times, all cultures, and all social conditions will be seized in the grace of the *kairos,* and the eschatological gifts (the *eschata*) will have been spread out in their integrity as *arrabōna* ("down payments") of life in the kingdom.

Because *eschata* are for everyone in each generation and place, all must receive their fullness. That is the way humanity is saved. But precisely because salvation does not concern abstract humanity but concrete people, who are characterized by a wide variety of forms, cultures, and historical circumstances, it is within this diversity in the human condition that the *eschata* must be *received* and actualized. Consequently, the one immutable truth that has been once-for-all "delivered to the saints" (Jude 3) will not be expressed identically in every human context and generation. This is clear already in the New Testament. The apostolic kerygma was fully *received* in the local church of Corinth exactly as it had been fully *received* by the community of Jerusalem. Nevertheless it is not actualized and expressed in the church of Corinth exactly the same way as it was actualized and expressed in Jerusalem. The apostolic message concerning the death and resurrection of Christ was fully *received* in all the local churches. However, for some, Christ Jesus was considered principally as the Servant of God (the *'ebed Yahweh*), for others as the eschatological Son of Man, and for a few as the High Priest. The Johannine tradition prefers to start with Christ's preexistence from the eternal presence of the *Logos* in the mystery of God, while the Pauline tradition prefers to start with the human condition of the son of a woman born under the law. These diverse actualizations in which the Spirit is at work unfold the richness of the *ephapax*.

The verb "unfold" and the noun "unfolding" used above are not exact synonyms of "develop" and "development." Both pairs of words do indicate a disclosure, a bringing into the open, a revelation of something not yet clearly recognized. But "development" is usually associated with the idea of progress, of stepping forward to increase the precision of the former steps. "Unfolding" means only the spreading out or unfurling of a rich reality that is already fully realized. Thanks to this operation it is evident that the knowledge people have of this reality is increased even when the reality itself does not necessarily change. This is why we believe that the idea of *unfolding* is more in harmony with the nature of Christian truth than the idea of development as it is usually defined. Through its actualization in the diversity of human cultural and historical contexts, the depth and richness of the truth *once-for-all* revealed are manifested and expressed. But what happens in one specific milieu or one specific period of human history is not necessarily an advance, a step forward, compared to what occurs in other places or in previous centuries. Quite often it may be the contrary. The history of the Church, when it is seen in its wholeness, is made up of many parallel streams (some expressing more perfectly the richness of the divine grace), and it cannot be described as one linear trend making its way through all the ages. Because it is necessarily catholic — that is, offering the integrity of God's gift to everyone in all places and at all times — the Church of God displays the fullness of divine truth precisely because of the diversity of its actualization and not because of some internal law of constant progress. Since it embraces the totality of time and human situations, the *katholou* of the eschatological grace is manifested through this simultaneous complex of forms. Sometimes it looks a little jumbled. It steps backward and is then followed by large steps forward; ardent communities coexist with mediocre communities; clever expressions of the faith are contemporaneous with poor expressions of the gospel. Must one say that even in the lowest ecclesiastical situations important dimensions of Christian faith are unfolded, especially God's mercy, patience, faithfulness, and constant call to conversion?

This is not a development of doctrine that leads to new propositions. It is, nevertheless, an important growth in the knowledge of Christian truth though an experience of its catholicity *(katholou)*. Let us give two examples, one liturgical the other theological: The varied liturgical traditions of the Eucharist make known the universality of the eschatological grace of God. Each tradition expresses a complete union with Christ that is in harmony with the soul, culture, and human experience of the people that celebrates it. No one would say that the most recent of these liturgies are more adequate than the oldest ones. Likewise, the coexistence in the past of the theological schools of Antioch and Alexandria reveals the transcendence of Christian truth. Likewise, the understanding of its content cannot become the privilege of one culture or one philosophical ethos. Many of the new African churches are now aware of this situation.

2. When the Church of God passes from one generation and culture to another, it knows that it has to offer each generation and culture the integrity of Christian Truth together with the *eschata* that God bestows on all those who *receive* this truth. But it is evident that there is a distinction between the truth as such and its various expressions and actualizations. On the one hand, the Church cannot transmit a catalogue of interpretations. It has to transmit the truth itself. On the other hand, as we have seen, many of the forms in which Christian Truth expressed itself in this or that local church in a given generation were the fruits of the efforts of that church and generation to cope with their own historical context and cultural environment. Gradually, in the context of a new milieu and a new historical situation, they will give place to different forms of interpretations and life. In the doctrinal history of the

(Roman) Catholic Church, the difficult issue of religious freedom is a clear example of this process. From Gregory XVI and Pius IX to the decree *Dignitatis Humanae* of Vatican II there is — with the basic principle remaining unchanged — a movement toward a new interpretation of this fundamental Christian conviction that is closely associated with the status of faith. The same is true, analogically, in the Eastern tradition concerning the way the Byzantine churches interpret the christology of what they called in the past "Monophysite" communities. What is lived out *hic et nunc* in the Church of God is not a replica of what was lived out five hundred years ago. What we call Christian Tradition is precisely the process of this constant *re*-reception, *re*-reading, *re*-interpretation, *re*-actualization of the one and unchangeable Christian truth — a process that is accomplished through the power of the Holy Spirit.

3. It so happens that, for many reasons, in some church of a given culture and period the result of this *re-reception* appears to be incoherent with what the churches elsewhere (in agreement with all the churches of the past) consider as the only correct understanding of Christian truth on an important point. Thus the *koinōnia* in faith and life in all the churches is threatened. Consequently the authentic nature of the Church of God — which is the *koinōnia* of all the local churches — is also threatened. This was already the case in the apostolic age when Jewish Christians challenged the manner in which converts from paganism understood the principles of "life in Christ." More dramatically, this was at the heart of the Arian crisis. Diversity always has to be encompassed within a strong confession of all the essential elements that together constitute the *catholic* faith, that is, faith in the *katholou* of the revealed truth. If one of these elements is lacking, then catholicity itself is at stake. For instance, a church ceases to be in the *catholic* faith if its teaching denies the divinity or the true humanity of Christ, if the common divine nature of the three divine persons is rejected, if the death and resurrection of the Lord are contradicted, and if the place of the Church in God's design is rejected. When the teaching or life of a community appear so extravagant that they seem to damage and perhaps even destroy the catholic *koinōnia*, other churches have to react. It is especially the mission of their bishops to discern together, but in *communion* with their local churches, "where the truth is" and, if it is clear, to declare solemnly that a certain teaching or interpretation of the Christian life can no longer be considered in harmony with the truth that is revealed in Christ Jesus.

Such a judgment indeed applies to all churches since it concerns their *communion* in the faith. Moreover, it is evident that it will continue to be valid for future generations since it concerns the faith itself in its essential elements, which must remain unchanged until the *parousia* of the Lord. This point will be preserved in the *memory* of the Church. The solemn declarations of the three hundred eighteen Fathers (in 325) continue to be valid precisely because their goal was to declare clearly the authentic content of the faith. To characterize this result, one may use the word progress and the image of a "step forward." One may also say that it is a development of the understanding of Christian truth. But it would be wrong to say that this development occurs because God wants the Church to be involved in a continuous process of evolution in such a way that from generation to generation truth has to become more and more explicit.

4. It is, as we have seen, the necessary *reception* and actualization of the *ephapax* of divine revelation in great and complex diversity of human cultures, situations, times, and generations which on certain more crucial occasions (where *communion* is at stake) constrains the churches to determine together the authentic meaning of the faith, or at least together reject false teachings. It happens because of what we have called the unfolding of Christian truth in the concrete situation of humanity. It is not the truth of a deliberate intellectual program of logical deductions. It is the consequence of the catholic nature of Christian truth to remain one and integral, *semper ipsa,* yet in need of being *received* and expressed in the concrete ethnic, cultural, and historical conditions of human groups that are profoundly diverse, *nunquam eadem.* The seed of truth does not give birth to a full-grown tree that gains more strength and splendor year after year. It gives birth to a shrub that has several stems growing from the same root but from different grounds. Because of the common root the stems are in *communion,* but they do not grow at the same rate. Each one is deeply marked by the quality of its own soil. When those who exercise the office of *episkopē* officially declare that an interpretation of the faith that is spreading in one of the local churches is wrong and must be eradicated they serve the "development" in the understanding of the truth more by purifying it of erroneous interpretations than by a peaceful explanation of its content. The main dogmas of the Church of God have always been defined solemnly to eliminate the danger that comes precisely from one group of local churches propagating a corrupt understanding of the revealed truth. That

is why it is correct to affirm that such a "development" belongs essentially to the pastoral realm of the Church's reality.

5. From this perspective, the role becomes much clearer for all those in the local churches who study the apostolic teachings with the help of the human sciences and especially philosophy. In their research they need to take into account not only the implicit richness of Christian revelation but also the concrete ways in which it has been, and still is, unfolded in the diversity of times and places. For not everything that is deduced from the affirmations of revealed traditions will necessarily become official doctrine. Many of the propositions or positions that one theological school firmly considers to be implicitly contained in the traditional teaching of the Church will remain theological opinion (or *theologoumenon*), never officially received nor refused. This, for instance, is the case of the Thomistic and Scotist views concerning the place of the incarnation in the divine purpose (the Thomistic and Molinist theology of grace still taught side by side in the Catholic schools). It is evident that the growth of an African theology will necessarily give birth to new theological positions that will probably coexist with the positions of Western theologies without being condemned or proclaimed everywhere as the only valid explanation of Christian truth.

In the face of this necessary pluriformity — which is a consequence of the catholicity of the truth on which the Church of God is founded, theologians have two crucial tasks. The first of these tasks is to discern as clearly as possible and to explain what are the elements of this truth that are impossible to contradict or deny in life and doctrine. The Vincentian canon (*Commonitorium* II.3), well understood, is an important guide here: to differentiate between false traditions and the true interpretation of the Christian faith, one has to test if the tradition or the doctrine has been believed "everywhere, always, by all" *(quod ubique, quod semper, quod ab omnibus creditum est)*. Such a discernment is not always easy since the same basic insight may be expressed with different words and in quite diverse systems of thought. It seems now that this was the case in the burning discussions of the nature *(physis)* of Christ, divine and human, and the confession of an orthodox christology in Monophysite vocabulary. Consequently it happens that a new generation — thanks to further linguistic or philosophical inquiry — changes the verdict of a past doctrinal trial. This process is crucial in ecumenism. But it has to be understood in all its complexity: being now recognized as a valid expression of the apostolic faith, the formerly rejected or even condemned proposition may seem *hic et nunc* more in tune with the whole of Christian truth than the official formulation. For instance, the rediscovery of the biblical and patristic meaning of *anamnēsis (zikkarōn),* understood as sacramental presence of the once-for-all offered sacrifice of Christ, showed that the affirmation that the Eucharist is the *memorial* of the paschal sacrifice (for a long time under suspicion in official Catholic teaching) is richer than the blunt proposition that "the Eucharist is a sacrifice." Here, progress appears sometimes to be a return to the past by overcoming all the polemical and passionate circumstances that brought about the rebuff of a doctrinal position. The weakest stem of the shrub, which is supposed to remain in the undergrowth, may become the most luxurious, while the rampant stem may lose its superiority.

But theologians also have to discover among the customs, aspirations, and cultural emphases what new perceptions of societies are really compatible with Christian truth and, consequently, what may be assumed by the local church without breaking or weakening its *koinōnia* with the other churches and its faithfulness to the apostolic faith. This is neither a compromise nor "a concession to the desires of the world." It belongs to the nature of catholicity *as such.* Here again, it is important to observe that such a process pertains to what we have called the unfolding of truth and that in the confrontation with the thinking of its generation or cultural context, very often a church perceives more deeply some of the implications of the Christian faith. The best illustration of this is probably the way the most ancient churches are now dealing with the very popular issue of "the place of women in the Church of God." It is evident that they rediscover and *re-receive,* after a long parenthesis, important facets of the role of women already recognized in the most ancient Christian tradition. This is true even if they resist the ordination of women to the episcopacy and presbyterate. The function of women as witnesses of the risen Lord, hostesses of the first Christian gatherings, and deaconesses especially involved in the ministry of compassion and the care of the poor are acknowledged again. The fact that some Orthodox theologians and bishops now take for granted the possibility of ordaining women to the diaconate is the sign that a strong devotion to the once-for-all of revelation is not a hindrance to the actualization of Christian truth in the perpetual newness of human history. Quite often, *re-reception* of the grace of the *kairos* ("time") of salvation means newness.

Here again it is necessary to say that when the fruit of these theological and pastoral researches will be *received* by the churches, it will not be only the result of a logical development of the content of divine truth. It will come also, and inseparably, from a careful examination of the manner in which local churches in *communion* have dealt with the issues at stake in their diversity and sometimes in their verbal conflicts. Ideas proposed by some churches as the most brilliant logical development of Christian doctrine will be considered only as legitimate opinions because the people of God — with its *sensus fidei* — will not be convinced that they need to be imposed upon all the local churches in *communion*. Moreover, it will happen that the proposition which a council (or the bishop of Rome in some of his statements) will consider as the most appropriate to express the mind of the whole Church of God will not be the best intellectual expression of the truth or say everything it would be possible to say. This will not come only because of the limitation of the culture or the weakness of skill but because Christian truth always involves more than clarity of thought. It has an inner relation to the *apophatic* character that belongs to the transcendent nature of God and his design.

6. It is this relation to the *apophatic* dimension of Christian truth that explains the role that mysticism, contemplation, and prayer play in the discernment of Christian truth. When we say that truth is unfolded in the life of the local churches but that the diversity of these communities needs to be always measured by reference to the elements that have to remain in their integrity no matter how they are expressed, we implicitly allude to the important place of the *lex orandi lex credendi* in this whole process. Here, *lex orandi* does not mean only the liturgical life of the community. It means also the so-called mystical experience of its members. Because of its relation to *the whole* of Christian reality, with its accent on *the whole* of human destiny, mysticism is certainly one of the richest sources of our knowledge concerning divine truth. Such a knowledge is of a differnt kind than the results of intellectual thinking. It affords insights on realms of divine truth that human reason cannot grasp because they cannot be confined to concepts and transcend the field of intellectual ability. Usually it is expressed with images, poetry, and symbols. Some of the Orthodox icons, for instance, express better than a theological treatise essential aspects of the divine mystery. On this basis we affirm that it is quite wrong to concentrate on the growth of intellectual propositions to measure the progress of the Church of God in the knowledge of revealed truth. This truth is also unfolded through the depth of mystical experience and, more generally, of mystical tradition.

But here again we are facing the same situation. The mystical experience of divine truth is diverse. It is, for example, obvious that Eastern mysticism rarely expresses itself with the help of psychological or introspective language. Russian mysticism is more in tune with a deep experience of human misery and poverty. Western mysticism, especially since Augustine, is usually marked by a highly personal character, an introspective inclination always at home with spiritual autobiographies (Augustine, Theresa of Avila, Teresa of Lisieux) or spiritual diaries (Ignatius of Loyola, John XXIII). The evangelical piety and devotion to the humanity of Jesus springs from a Christian heart and personal experience more than from the common experience of the liturgy. The mystical experience of Christ is also at the foundation of a strong desire to be identified with the poor and to serve them. None of these traditions is an intellectual synthesis; none is the fruit of an effort to express more distinctly the content of divine truth. Nevertheless in all these mystical approaches to God, revealed truth is made known; thanks to them it becomes more fully perceived. The richness of Christian revelation is unfolded and becomes more evident when Christians "stimulated by the love of Christ" consecrate their whole life to the service of the poor as well as when theologians deduce from the *depositum fidei* ("deposit of truth") a clearer understanding of the incarnation. This explains why we affirm that the relation of the Church of God to revealed truth varies according to the quality of its mystical or spiritual experience of the living God. It is impossible to judge it only from an intellectual point of view.

From this perspective, it is easier to understand why in Russian Christianity the experience of the *Humiliated Christ* — the history of which is beautifully studied by Nadejda Gorodetzky[3] — has been a disclosure of christology within the intuition of the presence of Christ still accessible to people under the form of all who suffer. Facets of christology already proclaimed in the first Christian generations but forgotten over long centuries have been *re-received* thanks to this mystical insight. In the Western Church it is certainly St. Francis of Assisi who, without any speculative interest, brought the expression of Christian truth to a profound and radical renewal.

7. While the consensus of the local churches on doctrinal propositions is usually contained in verbal declarations or creeds, their *communion* in what we called the mystical realm of Christian experience is expressed in the celebration of the liturgy. Liturgy is at the heart of the reality of Christian

3. Nadejda Gorodetzky, *The Humiliated Christ in Modern Russian Thought* (London, 1938).

truth. This is not only the consequence of the presence of Christ himself — who is the truth — in the midst of the congregation celebrating the divine mysteries. It comes also from the way in which the community expresses its response to the gift of God. The liturgical hymns, with their poetic language and symbolic images, do not proclaim the faith of the local church exactly the same way that the official documents this church *received* try to do it. The reaction of the human heart (the *lēb*), of personal and communal sensitivity in "the joy of the Spirit," is there. Sometimes it reveals a dimension of Christian truth that no dogmatic proposition is able to communicate. The gathering of the people of God around the Word and in the power of the Spirit says concretely what the Church of God is. But — especially in Western Christianity — religious hymns and liturgical songs are not the same everywhere. The celebration of Holy Friday in Kinshasa — with its canticles, its symbols, its colors — shows a dimension of the mystery of the cross that only an African community might discover. This is certainly progress in the unfolding of the *depositum fidei*. But it is impossible to write a proposition expressing the full equivalent of what it reveals: one has to share with the local church the experience of the celebration to perceive it. This concrete case illustrates very well the fact that even doctrinal development cannot be identified only with progress in the "intellectual" expression of Christian truth. Moreover, there is an important dimension to the mystery of Christ that all those who will not have the grace of celebrating the liturgy with the local church of Kinshasa will probably never grasp.

III

Our final conclusion is simple. It is only in the *koinōnia* of all the local churches, involving, in addition to doctrinal propositions, the concrete liturgy and the whole spiritual life of the community, that it is possible to discern progress or decline. Revealed truth is kept alive and unfolded not abstractly but in the common faithfulness of all the local churches to the revealed Word of God, which they must receive in its integrity *(katholou)* and actualize in the huge diversity of various times and places. Those who exercise *episkopē* declare officially that the understanding of this truth in one church or in a group of local churches is wrong and therefore cannot be considered as the doctrine of the catholic Church of God. This is, indeed, an important determination. It clarifies forever the Christian understanding of faith and makes progress in its expression. But this is not frequent. Normally, Christian Truth is unfolded in a "catholic way," that is, through its diverse expressions — remaining in *communion* — in the plurality of cultures, histories, and situations. In some places and some periods this actualization may be splendid, in other places and periods very weak. Moreover it happens that sometimes the spiritual life and quality of sacramental celebrations are regressing in some local churches.

In each local church, faith is nourished by the constant dynamic encounter of all its members (celebrating the liturgy, living in communion with God, confessing Christ in their social environment) with those among them who must *episkopein,* that is, oversee the manner in which the community is faithful to the apostolic faith, especially the local bishop in communion with the bishops of all other local churches. The Holy Spirit is at work in this continual interrelation, which is the source of a common awareness, a living agreement, a *consensus fidelium* (coming from the same *sensus fidei*), which manifests the evidence of divine truth. Always *re-receiving* the apostolic teaching, in the meanderings of its historical and social surroundings, together with its sister churches also confronted by the movements of humanity, the local church is therefore by the totality *(katholou)* of its concrete existence the authentic and trustworthy expresser of the content of revealed truth. But this concrete existence shows that the condition of this truth is not that of a seed led by its inner force toward an always more perfect development. It is the condition of a transcendent reality, delivered once for all *(ephapax)* with its whole richness (its *katholou*) in the *kairos* of Christ Jesus, always *re-received* in the *communion* of all the local churches of God, remaining the same in its inner perfection (its *katholou*) but expressed in the complex and constantly changing situation of humanity, sometimes advancing, sometimes regressing. Neither is this condition a rich proposition from which, thanks to logical reasoning, generation after generation the people of God will deduce the whole sum of truths or articles of faith it implies. It is the condition created by communion with Christ Jesus, the divine truth who reveals himself not only in the words that transmit the core of the *euangelion tou theou* (from *kērygma* to solemn definitions of faith) but also by the living experience of the *communion* of believers with the Father and by the celebration of the mysteries in the liturgy of the Church. How is it possible to evaluate the development of divine truth at these levels of spiritual and mystical life?

SPIRITUALITY AND LITURGY

God as Eros
Metaphysical Foundations
of Christian Mysticism[1]

BERNARD McGINN

"Everyone who has reached the age they call puberty loves something," as Origen observed in the third century.[2] There would be little disagreement with this in our own time. Since the investigations of Sigmund Freud, we would even be inclined to push the frontiers of eros back beyond puberty to the origins of psychic life. Yearning and desire, the pursuit of the beautiful and the pleasurable, are basic human experiences. To be erotic, in the sense of being in pursuit of what we find attractive, is not a bad definition of being human.

The forms of beauty pursued are many. Origen's observation about

---

1. An early version of this paper was first given in March 1989 as the annual "Thomas Aquinas Lecture" at the University of St. Thomas in St. Paul, Minnesota. Other versions were subsequently delivered at the University of Groningen in the Netherlands, at Washington University in St. Louis, at Boston College as part of the 1992 Lonergan Workshop, and to the faculty of the Divinity School of the University of Chicago. In each of these venues I received helpful criticisms and suggestions from persons too numerous to mention here, but to all of whom I am deeply grateful. Finally, it is with profound gratitude and a deep sense of loss that I contribute this essay to the memorial volume for my friend, Father John Meyendorff.

2. Origen, *Commentarium in Canticum Canticorum*, in *Origenes Werke*, vol. 8, ed. W. A. Baehrens (Die Griechischen Christlichen Schriftsteller; Leipzig: Hinrich, 1925), p. 72: "*Omnis namque, qui ad id aetatis venerit, quam pubertatem vocant, amat aliquid. . . .*" Unless otherwise noted, I will make use of the translation found in *The Song of Songs: Commentary and Homilies,* tr. and annotated R. P. Lawson (Westminster, MD: Newman, 1957), Prologue, p. 36.

the universality of eros prefaced a moral judgment that each person loves "either less rightly when he loves what he should not, or rightly and with profit when he loves what he should."[3] Popular culture, probably not essentially different today than when Origen wrote about love, tends to fixate on a mode of eros too well known to require further comment. Other conceptions of eros, more varied and refined both psychologically and philosophically, are central to the history of Western culture, and indeed to all human societies.

My concern here is not so much with eros as a universal human phenomenon, though obviously that cannot be left out of consideration; but rather with an even larger issue. In what sense is it legitimate to extend the domain — and the demands — of eros beyond the human sphere? Many moderns who would champion the universal role of eros understood as libido on the psychological level would find it very odd to speak of an erotic universe, thinking it at best a poetic fancy or misplaced metaphor, more likely a philosophical confusion. But the tradition of seeing eros as a cosmic principle goes deep in the history of Western speculation, at least as far back as Parmenides and Empedocles.[4]

The ancient Greeks, of course, also thought of eros as divine. In the polytheistic and polymorphic religious world of the Greeks it was easy enough to view eros as *some kind* of god, but as the conception of the divine in ancient philosophy became more unified and more purified, a truly erotic God became more problematic. How could the one, perfect, and immutable source of all things be described as possessing the characteristics of yearning desire that are the essence of eros?

The first Christians came up with a good answer. God was indeed love, but not love in the sense of eros. The New Testament teaching on the God who is love reached a climax in 1 John, where it is said not just that God gives love but that "God is love" (1 John 4:8). The word for love used here and elsewhere in the New Testament is *agapē*, not *erōs*, and it is difficult to think that the choice was not a conscious one on the part of the first

---

3. Ibid.: . . . "*seu minus recte, cum amat, quae non oportet, aut recte et utiliter, cum amat, quae oportet.*"

4. For Parmenides (fragment 12) the goddess of begetting (Aphrodite) "steers all things." Empedocles holds that "love" (*philia*) and strife govern all things (fragment 17). For an introduction to the use of *eros* in Greek philosophy, see the entry in F. E. Peters, *Greek Philosophical Terms: A Historical Lexicon* (New York: New York University Press, 1967), pp. 62-66.

Christian authors.[5] They certainly intended to distinguish their notion of a loving God from the little god of love (Eros or Amor) who flits through classical art and poetry in charming if fickle fashion. But did they also intend to exclude all aspects of eros from the Christian God?

The most famous modern investigation of the relations of agape and eros in the history of Christian thought answered the question with a resounding "yes." For the Swedish theologian Anders Nygren, eros is "a human love for the Divine . . . and in Eros-love man seeks God in order to satisfy his spiritual hunger by the possession and enjoyment of the Divine perfections."[6] Agape, on the contrary, "means a whole-hearted surrender to God, whereby man becomes God's willing slave . . . having entire trust and confidence in Him." It is "a response in gratitude for something freely and bountifully given, namely, God's own Agape."[7] Nygren's lengthy work is an account of the bad effects that deep draughts of the heady wine of Platonic eros had on the agapic sobriety of Christian thought, at least until Luther. Not only was eros the wrong kind of love to be directed to God; but, for Nygren at least, it was impossible from an authentic "biblical" perspective to think of God as erotic. Although he admitted that Christianity changed eros as much as eros changed Christianity,[8] his book was a long lament for this mutual contamination.

Students of ancient philosophy have sought to show that Nygren's understanding of Greek views of eros was erroneous,[9] just as perspectives based on other Christian theories of love have taken issue with his criticism of patristic and medieval attempts to relate agape and eros.[10] My purpose here

---

5. For a detailed study, see Ceslaus Spicq, *Agape in the New Testament* (3 vols.; St. Louis and London: Herder, 1963-67).

6. Anders Nygren, *Agape and Eros,* tr. Philip S. Watson (Philadelphia: Westminster, 1953), p. viii.

7. Ibid., pp. viii-ix.

8. See ibid., pp. 667, esp. p. 678, n. 2.

9. E.g., A. H. Armstrong, "Platonic *Eros* and Christian *Agape*," *Downside Review* 79 (1961), pp. 105-21; idem, "Platonic Love: A Reply to Professor Verdenius," *Downside Review* 82 (1964), pp. 199-208.

10. E.g., John Burnaby, *Amor Dei: A Study of the Religion of St. Augustine* (London: Hodder and Stoughton, 1938), esp. pp. 15ff., 92ff., 121ff., and 275ff.; Martin C. D'Arcy, *The Mind and Heart of Love* (New York: Meridien, 1956), chapter 2. On the level of theological perspective, the real difference between Armstrong and Nygren centers on the question of whether Eros-piety was Christianity's forerunner or its most dangerous rival (cf. Nygren, *Eros and Agape*, p. 162; Armstrong, "Platonic *Eros* and Christian *Agape*," pp. 118-20); between D'Arcy and Nygren it centers on the relation of nature

is not to offer yet another critique of Nygren, but to reformulate the issue. Such a reformulation, I believe, is needed not only to set the record straight, but also in order for Christians to understand an important element in their common traditions, the element that has been called the mystical, that which seeks the immediate presence of God in this life.[11] The conviction that God is the love that is *both* agape and eros was foundational to much Christian mysticism, both of the East and the West. In order to understand the metaphysical basis for Christian erotic mysticism, therefore, we must try to understand what some ancient and medieval Christian thinkers meant when they used the term *erōs* not only to describe human passion and love for God, but also when they expanded the frontiers of eros to include the entire cosmos and when they were even willing to ascribe eros to God.

We need to begin with Plato, not because he was a closet Christian, but because so much Christian theology found aspects of his thought helpful for the task of presenting a systematic account of Christian belief. Plato's presentation of eros, especially in the *Symposium* and the *Phaedrus,* is a rich mixture of *logos* and *mythos.* This helps explain, at least in part, the difficulties that centuries of philosophers have had in dealing with it. A key text for exploring Plato's typically subtle view is to be found in Socrates' famous speech recounting the female seer Diotima's teaching on *ta erotika,* or "love matters," that comes at the end of the *Symposium.*[12]

Diotima taught that love is not love "of the beautiful" itself, but rather is love "of engendering and begetting upon the beautiful" (*Symposium* 206E). She also insisted that "love loves the good to be one's own forever" (206A). These quotations suggest a number of the issues that students of Plato were to discuss over the centuries. What is the relation between desire and conception in the path of eros? How are both the Beautiful and the Good the objects of love's search? How can eros be an eternal longing when desire should cease after it has attained its object?

---

and grace. In the Preface to the 1953 English edition of his work, Nygren dismisses the objections of Burnaby and D'Arcy (whose book was first published in 1945) as starting from different premises. He therefore says that he has nothing to change.

11. This notion of mysticism is developed more fully in my book, *The Foundations of Mysticism: Origins to the Fifth Century* (New York: Crossroad, 1991), esp. pp. xiii-xx.

12. The texts and translations from Plato cited here are from *Plato: Works,* tr. Harold North Fowler, et al. (12 vols., Loeb Classical Library; Cambridge, MA: Harvard University Press).

There is general agreement, to be sure, that Plato conceived of eros as desire, that is, as the acquisitive longing for something that is not possessed. This longing always begins on the physical level, and Plato seems sometimes to approve and sometimes to disapprove of the role that interpersonal and physical love (of a homosexual nature) plays in the ascensional process.[13] For the most part — at least as he was read in both pagan and Christian tradition — Plato seems to support the view that sexual longing needs to be transformed into longing for spiritual beauty if the soul is to experience the true heights of eros. We have to start on the physical level, but we should end on the spiritual level. Eros is fundamentally an upward attraction, a kind of reverse gravity that draws the soul back to its true home (cf. *Phaedrus* 250). This is why the gods themselves can have no eros — hence, love is not a god, but a "great daimon," an intermediate being born of the union of Porus and Penia, as *Symposium* 203 tells us. The role of eros in Plato's universe is a partial one, being restricted to souls rather than the whole of nature and dealing only with the upward way; but it is still essential because eros alone makes possible the return to our true home.[14]

Disagreements over Plato's teaching begin when we ask if the fact that eros is acquisitive means that it is necessarily individualistic and egocentric, even solipsistic. For Nygren, as might be expected, eros, in opposition to agape, "always seeketh its own."[15] Other students of the history of love in Western culture, such as Irving Singer, while giving greater recognition to Plato's claim that the love of beauty includes the wish to bring forth beauty, still see Platonic eros as always self-interested. They also claim that Plato's higher eros is not fundamentally a merging with a person, either human or divine, but "basically a love of abstract science."[16] It seems to me, however, following an analysis of the *Symposium* given by R. A. Markus and A. H. Armstrong, that Plato winds up with "a desire that is no longer a desire for possession but the desire of the lover united with his beloved to

---

13. For some interesting reflections on two patterns of erotic fulfillment in Plato, see Martha C. Nussbaum, *The Fragility of Goodness* (Cambridge: Cambridge University Press, 1986), chapters 5 and 6.

14. See Nygren, *Agape and Eros*, p. 168.

15. Ibid., pp. 179-81.

16. Irving Singer, *The Nature of Love* (2nd ed., Chicago: University of Chicago, 1984), vol. 1, p. 73; cf. also p. 84.

produce, to 'bring forth beauty' — a desire which is no longer acquisitive but creative."[17] While this desire may not be explicitly personal in Plato, it is open to a personalistic interpretation once the goal — Beauty or the Good itself — comes to be conceived in some way as a transcendent subject.

Though there is no role for love in Plato's picture of the formation of the universe (how could the gods give what they do not have and do not need?), there is, perhaps, a point of access in Plato's creation myth that later Platonists could use to give credence to their own more universal views of eros. In *Timaeus* 29E the Demiurge is described as follows: "He was good, and in him that is good no envy ariseth ever concerning anything; and being devoid of envy He desired [*eboulēthē*] that all should be, so far as possible, like unto Himself."[18] Another text that later Platonists cited was *Phaedrus* 246B, where the higher soul is described as "having care [*epimeleitai*] of all that is soulless." If the desire to communicate and propagate beauty and the good can be seen as an object of eros on the human level, and if the supernal soul has a care for what is below it, then we should not be surprised that later Platonists, once they recognized that not all eros must be seen as need, could claim that there is a transcendent "Provident Eros" active in the universe.

Plato's student and critic Aristotle played an important role in making this development possible. Aristotle's Unmoved Mover, of course, has no provident love or concern for anything beneath it; but Aristotle's universe does have a place for cosmic desire lacking in Plato because "the final cause produces motion as being loved" (*Metaphysics* 12, 1072B3). Aristotle's notion of love as final cause applies throughout the entire physical universe, not just to the human soul, a point that became an essential part of later speculation on eros.

In the pagan Neoplatonists, especially in Plotinus and Proclus, eros was cosmicized, that is, it came to be seen as a fundamental governing force of the whole universe. It was also to some degree transcendentalized, that is, applied to the First Principle. This movement toward universal efficient, exemplary, and even final causality in the case of eros, however, was initiated

17. Armstrong, "Platonic *Eros* and Christian *Agape*," p. 107, following R. A. Markus, "The Dialectic of Eros in Plato's Symposium," *Downside Review* 74 (1955), pp. 219-30.

18. On this passage, see Armstrong, "Platonic *Eros* and Christian *Agape*," pp. 109-11.

by a Christian author, Origen, and completed by another Christian, the mysterious fifth-century writer we call the Pseudo-Dionysius. This development forms one of the primary illustrations of the dynamic and transformative interaction between pagan and Christian Platonism in late antiquity.

In the Prologue to his *Commentary on the Song of Songs,* written in the 230s, Origen argues the case for not leaving love to its perverters, either those who have understood it only in a sensual fashion, or even the philosophers like Plato who said much that was correct about it, but who still missed the essential truth. According to Origen, all the words used for love, either "charity/affection" *(caritas/dilectio,* reflecting the Greek *agapē)* or "desire/passion" *(amor/cupido,* that is *erōs)* have the same meaning.[19] Thus, Origen understands the Johannine claim that "God is *agapē*" to mean that all forms of love find their transcendent source in him. "So you must take whatever Scripture says about charity as if it had been said with reference to passionate love *(erōs),* taking no notice of the difference of terms; for the same meaning is conveyed by both."[20] This may be questionable exegesis (though Origen appeals to the appearance of *erōs* in the Septuagint in Prov. 4:6 and Wis. 8:2), but the point is essentially a theological one. If eros is not totally evil, it must be in some way related to God. One way to understand this relation is to conceive of the pure light of God's overwhelming love as necessarily refracted into a diversity of terms here below, all of which signify the same divine source. Although the moral value of our loves is judged according to the worthiness of the objects to which they are directed — unseemly ones of sensual delight, indifferent ones of human skills, and saving ones of the spiritual world — the power that motivates all love must be divine, according to Origen.[21]

The Alexandrian thinker went a step further, in daring, if tentative, fashion. If human passionate eros has its source in God, in what sense might God be thought of as erotic? Here Origen confronted a problem that has perplexed Christian thinkers down to the present. God's nature, at least as

19. Origen, *Commentarium,* Prologus (ed. Baehrens, p. 71; tr. Lawson, p. 35). An insightful study of eros in Origen can be found in John M. Rist, *Eros and Psyche: Studies in Plato, Plotinus and Origen* (Toronto: University of Toronto, 1975), pp. 195-212.

20. Origen, *Commentarium* (ed. Baehrens, pp. 70-71; tr. Lawson, p. 34): "*Sic ergo quaecumque de caritate scripta sunt, quasi de amore dicta suscipe nihil de nominibus curans; eadem namque in utroque virtus ostenditur.*"

21. *Commentarium,* p. 72.

conceived in classical Greek philosophical categories, seems to demand a
perfection whose essential concomitant is immutability or lack of change. But
if God is truly erotic, that is, if he not only gives love but is love in some sense,
a love of yearning or at least of going out of himself in his relation to creatures,
must not such a God also change and therefore not really be perfect? The main
thrust of Origen's theology, like that of most classical Christian authors, was
to protect divine perfection and immutability. But a measure of how seriously
he took his insistence that all forms of human love have their source in God
is to be found in the few texts where he suggests that God's eros makes God
capable of the suffering of love. The most powerful of these passages occurs
in the sixth of Origen's *Homilies on Ezekiel* where he sets up a threefold
comparison of the compassion we experience from another human being,
from the Savior, and finally from the Almighty Father. Employing a wordplay
(in the surviving Latin at least) between the stages of descent *(passus)* and the
suffering *(passio)* that God undergoes on behalf of the salvation of human
race, Origen concludes:

> The suffering is one of love. The Father himself and the God of the
> universe, "longsuffering and full of mercy" (Ps. 102:8) and merciful, does
> he not also suffer in a way? Do you not know that when he gives gifts to
> humans he undergoes human suffering? "The Lord your God has borne
> your deeds the way a man carries his child" (Deut. 1:31). Therefore, God
> bears our deeds just as God's Son bears our sufferings. The Father himself
> is not without suffering *(non est impassibilis)*. If he is asked, he has mercy
> and takes pity, feeling some love *(caritas)*. He undergoes change in the
> things in which he cannot exist due to the greatness of his nature. He
> undergoes human sufferings *(passiones)* for us.[22]

22. *In Ezechielem* 6.6 (ed. Baehrens, vol. 8, pp. 384-85):

*Caritatis est passio. Pater quoque ipse et Deus universitatis, "longanimis et multum
misericors" et miserator, nonne quodammodo patitur? An ignoras quia, quando
humana dispensat, passionem patitur humanam? "Supportavit" enim "mores tuos
Dominus Deus tuus, quomodo si quis supportet homo filium suum." Igitur "mores"
nostros "supportat Deus," sicut portat passiones nostras filius Dei. Ipse pater non est
impassibilis. Si rogetur, miseretur et condolet, patitur aliquid caritatis et fit in iis, in
quibus iuxta magnitudinem naturae suae non potest esse, et propter nos humanas
sustinet passiones.*

Cf. *Commentarium in Matthaeum* 10.23. In *De Principiis* 2.4.4 and *In Jeremiam* 18.6,
Origen advances a more spiritual interpretation of God's eros.

There are, then, at least hints of a "passionate" God in Origen, as well as a fully developed doctrine of the passionate soul. What Origen lacks is a sense of the entire universe suffused with eros. For the develoment of this idea we must turn to his successors, both pagan and Christian.

Plotinus, the founder of Neoplatonism, is usually thought of as an austere intellectual; but anyone who has read his *Enneads* will recognize not only that they are much concerned with eros but also that they are filled with a kind of erotic tension that is more than just an *amor intellectualis*. Plotinus's most detailed considerations of eros are found in his earliest work, the famous *Ennead* I.6 on Beauty, and in the late treatise, *Ennead* III.5, a detailed philosophical commentary on the *Symposium*. Important as such treatments are, the real innovations in Plotinus's thought appear in a number of scattered remarks taken from other places in the *Enneads*.

The important developments found in Plotinus's doctrine of eros in relation to the previous pagan Platonic tradition are twofold. First, if only in ambiguous fashion, Plotinus makes a place for eros in the downward way, that is, in the path of emanation or of the production of the universe, and not just on the road of the return of the soul to its source. Like Plato, Plotinus insists that in the case of the eros that is an affection in the soul, pure love of beauty is better than the mixed love that seeks to perpetuate itself in physical generation (III.5.1). But Plotinus also holds that the eros by which the soul loves the Good originates in the Good — a significant new emphasis in pagan thought. "In this way the soul also loves that Good," as he puts it, "moved by it to love from the beginning" (*Enn.* VI.7.31).[23] This claim that eros is in some way a gift from above has been interpreted in different ways by pro- and anti-Platonists. Nygren recognized the departure from Plato, but he denied that the downward way of Plotinus "bears any real resemblance to the condescending Agape of Christianity," because, first, "there is in Plotinus no real descent of the Divine" and, second, "the Descent, *in so far as it is a reality,* means not an act of Divine condescension, but the Fall of the soul into sin and guilt."[24] In other words, Nygren has to claim that Plotinus has a descending love that is not really descending in order to maintain his separation between Platonic eros and Christian agape.

---

23. All texts and translations from Plotinus will be cited according to *Plotinus: Works,* ed. and tr. A. H. Armstrong (7 vols., Loeb Classical Library; Cambridge, MA: Harvard University Press).

24. Nygren, *Eros and Agape,* pp. 196-97.

Though I would not want to suggest that the Neoplatonic philosopher's view of the "downward" movement of eros is the same in all respects as the Pauline notion of God's condescending agape, Nygren's self-contradictory reading misrepresents Plotinus in order to get him to fit the Procrustean bed of Nygren's theory.[25]

The second major new element found in Plotinus is less ambiguous in expression, but no less difficult to interpret. In *Ennead* VI.8.15 (cf. VI.7.22) Plotinus makes the astonishing statement that the Good, "he, that same self, is lovable and love and love of himself" *(kai erasmion kai erōs ho autos kai hautou erōs)*. Calling the Good eros would have made no sense to Plato. Single-minded interpreters of Platonic eros have been equally mystified by the statement. Nygren emphasizes the final phrase ("love of himself"), insisting that we have no basic change in the acquisitive and egocentric nature of love here. God's love can only be self-love, which is no different from what the Greeks had always held.[26] One can only wonder then what made Plotinus the first Hellene to assert that "God is Eros," if nothing had really changed.

Proclus, the last great pagan Neoplatonist, to the best of my knowledge never says that the First Principle, or even the Good, is Eros, and thus from the aspect of love's transcendentality he is less daring than Plotinus; but from another perspective he goes further. Proclus provides the first full cosmic interpretation of eros from a Platonic perspective.[27]

A study of the notion of eros in Proclus's commentary on the *First Alcibiades* (a text always ascribed to Plato in antiquity) shows that he conceived of eros as a power that is *partially* transcendent and *fully* cosmic. The transcendent character of eros is limited. "This god one should not

---

25. Nygren also fails to take account of that side of Plotinus's admittedly complex and often ambiguous thought according to which souls are said to descend by "spontaneous inclination" (e.g., *Enn.* IV.8.5) rather than through punishment for guilt. Armstrong, on the other hand ("Platonic *Eros* and Christian *Agape*," p. 113), seems to provide too Christianized a reading of Plotinus's hints about the role of eros in the downward path, even speaking of the Good as giving eros "in his eternal *creative* act."

26. Nygren, *Eros and Agape*, pp. 197-99. On this issue, see Rist, *Eros and Psyche*, p. 239.

27. Nygren, *Eros and Agape*, pp. 566-75, who provides a good summary of Proclus's views, escapes some of the problems raised by the Athenian's theory of love through an unhistorical assertion of Christian influence (p. 569). This seems unlikely on the part of such an anti-Christian thinker.

think to rank either among the first of the things that are or the last. . . . One must establish him mid-way between the object of love (that is, the Beautiful) and lovers."[28] To the three substantial natures that are found among the intelligible gods (that is, the Good, Wisdom, and Beauty) there are three corresponding monads of faith, truth, and love. "This triad proceeds thenceforward to all the divine orders and radiates to all union with the intelligible."[29] Universal eros gives harmony to the cosmos. "From above, then, love ranges from the intelligibles to the intra-mundane making everything revert to the divine beauty, truth illuminating the universe with knowledge, and faith establishing each reality in the good."[30]

The "whole series (or chain) of love," that which binds the universe together,[31] is definitely a two-way street, or more correctly we might call it a path of salvation. Love comes down from the gods above. "What origin do we ascribe to this characteristic love in the souls of men, unless it previously exists in the gods themselves? . . . How much more shall we suppose that the primary cause of love lies among the gods. . . . So gods love gods, the superior their inferiors providentially, and the inferior their superiors reflexively."[32] The distinction between "providential eros" *(pronoetikos erōs)* and "returning or reflexive eros" *(epistreptikos erōs)* reflecting the downward and the upward ways is new in Platonic thought. It summarizes the long evolution that finally came to see in eros not just an expression of human need, but a universal force binding together all levels of reality below the Unknown One. Proclus seems to have been helped in achieving this synthesis by his recognition that in its origin eros was not just a passivity, that is, a desire resulting from the beholding of a beautiful object that makes us want to possess it, but primarily an activity on the part of the higher causes. "We must observe," he says, "that divine love is an activity, wanton love a passivity; the one is coordinate with intellect and divine beauty, the other with bodies."[33]

The great Christian thinker we refer to as Pseudo-Dionysius adopted,

---

28. See *Proclus: Alcibiades I. A Translation and Commentary,* by William O'Neill (The Hague: Nijhoff, 1965), § 51 (p. 32).

29. Ibid., § 51 (pp. 32-33).

30. Ibid., § 52 (p. 34). Armstrong, "Platonic *Eros* and Christian *Agape,*" p. 116, seems to me mistaken in saying that Proclus limits the scope of eros more rigidly than Plotinus, forgetting the maxim "all things in everything, but appropriately."

31. O'Neill, § 26 (p. 16), §§ 30-31 (p. 19).

32. O'Neill, § 56 (p. 37).

33. O'Neill, §§ 117, 122 (pp. 77, 80).

developed, and transformed this universal conception of eros in his *Divine Names* IV.10-17. In the history of Christian thought this text, both by reason of its quasi-apostolic authority and also because of the depth of its theological insight, remains the classical source for all later views of God as eros.

Book IV of the *Divine Names* is devoted to Goodness *(to agathon)* as a preeminent positive or cataphatic name of God.[34] The self-diffusive nature of Goodness, for which light is the best metaphor (IV.4-6), as well as its power to move all things as final cause, introduces an analysis of the identity of the Good and the Beautiful (IV.7) and leads into a detailed discussion of eros, the force that not only draws us up to but also is identical with the Beautiful-Good.

Dionysius insists (IV.10) that just as the Good and the Beautiful is the cause of all the movements of the soul,[35] so "all being derives from, exists in, and is returned toward the Beautiful and the Good" (705D). All movement, then, comes from above, and can be described as love or eros. ". . . All things must desire, must yearn for, must love, the Beautiful and the Good. Because of it and for its sake, subordinate is returned to superior, equal keeps company with equal, superior turns providentially to subordinate" (708A, cf. 711A, 713AB). All of this can be found in Proclus's thoughts on cosmic eros, including the fact that at least some superior powers have a providential love for their inferiors. What follows is new. "And we may be so bold," Dionysius continues, "as to claim also that the Cause of all things loves all things [*panta erą*] in the superabundance of his goodness, that because of this goodness, he makes all things, brings all things to perfection, holds all things together, returns all things" (708A). Dionysius concludes the passage by providing the first and perhaps still the most pregnant definition of God as Eros — "Divine

---

34. The Dionysian corpus has recently appeared in a new critical edition, *Corpus Dionysiacum*, ed. Beate Regina Suchla, Gunther Heil, and Adolf Martin Ritter (Berlin: Walter De Gruyter, 1990-91), 2 vols. References given here have been checked against this new edition but make use of the standard column numbers found in the Cotelius edition reprinted in J.-P. Migne, *Patrologia Graeca* 3. The translations, unless otherwise noted, are from *Pseudo-Dionysius: The Complete Works*, tr. Colm Luibheid (New York: Paulist, 1987). For Pseudo-Dionysius's views on eros and agape, see Nygren, *Eros and Agape*, pp. 576-93; J. M. Rist, "A Note on Eros and Agape in Pseudo-Dionysius," *Vigiliae Christianae* 20 (1966), pp. 235-43; and Rosemary Ann Lees, *The Negative Language of the Dionysian School of Mystical Theology* (Salzburg: Universität Salzburg, 1983), vol. 1, pp. 116-22.

35. *Divine Names* IV.8-9 analyzes the three motions of the soul since soul is always the intermediary between the Beautiful-Good and the rest of reality.

Eros is the Good of the Good for the sake of the Good" [*esto kai ho theios erōs agathos agathou dia to agathon*].[36]

Like Origen before him, Dionysius found it necessary to defend the fact that eros and agape can be used interchangably because they signify the same reality (*Divine Names* IV.11). "Real Eros" [*to ontos erōs;* elsewhere *alēthēs erōs*] is not the empty image of physical attraction, "but the simplicity of the one divine Eros" (IV.12, 709C). In the created universe eros is any "capacity to effect a unity, an alliance, and a particular commingling in the Beautiful and the Good" (709D). But this capacity must preexist in the Beautiful and the Good itself and from there be spread forth into all creation in the great cosmic heartbeat of emanation and return.

Divine Eros is ecstatic, producing a situation in which "the lover belongs not to self but to the beloved" (IV.13, 712A). Here we come up against the root difficulty of ascribing eros to God. How can God become ecstatic? How can he go out of himself and belong to what he loves? Such an idea seems to produce not only a God who changes but also one who lowers himself to the level of creation. Dionysius's answer penetrates to the root of his understanding of God:

> It must be said that the very cause of the universe in the beautiful, good superabundance of his benign yearning for all is also carried outside of himself in the loving care he has for everything. He is, as it were, beguiled by goodness, by love and by yearning and is enticed away from his transcendent dwelling place and comes to abide within all things, and he does so by virtue of his supernatural and ecstatic capacity to remain, nevertheless, within himself."[37]

In other words, God alone is capable of going totally out of self in a complete ecstasy of self-giving because he alone has the supreme ecstatic power to remain absolutely within self, utterly transcendent to all things. He loves himself in all things from the same ground and for the same reason that he loves himself apart from all things. This dialectically transcendent view of eros also guarantees its fully cosmic character. Because God is totally and perfectly erotic, the universe that is his theophany must also be erotic in essence. God is both the ultimate object of the yearning of all things and

36. My translation. Luibheid (p. 79) translates "The divine longing is Good seeking good for the sake of the Good." On this passage, see Rist, "A Note," pp. 240-41.

37. *Divine Names* IV.13 (712AB).

that very yearning itself. "He is yearning on the move, simple, self-moved, self-acting, preexistent in the Good, flowing out from the Good onto all that is and returning once again to the Good" (IV.14, 712CD).

Dionysius's view of the personal Creator, in the words of John Meyendorff, "is . . . the living God of the Bible and not the One of Plotinus."[38] The full import of this dialectical view of God framed in terms of love rather than of being cannot be investigated here. Suffice it to say that Dionysius was the first Christian thinker to give metaphysical expression to such a position, and that given the immense role of eros/agape in the Christian tradition, his text was to remain a potent resource for later thinkers who sought to provide a systematic grounding for the expression of their yearning desire for God. The fruitful interchanges between the sensuously erotic language of the Song of Songs and the metaphysical eroticism of the Dionysian corpus played a large role in the mystical theology of Western Christendom. My purpose here is not to try to sketch this complex history,[39] but only to point to how this creative moment in Byzantine theology provided a foundation for later discussion of God as *amor/caritas*.

In Latin Christianity, the Dionysian strand, after its entry in the ninth century through translations by John Scottus Eriugena, found ready acceptance, not least because it enforced the efforts of another Christian Platonist, Boethius. This "last Roman" and "first Scholastic" provided a simpler but still influential picture of the erotic God ruling an erotic world. The eighth poem of the second book of Boethius's *Consolation of Philosophy* is a beautiful evocation of cosmic eros, one which had as strong an influence on medieval poets as Dionysius had on medieval theologians. Beginning on the note of the harmony of the physical universe, a theme dear to ancient philosophers of all stripes, Boethius proceeds to identify this universal concordance with the love (*amor*, not *caritas*) that commands even the heavens:

Hanc rerum seriem ligat	Love commanding the heavens
Terras ac pelagus regens	And ruling earth and sea
Et caelo imperitans amor.	Binds this chain of things.

38. John Meyendorff, *Byzantine Theology: Historical Trends and Doctrinal Themes* (New York: Fordham University Press, 1974), p. 28.

39. For an interesting interpretation of the interaction between Dionysian erotic metaphysics and commentaries on the Song of Songs, see Denys Turner, *Eros and Allegory* (forthcoming from Cistercian Publications).

The second part of the poem reverses the initial picture of harmony with a brief presentation of the chaos and mutual destruction that would result if Love were to let the reins slip. The final third of the poem returns to the theme of unity, but this time on the human level. *Amor* is the source of all social conjunction, including those of the "chaste loves" of holy matrimony. Boethius concludes with the hope that human loves will reflect the Love that rules all, thus suggesting the divine nature of ultimate principle:

O felix hominum genus,	O blessed humankind,
Si vestros animos amor	If the Love who rules heaven
Quo caelum regitur regat.	Could rule your souls too.[40]

A carping critic might suggest that Boethius's noble poem does not go beyond traditional expressions of cosmic harmony found in earlier Latin literature. But it is difficult to think that someone who knew late Neoplatonism as well as Boethius did was not reflecting the new view of eros, though in fairly traditional garb.

By the beginning of the sixth century, then, a distinctive Christian view of God as eros had been created, one that owed much to developments within the pagan Platonic tradition, but attained its full expression in Christian authors. This understanding of an eros both cosmic and transcendent has interesting analogies in the other monotheistic religions deeply influenced by Platonism, as the examples of the great eleventh-century Muslim philosopher Avicenna's *Treatise on Love*[41] and the Jewish sage Leone Ebreo's *Dialogues of Love* of the early sixteenth century show.[42] In a brief presentation, however, I cannot hope to give even the broadest

40. Boethius, *Consolatio Philosophiae* II, m. 8, lines 13-15 and 28-30, following the edition of H. F. Stewart and E. K. Rand in the Loeb Classical Library, p. 222. On the Neoplatonic background to Boethius's poem, see C. de Vogel, "'Amor quo caelum regitur,'" *Vivarium* 1 (1963), pp. 1-34; and Gilles Quispel, "God is Eros," *Early Christian Literature and the Classical Tradition: In Honorem Robert M. Grant,* ed. W. R. Schoedel and R. L. Wilken (Paris: Beauchesne, 1979), pp. 189-205.

41. See the translation and study of this text by Emil Fackenheim, "A Treatise on Love by Ibn Sina," *Mediaeval Studies* 7 (1945), pp. 208-28.

42. Leone Ebreo, *Dialoghi d'Amore,* ed. Santino Caramella (Bari: Laterza & Figli, 1929). On Leone's relation to his sources, see Shlomo Pines, "Medieval Doctrines in Renaissance Garb? Some Jewish and Arabic Sources of Leone Ebreo's Doctrines," in *Jewish Thought in the Sixteenth Century,* ed. B. D. Cooperman (Cambridge: Harvard, 1983), pp. 365-98.

sketch of the later history of the erotic God, whether in the Middle Ages, the Renaissance, or in its modern transpositions. Given the role of Thomas Aquinas in the history of medieval thought, however, it is instructive to take a look at how the Angelic Doctor both adopted and qualified the erotic God of Christian Neoplatonists and mystics.

Some might think that Thomas would have little to say on a topic as juicy as God as eros. They are as mistaken as those who insist that he has everything to say on this and on all other topics. There can be no question, of course, of doing full justice to all of what St. Thomas has to say about love, an intricate combination of complacency and concern, as Frederick Crowe termed it in a series of articles that are still unsurpassed as an overall presentation of Thomas's thought on the nature of love.[43] Fortunately, Thomas's explicit treatments of the cosmic and transcendent aspects of *erōs/amor* are fairly limited, the most important coming in *Summa Theologiae* Ia, q. 20, and in his commentary on the fourth book of Dionysius's *Divine Names*, lectures 9-12.[44]

We can start with article 1 of q. 20, which asks the root question "Whether there is love *(amor)* in God." But in order to grasp fully Thomas's dependence on as well as his differences from Dionysius, it will also be necessary to look at the rich treatment contained in the Dionysian commentary. The Dominican begins article 1 in typical fashion by noting the objections of those who deny that love can be found in God. Love is a passion *(passio)* and there can be no passion in God. His response is that because God is Will (Ia, q. 19, a. 1), love must also be ascribed to him, because "the first movement of the will and of any appetitive power is love" (q. 20, a. 1c). Love is what looks to the good in general. It grounds all specific acts of will directed toward the good under its various aspects, such as the good as absent *(desiderium/spes)* or the good as present *(gaudium/delectatio)*. The response to the first and main objection distinguishes between acts of the sensitive appetite, which are always accompanied by bodily change and hence are passions in the sense of something the body *under-*

---

43. Frederick Crowe, S.J., "Complacency and Concern in the Thought of St. Thomas," *Theological Studies* 20 (1959), pp. 1-39, 198-230, 343-95.

44. I will cite the *Summa Theologiae* according to the edition found in *Sancti Thomae Aquinatis. Summa Theologiae* (Madrid: Biblioteca de Autores Cristianos, 1955). The *Expositio de Divinis Nominibus* will be cited following the Marietti edition of C. Pera (Rome: Marietti, 1950).

goes, and those acts of the intellective appetite that do not imply change and therefore are not passions properly speaking. The latter may be predicated of God.

This distinction is made more precise in Aquinas's answer to the second objection, where he shows that even with regard to the intellective appetite some movements imply imperfection, "as in the case of desire which is of a good not possessed," while others, such as love and joy *(amor et gaudium)* imply no lack or imperfection. The former can be applied to God only metaphorically; the latter are properly predicated of him — that is, they are truly transcendental terms. We see here the first point of departure from Origen and Dionysius — for Thomas, God as *amor* is not truly characterized by *desiderium.* And yet in the reply to the third objection we can sense a possible qualification of this as Thomas discusses God's love for his creatures. Here the Dominican defends Dionysius's description of God's love as both unitive *(unitiva)* and binding *(concretiva)* by ascribing the former term to the divine self-love and the latter to the love by which God loves others and wishes them good. "And thus he puts the other in his place *(utitur eo tamquam seipso),* referring the good to the other just as he does to himself. . . . [This love] joins the other to itself and relates itself to the other just as it relates itself to itself."[45] Thomas wants to exclude any lack, imperfection, or need in God, but he also wants God's love for creatures to be a real love.

There is no need to detail how Thomas demonstrates the universality of God's love (a. 2), or how he lays down general principles concerning the differing modes in which this universal love is expressed (aa. 3-4). It is important, however, to follow, if only briefly, how he wrestles with the issue of God's eros as he comments on the fourth book of Dionysius's *Divine Names.* Thomas has no problem in agreeing with the essential conclusions of his Neoplatonic forbear. God is both the object and the subject of love. Indeed, he is the former because he is first of all the latter. All things love God because it is his love of his own goodness that moves him to communicate that good to others insofar as this is possible (lecture IX, § 409, p. 135). The Dionysian circle of love is underscored throughout by the Dominican,[46] but in the tenth lecture on book IV, where Aquinas treats

---

45. *Summa Theologiae* Ia, 20, 1, ad 3: "*Et sic utitur eo tamquam seipso, referens bonum ad illum, sicut ad seipsum. Et pro tanto dicitur amor* vis concretiva: *quia alium aggregat sibi, habens se ad eum sicut ad seipsum.*"

46. E.g., lecture XI, § 450 (p. 148); lecture XII, § 459-60 (p. 152).

what Dionysius has to say about God's ecstasy or "jealousy" (*zelus*), we can detect some interesting shifts.

A distinction not found in Dionysius, but central to Thomas, provides a way into the difference. The love of desire (*amor concupiscentiae*) is when we love something as an accidental good, that is, insofar as it is of use to something else, the way we love virtue, for instance, because it makes us good. But the love of friendship (*amor amicitiae* or *benevolentiae*) is when we tend toward the other as a substantial good, that is, as a good in itself and not for its usefulness for us (lecture X, § 428, p. 142). The first form of love cannot be truly ecstatic, that is, leading the subject outside itself, because "through intention the movement (*affectus*) returns to itself" (§ 430, p. 142). But *amor amicitiae* "does not return to itself, because it wishes good to the thing loved, not because something is gained from that thing. Such a love effects an ecstasy because it places the lover outside the self."[47] Thus far we have only a new precision, not a position contrary to Dionysius. However, Thomas, following the Neoplatonic triple division that Dionysius took over from Proclus, goes on to distinguish three types of *amor amicitiae* — love of inferiors for superiors, love of equals for equals, and love of superiors toward inferiors — and to claim that *real* ecstasy belongs only to the first type.[48] Since God's love is always of the third variety, this would exclude a true ecstatic love on God's part for creatures and thus contradict Dionysius. *Amor divinus* is, of course, ecstatic insofar as it signifies *our* love for God, a love of the inferior for the superior; but it is only equivocally applied to the provident love by which superiors love inferiors, that is, how God loves us. The most that Thomas will say about the metaphorical ecstasy of provident love is that as superiors love inferiors, "because they intend other things, they are *in a way* outside themselves."[49] But what about the text in Dionysius that explicitly affirms that God's love is ecstatic? This is how Thomas interprets it:

> . . . [God] is "in all things" through the effects of his goodness according to a kind of ecstasy which makes him to be in all inferiors in such a way

47. Lecture X, § 430 (p. 142): ". . . *non recurrit in seipsum, quia ipsi rei amatae vult bonum, non ex ea ratione quia ei exinde aliquid accidat. Sic igitur talis amor extasim facit, quia ponit amantem extra seipsum.*"

48. Lecture X, §§ 431-32 (pp. 142-43).

49. Lecture X, § 435 (p. 143): "*in hoc enim quodammodo extra se ponuntur, quod aliis intendunt. . . .*"

that his supersubstantial power does not leave him. He fills all things in such a way that nothing is bereft of his power. Dionysius adds this when he says "lets down" *(deponitur),* which is not to be understood as some lessening, but only in that [God] pours himself into inferior things so that they can participate in his goodness.[50]

This appeal to the notion of participation as the best way to understand the relation of Creator and creation at the end of this text is significant. Also revealing is the way in which Aquinas summarizes his teaching on God as both *amor* and *amabilis* in the following eleventh lecture. Here he analyzes the two terms in relation to the love by which all things love God, as well as in relation to the love by which God loves himself. What is missing is a treatment of how God is both *amor* and *amabilis* from the perspective of the love by which he loves all that he has created.[51]

So-called classical theism, as represented by Thomas Aquinas, has been criticized, especially by modern process theologians such as Charles Hartshorne and Schubert Ogden, for its static conception of God and for God's lack of real involvement with creation. Defenders of Thomas have demonstrated that his identification of God with *ipsum esse subsistens* ("to be itself as subsisting") can scarcely be described as static. They have also tried to show that the Dominican's conception of how God is related to the world has often been misconstrued. The famous formulation in *Summa Theologiae* Ia, q. 13, a. 7, in which Thomas speaks of things as being related to God through a *relatio realis,* a real relation, while God is related to things by means of a *relatio secundum rationem,* a relation of mind or reason, is a *locus classicus* of this debate. David Burrell has argued that Thomas's main purpose in invoking this perhaps unhelpful or at least easily misunderstood

---

50. Lecture X, § 437 (p. 143): ". . . *sit in omnibus, per effectus suae bonitatis, secundum quamdam extasim, quae tamen sic ipsum facit in omnibus inferioribus esse, ut supersubstantialis eius virtus non egrediatur ab ipso. Sic enim implet omnia quod ipse in nullo evacuetur sua virtute. Quod quidem addit, ut per hoc quod dixerat: deponitur, non intelligatur aliqua minoratio, sed hoc solum quod se inferioribus ingerit propter suae bonitatis participationem."* A similar explanation is given in §§ 438-39 for the use of the language of "zelus" in relation to God. *Zelus* signifies the intensity of God's love, but it must be understood as excluding all jealousy and as causing beauty and goodness rather than being caused by them.

51. Lecture XI, § 444 (p. 147) says that from the perspective of the first type of love God is love "causaliter," that is, insofar as he is the cause of the love by which creatures love him.

distinction was to emphasize that God is not naturally or necessarily related
to the world, but that his relation to things is an intentional one characteristic of his supreme freedom.[52] Like Origen and Dionysius before him,
Thomas understood this intentional relation to creation as a love relation,
a love that he was as willing to refer to as both *amor/erōs* and *caritas/agapē*.
Building on the long tradition of the transformation of Platonic eros in
Christian service, Thomas identified God with *amor* and insisted that *amor*
was the fundamental dynamic law of the universe — ". . . this love is first
in the Good itself, which is God, and from this Good it emanates into
existence, and then, in its participated form in existences, it returns itself
to its source which is the Good."[53] But the thirteenth-century Dominican
was more anxious to protect God's immutability than his predecessors had
been, and hence we have seen him introduce important qualifications in
the way in which *amor* can be ascribed to God. God is *amor,* but this *amor*
must not be understood as involving any yearning or desire. Further, it is
not really ecstatic since both yearning and ecstasy seem to imply either a
lack in God or his dependence on something outside himself.

Origen, in places at least, and Dionysius more expansively had been
less hesitant about ascribing both desire and ecstasy to God. Perhaps this
is merely because they were less careful and observant than Thomas was
of the complications and difficulties that such a view might entail for
traditional conceptions of divine perfection. But I think it more likely,
especially in the case of Dionysius and his followers, that we are dealing
with a different way of conceiving God. However much St. Thomas was
influenced by pseudo-Dionysius and the Neoplatonic tradition in general
(and we are in the midst of a major reevaluation of this influence),[54] his
view of God and of God's relation to the world is not dialectical in the way
that pseudo-Dionysius's is.

This is not the place to try to compare what I would call the dialectical

52. David Burrell, *Aquinas: God and Action* (Notre Dame: University of Notre
Dame, 1979), pp. 84-87.

53. Lecture XI, § 450 (p. 148): ". . . *et dicit quod iste amor, primo, est* in *ipso* bono
quod est *Deus et* ex *isto* bono *emanavit in existentia et, iterum, in existentibus participatus
convertit se* ad *suum principium quod est* bonum. . . ."

54. E.g., Edward Booth, *Aristotelian Aporetic Ontology in Islamic and Christian
Thinkers* (Cambridge: Cambridge University Press, 1983); and W. J. Hankey, *God in
Himself: Aquinas' Doctrine of God as Expounded in the 'Summa Theologiae'* (Oxford:
Oxford University Press, 1987).

model of the God-world relation found in Dionysius and his followers, like Maximus the Confessor in the East and John Scotus Eriugena in the West, with the participatory or analogical model of this relation that I believe is characteristic of Thomas Aquinas and the Thomist tradition. Nor is it possible to give any easy evaluation of the relative success or possible validity of these different but in many ways overlapping attempts to describe how God can be said to be in love with the world. All that I have tried to do is to give a brief sketch of how eros not only was baptized but also came to play an important role in the way in which Christian theologians understood God and the universe. This role was especially significant for those mystical thinkers (not all, to be sure) who wished to ground their accounts of the consciousness of the presence of the Divine Lover in a metaphysical theory of how erotic love rules the universe because it is the most adequate positive name for God. Even the name "Love," of course, is not really sufficient. Confronted by the mystery of the God who addresses himself to us as love, the powers of even the deepest of theologians and the greatest of poets have had to grow silent, as Dante says at the end of the *Divine Comedy*:

> *A l'alta fantasia qui mancò possa;*
> *ma già volgeva il mio disio e 'l velle,*
> *sì come rota ch'igualmente è mossa*
> *l'amor che move il sole e l'altre stelle.*[55]

---

55. Dante, *Paradiso* XXXIII, lines 142-45. In the translation of Charles S. Singleton, *Dante Alighieri, The Divine Comedy: Paradiso* (Princeton: Princeton University Press, 1975), p. 381: "Here power failed the lofty phantasy; but already my desire and my will were revolved, like a wheel that is evenly moved, by the Love which moves the sun and the other stars."

The Epiclesis Question in the Light of the Orthodox and Catholic *Lex Orandi* Traditions[1]

ROBERT F. TAFT, S.J.

The Latin adage of Prosper of Aquitaine (d. *ca.* 463), "*legem credendi lex statuat supplicandi* — let the rule of prayer set the rule of belief,"[2] often collapsed to the shorthand "*lex orandi est lex credendi* — the rule of prayer is the rule of faith," summarizes the relationship between a community's

1. I began work on this article during July-August 1988 as a Summer Fellow in Byzantine Studies at the Dumbarton Oaks Center for Byzantine Studies in Washington, D.C. I wish to express my gratitude to the Trustees of Harvard University who awarded me this fellowship and to the director and staff of Dumbarton Oaks, as well as to the community of Summer Fellows, for their kindness and cooperation. A special word of thanks is due to Jill Bonner, Assistant for Technical Services, and Mark Zapatka, Assistant for Readers' Services, in the Byzantine Library of Dumbarton Oaks. Their unfailingly kind, generous, and prompt assistance in obtaining materials rapidly and efficiently greatly facilitated my work.

The following abbreviations are used in subsequent notes:

AP	The no-longer extant Antiochene Greek Liturgy of the Apostles from which CHR and APSyr are presumed to derive
APSyr	The Syriac Anaphora of the Twelve Apostles (I)
BAS	The Liturgy of St. Basil (the Byzantine redaction unless otherwise specified)
CHR	The Byzantine Liturgy of St. John Chrysostom
CPG	*Clavis Patrum Graecorum* I-V, ed. M. Geerard, F. Glorie (Corpus Christianorum, Turnhout: Brepols, 1983-87)
CSEL	Corpus Scriptorum Ecclesiasticorum Latinorum (Vienna, 1866-)
LEW	F. E. Brightman, *Liturgies Eastern and Western* (Oxford: Clarendon Press, 1896)

worship and its beliefs. As you pray, so do you believe. If you want to know what Christians are all about, observe what they do and say when they gather in church to express before God and one another what they think about him, themselves, and their relation to one another and to him. Gerhard Delling has put it in contemporary terms:

> Worship is the self-portrayal of religion. In worship the sources by which religion lives are made visible, its expectations and hopes are expressed, and the forces which sustain it are made known. In many respects the essence of a religion is more directly intelligible in its worship than in statements of its basic principles or even in descriptions of its sentiments.[3]

This is what the theologians call *"theologia prima"* or first-level theology, the faith expressed in the life of the Church antecedent to speculative questioning of its implications, prior to its formulation in dogmatic propositions resulting from *"theologia secunda"* or second-level theology, systematic reflection on the lived mystery in the Church.

In these pages I would like to reflect on the *lex orandi* traditions of the traditional Byzantine and Roman anaphoras (prayers of the eucharistic offering) in the light of presumed or perceived differences between the Orthodox and Catholic *leges credendi* on the issue of the form(ula) of eucharistic consecration.

Mansi   J. D. Mansi, *Sacrorum conciliorum nova et amplissima collectio* (53 vols., 1st ed. Florence, 1759-; reprinted Paris/Leipzig: H. Welter, 1901)

OCP   *Orientalia Christiana Periodica* (Rome: Pontificio Istituto Orientale, 1935-)

PE   A. Hänggi and I. Pahl, *Prex Eucharistica* (Spicilegium Friburgense 12, Fribourg: Ed. Universitaires, 1968)

PG   J.-P. Migne (ed.), *Patrologia cursus completus, series graeco-latina* (161 vols., Paris: Migne, 1857-66)

PL   J.-P. Migne (ed.), *Patrologia cursus completus, series latina* (221 vols, Paris: Migne, 1844-65)

SC   Sources chrétiennes (Paris: Cerf, 1941-)

2. It appears around 435-440 in the *Indiculus* of Pseudo-Celestine (Mansi 4:461), which is now attributed to Prosper.

3. *Worship in the New Testament* (London, 1961), p. xi.

I. "Epiclesis"

The Greek substantive ἐπίκλησις, "invocation," from the verb ἐπικαλέω, "call upon" or "invoke," has given rise to the English term "epiclesis," which is used in liturgical nomenclature for a prayer calling down the Holy Spirit upon an object — e.g., the water of baptism — to sanctify it and render it fruitful for its destined use. In particular, "epiclesis" has become the technical term for that section or sections of the anaphora or eucharistic prayer in which the priest prays God the Father to send the Holy Spirit or Logos, or directly calls on the Holy Spirit or the Logos to come upon the oblation in order that it might attain the purpose for which Jesus is believed to have instituted it and ordered it repeated. This latter sense is the one in which I use the term "epiclesis" here.

The prehistory of the eucharistic epiclesis, before the emergence of its present form, I have treated elsewhere.[4] The evidence from Palestine, Syria, and Egypt points unmistakably to an anaphoral Spirit epiclesis by the second half of the fourth century, and it has sometimes been presumed that the Spirit epiclesis is a fourth-century development.[5] But what we now know from third-century sources like the anaphora of *Apostolic Tradition* 4,[6] and especially the *Didaskalia*, which assigns a notable role to the Holy Spirit in the Church,[7] specifically in the ministry of word and sacrament, including the sanctification of the eucharist (VI.21-22),[8] has rendered untenable the view that a Spirit epiclesis *could not* have existed before the second half of the fourth century. Whether or not one actually did remains moot because of unresolved disputes concerning the epiclesis text of *Apostolic Tradition* 4.

At any rate, "epiclesis" is used in our modern, eucharistic sense — though not exclusively — from at least the fourth century. Also germane for our purposes is the earlier use of the term "epiclesis" for the entire prayer over the gifts, a point I will return to later.[9]

---

4. R. F. Taft, "From Logos to Spirit: On the Early History of the Epiclesis," in A. Heitz and H. Rennings (eds.), *Gratias agamus. Studien zum eucharistischen Hochgebet. Für Balthasar Fischer* (Freiburg/Basel/Vienna: Herder, 1992), pp. 489-501.

5. Ibid., pp. 494-98.

6. Cited below at note 11.

7. I.1.8; IV.5; V.1; VI.7.14, 23, *Didascalia apostolorum: The Syriac Version Translated and Accompanied by the Verona Fragments, with an Introduction and Notes, by R. H. Connolly* (Oxford: Clarendon, 1929), pp. 3, 20, 156, 161, 200, 212, 258.

8. Ibid., pp. 242-52.

9. See below at notes 81-85.

II. From Communion to Consecratory Epiclesis

The epiclesis immediately follows the anamnesis in anaphoras of the Antiochene type. In its evolved form in prayers like the Byzantine anaphoras of St. Basil (BAS) and St. John Chrysostom (CHR), this Antiochene epiclesis comprises three easily identifiable parts: (1) the petition for the coming or sending of the Spirit, (2) the petition that this coming effect the consecration of the gifts, and (3) the petition that this coming make these consecrated gifts fruitful unto salvation for those who receive them in communion.

The earliest anaphoral epicleses, however, contained only parts 1 and 3 of this structure of the the later, developed consecratory-type epiclesis, with no part 2, i.e., no explicit petition for the consecration of the elements. The apocryphal *Acts of Thomas* 133, from the first half of the third century, for example, has this eucharistic epiclesis: "May the power of blessing come and dwell in the bread, so that all the souls who partake of it may be washed free of sin."[10] Our earliest extant complete anaphoral text, *Apostolic Tradition* 4 (*ca.* 215), concludes the eucharistic prayer with a similar primitive epiclesis: "And we ask you to send your Holy Spirit upon the offering of the holy Church. Congregating [them] into one, to all the saints who receive [it] grant [it to be] for the fulfillment of the Holy Spirit unto the confirmation of faith in truth. . . ."[11] Likewise the original epiclesis of the fifth-century *Testamentum Domini* I.23,[12] would read, according to Botte's convincing reconstitution of the original Greek text: "Lord, Father of our Lord Jesus Christ, send the Holy Spirit upon this drink and upon this your holy food. Make it be for us not unto judgement, shame, or condemnation, but for the healing and strength of our spirit."[13]

Disputes about the original shape of these texts notwithstanding[14] —

10. *PE* 78.

11. B. Botte (ed.), *La Tradition apostolique de S. Hippolyte. Essai de reconstitution* (Liturgiewissenschaftliche Quellen und Forschungen 39, Münster: Aschendorff, 1963), p. 16; see also B. Botte, "L'épiclèse de l'anaphore d'Hippolyte," *Recherches de théologie ancienne et médièvale* 14 (1947), pp. 241-51.

12. *Testamentum Domini nostri Jesu Christi*, ed. I. E. Rahmani (Mainz: Kirchheim, 1899), p. 43.

13. Botte, "L'épiclèse," pp. 245-48.

14. E.g., the *Apostolic Tradition* Spirit epiclesis is considered a fourth-century interpolation by such authoritative commentators as Dix and Bouyer: G. Dix, *The*

they concern the question whether the petition for the fruits of communion originally commenced with a prayer for the coming of the Spirit — the point I wish to make remains unaffected: the original petition was not explicitly consecratory, regardless of whether the coming of the Spirit was considered the cause of these benefits.

So the pristine epiclesis was primarily a prayer for communion, not for consecration. It was directed at the sanctification of the *communicants*, not of the *gifts*. Or, better, it was a prayer for the sanctification of the *ecclesial communion*, not for the sanctification of its sacramental sign, the *Holy Communion.*

The old Roman canon retains such an ancient communion-type epiclesis following the institution. It is a text redolent of the *Testamentum Domini* I.23 epiclesis in Botte's reconstruction just cited:

Supplices te rogamus, omnipotens Deus, iube haec perferri per manus sancti angeli tui in sublime altare tuum in conspectu divinae majestatis tuae, ut quotquot ex hac altaris participatione sacrosanctum Filii tui corpus et sanguinem sumpserimus, omni benedictioni caelesti et gratia repleamur.[15]	Humbly we implore you, almighty God, bid these offerings be carried by the hands of your holy angel to your altar on high in the presence of your divine majesty, so that those of us who, sharing in the sacrifice at this altar, shall have received the sacred body and blood of your Son, may be filled with every heavenly blessing and grace.

Modern commentators are right, then, to distinguish the more primitive "communion epiclesis" from the "developed" or "consecratory epiclesis" containing the later interpolated explicit prayer for the hallowing of the gifts and their change into the body and blood of Christ.

If this distinction has proved useful for the history and interpretation of liturgy, its *theological implications* must not be pushed beyond the evidence. For it is clear that *any prayer* for the power of God to come upon something in order that it be unto salvation for those who partake of it or participate in it as God intended necessarily implies that God *do something*

Treatise on the Apostolic Tradition of St Hippolytus of Rome, Bishop and Martyr (London: SPCK, 1937), pp. 75-79; L. Bouyer, *Eucharist: Theology and Spirituality of the Eucharistic Prayer* (Notre Dame/London: University of Notre Dame, 1968), pp. 170-77.

15. *PE* 435.

by his coming to make that object salvific — in this case, to make bread and wine the body and blood of Christ. Hence to call a text a "communion epiclesis," not a "consecration epiclesis," is only to comment on the structure of its text and not in any way to infer that such a more primitive, less explicit epicletic prayer is not, in fact, implicitly consecratory.

This realization led early on to rendering this theology explicit. For if the petition of the earlier Spirit epiclesis in *Apostolic Tradition* 4[16] is directed at the benefits of communion rather than the consecration of the gifts, already in Cyril/John II, *Catechesis* 5.7 (cf. 1.7; 3.3),[17] Theodore of Mopsuestia, *Homily* 16.12,[18] and *Apostolic Constitutions* VIII.12.39,[19] our earliest witnesses to the Spirit epiclesis after *Apostolic Tradition* 4, the prayer is expressly consecratory.

III. The Byzantine Epiclesis Texts

The epiclesis texts of CHR and BAS read as follows. I give the CHR text from the earliest manuscript, the eighth-century Vatican codex *Barberini Gr. 336* (ff. 31v-32r).[20] Italicized texts are peculiar to one or the other

16. Note 10 above.

17. Cyrille de Jérusalem, *Catéchèses mystagogiques*, introduction, critical text, and notes by A. Piédangel, tr. P. Paris (SC 126bis, Paris: Cerf, 1988), pp. 94, 124, 154. The date of this witness to the intercessions/commemorations in the hagiopolite eucharistic anaphora depends on the much controverted question of authorship between Cyril during his turbulent episcopacy (348-357, 362-367, 378-386) and his successor John II (386-417). Piédagnel has reviewed the evidence, and the weight of opinion seems to be leaning toward the following conclusions: the catecheses are from the end of the century, most likely after 380 (Cyril died in 387); *in their present form* they are attributable to John as their final redactor; but they probably go back to texts of Cyril that were used year after year, undergoing redactional emendations in the process; they still retain elements derived directly from Cyril (ibid., Introduction pp. 21-28, Appendix I: "L'auteur des Catéchèses Mystagogiques," pp. 177-87, esp. pp. 185-87).

18. R. Tonneau and R. Devreesse, *Les homélies catéchétiques de Théodore de Mopsueste* (Studi e testi 145, Vatican City: Vatican Polyglott Press, 1949), p. 553.

19. *Les Constitutions apostoliques*, ed. M. Metzger, vol. 3: V-VIII (SC 336, Paris 1987), pp. 198-200.

20. Since the same parallel passages of these two anaphoras will be referred to often in the following pages, I give here once and for all the editions where they may be found in the original Syriac and Greek: APSyr: *Anaphorae Syriacae, quotquot in*

redaction and are presumed not to be part of the lost *Urtext,* the Greek Anaphora of the Apostles (AP), from which both CHR and APSyr derive.[21] The final section [8], the petition for the fruits of communion, I have already treated elsewhere.[22]

CHR	APSyr
1. *Again we offer you this reasonable and unbloody worship,*	1. *So then,*
2. *and we invoke and pray* and beseech [you],	2. we ask *of you, Lord almighty and God of the holy virtues, prostrate on our faces before you,*
3. send down your Holy Spirit *upon us, and* upon these offered gifts,	3. that you send your Holy Spirit upon these offered gifts
4. and make this bread the precious body of *your* Christ,	4. and *show* this bread [to be] the precious body of *our Lord Jesus* Christ,
5. *changing [it] by your Holy Spirit,*	
6. *and that [which is] in* this chalice the *precious* blood of *your* Christ,	6. and this chalice [to be] the blood *of our Lord Jesus* Christ,

codicibus adhuc repertae sunt, cura Pontificii Instituti Studiorum Orientalium editae et latinae versae, I-III (Rome: Pontificio Istituto Orientale, 1939-81) 1.2, pp. 203-27, here pp. 218-20 = H. Engberding, "Die syrische Anaphora der zwölf Apostel und ihre Paralleltexte einander gegenüberstellt und mit neuen Untersuchungen zur Urgeschichte der Chrysostomosliturgie begleitet," *Oriens Christianus* 34 = series 3, vol. 12 (1938), pp. 213-47; here 224-28 = *PE* 267; CHR: *LEW,* 329-30 = *PE* 226.

21. On this whole question see R. F. Taft, "The Authenticity of the Chrysostom Anaphora Revisited: Determining the Authorship of Liturgical Texts by Computer," *OCP* 56 (1990), pp. 5-55, esp. pp. 5-21, 48-55.

22. R. F. Taft, "The Fruits of Communion in the Anaphora of St. John Chrysostom," in I. Scicolone (ed.), *Psallendum. Miscellanea di studi in onore del Prof. Jordi Pinell i Pons, O.S.B.* (Analecta liturgica 15 = Studia Anselmiana 105; Rome: Pontificio Istituto Liturgico Sant' Anselmo, 1992), pp. 275-302.

7. changing [it] by your Holy Spirit,

8. so that for those who receive [them] they might be for *sobriety of soul,* for forgiveness of sins, for *communion in your Holy Spirit, for fullness of the kingdom, for filial confidence before you, and not unto judgement or damnation.*

so that for *all* those who receive them they might be for *life and resurrection, and* the forgiveness of sins, *and the health of soul and body, and the enlightening of the mind, and for a good defense before the dread judgement seat of your Christ, and that no one of your people might perish, Lord, but make us all worthy . . . etc.*

The corresponding text of BAS reads as follows. The segments in brackets are found in the Byzantine redaction but not in the *Urtext* extant in the Sahidic BAS:[23]

1. Wherefore, all-holy Master, we too, your sinful and unworthy servants, deemed worthy to serve at your holy altar . . . because of your mercies and compassions which you have so abundantly showered upon us, dare to approach your holy altar and, offering you the figures (τὰ ἀντίτυπα) of the holy body and blood of your Christ,

2. we pray you and beseech you, O holy of holies, that, by the favor of your goodness,

3. your Holy Spirit may come upon us, and upon these offered gifts,

4. [and bless] and hallow and show (ἀναδεῖξαι) this bread to be [indeed the precious body of our Lord and God and Savior Jesus Christ,

6. and this cup to be indeed the precious blood of our Lord and God and Savior Jesus Christ shed for the life of the world],

8. so that all of us who partake of this one bread and chalice may be united to one another in the communion of the one Holy Spirit, and that the partaking of the holy body and blood of your Christ may be for none of us unto judgment or condemnation, but that we might find

---

23. Sahidic UrBAS: J. Doresse, E. Lanne, *Un témoin archaique de la liturgie copte de S. Basile* (Bibliothèque du *Muséon* 47; Louvain: Publications Universitaires/Institut Orientaliste, 1960), pp. 21-22; Byzantine BAS: *LEW,* 329-30 = *PE* 236, cf. 352.

mercy and grace together with all the saints . . . [there follows the com-
memoration of the saints and of the dead].

IV. Animadversions on the Texts

1. The Consecratory Petition of BAS [4, 6]

In the BAS *Urtext* extant in the ancient Sahidic redaction, the object of the
consecratory verbs is simply "the holy of holies," replacing the entire
bracketed segment so that the relevant consecratory expression reads:
". . . and we pray you our God, sinful and unworthy and miserable as we
are, and we adore you: by the favor of your goodness may your Holy Spirit
come upon us and upon these offered gifts and sanctify and show [them
to be] the holy of holies." There are also variants in the petition for the
fruits of communion, but that section does not concern us here.

2. The Consecratory Petitions of CHR [4-7]

I have already discussed certain redactional emendations in the CHR text
necessitated by the later reworking of the transition from anamnesis to
epiclesis.[24] But this issue does not affect the point under discussion here,
which concerns the explicitly consecratory petitions [4-7]. I would consider
this entire formula, and not just where CHR departs from APSyr, not to
have been a part of UrAP — which is also UrCHR — but a later interpolation into both recensions, with APSyr giving the earlier, first stage of the
expanded redaction. The formula is designed to explicitate the consecratory
action of the Holy Spirit in changing the elements, transforming an earlier
"communion epiclesis" into a later, more evolved "consecratory epiclesis."

The reader should please note that my view here is not dictated by

24. R. F. Taft, "Some Structural Problems in the Syriac Anaphora of the Apostles
I," to appear in a Festschrift for Sebastian Brock (a special number of *ARAM Periodical*);
"Understanding the Byzantine Anaphoral Oblation," to appear in a Festschrift for Aidan
Kavanagh; "The Oblation and Hymn of the Chrysostom Anaphora: Its Text and Ante-
cedents," *Bolletino della Badia Greca di Grottaferrata* 46 (1992), pp. 319-45; "Reconsti-
tuting the Oblation of the Chrysostom Anaphora: An Exercise in Comparative Liturgy,"
OCP 59 (1993), pp. 387-402.

any Catholic vs. Orthodox polemic in the epiclesis vs. institution narrative question. As I explain below, I consider the extreme position of both sides to be equally erroneous. What interests me here is the text history of the formula. It is perfectly clear not only that the Holy Spirit epiclesis, in its most explicitly consecratory sense as a petition to change the gifts, had evolved long before any East-West dispute over the question. It is also clear that this development does no more than explicitate the meaning already implied in the more primitive communion epiclesis — and indeed, in the New Testament words of institution themselves ("this is my body, this is my blood"), as the saner theologians of East and West have held all along.

In my view, far too much has been made of the (per se undeniable) difference between the two types of epiclesis, for as Cyril/John II, the earliest witness to an expressly consecratory Holy Spirit epiclesis, says in *Catechesis* 5.7, "Whatever the Holy Spirit has touched is sanctified and changed,"[25] and that remains true whether the prayer asks for that change expressly or only implicitly. Hence a simple petition for the Spirit to come upon the gifts so that they may be for us unto sanctification implies that this is not an empty petition without effect.

But the explicitation of this effect via the insertion into the anaphoral epiclesis of a change petition is a later development, and since APSyr and CHR diverge at this point, I consider the entire "and make . . ." formula a later interpolation.

3. The Consecratory Verbs: "Show" vs. "Make" [4]

Over against the strong CHR verb "make" [4], the petition of APSyr [4] for the Spirit to "show" or have the gifts "appear" to be the body and blood of Christ[26] seems a more subtle, sacramentally sensitive term, referring to the "mystery of faith" to be "seen" only with the eyes of faith. I would consider it more primitive than the CHR reading, especially since it is supported by analogous expressions in *Apostolic Constitutions* VIII.12.39 ("so that [the Holy Spirit] make this bread appear [ἀποφήνη] as the body

25. Ed. Piédagnel, SC 126bis:154.
26. *PE* 267. The reading is not, like so many of APSyr's divergences from CHR, a Syriacism from the Syriac redaction of the anaphora of St. James, which has "make": *PE* 271.

of your Christ"), BAS 4-6 above ("bless and sanctify and show [ἀναδεῖξαι] this bread [to be] indeed the precious body of our Lord . . ."),[27] and Theophilus of Alexandria, *Epistula Paschalis* 13 (A.D. 402), preserved in Jerome's Latin version ("The dominical bread in which the body of the Savior is shown [*ostenditur*] and the holy chalice . . . are sanctified through the invocation and coming of the Holy Spirit").[28]

Jugie has pointed out the parallelism between the "show" (ἀναδεῖξαι) reading of the BAS epiclesis and the words of institution in the same anaphora.[29] Jesus, "taking bread in his holy and immaculate hands, and having presented (ἀναδεῖξας) it to you, the God and Father. . . ."[30] In the institution, together with Jesus we dedicate to the Father the gifts that the Father will then present to us in communion as Jesus' body and blood.[31]

But any attempt to exploit such expressions to weaken the con-secratory thrust of the formula would be anachronistic and without theological foundation. If sacramental signs as manifestations of a mys-tery of faith are to have any meaning at all, then to ask God to *show the gifts to be* the body and blood of Christ is to ask him that they, in fact, be what we believe them to be. It has already been shown, and is now generally accepted, that ἀναδείκνυμι, literally "show, show forth, manifest as," was used in pagan Greek as a sacral term meaning "dedicate" or "consecrate" something to a god, and in patristic Greek to mean "bring forth, produce."[32] The Byzantine marriage rite uses it several times in

---

27. *PE* 92, 236.

28. "Panis dominicus quo Salvatoris corpus *ostenditur* et sacer calix . . . per invocationem et adventum Spiritus Sancti sanctificantur." *PL* 20:801; cf. M. Jugie, "De epiclesi eucharistica secundum Basilium Magnum," *Acta Academiae Velehradensis* 19 (1948), p. 204.

29. Jugie, "De epiclesi," pp. 205-6.

30. *PE* 234.

31. For ἀναδείκνυμι in this sense of "offer, dedicate," see also *Apostolic Consti-tutions* VIII.12.44, ed. Metzger, SC 336:202.

32. Literature and references in J. H. McKenna, *Eucharist and Holy Spirit: The Eucharistic Epiclesis in 20th Century Theology* (Alcuin Club Collections 57; Great Waker-ing, Essex: Mayhew-McCrimmon, 1975), p. 108 and p. 215, n. 18; J. Moreau, *Les ana-phores des Liturgies de Saint Jean Chysostome et de Saint Basile comparées aux canons romain et gallican* (Paris: Bloud & Gay, 1927), p. 59, n. 1; E. Peterson, "Die Bedeutung von ἀναδείκνυμι in den griechischen Liturgien," in *Festgabe für Adolf Deissmann* (Tü-bingen: J. C. B. Mohr, 1927), pp. 320-26; G. W. H. Lampe, *A Patristic Greek Lexicon* (Oxford: Clarendon Press, 1961), p. 101.

this sense, for God having joined Adam and Eve in one body, (ἀμφοτέρους αὐτοὺς ἓν μέλος ἀναδείξας διὰ τῆς συβυγίας), having produced (ἀναδείξας) the twelve patriarchs from the union of Jacob and Rachel, and making the marriage being celebrated an honorable one (τίμιον αὐτοῖς τὸν γάμον ἀνάδειξον).[33] So ἀναδεῖξαι can be taken as a synonym for the "make" (ποίησον) of the epicletic blessing in CHR [4], the Greek anaphora of St. James, and numerous other anaphoras, a reading which is only *apparently* stronger because of our modern ratio-nalistic disjunction between the symbolic and the real, a disjunction completely foreign to the patristic mentality in both East and West.[34] But in BAS, too, the explicit request to send the Spirit on the bread and cup is a later interpolation not found in UrBAS. This strengthens my hy-pothesis that the parallel formula in CHR is a later addition as well.

4. The Change Petition of CHR [5, 7]

The phrase "changing [it/them] by your Holy Spirit," with the direct object understood but not expressed, is repeated twice in *Barberini Gr. 336*, once over the bread and once over the cup [5, 7],[35] though not in other manu-scripts of the ancient recension of CHR, which just give it once, over both bread and cup together, as in the *textus receptus*. The Constantinopolitan

33. J. Goar, Εὐχολόγιον *sive Rituale Graecorum* . . . (2nd ed., Venice: Bar-tholomaeus Javarina, 1730, reprinted Graz: Akademische Druck- u. Verlagsanstalt, 1960), pp. 315-16, 318, 320.

34. Recall the famous dictum of Adolf von Harnack concerning the difference between the symbolic theology of the patristic period and the later rationalism: "*Wir verstehen heute unter Symbole eine Sache, die das nicht ist, was sie bedeutet; damals verstand man unter Symbol eine Sache, die das in irgend welchem Sinne wirklich ist, was sie bedeutet. . . .*" (Today we understand by symbol something which is not that which it represents; previously one understood by symbol something that in some sense really was that which it symbolized . . .), *Lehrbuch der Dogmengeschichte* (4th ed., Tübingen: Mohr, 1909-10), 1:476. For the sort of thing the loss of this mentality led to in East and West, see Bishop Kallistos (Ware), "The Meaning of the Divine Liturgy for the Byzantine Worshipper," in Rosemary Morris (ed.), *Church and People in Byzantium. Society for the Promotion of Byzantine Studies, Twentieth Spring Symposium of Byzantine Studies, Manchester, 1986* (Birmingham: Centre for Byzantine, Ottoman and Modern Greek Studies, University of Birmingham, 1980), pp. 18-19.

35. *LEW* 330.5-6, 9-10 = *PE* 226.

euchology roll *Stavrou 109* omits the formula entirely,[36] but this is an eleventh-century manuscript and all earlier witnesses I have examined contain it. So from the manuscript tradition alone the reading cannot be challenged.[37]

Nevertheless, this formula is clearly superfluous to the consecratory sense of the CHR epiclesis, being already adequately explicit in the "and make" petition. Furthermore, its variant form in APSyr shows it to be a later interpolation not found in UrAP. Since it does appear in NES,[38] a formulary, recognized as dependent on CHR, which dates from the first half of the sixth century, it had probably been interpolated into CHR at least by that time. The novel character of the expression is confirmed by the fact that it is not found in other anaphoras and is not part of the liturgical *Formelgut,* that common stock of vocabulary, phraseology, and set formulas used repeatedly in the Christian liturgical Greek of Late Antiquity.

Its presence in the Armenian anaphora of St. Athanasius[39] is doubtless the result of later Byzantine influence, commonly exerted on the Armenian Rite especially from around the tenth century, since it is not witnessed to in the commentary on the Armenian eucharist by Xosrov Anjewacʻi (who died 965), written about A.D. 950.[40] Its presence in some Greek manuscripts of BAS, as well as in the *editio princeps* of Rome, 1526, and other early printed editions of the Basilian liturgy,[41] is an obvious interpolation from

36. A. Grabar, "Un rouleau liturgique constantinopolitain et ses peintures," *Dumbarton Oaks Papers* 8 (1954), plate 15, following p. 166.

37. Indeed, even in *Stavrou 109* there is in the right margin an interpolation, visible but illegible to me in both Grabar's plate and in the microfilm, which may well be the copyist's or a later hand's correction of this oversight.

38. *PE* 395.

39. *PE* 323.

40. *Commentary on the Divine Liturgy by Xosrov Anjewacʻi,* translated with an introduction by S. Peter Cowe (Armenian Church Classics, New York: St. Vartan Press, 1991), pp. 176-81 (nos. 103-105). On Xosrov and his commentary, see S. Salaville, "L'ʻExplication de la Messe' de l'arménien Chosrov (950). Théologie et liturgie," *Echos d'Orient* 39 (1940-42), pp. 349-82.

41. P. N. Trempelas, Αἱ τρεῖς Λειτουργίαι κατὰ τοὺς ἐν Ἀθήναις κώδικας (Texte und Forschungen zur byzantinisch-neugriechischen Philologie 15, Athens: Verlag der byzantinisch-neugriechischen Jahrbücher, 1935), p. 184 (apparatus); and esp. M. I. Orlov, *Liturgija sv. Vasilija Velikago* (St. Petersburg: Sinodal'naja Tipografia, 1909), pp. xxiv-xxv, 208. The earliest manuscript listed by Orlov is *Grottaferrata Arsenii* (= *Cryptof.*

CHR. From there it entered the Slavonic recension,[42] where it is still found in the *textus receptus* of the Slavonic Orthodox books, though it was rightly excised from the modern Roman editions,[43] and is not part of the Greek Orthodox *textus receptus*.[44] The 1927 Athens edition of the euchology even has a note to that effect.[45]

5. The Chalice Petition [6]

The CHR text, "what is in this chalice," instead of the surely more primitive "this chalice" of APSyr and BAS as well as *Apostolic Constitutions* VIII.12.39[46] and the Greek anaphoras of St. James, Sarapion, St. Mark, the Der-Balizeh fragment, etc.,[47] I take to be a later refinement.

V. Ecumenical Reflections

1. Two Liturgical Expressions of Two Liturgical Theologies

Since one must reject any attempt to press texts beyond what they can bear, the most one can say is that the anaphoral texts surrounding the institution and epiclesis in BAS and CHR neither confirm nor exclude any particular

---

Arsenii), A.D. 1001, a now lost roll of BAS described by Goar, Εὐχολόγιον 151 note Y. On this manuscript and its dating see A. Strittmatter, "Notes on the Byzantine Synapte," *Traditio* 10 (1954), p. 89-90 and n. 18. Among other manuscripts Orlov notes with the variant are *Sinai Gr. 971* (13-14th c.) = A. Dmitrievskij, *Opisanie liturgicheskix rukopisej xranjashchixsja v bibliotekax pravoslavnago vostoka*, I-II (Kiev: Tipografia Imperator-skago Universiteta Sv. Vladimira N. T. Korchak-Novitskago, 1895, 1901), III (Petrograd: no press indicated, 1917; all 3 vols. reprinted Hildesheim: G. Olms Verlagsbuchhan-dlung, 1965) 2:249; *Petersburg Imperial Public Library Gr. 558* (14-15th c.) and *561* (A.D. 1561); *Moscow Synod Gr. 264 (554)* (A.D. 1602). On this question see also *LEW*, 406, note a.

42. Orlov, *Liturgija* 209.

43. *Sluzebnik* (Rome: Grottaferrata Abbey Press, 1956), pp. 372-73.

44. For instance, see Εὐχολόγιον τὸ μέγα (Athens: M. I. Saliveros, 1927), p. 64; Ἱερατικόν (Athens: Apostolike Diakonia, 1951), pp. 126-27; (1956), p. 186.

45. Εὐχολόγιον τὸ μέγα (see previous note).

46. Ed. Metzger, SC 336:198-200.

47. *PE* 92, 122, 126, 130, 236, 250, 267, etc.

theological thesis of when or by what particular part of the anaphoral prayer the consecration is effected.[48] My own view is that later precisions, in the sense in which they are sometimes posed today as the result of confessional disputes, are sterile and pointless. They were in no one's mind in the fourth century. Earlier liturgical language is metaphorical and evocative, not philosophical and ontological. Only later doctrinal problems will lead to the sorting out of what, exactly, this language meant in the more dogmatically precise terms of *theologia secunda*.

When that sorting out does occur, I think it fair to say that the overall flow, the thrust and sequence of idea and expression of the Roman Canon on the one hand and of BAS and CHR on the other are more patient of the distinct consecration theologies of the Latin and Byzantine traditions respectively. In short, what we are dealing with here, as in other dogmatic or theological issues that are thought to divide Catholic and Orthodox today are two distinct but complementary *and equally ancient* liturgical expressions of what the Church does in the eucharist. The eagerness with which some theologians, even today, attempt to magnify these issues into major doctrinal differences, even dire portents of defective dogma at the very heart of trinitarian faith, is reflective of little more than their need to bolster their self-identity by showing how different they are from everyone else.

For the Byzantines to denigrate the Roman view because it has no Holy Spirit epiclesis is simply untenable, for the Roman Canon is a prayer more primitive than any anaphora with an explicitly consecratory Spirit epiclesis. As we have seen above, the textual evidence for that is no earlier than the second half of the fourth century, and it would have been unthinkable before the developments in pneumatology in the third century, when we first see the sanctification of the eucharist attributed to the Holy Spirit in Christian writings. Anyone who would wish to argue that such an epiclesis is of the essence of a Christian eucharist must ineluctably conclude that no eucharist could have existed before the third or fourth century.

Equally fatuous would be any attempt to dismiss the consecratory epiclesis by arguing that it is a fourth-century innovation, whereas the institution narrative is found in the New Testament itself.[49] For the con-

---

48. I discuss these issues at greater length in Taft, "Understanding the Byzantine Anaphoral Oblation," cited in note 24.

49. However, this sort of thing caused problems for the sixteenth-century Reformers. See D. N. Power, "The Priestly Prayer: The Tridentine Theologians and the

secratory Spirit epiclesis simply makes explicit a theology already implicit in more primitive invocations and is a logical, indeed, perhaps inevitable development, given the later evolution of pneumatology and sacramental theology. Furthermore, today few reputable historians of the anaphora would hold it for certain that the earliest eucharistic prayers included, necessarily, an institution narrative.[50]

Is there any way out of the impasse created by the later hardening of different liturgical systems into doctrinal disputes? It is not the task of the liturgical historian to sort such things out. It is the historian's duty, however, to draw attention to the *facts,* insofar as they can be attained. And on the basis of the facts, neither Latins nor Greeks can sustain, without being simply ridiculous in the face of their own history, a position that their view is the only legitimate one. In Christianity, tradition is the gauge of legitimacy. Both the Latin and Greek liturgical expressions of the eucharistic prayer of blessing over the bread and wine, and the implicit theologies that they unself-consciously expressed, coexisted peacefully for centuries not only in the liturgical celebrations of the one undivided Church. They were also explicitly formulated in the theologies of saints like Ambrose and John Damascene, still revered as saints and Fathers of the Church by both East and West. This means, I would think, that each Church must accept both expressions as legitimate, or render their pretense to orthodoxy untenable for having remained in communion for well over a millennium with a Church, and for continuing even today to venerate in their liturgical calendars its saints, that held, celebrated, and professed heretical views on so fundamental an issue as the eucharist.

In the less irenic past, as well, of course, as in our somewhat more ecumenical today,[51] liturgical theologians with a modicum of historical

---

Roman Canon," in G. Austin (ed.), *Fountain of Life: In memory of Niels K. Rasmussen, O.P.* (NPM Studies in Church Music and Liturgy, Washington, D.C.: The Pastoral Press, 1991), pp. 133-38.

50. See the discussion and relevant literature in R. F. Taft, "The Interpolation of the Sanctus into the Anaphora: When and Where? A Review of the Dossier," Part I, *OCP* 57 (1991), pp. 289-95.

51. Though the late Timothy S. Healy, S.J., former president of Georgetown University and Librarian of the New York Public Library, rightly said, "anti-Catholicism seems to be the one allowable bigotry," I remain sanguine that the anti-Roman hysteria rife at the moment in certain Orthodox circles is a transitory phenomenon provoked by recent traumas.

knowledge and common sense have adopted a balanced, nonpolemical view of this issue. As early as the seventeenth century, no less a savant than the famous Bossuet (1627-1704) raised his voice in favor of sanity "without inquiring about precise moments" in this issue,[52] sagely reminding us that

> the intent of liturgies, and, in general, of consecratory prayers, is not to focus our attention on precise moments, but to have us attend to the action in its entirety and to its complete effect. . . . It is to render more vivid what is being done that the Church speaks at each moment as though it were accomplishing the entire action then and there, without asking whether the action has already been accomplished or is perhaps still to be accomplished.[53]

And Dom Charles Chardon, O.S.B., in his *Histoire des sacrements* (Paris 1745) expressed this balanced view of the situation:

> Despite this diversity [over the form or moment of consecration] there was formerly no dispute over this subject. The Greeks and Latins were convinced that the species [of bread and wine] were changed into the body and blood of our Savior in virtue of the words of the Canon of the Mass, without examining the precise moment at which this change occurred, nor just which of the words [of the anaphora] effected it as over against other [words]. One side said the change was effected by the prayer and invocation of the priest; the others said that it was the result of the words of Our Lord when he instituted this august sacrament. And they in no way believed that these different ways of expressing themselves were opposed to each other (and indeed they are not, as would be easy to show). But we shall leave that to the theologians to treat.[54]

52. J.-B. Bossuet, *Explication de quelques difficultés sur les prières de la messe à un nouveau catholique* (Paris, 1710), pp. xlvi-xlvii, 1, cited in McKenna, *Eucharist and Holy Spirit* 139.

53. Bossuet, *Explication de quelques difficultés*, 45, ed. F. Lachat, *Oeuvres* 17 (Paris: L. Vives, 1864), pp. 74-75, tr. in R. Cabié, *The Eucharist* = A. G. Martimort (ed.), *The Church at Prayer*, vol. II (new edition, Collegeville: Liturgical Press, 1986), p. 147.

54. "*Nonobstant cette diversité, il n'y a eu autrefois aucune dispute sur ce sujet. Les Grecs et les Latins étaient persuadés que les espèces étaient changés au corps et au sang de notre Sauveur, en vertu des paroles du canon de la messe, sans examiner le moment précis auquel se faisait cette transmutation, ni les paroles qui l'opéraient plutôt les unes que les autres. Les uns disaient qu'elle se faisait par la prière et l'invocation du prêtre, les autres*

2. Two Irreducible Expressions of One Common Faith

But are these two liturgical expressions, Roman and Byzantine, indeed *reconcilable?* Or are they rather two irreducible[55] if equally ancient and legitimate ways of expressing what everyone agrees is the same underlying reality? I do not think there can be any doubt about the reconcilability of the eucharistic *doctrine* of the two traditions as expressed in their liturgies and interpreted by their moderate exponents. Much has been made of the fact that long before the dispute began, John Chrysostom attributes con- secratory efficacy both to the words of institution and to the epiclesis.[56] For Chrysostom, what happens in the eucharist happens by the power of the Holy Spirit, a teaching common to both the Greek and Latin Churches.[57] In *De coemet. et de cruce* 3, Chrysostom is clearly speaking of the epiclesis.[58] But in *De proditione Judae hom.* 1-2.6, he attributes the consecration to Christ in the words of institution:

> It is not man who causes what is present to become the body and blood of Christ, but Christ himself, who was crucified for us. The priest is the representative when he pronounces those words, but the power and the grace are those of the Lord. "This is my body," he says. This word changes the things that lie before us; and just as that sentence, "increase and

---

disaient qu'elle était l'effet des paroles de Notre-Seigneur quand il institua cet auguste sacrement; et ils ne croyaient point que ces diverses manières de s'exprimer fussent opposées entre elles, comme elles ne le sont pas effectivement, ce qu'il serait aisé de montrer; mais nous laissons cela à traiter aux théologiens." I cite it from the re-edition of J.-P. Migne, *Theologiae cursus completus,* 28 vols. (Paris: Migne, 1839-43), 20:249.

55. By "irreducible" I mean that one cannot simply be identified with or combined with the other without each losing its distinct and proper systems, which are neither identical nor reducible to a least common denominator without distortion.

56. See Salaville in Nicolas Cabasilas, *Explication de la Divine Liturgie,* tr. and notes by S. Salaville, 2nd ed. by R. Bornert, J. Gouillard, and P. Périchon (SC 4bis; Paris: Cerf, 1967), pp. 314-15.

57. *De sacerdotio* III.4.40-50; VI.4.34-44, Jean Chrysostome, *Sur le sacerdoce (Dia- logue et Homélie),* ed. A.-M. Malingrey (SC 272, Paris 1980), pp. 142-46, 316 = *PG* 48:642-45, 681 (= *CPG* 4316); *Oratio de beato Philogonio* 3, *PG* 48:753 (= *CPG* 4319); *De resurr. mortuorum* 8, *PG* 50:432 (= *CPG* 4340); *In pentec. hom. 1,* 4, *PG* 50:458-59 (= *CPG* 4343); *In Ioh. hom.* 45.2, *PG* 59:253 (= *CPG* 4425); *In 1 Cor hom.* 24.5, *PG* 61:204 (= *CPG* 4428).

58. *PG* 49:397-98 (= *CPG* 4337).

multiply," once spoken, extends through all time and gives to our nature
the power to reproduce itself; likewise that saying, "This is my body,"
once uttered, from that time to the present day, and even until Christ's
coming, makes the sacrifice complete at every table in the churches.[59]

Nicholas Cabasilas (ca. 1350) and numerous Orthodox theologians
after him have attempted to weaken the force of this text by arguing that
Chrysostom assigns consecratory power not to the priest's *liturgical repetition* of Jesus' words now, but to the *historical institution itself*, that is, to the
original utterance of Jesus, the force of which extends to all subsequent
eucharistic celebrations.[60] But is this saying anything different from the
position of the Latins, who obviously attribute the efficacy of these words
not to the prayer of the priest, as Cabasilas accuses them, but to the inde-
fectible effectiveness of the Word of God? Certainly not, as is perfectly clear
in Ambrose, *De sacramentis* IV.4.14-17:

> 14 . . . to produce the venerable sacrament, the priest does not use his
> own words but the words of Christ. So it is the word of Christ which
> produces this sacrament. 15. Which word of Christ? The one by which
> all things were made. The Lord commanded and the heavens were made,
> the Lord commanded and the earth was made, the Lord commanded
> and the seas were made, the Lord commanded and all creatures were
> brought into being. You see, then, how effective the word of Christ is. If
> then there is such power in the word of the Lord Jesus that things which
> were not began to be, how much more effective must they be in changing
> what already exists into something else! . . . 17. Hear, then, how the word
> of Christ is accustomed to change all creatures and to change, when it
> will, the laws of nature. . . .[61]

---

59. *PG* 49:380, 389-90 (= *CPG* 4336); English adapted from J. Quasten, *Patrology*,
3 vols. (Utrecht-Antwerp: Spectrum Publishers, 1975), 3:481. This teaching of Chrysostom influenced the consecration theology of the East Syrian liturgical commentator
Gabriel Qatraya bar Lipah (ca. 615): E. J. Kilmartin, "John Chrysostom's Influence on
Gabriel Qatraya's Theology of Eucharistic Consecration," *Theological Studies* 42 (1981),
pp. 444-57.

60. Chapter 29, ed. Salaville, SC 4bis:178-90; cf. the commentary of Salaville, ibid.
pp. 314-15; McKenna, *Eucharist and Holy Spirit*, p. 59.

61. "14. . . . *ut conficiatur uenerabile sacramentum, iam non suis sermonibus
utitur sacerdos, sed utitur sermonibus Christi. Ergo sermo Christi hoc conficit sacramentum. 15. Quis est sermo Christi? Nempe is quo facta sunt omnia. Iussit dominus factum*

So it seems to me that Latin theology would be in full agreement with what Chrysostom says on other occasions: the same Jesus accomplishes the same eucharist, the same marvels, in the liturgy as at the Last Supper.[62] For instance, Chrysostom, in *In 2 Tim hom.* 2.4, affirms:

> The gifts which God bestows are not such as to be the effects of the virtue of the priest. All is from grace. His part is but to open his mouth, while God works all. He [the priest] only completes the sign (σύμβολον πληροῖ). The offering is the same whoever offers it, Paul or Peter. It is the same one Christ gave to his disciples, and which priests now accomplish. The latter is in no way inferior to the former, because the same one who sanctified the one, sanctifies the other, too. For just as the words which God spoke are the same as the ones the priest pronounces now, so is the offering the same, just like the baptism which he gave.[63]

Here we find all the elements of the classic Eastern Orthodox theology of consecration, which, except in some of its extreme polemical expressions, does not attribute the sanctification of the gifts to the Holy Spirit epiclesis *alone,* that is, *sensu negante,* in deliberate exclusion of Jesus and his words. Cabasilas, for instance, says of the words of institution:

> Repeating those words, he [the priest] prostrates himself and prays and beseeches, while applying to the offered gifts these divine words of his Only-Begotten Son, the Savior, that they may, after having received his most holy and all-powerful Spirit, be transformed (μεταβληθῆναι) —

---

est caelum, iussit dominus facta est terra, iussit dominus facta sunt maria, iussit dominus omnis creatura generatus est. Vides ergo quam operatorius sermo sit Christi. Si ergo tanta uis est in sermone domine Iesu ut inciperent esse quae non erant, quanto magis operatorius est ut sint quae erant et in aliud commutentur. . . . 17. Accipe ergo quemadmodum sermo Christi creaturam omnem mutare consueuerit et mutet quando uult instituta naturae. . . ." Ambroise de Milan, *Des Sacrements, Des mystères,* ed. B. Botte (2nd ed., SC 25bis: Paris, Cerf 1961), p. 110 = CSEL 73:52-53; English tr. adapted in part from E. Mazza, *Mystagogy* (New York: Pueblo, 1989), p. 183; cf. *De mysteriis* IX.52: "The sacrament you receive is produced by the word of Christ" (SC 25 bis:186 = CSEL 73:112).

62. *In Mt hom.* 50(51).3; 82(83).5, *PG* 58:507, 744 (= *CPG* 4424).

63. *PG* 62:612 (= *CPG* 4437); tr. adapted from *A Select Library of the Nicene and Post-Nicene Fathers of the Christian Church,* ed. P. Schaff (reprint, Grand Rapids: W. B. Eerdmans), series 1, 13:483.

the bread into his precious and sacred Body, the wine into his immaculate and sacred blood.[64]

Here [in the liturgy] we believe that the Lord's words do indeed accomplish the mystery, but through the medium of the priest, his invocation, and his prayer.[65]

So for Cabasilas, neither epiclesis nor institution narrative stands alone; they are interdependent in the context of the anaphora, as we would say today. If one prescinds from the polemical context of Cabasilas's remarks, forced on him by Latin impugning of the Byzantine consecratory epiclesis, one will see a balanced view of the anaphora and of the interrelatedness of its constituent parts: "The words [of institution] do not take effect simply of themselves or under any circumstances, but there are many essential conditions, and without those they do not achieve their end."[66]

Reputable Catholic theologians today would say the same thing, rejecting theologies that would isolate the institution narrative from its essential setting within the anaphora.[67] Nor is that a novelty in Catholic thought. Similar views can be found in the Latin Fathers in the period anterior to the fourteenth-century epiclesis dispute between Byzantines and Latins. Isidore (ca. 560–636), bishop of Seville from 600-601 to 636, says in *De officiis ecclesiae* I.15.3 that the consecration occurs in the canon. Isidore calls it the "sixth prayer" of the "ordo of the mass and prayers by which the sacrifices offered to God are consecrated" (I.15.1).[68] From the

---

64. Chapter 27, ed. Salaville, SC 4bis:174; tr. adapted from Nicholas Cabasilas, *A Commentary on the Divine Liturgy*, tr. by J. M. Hussey and P. A. McNulty (London: SPCK, 1960), p. 70.

65. Chapter 29.4, SC 4bis:182; tr. Hussey-McNulty, p. 72.

66. Ibid.

67. For an excellent, fresh Catholic discussion of these issues, see E. J. Kilmartin, "The Active Role of Christ and the Holy Spirit in the Sanctification of the Eucharistic Elements," *Theological Studies* 45 (1984), pp. 225-53; earlier views are summarized both excellently and in truly ecumenical and irenic fashion by McKenna, *Eucharist and Holy Spirit*, the standard work on the topic. See also his more recent "Eucharistic Prayer: Epiclesis," in A. Heitz and H. Rennings (eds.), *Gratias agamus. Studien zum eucharistischen Hochgebet. Für Balthasar Fischer* (Freiburg/Basel/Wien: Herder, 1992), pp. 283-91, which, I think, is in basic agreement with the point of view I develop in this article.

68. "*Ordo . . . missae et orationum quibus oblata Deo sacrificia consecrantur.*" PL 83:732.

context it is clear that he is referring to that section of the anaphora following the preface that extends from the Sanctus to the Our Father inclusive (I.15.2):

> Then [comes] *the sixth prayer* [of the eucharist], from which results the formation of the sacrament as an oblation that is offered to God, sanctified through the Holy Spirit, formed into the body and blood of Christ. The last of these is the prayer by which our Lord instructed his disciples to pray, saying: "Our Father, who art in heaven."[69]

Isidore is usually considered the "last of the Latin Fathers," so right through to the end of the patristic period the view was current in Latin theology that the eucharistic consecration was the work of the Holy Spirit and that the prayer that effected it was the canon or anaphora, without further specification of one of its component parts as the "form" of the sacrament. Fulgentius of Ruspe (died 533) is another Latin author clearly to be understood in this sense.[70]

Nor is this view much different from that of the medieval Latin

---

69. "*Porro sexta* [*oratio*] *exhinc succedit conformatio sacramenti, ut oblatio, quae Deo offertur, sanctificata per Spiritum sanctum, Christi corpori et sanguini conformetur. Harum ultima est oratio, qua Dominus noster discipulos suos orare instituit, dicens:* Pater noster, qui es in coelis." PL 83:733. For a full exposition of Isidore's views on this question, see J. R. Geiselmann, *Die Abendmahlslehre an der Wende der christlichen Spätantike zum Frühmittelalter. Isidor von Sevilla und das Sakrament der Eucharistie* (Munich: Max Hueber, 1930), pp. 180-97, 244-47; also S. Salaville, "Épiclèse," *Dictionnaire de théologie catholique* 5:246.

70. *Ad Monimum* II.6, 9-10, *PL* 65:184-85, 187-88. Geiselmann, *Abendmahlslehre* 198-224 cites as reflecting this view numerous other Latin exponents, but many of the texts he adduces are far from probative. One is the much-discussed fragment of Pope Gelasius I (492-496), *Letter to Elpidius, bishop of Volterra* 2: "*Nam quomodo ad divini mysterii consecrationem coelestis Spiritus invocatus adveniet, si sacerdos, et qui eum adesse deprecatur, criminosis plenus actionibus reprobetur?*" ("For how can the Holy Spirit come who is invoked for the consecration of the divine mystery, if the priest, who calls upon him to be present stands condemned because he is filled with wicked deeds?") = Frag. 7, *Gelasius Elpidio episcopo Volaterrano* 2, ed. A. Thiel, *Epistolae Romanorum pontificum genuinae et quae ad eos scriptae sunt*, vol. I: *A S. Hilaro usque ad S. Hormisdam, ann. 461-523* (Braunsberg: E. Peter, 1868), p. 486 = PL 59:143A; tr. McKenna, *Eucharist and Holy Spirit*, p. 66. But a posthumously published study of C. Callewaert has demonstrated that this text does not necessarily refer to the Canon Missae: "Histoire positive du Canon romain. Une épiclèse à Rome?" *Sacris erudiri* 2 (1949), pp. 95-110, esp. pp. 95-98.

commentators, as Cabasilas himself recognized when he cited the *Supplices* prayer following the institution in the Roman Canon[71] as saying basically the same thing as the Byzantine epiclesis.[72] Peter Lombard (ca. 1095–1160), speaking of the *Supplices*, says in his *Sentences* IV.13:

> It is called "Missa" that the heavenly messenger *might come to consecrate the lifegiving body*, according to the expression of the priest: "Almighty God, bid that this be borne by the hand of your holy angel to your altar on high. . . ."[73]

Even more explicitly, shortly after 1215, John Teutonicus's comment on the same prayer in the *Glossa ordinaria ad Decretum Gratiani* — and its inclusion in such an anthology shows how common and acceptable such a view must have been — says: " 'Bid,' that is: *make*. 'Be borne,' that is: *be transubstantiated*. Or: 'be borne,' that is, be assumed, that is: *be changed*. . . ."[74] Note, please, that both these authoritative medieval Latin commentators are speaking here of a prayer said *after* the words of institution in the Roman Canon.

Finally, a modern Catholic classic on the eucharist, Maurice de la Taille's *Mysterium fidei*, while rejecting some of Cabasilas's affirmations made in the heat of anti-Latin polemic, accepts his identification of the *Supplices* prayer as "a Roman epiclesis that corresponds both in the place it occupies and in its meaning — though not in its external form — to the Eastern epicleses."[75]

So if the classic Latin doctrine on the words of institution as the form of consecration can be traced back to Ambrose, who states the teaching

---

71. Cited in full above at note 15.

72. Chapter 30, ed. Salaville, SC 4bis:190-99; tr. Hussey-McNulty 76-79.

73. "*Missa enim dicitur eo quod caelestis nuntius ad consecrandum vivificum corpus adveniat, juxta dictum sacerdotis: Omnipotens Deus, jube haec perferri per manus sancti Angeli tui in sublime altare tuum.* . . ." *PL* 192:868.

74. "*Jube*, id est: *fac*. Perferri, id est: *transsubstantiari*. Vel: perferri, id est sursum efferri, id est *converti*. . . ." *Decretum de consecratione* 2.72, in *Glossa ordinaria* (Rome, 1582) II, 1813, cited in Salaville, SC 4bis:322. Salaville cites numerous other ninth to sixteenth-century Latin authors in his classic (if one-sided) study "Épiclèse," pp. 265-70.

75. ". . . épiclèse romaine, répondant, pour la place qu'elle occupe et pour le sens qu'elle a, quoique non par sa forme extérieure, aux épiclèses orientales." M. de la Taille, *Mysterium fidei* (3rd ed., Paris: Beauchesne, 1931), p. 276; cf. Salaville, SC 4bis:319-20, for similar modern Latin views.

unambiguously in his *De sacramentis* IV.4.14-17, 5.21-23, and *De mysteriis* IX.52-54,[76] not until the twelfth century do the scholastics formulate the thesis that the words of institution are the essential "form of the sacrament" that alone effect the consecration of the bread and wine.[77] This, of course, poses a problem of method. As Hughes notes, if the idea that the eucharistic consecration takes place through the recitation of the words of institution alone did not become general in the West until well into the Middle Ages, centuries after the Roman Canon was first formulated, it is illegitimate to read into its prayers a meaning that was unknown when those texts originated.[78]

Nonetheless, it is equally clear that we are dealing with two distinct liturgical traditions both then and now. Following long Catholic tradition, the prayers of the "split" or "double" epiclesis in which the traditional Roman anaphoral structure embeds the institution narrative — prayers which, in Cabasilas's words, "apply" the words of Jesus to the gifts — place the overtly consecratory petition *before* the institution narrative, giving a more explicit "formulary" character to Jesus' words. This cannot be said of the Byzantine anaphoras, which tell the story and *then* ask for the consecration of the gifts. Hence when Orthodox authors say that the institution account of CHR and BAS is pronounced *narratively,* not significatively,[79] they are simply affirming what is clear from the text of their prayers, as H.-J. Schulz's recent serenely objective Catholic commentary, devoid of all polemics, admits, *pace* earlier Catholic apologists.[80]

76. Ed. Botte, SC 25bis:110, 114, 186-88 = CSEL 73:51-53, 55-56, 112-13.

77. Geiselmann, *Abendmahlslehre* pp. 192-94, 144-47; J. J. Hughes, "Eucharistic Sacrifice: Transcending the Reformation Deadlock," *Worship* 13 (1969), p. 540; J. A. Jungmann, *The Mass of the Roman Rite: Missarum sollemnia,* 2 vols. (New York: Benzinger Brothers, 1951, 1955), 2:203-4, n. 9: "In general Christian antiquity, even until way into the Middle Ages, manifested no particular interest regarding the determination of the precise moment of the consecration. Often reference was made merely to the entire Eucharistic prayer. It is Florus Diaconus, *De actione miss.,* c. 60 (*PL* 119:52f.), in the Carolingian period, who with particular stress brought out the significance of the words of consecration; *ille in suis sacerdotibus quotidie loquitur.*"

78. Hughes, "Eucharistic Sacrifice," p. 539.

79. Cabasilas 29.22, ed. Salaville, SC 4bis:190; tr. Hussey-McNulty, p. 76.

80. *Ökumenische Glaubenseinheit aus eucharistischer Überlieferung* (Konfessionskundliche u. kontroverstheologische Studien 39; Paderborn: Bonifacius-Druckerei, 1976); "Liturgischer Vollzug und sakramentale Wirklichkeit des eucharistischen Opfers," *OCP* 45 (1979), pp. 245-66; 46 (1980), pp. 5-19. Also "Ökumenische Aspekte der Darbrin-

VI. Conclusion

So I believe that there *are* irreducible local differences in the *liturgical expression* of what I would take to be the fully reconcilable *teaching* of both Churches on the eucharist: that the gifts of bread and wine are sanctified via a prayer (the anaphora), which applies to the present gifts of bread and wine the words of Jesus narrated in the institution account. *How* the individual anaphoras make this application has varied widely across the traditions. Broadly speaking, that reality is expressed:

1. by narrating the story of the Last Supper — the institution account — which provides the biblical warrant for what is being done; and
2. by asking, in some way or other, that God receive or accept or bless or sanctify the gifts or oblation, so that they may be unto salvation for the communicants and for the benefit of all the living and dead.

Just how these two pieces are arranged and articulated and how they express what they express, is a matter of local tradition, particular history, the doctrinal concerns of time and place. These should not, indeed in my view cannot, with any historical legitimacy be seen in conflict with parallel but divergent expressions of the same basic realities in a different historico-ecclesial milieu. Orthodox theologies that attempt to restrict the consecration to the epiclesis only; Catholic theologies that wish to isolate the words of institution from its context as a "form of consecration" independent of the anaphoral setting in which they are embedded and that reveal their meaning and apply them to the rite being celebrated; Orthodox or Catholic theologies that attempt to identify within the anaphora a particular "moment of consecration" not merely as an explanation of the most significant portions of

---

gungsaussagungen in der erneuerten römischen und in der byzantinischen Liturgie," *Archiv für Liturgiewissenschaft* 19 (1978), pp. 7-28; "Orthodoxe Eucharistiefeier und ökumenisches Glaubenszeugnis," *Der christliche Osten* 34/1 (1979), pp. 10-15; "Das frühchristlich-altkirchliche Eucharistigebet. Überlieferungskontinuität und Glaubenszeugnis," *Internationale Kirchliche Zeitschrift* 70 (1980), pp. 139-53; "Patterns of Offering and Sacrifice," *Studia Liturgica* (1982), pp. 34-48. On BAS see also the recent study of R. Meßner, "Prex Eucharistica. Zur Frühgeschichte der Basileios-Anaphora. Beobachtungen und Hypothesen," in E. Renhart and A. Schnider (eds.), *Sursum corda. Variationen einem liturgischen Motiv. Für Philipp Harnoncourt zum 60. Geburtstag* (Graz: Akademische Druck- und Verlaganstalt und Andreas Schnider Verlags-Atelier, 1990), pp. 121-29.

their prayer tradition, but in polemical opposition to another "moment" in another tradition and that then interpret in function of this "moment" whatever precedes and follows it in the anaphoral text — none of these tendencies represent the best of the common tradition of the undivided Church of the first millennium, and they are to be resolutely rejected.

This view, that the prayer of consecration is the anaphora in its entirety, not just some segment of it set apart as an isolated "formula," is, I think, more faithful to the earlier common tradition of the undivided Church. Several patristic texts lend themselves to this interpretation, using the term "epiclesis" for the whole prayer over the gifts. Among the earliest second-century witnesses to the eucharist in the period following the New Testament, Justin's *Apology* I.65-67,[81] written ca. A.D. 150, testifies to a prayer over the gifts that included the institution narrative (I.66). After that prayer, the gifts were no longer "ordinary food or ordinary drink but . . . flesh and blood of that same Jesus who was made flesh" (I.66). From the same period (ca. 185), Irenaeus, *Adversus haereses* IV.18.5, calls this consecration prayer "the invocation (τὴν ἐπίκλησιν) of God."[82] Indeed, "epiclesis" is commonly used for the entire prayer over the gifts even in sources as late as the fourth century.[83] For although Cyril/John II of Jeru-

---

81. *PG* 68-72.

82. Irenée de Lyon, *Contre les hérésies,* ed. A. Rousseau and L. Doutreleau, I/1-2 (SC 263-64, Paris: Cerf, 1979), SC 264:611; cf. also *Adv. haer.* I.13.2, ibid. I/1-2, ed. A. Rousseau (SC 263-64, Paris: Cerf, 1979), SC 264:190-91.

83. Hippolytus, *Refutatio omnium haeresium (Philosophoumena)* VI.39.2, *PG* 16/3:3258 (= *CPG* 1899; on its disputed authenticity cf. *CPG* 1870); Firmilian of Caesarea, cited in Cyprian, *Ep.* 75.10, CSEL 3/2:818 (tr. and discussion of this text with relevant literature in A. Bouley, *From Freedom to Formula: The Evolution of the Eucharistic Prayer from Oral Improvisation to Written Texts* [Catholic University of America Studies in Christian Antiquity 21; Washington, D.C.: Catholic University of America Press, 1981], pp. 143-45; G. A. Michell, "Firmilian and Eucharistic Consecration," *Journal of Theological Studies* 5 [1954], pp. 215-20; *Didaskalia* VI.22.2, Connolly, *Didascalia apostolorum,* pp. 252-53; cf. J. W. Tyrer, "The Meaning of ἐπίκλησις," *Journal of Theological Studies* 25 (1923-24), pp. 139-50; esp. pp. 142-45, 148; O. Casel, "Neuere Beiträge zur Epiklesenfrage," *Jahrbuch für Liturgiewissenschaft* 4 (1924), pp. 169-78, esp. pp. 170-71. Some authors would also include in this list Basil, *De Spiritu Sancto* 27, Basile de Césarée, *Sur le Saint-Esprit,* ed. B. Pruche (SC 17bis, Paris: Cerf, 1968), p. 480 = *PG* 32:188 = *CPG* 2839. But I would agree with A. Gelston, *The Eucharistic Prayer of Addai and Mari* (Oxford: Clarendon, 1992), pp. 15-17, that Basil is probably referring to the epiclesis in the narrow sense of the term.

salem, *Catechesis* 3.3; 5.7, also uses the term *epiclesis* in its present restricted sense,[84] in another passage, *Catechesis* 1.7, the word is usually interpreted as referring to the entire anaphora:

> Before the holy epiclesis of the adorable Trinity the bread and wine of the eucharist was ordinary bread and wine, whereas after the epiclesis the bread becomes the body of Christ and the wine the blood of Christ.[85]

But is there not still a contradiction in Cyril/John II, at one time seeming to consider the entire anaphora as the consecration, in another assigning this role to the "epiclesis of the Holy Spirit"? We saw something similar in Chrysostom. In one text he attributes the consecration to the epiclesis, in another to the words of institution. Casel is probably closest to the truth when he asserts that

> we have to make it much clearer to ourselves . . . that the epiclesis of the Trinity, which was common to all the sacraments, required a definition of its purpose for each particular consecration. In the mass this occurred via the words of institution. Hence one can ascribe the consecration now to the whole eucharistic prayer, now to the epiclesis, now to the words of institution, *without contradicting oneself.*[86]

In short, one and the same early Father of the Church — Chrysostom is the perfect example — might speak now of the anaphora, now of one or another or even both sections of the anaphora wherein its consecratory purpose was stated most explicitly, as the prayer of consecration without seeing any contradiction in his assertions. For he was not identifying a *forma sacramenti* or isolating a "moment of consecration," but simply affirming that before the gifts are blessed they are not blessed, and after they have been blessed, they are. Hence I think it anachronistic to interpret

---

84. Ed. Piédagnel, SC 126bis:124, 154.

85. Ibid. 94.

86. "*Wir müssen uns vielmehr . . . klarmachen, daß die E. der Trinität, die allen Mysterien gemeinsam war, je nach der speziellen Weihe eines näheren Zweckbestimmung bedurfte; diese erfolgte in der Messe durch die Einsetzungsworte. Man kann demnach bald der Eucharistia, bald der Epiklese, bald den Einsetzungsworten die Konsekration zuschreiben,* ohne sich zu wiedersprechen" (emphasis added): O. Casel, "Neue Beiträge zur Epiklesenfrage," *Jahrbuch für Liturgiewissenschaft* 4 (1924), p. 173. Cf. *idem*, "Zur Epiklese," *Jahrbuch für Liturgiewissenschaft* 3 (1923), pp. 101-2.

Ambrose as meaning that *only* the institution is consecratory, or to maintain that such early Greek Fathers as Cyril/John II of Jerusalem and Basil, or the early anaphoras, considered the epiclesis consecratory in the negative sense of *ante quem non* rather than affirmatively, *post quem* yes. In other words, affirming that the gifts are consecrated after the epiclesis does not justify inferring that they meant that the epiclesis *alone* is consecratory and that the gifts remained ordinary bread and wine until just before it.

That precision is not seen in Greek theology until the dispute over, and ultimate rejection of, the primitive understanding of "antitype" and "symbol" by John Damascene (ca. 675-753/4),[87] and the iconodule Council of Nicaea II in 787, which condemned the iconoclast Council of 754.[88] But as I have shown elsewhere, John Damascene's interpretation of the term "figures" or "antitypes" (ἀντίτυπα) for the gifts in BAS [1] before the epicletic consecratory petition is simply wrong.[89] And the Nicaea II definition was the fruit of the iconoclastic troubles and not directly concerned with the later formula of consecration dispute between East and West in the fourteenth century.

87. John Damascene, *Expositio fidei* 86.163-166, interprets BAS thus: "Moreover, although some may have called the bread and wine *antitypes* of the body and blood of the Lord, as did the inspired Basil, they did not say this as referring to after the consecration (τὸ ἁγιασθῆναι), but to before the consecration, and it was thus that they called the [unconsecrated] offertory bread (προσφοράν) itself." B. Kotter (ed.), *Die Schriften des Iohannes von Damaskos* II (Patristische Text u. Studien 12, Berlin: W. de Gruyter, 1973), p. 197 = *De fide orthodoxa* IV.13, *PG* 94:1152C-53B; tr. from Saint John of Damascus, *Writings*, tr. F. H. Chase, Jr. (The Fathers of the Church 37; Washington, D.C.: Catholic University of America Press, 1981), pp. 360-61. The glosses are mine; "prosphora (offering)" is the ordinary Byzantine Greek term for the unconsecrated eucharistic loaves used at the liturgy.

88. Cf. the debate at Nicaea II, session 6 (Mansi 13:261E-268A), where the relevant texts of the Council of 754 are preserved because they were read into the Acts of Nicaea II and condemned. A complete English tr. of these texts, with the sections from the Acta of 754 set off in italics, is conveniently provided in D. J. Sahas, *Icon and Logos: Sources in Eighth-Century Iconoclasm* (Toronto Medieval Texts and Translations 4; Toronto/Buffalo/New York: University of Toronto Press, 1986), pp. 92-96. For the debate on the use of "antitype" for the eucharistic species, see Mansi 13:265C = Sahas 95.

89. In my study "Understanding the Byzantine Anaphoral Oblation" cited above, note 24, I bring forward textual evidence proving beyond any doubt that "type" or "antitype" were used for the consecrated gifts. On "antitypes" in BAS see also the discussion in Meßner, "Prex Eucharistica," pp. 123-25; M. Jugie, "L'épiclèse et le mot antitype de la messe de saint Basile," *Echos d'Orient* 9 (1906), pp. 193-98, with references to later Greek authors on the topic, though Jugie exaggerates on the other side of the issue.

Grace and the Knowledge of God

ROBERT L. WILKEN

Father John Meyendorff was cochair of the Orthodox-Lutheran dialogue in the United States. In 1989, after the commission had completed six years of study, a press conference was called in St. Paul, Minnesota to present the results of that work. At that gathering Father Meyendorff and the Lutheran cochair described the work of the commission and then invited the reporters to ask questions. I recall that the first question addressed to Father John was: "What do the Orthodox and the Lutherans have in common?" He thought for a moment, and with a wry smile, replied: "We worship the one true God." It was a surprising response, yet characteristically to the point, profound, and, one might add, timely in the secular culture of late twentieth-century America.

Christian faith has to do with knowing and loving the one true God revealed in Jesus Christ. St. John of Damascus, sometimes called the Aquinas of the East, begins his *Exposition of the Orthodox Faith* with these words from the prologue of the Gospel of John: "No one has ever seen God. It is God the only Son, who is close to the Father's heart, who had made him known" (John 1:18). God, says John of Damascus, is incomprehensible, and even though human beings are made in God's image, they cannot know God unless he discloses himself to us. Not even the angels and cherubim and seraphim know God as he is. Only the Son (Matt. 11:17) and the Holy Spirit know the things that are of God (1 Cor. 2:11). God, John writes, is known only by those "to whom he has revealed himself."[1]

1. *Expositio Fidei* 1.1 (ed. Kotter, vol. 12:7).

The first topic to be addressed in any presentation of Christian teaching is the question "how God is known," and it is significant that St. John begins his work with the citation of John 1:18. It is also noteworthy that he renders the phrase "who has made him known" with the words "to whom [God] has revealed himself." John's choice of terms is not accidental and in this essay I should like to discuss several passages in the homilies of Origen that illuminate John's formulation.

As is well known, one of the most familiar citations of Plato in Greco-Roman philosophy during the early centuries of the Christian era was a passage from the Timaeus: "It is difficult to discover the Father and Maker of this universe; and having found him, it is impossible to declare him to all."[2] This text was understood to mean that God was beyond our comprehension, though by the activity of enlightened minds it was possible to have some knowledge of God. In his work against the Christians, Celsus had cited this passage from Plato, and in his response Origen agreed that Plato's statement "is noble and impressive."[3] Nevertheless, Origen claims that the philosophical approach to God betrays a theological agnosticism. As evidence for this view, he argues that the philosophers did not change their lives or their manner of worship on the basis of their knowledge of God. Though they claimed to know the true God, they went on worshiping the many gods of Greece and Rome (and defending such piety).

For Origen, as for Augustine and other critics of philosophical religion, the persistence of veneration of lesser gods among the philosophers was a powerful argument against their theological views. In the view of the early Christian apologists the knowledge of God possessed by the philosophers was limited to what could be known by the activity of the mind (e.g., by deduction or inference).[4] As as a consequence they never came to a genuine knowledge of God and kept falling back into idolatry. Had Plato known the true God, writes Origen, he "would not have reverenced anything else and called it God and worshiped it, either abandoning the true

---

2. *Timaeus* 28c.

3. *Contra Celsum* 7.42. On the knowledge of God in Origen, see M. Harl, *Origène et la fonction révélatrice du Verbe Incarné* (Paris, 1958); H. Crouzel, *Origène et la "connaissance mystique"* (Paris, 1956); John Dillon, "The Knowledge of God in Origen," in *Knowledge of God in the Graeco-Roman World*, ed. R. van den Broek, T. Baarda, and J. Mansfeld (Leiden, 1988), pp. 219-28.

4. For a statement of the conventional philosophical view that is the object of Origen's criticism see the passage on how God is known in Albinus, *Didaskalikos* 10.

God or combining with the majesty of God things which ought not to be associated with him."

The philosophers would not acknowledge that by "becoming flesh" the divine Logos made it possible for human beings to know God more fully than they could by means of human reasoning alone. "We affirm," writes Origen, "that human nature is not sufficient in any way to seek for God and to find him in his pure nature, unless it is helped by the God who is the object of the search."[5] Unlike other forms of knowledge, the knowledge of God begins with God's action, not with human reasoning, and what we know is dependent on the nature of the reality that is presented to us.

How Christians would come to such a view can be seen in several provocative passages from Origen's *Homilies on the Gospel of Luke*. Luke 1:11 reads: "There appeared to him an angel of the Lord, standing at the right side of the altar of incense." Origen comments: "In order to see sensible things *(ta aisthēta)* nothing is required other than a healthy eye directed [at the sensible object]. Whether the eye wishes to see the object or not, it sees it. But that is not the way it is with divine matters *(ta theia)*. Even when present they are seen only only by their own initiative *(energeia)*."[6] God's appearance to human beings is always a matter of grace. "By grace God appeared to Abraham and to certain other saints." It was not Abraham's "spiritual perception" that was the "cause" of his seeing God but that "God presented himself to a just man, to one who was worthy of the vision."[7]

When the Scriptures say that God "appears" to someone, that means that God appears to those to whom he "wills" to appear. In similar words Irenaeus had made the same point a generation earlier. The one and true God, says Irenaeus, is beyond our powers of knowing. How can the human mind comprehend the one who has "measured the waters in the hollow of his hand and marked off the heavens with a span . . ." (Isa. 40:12)? It is not possible for human beings to know the God who is above and beyond all things and cannot be known fully even on the basis of the things he has made. As a consequence, says Irenaeus, the knowledge of God must begin

---

5. *Contra Celsum* 7.42.

6. Origen's observation that the healthy eye sees what is presented to it is commonplace. Plutarch, for example, observes that the senses must receive everything that presents itself whether useful or useless (*Pericles* 1-4).

7. *Contra Celsum* 2.72. So also Clement of Alexandria: God is known "only by divine grace and the word that comes from God." Only by "exceptional grace" does the soul receive wings and soar (*Stromata* 5.12.78–13.88).

with God, not with the human capacity to know. For human beings are not capable of "seeing [i.e. knowing] God by [their] own powers." God, Irenaeus writes, "is seen when he wishes to be seen, by whom he wishes to be seen, when he wills, and as he wills."[8]

For Irenaeus, as for Origen, the knowledge of God begins with the divine initiative. Indeed, Irenaeus uses the rather strong term "will," repeating it several times, to explain how God is known by humans. God is known only by those to whom God *wills* to appear. Just as the world came into being by an act of God's will, so according to the Scriptures the knowledge human beings have of God has its beginning in an act of self-disclosure on the part of God. The biblical language implies an action in which God is the agent. This feature of the Scriptures made a deep impact on Christian thinkers. Commenting on John 1:18, Augustine wrote: "They saw — those of them who did see God — because to whomever he wished, as he wished, he appeared in that form which his will chose. . . ."[9]

For the Church Fathers knowledge of God is a form of seeing.[10] In another homily on Luke, this one dealing with the prologue to the Gospel, Origen notes the unusual use of the term "eyewitnesses." The prologue to Luke reads:

> Since many have undertaken to set down an orderly account of the events that have been fulfilled among us, just as they were handed on to us by those who from the beginning were *eyewitnesses* and servants of the word, I too decided, after investigating everything carefully from the very first, to write an orderly account for you, most excellent Theophilus, so that you may know the truth concerning the things about which you have been instructed.

Origen observed that in the account of the giving of the Law on Mount Sinai the Scriptures say that the people "saw the voice of the Lord" (Exod. 20:18, LXX). Obviously a voice cannot be seen with the eyes. The biblical expression, says Origen, means that the voice of the Lord is "seen by those to whom it is given to see," that is, those who have the capacity to see what is dis-

---

8. *Ad Haereses* 4.20.5.
9. *Epistle* 147.19.
10. "What is called 'seeing' and 'being seen' in the case of bodily existences is with the Father and the Son called 'knowing' and 'being known,' through the faculty of knowledge and not through our frail sense of sight" (Origen, *De Principiis* 1.1.8).

closed.[11] Hence the term "eyewitnesses" in the prologue to the Gospel of Luke cannot simply mean seeing Christ with the eyes. When Luke says that they were "eyewitnesses of the *word*," he means "not only that they saw Jesus in his bodily form, but also that they were eyewitnesses of the *Word of God*." For if seeing Jesus in his bodily form is the meaning of "eyewitness," then Pilate or Judas or those who cried out "crucify him, crucify him" would also be "eyewitnesses," and that is patently false. When the Scriptures speak of "seeing God," that must be understood in the sense of the words from the Gospel of John: "Whoever has seen me has seen the Father who sent me."[12]

The knowledge of God, then, implies a reciprocal relation between God and the knower, for one cannot see God unless God wills to be seen and the knower is capable of seeing what there is to see. Hence only a heart that is pure can "see" God. If, for example, two people are standing in the same place, writes Origen, one with a pure heart and one whose heart is stained, only the one with a pure heart will see God.[13] For this reason, when Christ was living among human beings, says Origen, not everyone "saw" what was being disclosed in him. Some saw only bits and pieces, a word or saying, a gesture, Christ's body, signs of what there was to see, but they did not see the "form of Christ," to use von Balthasar's term,[14] the objective whole that was present in the signs. Which means

---

11. *Hom. in Luc* 1 (ed. Rauer, p. 7).

12. Augustine makes a similar point in a sermon on the prologue to the First Epistle of John. John does not simply say that he is bearing witness to what he has seen and touched; he says that he is bearing witness to the "Word of Life." It does not escape Augustine that the phrase *Word of Life* does not refer to the body of Christ, which could be seen and handled. "The life itself has been manifested in flesh — set in manifestation, that what can be seen by the heart alone might be seen also by the eyes for the healing of hearts. Only by the heart is the Word seen; flesh is seen by the bodily eyes. We had the means of seeing the flesh, but not of seeing the Word: the Word was made flesh which we could see, that the heart, by which we should see the Word, might be healed" (*Patrologia Latina* 35:1978-79).

13. "It is not right for a heart that has been defiled to look upon God" (*Contra Celsum* 6.69; cf. 6.4).

14. Hans Urs von Balthasar, *The Glory of the Lord* (San Francisco: Ignatius Press, 1982), p. 467 (see also p. 30):

The first prerequisite for understanding is to accept what is given just as it offers itself. If certain excisions are practiced on the Gospel from the outset, the integrity of the phenomenon is lost and it has already become incomprehensible. The Gospel presents Christ's form in such a way that "flesh" and "spirit," Incarnation

that even though they heard Christ and observed him, they did not "see" him (that is, know him). His disciples, however, saw Christ as he was and marveled at what they saw. Philip said to Christ, "Lord show us the Father and we will be satisfied." But Christ responded: "Have I been with you all this time, Philip, and you still do not know me? Whoever sees me sees the Father." "Pilate and the betrayer saw Jesus, but neither perceived the Father, because neither Pilate nor Judas saw Christ in so far as he was Christ."[15] Only those who are capable of seeing can see the Christ. In the words of the Wisdom of Solomon, "He is found by those who do not put him to the test, and manifests himself to those who do not distrust him" (Wisdom 1:2).

In these few comments in his *Homilies on the Gospel according to St. Luke* Origen sets forth a general theological framework for understanding how God is known by human beings, a kind of theological epistemology. Several observations are in order. First, even though there was a well developed "theological epistemology" in the Greco-Roman world, Christian thinking on this topic began with the Scriptures.[16] The preeminent instance of God's appearing to human beings was the revelation in Christ, and this was set within the framework of earlier appearances of God to those who sought the Lord with sincerity of heart. Abraham was the premier example in the Septuagint, but there were many other incidents that formed Christian thinking on this matter, for example the appearances to Isaac, Jacob, Joseph, Moses, the prophets

---

to the point of suffering and death, and resurrected life are all interrelated down to the smallest details. If the Resurrection is excised, then not only certain things but simply everything about Jesus' earthly life becomes incomprehensible. . . . Of if the trinitarian dimension is excluded from the objective form of revelation, then again everything becomes incomprehensible.

15. *Hom. in Luc.* 3, Latin text (ed. Rauer, pp. 21-22). Origen makes a similar point commenting on John 8:45. Pilate, for example, believed that Christ was crucified in Judea, but did not believe in the one begotten from the Virgin Mary (*Comm. Jo.* 20.268-272).

16. There are, of course, parallels between Christian and Greco-Roman ways of speaking about the knowledge of God, for example the idea that "like is known by like." See for example Albinus, *Didaskalikos* 2, 27. See Heinrich Doerrie, "Die platonische Theologie des Kelsos in ihrer Auseinandersetzung mit der christlichen Theologie," *Nachrichten der Akademie der Wissenschaften in Göttingen. Philologisch-historische Klasse* (Göttingen: Vandenhoeck & Ruprecht, 1967), pp. 19-55.

Elijah and Nathan, David, the prophets of the exile, and many other figures in the Bible.[17]

Second, the presumption behind this understanding of how God is known is that knowledge of God is an act of divine self-giving, of grace, that has its origins in God's movement toward human beings. In the words of the *Contra Celsum,* humans are not able to seek God and find him unless they are "helped by the God who is the object of the search."[18] The biblical expressions that describe God's disclosure are active, God acting as agent. Thus when St. Paul writes, "God manifested himself" (Rom. 1:19), this means, says Origen, that we do not come to the knowledge of God "without God's help."[19] And when St. Paul speaks of the knowledge of divine things, he presents spiritual knowledge as a "gift bestowed on us by God" (1 Cor. 2:12). Human knowledge is based on principles learned by someone skilled in one of the arts of knowing; the knowledge of God is given to us by the Holy Spirit.[20]

Further, a person cannot know God without undergoing a change. In some texts, as in the homily on the vision of Zechariah, early Christian thinkers put the accent on purity of heart.[21] In other texts the emphasis is on obedience. The knowledge of God is a light kindled in the soul as a result of obedience to the commandments, the fruit of behavior, not talk.[22] Yet even our response to God is God's work. "Our will does not suffice to give us a heart wholly pure. We need God to make it so. That is why he who has that truth asks: '*Create* in me a clean heart O God.'"[23] Without a

17. Augustine says that God was seen by Abraham, Isaac, Jacob, Job, Moses, Michah, Isaiah, and others (*Epistle* 147.14).

18. *Contra Celsum* 7.42.

19. *Contra Celsum* 3.47.

20. On the trinitarian character of the knowledge of God, see Origen, *Comm. in 1 Cor.* 2:12-15 (ed. Claude Jenkins, *Journal of Theological Studies* 9 [1908], p. 240).

21. See also Origen, *Hom. in Num.* 5.1 on Numbers 4, the covering of the sanctuary and the vessels of blue cloth. Kohathites are to carry but not touch the holy things. The passage has to do with seeing divine things; only those who are pure are worthy of access.

22. Clement of Alexandria, *Stromata* 3.5.44.

23. *Contra Celsum* 7.33; cf. 6.69; *Hom. in Gen.* 16.4. Origen is speaking about discernment, the spiritual sense that is capable not only of seeing what is to be seen by the eyes, but of knowing what it is that they see — in Origen's words, "to hear God's words in a manner worthy of God" (*Com. Jo.* 6.20). In modern times, Pierre Rousselot, the French Jesuit who wrote early in this century, saw this point clearly in his classic

receptive human being, a heart that is pure and that seeks God, there can be no knowledge of God. At one point in the *Contra Celsum* Origen uses the term "reciprocal" *(antipeponthoton)* to speak of how humans come to know God. Not only must there be an initiative on God's part; there must also be a disposition on the part of the knower to see what is disclosed. The talk about the pride of the philosophers in early Christian texts, notably in St. Augustine, is directed at this point. Epistemology is linked to character. As biblical support for the place of receptivity, Origen cites Galatians 5:8, "persuasion is not of him who calls," and Isaiah 1:19-20, "If you are willing and listen to me, you will eat the good things of earth," as well as Deuteronomy 10:12-13, "What does God require of you but to fear the Lord, walk in his commandments, and love him."[24] The knowledge of God requires collaboration on the part of humans; not all are receptive to the things of the Spirit of God. The reason for this is not, as the Gnostics claimed, that by nature some are incapable of knowing God, but that "they have not readied themselves for such knowledge."[25] In a happy phrase Gregory of Nyssa said that the bride's love is a "reciprocating love" *(anterastheisa),*" a love that is disposed to embrace the affections of the beloved.[26]

God's self-disclosure has as its goal fellowship with God. God revealed himself in Christ, writes Origen, to "implant in us the blessedness which comes . . . from knowing him." It was God's desire that human beings have "closeness" *(oikeiosis)* with him, that is, that they share in the divine life.[27] One of the most prominent images for the knowledge of God in early Christian texts is light. A distinctive feature of light is that there is no way to "see" light without sharing in it. One cannot be a spectator with respect

---

essay, "The Eyes of Faith." When one fails to see, "his not seeing is culpable." "The state of mind Christ reproaches is not that of someone who has understood the miracle as a clue to divine power at work, and refuses to submit his will, but that of someone who has witnessed an astonishing occurrence, merely registers the raw fact, and fails to take a loftier view of it." Pierre Rousselot, S.J., *The Eyes of Faith*, tr. Joseph Donceel, S.J. (New York: Fordham University Press, 1990), pp. 66-67.

24. *Contra Celsum* 6.57.

25. *Comm. in 1 Cor.* 2:12-15 (ed. Jenkins, p. 240, lines 27-28). See also Augustine: One cannot attain truth without believing one will reach the goal, "then by presenting his mind as a suppliant; finally by purifying his life by action in obedience to certain great and necessary precepts" (*Util. cred.* 24).

26. Gregory of Nyssa, *Cant.* 13 (Jaeger, 378:14).

27. *Contra Celsum* 4.6.

to light. To see light is always to be illuminated, that is, changed, hence knowing God is always participatory. Commenting on John 8:19, "You know neither me nor my Father. If you knew me, you would know my Father also," Origen explains how the term "know" is used in John and in the Bible as a whole. "One should take note," he says, "that the Scripture says that those who are united to something or participate in something are said to *know* that to which they are united or in which they participate. Before such union and fellowship, even if they understand the reasons given for something, they do not know it." As illustration he mentions the union between Adam and Eve, which the Bible describes as "Adam knew his wife Eve," and 1 Corinthians 6:16-17, which speaks of union with a prostitute. This shows, he says, that "knowing" means "being joined to" or "united with."[28] The knowledge of God is experiential.

Finally, faith is not something added to knowledge, but is constitutive of the act of knowing. When Luke says that "these things have been accomplished among us" (Luke 1:1), he speaks confidently, says Origen, without doubting, as "one who knows well" what he saw and heard. This kind of certainty is possible only "to those who believe firmly." For it is not the "eyes of flesh," but the "understanding" and "reason" that give "firmness to faith."[29] One of the great accomplishments of patristic theology, as Hans Urs von Balthasar has reminded us, was to restore the biblical understanding of the complementarity of faith and knowledge after the disjunction brought about by the Gnostics. "If the spirit is to see and understand the facts as indicators of revelation, then it must receive as well the faculty to see what the signs are intended to expresss. . . . The act of faith is, thus, rational precisely at the moment that it is made truly as an act of faith."[30] For this reason there can be no genuine knowledge of God without faith.

In his commentary on the Gospel of John Origen noted the evangelist's distinctive use of the term "believe." One of his most arresting comments occurs at John 2:22. The text reads: "After he was raised from the dead, his disciples remembered that he had said this; and they *believed* in the Scripture and the word that Jesus had spoken" (John 2:22). Origen

---

28. *Comm. in Jo.* 19.4.21-25.

29. In his Latin translation Jerome renders Origen's "know well" as "know with certain faith *and* reason" (*Hom. in Luc 1*, Rauer, 5-6).

30. Hans Urs von Balthasar, *The Glory of the Lord* (San Francisco: Ignatius Press, 1982), 1:175-76.

is puzzled by the term "believe" in this passage by contrast to the words spoken to Thomas in John 20, "Blessed are those who have *not seen* and yet have come to *believe*." He asks: How could it be that those who have not seen and have believed are more blessed than those who have seen and believed (as in John 2:22)? If that were true, those who came after the apostles would be more blessed than the apostles.

Origen is dissatisfied with such an answer and he cites several texts in the Scriptures that suggest that seeing and believing are not exclusive of one another. For example, he mentions the words of Jesus to the apostles, "Blessed are your eyes for they *see* [= believe] and your ears, for they hear" (Matt. 13:16), and the words of Simeon when he saw the infant Christ: "Lord, now let your servant depart in peace, for my eyes have *seen* [= believed] your salvation" (Luke 2:29-30). Origen's proposes that John 2:22, "*believed* in the Scripture and the word Jesus had spoken," is referring to the kind of faith that will be present in the resurrection but that was already present in the apostles when Christ was on earth, that is, faith that is completed by sight. Since Christ is no longer on earth, faith, lacking sight, is imperfect; but the faith of the apostles (and of Simeon) was not imperfect. For them faith and sight converged; what they saw they believed, and what they believed they saw. Consequently it is possible to say of faith what Paul says of knowledge, "now we believe in part"; but when the "perfection of faith comes," that which is partial will disappear. "For faith complemented by vision is far superior to faith through a mirror."[31] For Origen faith implies fellowship with God, so that it is necessary to *believe* as well as *see*.[32]

To recapitulate: For early Christian thinkers the knowledge of God had its origin in God's grace, in those actions by which God brings human beings to share in the divine life, preeminently in the sending of the Word of God into human flesh. Any discussion of the knowledge of God in Christian thought must begin with God's movement toward human beings. Against the intellectualism of ancient philosophical ways of knowing God,[33]

31. *Comm. in Jo.* 10.301-6.

32. It is not possible, writes Gregory of Nyssa, "to draw near to God unless faith mediates and unites the soul that seeks God to that [divine nature] that is beyond our comprehension" (*Contra Eunomium* 2.91, Jaeger, 1:253).

33. See for example, Plotinus, *Enneads* 6.7.36, where he speaks of knowledge of the good by a process of rational discourse, e.g., comparisons, negations, and ascent by degrees. He does, however, mention virtues and purifications that give one a foothold in the intelligible.

Christian thinkers argued that the knowledge of God rested not on "human sagacity" but on "divine action" and on "God's appearance" among human beings in the person of Christ.[34] That we know God and how we conceive of God is dependent on the nature of the reality that is presented to us — in the language of the Bible, that which is "seen." Hence the importance in patristic literature of the text cited by John of Damascus at the beginning of his *Exposition of the Orthodox Faith:* "No one has ever seen God; the only Son, who is in the bosom of the Father, he has made him known."

With the coming of Christ, reason had to attend to something new in human experience. In the earliest period of the Church's history Christian thinkers did not become philosophers to engage the philosophers. Or, to put the matter more accurately, they did not assume a traditional philosophical starting point in order to engage in philosophical discussion. Even when speaking to the outsider, they insisted that that it was more reasonable to begin with the history of Jesus (and of Israel) than with abstract reasoning. In the words of Ignatius of Antioch: "The gospel has something distinctive: the coming of the Savior, our Lord Jesus Christ, his suffering and resurrection" (*Philadelphians* 9.2).

As the Church sought to respond to the many intellectual challenges faced in the early centuries, Christian thinkers turned first to the Bible, to the history it recorded, to its language and images, to understand and express what they had come to know in Christ. In many ways Christians borrowed deeply from the philosophical tradition, but it was the Scriptures that provided the language as well as the criteria by which the philosophical tradition was to be evaluated.[35] God, in the words of St. John of Damascus, is known by those "to whom he has revealed himself." The theological problems inherent in such theological voluntarism (with its intimation of predestination) are evident, yet the consistency of the theological tradition on this point is remarkable. In the context of contemporary thought, with its epistemological assumptions about the role of the subject in human knowing, it is well to be reminded that classical Christian thinkers insisted that all discussion of the knowledge of God must begin not with the knower but with the object of the search, with God. In the words of St. Thomas

---

34. *Contra Celsum* 3.14.

35. On this point see Wolfhart Pannenberg, "The Appropriation of the Philosophical Concept of God as a Dogmatic Problem of Early Christian Theology," *Basic Questions in Theology* (Philadelphia: Westminster, 1971), pp. 119-83.

Aquinas, "It is impossible for any created intellect to see the essence of God by its own natural power. . . . The created intellect cannot see the essence of God unless God by his *grace* unites himself to the created intellect, as an object made intelligible to it."[36] But perhaps it is fitting to end this tribute to Father John with a passage from the theologian and saint whom he loved and whom he taught us in the West to love as well. I mean, of course, Gregory Palamas. "Experiential knowledge of God," writes Gregory, "comes from the *grace* that makes man like God."[37]

36. *Summa Theologiae* Ia, q. 12, a. 4. Thomas's use of the term "essence" in this context will strike the Orthodox reader as strange and confusing. He seems oblivious to the distinction in Byzantine theology between the essence and the energies of God. As Father Meyendorff wrote in *St. Gregory Palamas and Orthodox Spirituality* (1974), "For 'to see God face to face' did not mean to Palamas 'to see the divine Essence.' The 'superessential' God can in no way be identified with any created concept, above all with the philosophical concept of essence" (p. 122). Of course St. Thomas recognized this and in the same question, in article seven, he distinguishes between "seeing" and "comprehending," by which he means something very similar. Thomas asks whether those who see the essence of God comprehend him. And he answers: "It is written: 'O most mighty, great, and powerful, the Lord of hosts is your name. Great in counsel, and incomprehensible in thought (Jer. 32.18-19). Therefore He cannot be comprehended. I answer that, It is impossible for any created intellect to comprehend God" (Ia, q. 12, a. 7).

37. *Grégoire Palamas. Défense des saints hésychastes. Introduction, texte critique, traduction et notes,* ed. John Meyendorff (Spicilegium Sacrum Lovaniense 21. Leuven, 1973), p. 719. For the English translation of this work, see *Gregory Palamas: The Triads,* introduction by John Meyendorff, tr. Nicholas Gendle (New York: Paulist Press, 1983). In a footnote Meyendorff wrote: ". . . the knowledge of God is not an intellectual matter (in the modern sense), but is acquired by *grace* and obedience to God's commands" (p. 123, n. 31).

Hierarchy versus Anarchy?
Dionysius Areopagita, Symeon the New
Theologian, and Nicetas Stethatos[1]

ALEXANDER GOLITZIN

The late Father John Meyendorff did not have much use for Dionysius the Areopagite. It was Dionysius's theory of hierarchy that he found particularly objectionable, characterizing it as oscillating between, on the one hand, a "magical clericalism" and, on the other, a failure to distinguish the "objective presence of grace" from "the personal perfection of the initiator."[2] Meyendorff felt that there was no difference between the role of the Dionysian hierarch "and that of a charismatic."[3] Dionysius thus represented "a tendency in one line of spirituality, linked to Evagrius [of Pontus],"

1. This is an abridged version of an article under the same title that appeared in *St. Vladimir's Theological Quarterly* 38/2 (1994), pp. 131-79. For more ample discussion of the issues and a wider selection of references, the reader is advised to consult the original version.

The following abbreviations are used in subsequent notes:

CH	*Celestial Hierarchy* (Pseudo-Dionysius)
DN	*Divine Names* (Pseudo-Dionysius)
EH	*Ecclesiastical Hierarchy* (Pseudo-Dionysius)
KG	*Kephalaia Gnostica* (Evagrius)
PG	J.-P. Migne (ed.), *Patrologia cursus completus, series graeco-latina* (161 vols., Paris: Migne, 1857-66)
PS	*Patrologia Syriaca* (Paris, 1897-1926)
SC	Sources chrétiennes (Paris, 1941-)

2. See *Christ in Eastern Christian Thought* (Washington, DC, 1969), p. 82.

3. *Byzantine Theology: Historical Trends and Doctrinal Themes* (London, 1974), p. 28.

that culminated in Nicetas Stethatos's "conclusion in the eleventh century that the real bishop is the one who has knowledge . . . not the one ordained by men."[4] Now it happens that Nicetas, for whom Father John also cared rather little, was the lifelong disciple, editor, and promoter of a man for whom he and Meyendorff shared a very high regard: the great Byzantine mystic Symeon the New Theologian. Even Symeon, though, was not without his problems. His fierce opposition of "the charismatic personality of the saint to the institution" of the Church drew from Father John the observation that, in this regard, the New Theologian was "reflecting a frame of mind which had existed in both ancient and Byzantine Christianity, in Pseudo-Dionysius and the Macarian tradition."[5]

A Paradoxical Relationship?

Aside from the interesting way these observations juxtapose the works of Dionysius and Evagrius with the *Macarian Homilies,* two sets of writings that he normally saw in opposition to each other,[6] Father John's usual perspicacity does shed a certain light on the problem of a three-cornered relationship — that between Dionysius, Symeon, and the latter's disciple, Nicetas — that has puzzled scholars for some time. Jan Koder, editor of the *Sources chrétiennes* edition of Symeon's *Hymns,* wonders for example how Nicetas could have placed himself in the "paradoxical position of defending simultaneously both the anarchical mysticism of Symeon and the unilateral theoretician of hierarchy," Dionysius.[7] Why, Koder continues, should Nicetas have sought, as he did in his own introduction to Symeon's *Hymns,*[8] to assimilate his master to the Areopagite's supposed teacher, Hierotheos?[9] And why do we find Stethatos's curious treatise, *On the Hierarchy,* trying to postulate the "exact coincidence of each person's hierarchical position

---

4. *Christ in Eastern Christian Thought,* p. 82, quoting Nicetas's *On Hierarchy* 5.32 (SC 81:340).

5. *Byzantine Theology,* p. 75.

6. For example, ibid., pp. 67-69.

7. From J. Koder's Introduction to *Syméon le nouveau théologien: Hymnes* (SC 156), pp. 60-61, n. 2.

8. See Nicetas's Preface, ibid., pp. 106-32, with its frequent and copious references to Dionysius's *Divine Names.*

9. Ibid., pp. 60-64.

with his illumination by the Spirit?"[10] Indeed, why should Nicetas have written such a treatise at all? What possible relation could he have seen his master, the charismatic anarchist, having with the apostle of hierarchical mediation — a system, moreover, borrowed from the pagan Neoplatonism of Iamblichus and Proclus?[11]

In reply to these questions, most scholars have held that there is no relation between Symeon and Dionysius, or at least very little. Nicetas, in this view, is quite on his own and, equally, quite in contradiction with his elder. He was a man, they point out, who was very much in the center of church life in the imperial capital, a hobnobber with the city's ecclesiastical and civil elite, and who ended up as abbot of the Studion and thus a very important person in his own right.[12] But, so this thinking goes, he was not a particularly original or even very clear thinker. Hence his "ludicrous" attempt to link two men of radically different persuasion was the result, first, of an effort to show off his own learning that was quite consonant with the anitquarian enthusiasm of upper class pretensions and, second, a clumsy effort to clothe the "quite personal system" of his still controversial master with the apostolic mantle of the divine Dionysius.[13] Others have suggested that perhaps there was a connection between Dionysius and Symeon that the latter handed on, not in his published writings, but in "detailed instruction of a more esoteric nature" to his disciple, and which Nicetas subsequently articulated in his peculiar treatise, On Hierarchy.[14]

While I think that there is something to be said for all these suggestions about Stethatos — Nicetas did occasionally have something of the snob about him, he is not always perfectly consistent, and it is likely that his master had some private things to say to him — I do not believe that we need to

---

10. Ibid., pp. 60-61, n. 1.

11. This, at any rate, is the usual picture of Dionysius since, in particular, the publication of H. Koch's Pseudo-Dionysius in seinen Beziehungen zum Neuplatonismus und Mysterienwesen (Mainz, 1900), and one may find it faithfully reflected in the most recent book in English on the Areopagite, P. Rorem's Pseudo-Dionysius: A Commentary on the Texts and an Introduction to Their Influence (Oxford, 1993).

12. For sketches of Nicetas's life, see J. Darrouzès in SC 81:7-10; I. Hausherr, Vie de Syméon le nouveau théologien (Rome, 1938), pp. xv-xxiv.

13. See Darrouzès, SC 81:37. The latter does, though, allow for some such possibility as Turner (below) suggests.

14. H. J. M. Turner, St. Symeon the New Theologian and Spiritual Fatherhood (Leiden, 1990), p. 116.

assume either his ego or his confusion, or even secret teachings, in order to see a relationship between the New Theologian and the Areopagite. Father John's emphasis on what we might call the "charismatic principle" is certainly one clue to Symeon's conscious use of Dionysius, but there are others as well. I have in mind particularly the note of "apostolic authority" struck above and, even more importantly (and never mentioned in the literature), the idea of the hierarchy — and so the whole church at worship — as the icon of the inner man. The latter is a notion that has common roots for both Symeon and Dionysius in the Macarian and Evagrian writings, which is to say in just that curious and uncharacteristic juxtaposition that we saw Meyendorff making above, and to which we shall return in the latter part of this essay. For now, the faithful disciple, Nicetas, will help us by supplying clues to the presence of the motifs just noted in two textual pairings taken from the works of the Areopagite and the New Theologian. We shall first examine Dionysius's *Eighth Epistle,* "To Demophilus, a monk," in parallel with Symeon's famous (or infamous) *Letter on Confession* and, second, the opening chapter and third paragraph of *The Celestial Hierarchy* in comparison with Symeon's *Fourteenth Ethical Discourse.*

Two Epistles: Dionysius's *To Demophilus* and Symeon's *On Confession*

These two letters appear at first as a study in contrast. They advocate positions in diametric opposition. As pointed out by Roland Hathaway, Dionysius's *Eighth Epistle* is a kind of interruption in the sequence of ten letters concluding the *corpus.*[15] The addressees of the first four letters are monks, of the fifth letter a deacon, of the sixth a priest, of the seventh a bishop, while the ninth and tenth are addressed to Timothy, St. Paul's disciple and a bishop, and finally the Apostle John in exile at Patmos.[16] The

---

15. R. F. Hathaway, *Hierarchy and the Definition of Order in the Letters of Pseudo-Dionysius* (The Hague, 1969), esp. pp. 64-65 and 86-102.

16. The Migne text of the ten letters is in *PG* 3:1065A-1120A. The critical text of Dionysius is the *Corpus Dionysiacum* I (the *Divine Names,* ed. B. M. Suchla) and II (everything else, ed. H. Ritter and G. Heil), published by de Gruyter (Berlin, 1990-91). The letters are in volume II, pp. 156-210. In future citations I shall give only the *PG* column number and, in parentheses, the page numbers and, where necessary, the line numbers of the critical text.

eighth is thus a disruption, and disruption is precisely its subject. An unruly monk, Demophilus ("lover of the mob"), has broken into the sanctuary to discipline a priest in the process of hearing a confession. He has chased the priest out, beaten up the penitent, grabbed the consecrated elements *(ta hagia)*, and is standing guard over them in order to prevent their profana-tion.[17] This scenario provides Dionysius with an occasion to expand on the importance of the divinely established order of the Church. Like someone who presumes to occupy an imperial office without the emperor's writ, Demophilus has been audacious *(tolmeros)*.[18] He has forgotten his place and calling, and has intruded upon a function not his in defiance of God and God's hierarchy. First of all, a monk has no place within the sanctuary veils. That is only for the clergy, who alone have the right to stand before the altar. Monks belong at the doors, outside the sanctuary, ahead of but not wholly removed from the rest of the laity.[19] To be sure, Dionysius agrees, the priest who is unillumined *(aphotistos)* is not a true priest, but that does not give a bossy monk the right to correct him.[20] And do not, he adds, quote the example of Elijah to me (a reference, clearly, to the prophetic role assumed by the monastic movement from its first appearance).[21] It is Demophilus's task instead to establish order *(taxis)* in his own house, and this means giving the proper place *(ta kat' axian)* to appetite, emotion, and reason *(epithymia, thymos,* and *logos)*.[22] Once he has truly "done his own thing" *(dran to heautou)*, then perhaps he may be given authority over home, city, and nation — but not before God has clearly singled him out for it.[23] For the present, however, he is clearly lacking in the virtues neces-sary for the vision of God, and Dionysius has begun his epistle with an encomium on the virtues of humility and compassion, which he presents as having been embodied in Moses and David.[24] In the meantime,

---

17. *Epistle* 8, 1084A-1100D (pp. 171-92).

18. *Tolmeros, tolmeo,* and the reference to the emperor are in 1089B (p. 178, ll. 1-6).

19. 1088D-1089A (p. 176, l. 9–p. 77, l. 10).

20. 1092C (p. 181, ll. 7-10).

21. 1096C (p. 186, l. 12). On early monastic claims to the mantle of the prophets see, for example, P. Rousseau, *Ascetics, Authority, and the Church* (Oxford, 1978), pp. 18-67.

22. 1093A-C (p. 182, l. 6–p. 183, l. 11).

23. 1093B (p. 183, ll. 6-10).

24. 1084B-1085B (p. 171, l. 3–p. 172, l. 10) for Moses and David.

Demophilus is to obey his superiors. Those whom God has given rule distribute his providence to their subordinates.[25] As examples of good shepherds, Dionysius points first to "our divine and sacred initiator, Christ."[26] Jesus forgives the sinner, but he has no patience with those who seek vengeance. He even, Dionysius adds in quoting Matthew 7:22-23, rejects people who have worked miracles in his name if they are lacking the virtues.[27] Secondly, the Areopagite turns to the example of a righteous bishop, Carpus, who knew the sight of God *(theoptia)* and, indeed, never celebrated the liturgy without having such a vision beforehand.[28] When Carpus was at one time tempted by thoughts of vengeance, he was vouchsafed a sudden *(aphno)* visitation from Christ.[29] The roof opened over him while he was at midnight prayer and the Lord himself gave him an unforgettable lesson about the virtues of mercy, patience, and longsuffering.

In direct opposition to Dionysius, Symeon's *Letter on Confession*[30] is devoted to the defense of the proposition that not only priests, but also — even especially — monks have the right to hear confessions and absolve sinners. Confession, Symeon begins, is a necessity since everyone sins, and sin is death.[31] The sinner cannot atone of himself or recover by his own efforts the things that Christ "came down from heaven — and daily comes down — to distribute" to the faithful.[32] One must therefore look for "an

25. 1093A (p. 182, ll. 3-6).

26. 1096A (p. 185, l. 7).

27. For Christ as forgiving and patient, 1096B (p. 185, l. 10–p. 187, l. 8). Mercy and vengeance or hatred is the difference between the angels and devils, 1097A (p. 187, l. 10–p. 188, l. 2). It is earlier, 1089D (p. 179, ll. 8-10), that Dionysius quotes Matthew 7. God does not permit the lawless, the *paranomoi,* approach him.

28. 1097BC (p. 188, ll. 9-13).

29. For the vision, 1096D-1100D (pp. 189, l. 10–p. 192, l. 2). For *aphno,* 1100A (p. 190, l. 5).

30. The text of the *Letter on Confession* and its ascription to Symeon were established by K. Holl, *Enthusiasmus und Bußgewalt beim griechischen Mönchtum. Eine Studie zum Symeon dem neuen Theologen* (Leipzig, 1898). The *Letter* is on pp. 110-27, and was recently reprinted by Orthodox Kypseli in *Tou hosiou patros hemon Symeonos tou neou theologou. Erga* III: *Hymnoi kai Epistolai* (Thessalonica, 1990), pp. 423-39. Paragraph and page numbers will be from Holl, page and line numbers in parentheses from the reprint.

31. *Letter* 3-4, pp. 111-13 (pp. 424-26).

32. *Letter* 4, pp. 113-14 (p. 425, l. 26–p. 427, l. 12).

intercessor, a physician, and a good counselor,"[33] "a friend of God . . . capable of restoring" him to his former state.[34] But such people are rare and, while there are many pretenders, Christ will reject these false authorities even as he will those who cast out demons in his name — and here Symeon quotes Matthew 7:22-23.[35] To presume upon what the New Theologian calls the "Apostolic rank" (axioma) of "binding and loosing" is comparable to the man who "has had the audacity [tolmeo] to dare represent himself as the representative of the earthly emperor" without the latter's permission. We must observe the proper rank [taxis]. To do otherwise is an act of dreadful presumption [tolma].[36] Pretenders are rightly and dreadfully punished on earth, and so will their ecclesiastical equivalents be at the Last Judgment.[37]

This brings Symeon to the heart of his argument, that it is permissible for unordained monks to hear confessions. While, he admits, it is true that only bishops used to have the authority to bind and to loose, that original situation has changed because of human corruption. Originally, and here he cites John 20:22-23, Christ gave this authority together with the Holy Spirit to his disciples, and they in turn to their successors, the bishops. But this initial situation changed because

> when time had passed and the bishops became useless, this dread authority passed on to priests of blameless life . . . [and] when the latter in their turn had become polluted . . . it was transferred . . . to God's elect people, I mean to the monks.[38]

Not to all the monks, Symeon hastens to add, since the devil got to most of them as well. Thus today, he concludes, while the clergy still have the presumably unique authority to celebrate (hierourgein) the rest of the sacraments,

33. Letter 7, p. 117 (p. 429, l. 21). The three characteristics of the spiritual father are taken from "The Pastor" in John of Sinai's The Ladder. See K. T. Ware, "Forward" to I. Hausherr, Spiritual Direction in the Early Christian East, tr. A. Gythiel (Kalamazoo, 1990), pp. vii-xxxiii, esp. xi-xv.

34. Letter 5, p. 115 (p. 428, l. 3-5).

35. Letter 7, p. 117 (p. 430, 1. 4-17).

36. Letter 9, p. 118 (p. 431, ll. 17-20) for the emperor, and 10, p. 119 (p. 432, ll. 3-8) for taxis and tolma.

37. Letter 9, pp. 118-19 and 10, p. 119 (p. 431, ll. 20-24, and 432, ll. 9-11).

38. Letter 11, p. 120 (p. 432, l. 22-31).

The grace [of binding and loosing] is given alone to those, as many as there are among priests and bishops and monks, who have been numbered among Christ's disciples on account of their purity of life.[39]

Only the person who has "been borne aloft to the divine glory . . . [and] become a participant of God," who has seen "the light unapproachable, God himself," can say to another, "Be reconciled with God."[40] For Symeon the vision of God is thus the *sine qua non* of authority in the Church and, conversely, authority belongs only to those who have had this experience. These people are recognized by the apostolic virtues that they exhibit, among them "compassion, brotherly love, and humility."[41] They have found within themselves "the intelligible light," and each of them has thus "discovered his own soul."[42] Symeon concludes the epistle by citing the example of his own spiritual father, Symeon the Pious, "who did not have the ordination from men," but who had encouraged him to receive it.[43]

We do not need Nicetas's help to note for ourselves a number of interesting parallels between these two documents. First, the very contrast is itself suggestive. Dionysius is telling a monk to get out of the priestly business of confession while Symeon argues that, properly qualified by illumination, the monk has a divine right — even obligation — to be thus involved. Second, both writers hold in common that illumination is an essential qualification for the true confessor. Dionysius agrees with Demophilus that the unillumined priest is not a priest, and Symeon speaks of the saint as in the light and glory of God. The lists of virtues, third, that accompany this grace are also similar. Dionysius begins with humility as that which enabled Moses to see God, and he concludes with the example of Carpus as an illustration of the same virtue, together with longsuffering and mercy. Likewise, Symeon begins the body of his *Letter* by stressing the observance of the commandments,[44] denounces like Dionysius the judgment of others uninformed by grace,[45] and returns at the *Letter's* end to

---

39. *Letter* 14, l. 124 (p. 436, ll. 10-15, *hierourgein* in line 10).
40. *Letter* 15, pp. 125 (p. 437, l. 29–p. 438, l. 3).
41. P. 436, ll. 27-29 in the 1990 reprint.
42. P. 126 (p. 438, ll. 9-12).
43. *Letter* 16, p. 127 (p. 438, l. 28–p. 439, l. 2).
44. *Letter* 4, pp. 112-14 (p. 425, l. 9–p. 427, l. 11).
45. *Letter* 8, p. 118 (p. 430, l. 18–p. 431, l. 6).

the list of virtues, humility and longsuffering prominent among them, that characterize the holy man. Fourth, both Symeon's saint and Dionysius's holy man, Carpus in this case, are singled out by visions. Carpus never celebrated without one, and the charismatic holy man sees Christ within (we might also recall Nicetas's description of his master in the *Vita* as never having presided at liturgy without seeing the fire of the Spirit descending at the *anaphora*).[46] Fifth, without this divine sanction and its accompanying virtues, even those who work wonders in Christ's name are dismissed with the same quotation from Matthew 7:22-23. To presume, sixth, upon the apostolic dignity *(taxis/taxis)* of reconciliation is an act of audacity *(tolmeros/tolmeo, tolma)*. Seventh, both writers offer the same illustration of this effrontery, that of pretending to imperial office without having been appointed by the emperor. We might also point out, eighth, that where Symeon does — grudgingly, it is true — allow that the clergy are still uniquely empowered to celebrate the other sacraments, he is obedient to the Dionysian (and generally traditional) *taxis* and, moreover, uses a strikingly Dionysian term, *hierourgein*,[47] to describe the clergy's function.

It is difficult to see these parallels as accidental. I think it clear that Symeon had the *Epistle to Demophilus* very much in mind when composing his own *Letter* — just as, indeed, I believe the Areopagite is in general far more important to the New Theologian's thinking than has generally been admitted, and we shall turn to one other such instance in a moment. For now, though, the one glaring difference between the two letters remains to be explained. This is of course Symeon's thesis of monastic authority and the argument he uses to defend it, that is, the history that he offers of the corruption of the bishop's office and the consequent devolution upon the monks of the authority to bind and loose. It is here that we might look to Nicetas to give us a clue as to the relationship obtaining between our two texts. In his *Eighth Epistle*, accompanying his own treatise *On the Hierarchy*, Nicetas quotes the *Epistle to Demophilus* altogether approvingly on the relative placement within the church building of the clergy (inside the sanctuary), the monks (on the *bema*), and the laity (in the nave). This, Stethatos concludes, is the order given by Christ to the Church and written

46. *Vie de Syméon* 30 (p. 40).

47. For *hierourgein* and its cognates in Dionysius, see the "Register: griechische Wörter" in *Corpus Dionysiacum* II, p. 286. I count *hierourgeo* twenty-three times, *hierourgia* thirty-eight, *hierourgikos* four, and *hierourgos* five.

down by Dionysius, the disciple of St. Paul.[48] In other words, Dionysius's authority, thanks to his pseudonym, is precisely "apostolic." We thus recall Symeon's *Letter* and his admission that the authority to bind and loose was originally given by Christ to the disciples and then to the bishops. Only the latter, he says, used to have it. Given the relationship between his *Letter on Confession* and Dionysius's to Demophilus that we have just noted, it is surely here that we find the reason for Symeon's historical theory of episcopal decline and monastic election. Things are not the same, he is arguing, as when the divine Dionyius was writing. There have been changes since the time of the Apostles. Perhaps it is only fair to add that Symeon's historical instincts were not all that far off the mark. The fourth century did see some singular developments along just the lines that he is defending.[49] What he did not know, of course, was that Dionysius may well have himself been responding to some of the problems (recall the allusion to Elijah) to which those same developments gave rise.[50] The point in any case is that Symeon's historical excursus fits well within the argument that his *Letter* was written with Dionyius' *Epistle* primarily in mind.

The Church as Macrocosm and the Saint as Microcosm: Nicetas and Dionysius on Hierarchy and Symeon *On the Feasts*

Yet the Areopagite is more for the New Theologian than simply an authority who must somehow be navigated. There are much deeper affinities between the two men. Authority itself as a personal and charismatic endowment is certainly one of these, as we have just seen, but this in turn involves the larger issue of hierarchy per se with which we began this essay. Here again we may take a clue from a passing remark in Nicetas's *Eighth Epistle*, together with some other passages from his treatises *On the Soul, On Paradise,* and *On Hierarchy.* In his epistle, we saw him approve Dionysius's

48. Nicetas, *Epistle* 8.1-5 (SC 81:281-286). Dionysius is cited in 8.3 (p. 286) together with *Apostolic Constitutions* 2.57.

49. See Holl, *Enthusiasmus,* pp. 225-330, and H. Dörries, "The Place of Confession in Ancient Monasticism," *Studia Patristica* 5 (1962), pp. 284-311, esp. 291-97.

50. See again Holl, *Enthusiasmus,* pp. 205-11, and, for the (monastic) holy man as locus of supernatural authority in late Roman times, P. Brown's series of studies in *Society and the Holy in Late Antiquity* (Berkeley, 1982), esp. pp. 103-95.

ordering of the different ranks of clergy and faithful. He then follows up this approval with an allusion to the phrase from the Divine Liturgy, "The doors, the doors! In wisdom, let us attend," and goes on to observe that the Christian is always to "guard the doors of the intellect [*nous*]," since it is the latter that is "the altar within us" [*to entos hemon thysiasterion*].[51] The connection of the intellect with the altar, the liturgy, and the ordering of celebrants and believers is not accidental. It points instead to a theme that is central to all three of our writers: microcosm and macrocosm. In Book 3 of his treatise *On the Soul*, Nicetas brings this out expressly. The human being stands on the dividing line *(methorion)* "of intelligible and sensible,"[52] "as a kind of other world . . . [at once] visible and intelligible . . . mortal and immortal . . . an angelic contemplator and initiate [*mystes*] of divine and human things."[53] In Book 4, he tells us that it is in this "other world" that God has established a paradise greater than Eden:

> The human being [*anthropos*] is seen indeed as a kind of great [world] in the small. . . . God creates together with the soul, in the whole of the human being made according to his image, the intelligible and invisible world in order that it may be contemplated here [i.e., in the human person] as neighbor to the perceptible.[54]

The "sun" of this inner and greater world is not a physical luminary, "but the primordial and divine light of the Holy Spirit."[55] Nicetas will therefore add in his treatise *On Paradise*:

> God made the human being in the beginning as a great world . . . thus, as in a greater world, he planted intelligibly in him another divine paradise greatly transcending the perceptible one . . . [which] is illumined by the sun of righteousness. This, indeed, is the place of the Kingdom of Heaven.[56]

It is against this background of the perfected human being as the great world and spiritual paradise, together with the eschatological sense of the

51. Nicetas, *Epistle* 8.6-7 (p. 288).
52. *On the Soul* 3.4 (pp. 76-78).
53. *On the Soul* 16 (p. 78).
54. *On the Soul* 27 (pp. 88-90).
55. *On the Soul* 27 (pp. 88-90).
56. *On Paradise* 2.19 (p. 176).

Eucharist, that we should look for Nicetas's understanding of hierarchy. In the introduction to his treatise on the subject, he tells us that he has been inspired by Dionysius's works on the hierarchies to write about the banquet of heavenly and earthly intellects *(noes)* around the one table and Host, the unique banquet of Christ.[57] The hierarchy he has in mind throughout the treatise is therefore not the present, canonical order of bishop, priest, deacon, etc., but that reality toward which the order of the Church here below points and which it — to a degree — embodies: the heavenly and eschatological meal and liturgy of the Messiah Word. Hence Nicetas's infamous addition of the triad, patriarchs-metropolitans-archbishops, to Dionysius's bishop-priest-deacon, and monks, baptized laity, catechumens, and penitents. Nicetas's nine ranks thus parallel the nine orders of angels,[58] but they also and at the same time parallel the nine orders of saints that he has mentioned just before: apostles-patriarchs-prophets, ecumenical teachers–martyrs/confessors-ascetics, and holy rulers–pious abbots–devout laity, the first two triads of which would have been familiar to him (as they still are to us) from the Byzantine liturgy.[59] He is not therefore proposing some sort of super clericalism, but simply providing another set of names for the more conventional taxonomy of saints celebrating the liturgy of heaven. It might seem a little odd to us, and it is perhaps a bit fanciful, but it is scarcely ludicrous.

This banquet is not just a cosmic reality, however. It is also a personal and subjective truth. The eschaton has already begun in Christ and, in light of the notion of the microcosm sketched above, it is even now present in the spiritual man, the saint. Asking the reader to note Nicetas's allusion to Ephesians 4:13, we therefore find him describing the "true bishop" as

> the man whose intellect, by unstinting participation in the Holy Spirit, has been purified of every impurity and illumined richly by the Spirit's superradiant illuminations, and who has attained to the measure of the fullness of Christ and been perfected into the perfect man.[60]

Such a person is the true initiate and mystagogue of the hidden mysteries of God.[61] In this man, "the true bishop," the heavenly liturgy is already dis-

---

57. *On Hierarchy* (p. 300).
58. *On Hierarchy* 3.21-23 (pp. 326-28).
59. *On Hierarchy* 17-19 (pp. 320-22).
60. *On Hierarchy* 4.38 (p. 340).
61. *On Hierarchy* 39 (p. 342).

cernable.[62] Jean Darrouzès is certainly correct to point to Gregory of Nazianzus and John Damascene as sources for Nicetas's idea of the microcosm.[63] Rather curiously, though, he seems to miss Stethatos's more proximate sources in Symeon and, so I would hold, in Dionysius. More often than not, the disciple is simply quoting or paraphrasing his master. The greatest part of Symeon's *First Ethical Discourse* is devoted to the themes of paradise, the mystical sun, the Church, and the heavenly marriage feast, which reappear in Nicetas.[64] The Church as the new and heavenly cosmos appears prominently in *Discourse* 2, and this eschatological reality is identified with the Eucharist in *Discourse* 3.[65] *Discourse* 10 is devoted to the theme of the "Day of the Lord," and the burden of its argument is that this same "Eighth Day" already shines in the heart of the perfected Christian.[66] Again in *Discourse* 3, Symeon assumes a parallel between the individual Christian as the throne of God and the Seraphim and Cherubim, as in the visions of Isaiah and Ezekiel, who bear aloft the God of Israel present in his Temple — an image that is certainly indebted to the *Cherubikon* of the Byzantine offertory.[67] The Church, which is the Body of Christ, is mirrored in *Discourse* 4 by the "body of virtues" that comprise the Christian who has arrived at the stature of the fullness of Christ and the perfected man[68] — and we note the same reference as in Nicetas to Ephesians 4:13. We also find Symeon making use here of the same source in Gregory of Nazianzus that we saw Nicetas quoting in his description of the human microcosm: "Each one of us . . . [is] created by God as a second world, a great world in this small and visible one."[69] Again, the disciple's chain or ladder of beatified souls, the human

62. See esp. *On Hierarchy* 4.36 (p. 338).

63. *On the Soul* 6.27 (p. 88, n. 1); and see his "Index analytique" for *kosmos*, p. 538. Gregory's "great world in the small" in *Oration* 38.11 (*PG* 36:324A) and in John Damascene, *De fide* 26 (Kotter II, pp. 76, 79), though John, as Darrouzès observes, reverses Gregory to speak of the human being as the "little world." Nicetas and Symeon both reverse this again in order to go back to Gregory.

64. *Ethical Discourse* 1, SC 122:170-309. For Paradise, see pp. 172-95; for the Church, pp. 206-41; for the heavenly marriage feast, pp. 241-71; for the mystical sun, see esp. the "Allegory of the Prisoner," pp. 297-305.

65. For the Church as the new, heavenly cosmos, see *Discourse* 2, SC 122, ll. 367-89; and for the Eucharist as the same eschatological reality, 3.421-29.

66. *Discourse* 10, SC 129, ll. 258-327, esp. 308-23.

67. *Discourse* 3, SC 122, p. 436:649-68.

68. *Discourse* 4, SC 129, 34:364–45:514.

69. *Discourse* 64:799-801 and, for the sanctified believer as the "new sun and new day," 66:826–68:834.

hierarchy of heaven paralleling the hierarchy of the angels, finds its equivalent at once in Symeon's description of the single, golden chain of saints stretching from heaven to earth in his *Theological Centuries* 3.4[70] and in the ladder of virtues, on which the angels ascend and descend, by which the holy man draws near and is united to God,[71] and through which he becomes the "new paradise" and dwelling place *(oikos)* of the Holy Trinity.[72]

There is therefore nothing in Nicetas's basic picture of hierarchy that cannot be found in Symeon. The fundamental presupposition, the saint as microcosm in whom the heavenly and earthly liturgies are present and mirrored, is identical. But what about that Dionysius to whom both men refer, the disciple directly and the master — as is his wont in virtually all his borrowings from the Church Fathers[73] — indirectly? I think that we can find the same theme at work here, too. Everyone admits that the Areopagite was deeply impressed by late Neoplatonism, although I must add that I do not think that Proclus was Dionysius's only source, or even the primary one — but more of that later on. Now it is a feature of all Neoplatonists, from Plotinus to Damascius, that the motif of microcosm and macrocosm plays an important, not to say central, role. We are, says Plotinus, all of us a *kosmos noetos,* existing here below and yet linked to the spiritual.[74] According to Stephen Gersh, the Neoplatonist vision of reality is at once an analysis in detail of the "great chain of being" and a dissection of the individual human being as reflecting the structures of both the phenomenal and intelligible worlds.[75] I am convinced that the same applies to Dionysius, but with a very important difference. Dionysius's world is the "new creation" of the Church — an insight, by the way, that is foundational for René Roques's magisterial study, *L'univers dionysien.*[76] In addition, the

---

70. *Chapitres théologiques, gnostiques, et pratiques* 3.4; SC 51, p. 81. Compare this passage with Nicetas above, *On Hierarchy* 3.17-21.

71. *On Hierarchy* 3.70-71, pp. 101-2.

72. *On Hierarchy* 3.72, p. 102 for the "new paradise"; 1.79, p. 64 for the "dwelling place of the Trinity."

73. See W. Völker, *Praxis und theorie bei Symeon dem neuen Theologen* (Wiesbaden, 1974), pp. 72-74 on the infrequency of Symeon's direct citations.

74. *Enneads* 3.4.3 (pp. 248-50 in the Loeb edition).

75. S. Gersh, *From Iamblichus to Eriugena: An Investigation of the Prehistory and Evolution of the Pseudo-Dionysian Tradition* (Leiden, 1978), pp. 27-120.

76. R. Roques, *L'univers dionysien. Structure hiérarchique du monde selon le pseudo-Denys* (Paris, 1954), esp. pp. 36-131.

obverse also applies. The human being, specifically the man or woman redeemed or renewed in Christ, is this new world in miniature. The outer hierarchy mirrors and is the model for what should obtain within. We have already come across a hint of this in summarizing Dionysius's *Epistle* 8. Demophilus has upset the God-ordained *taxis* of the Church because his own, inner being was also out of true, and Dionysius therefore admonishes him to put his house in order, and to "give what is proper [or deserving] to appetite, emotion, and reason." The hierarchy of the soul, here in terms taken from Plato's *Phaedrus* (though long familiar to the Christian ascetic tradition since at least Evagrius, if not Clement of Alexandria[77]), must reflect the harmony and peace of the *taxis* obtaining in the Church, and that means in the liturgy.[78] Only thus may one see God, as Dionysius tells his turbulent monk, and then perhaps be granted authority over city and nation. Nicetas's and Symeon's picture of the holy man as the "true bishop," the very "place" of the Kingdom of God and spiritual paradise, is surely then indebted in good part to Dionysius's description of the hierarch as "the inspired and divine man learned in all sacred knowledge, in whom his own hierarchy [*he kat'auton hierarchia*] . . . is both perfected and made known."[79] Likewise, both later writers must have found a sympathetic chord being struck in Dionysius's description of the divine man (presumably again the hierarch) in *Ecclesiastical Hierarchy* as one who, wholly in conformity with God, has become "at once an attendant and temple [*naos*] . . . of the divine Spirit," and thus, "by virtue of the dispassion [*apatheia*] of his own state of mind [*hexis*] . . . is beheld a physician to others."[80]

The references to "temple," with its echo of church and liturgy,[81] and to

77. The soul as the chariot steered by reason *(logos)* as the charioteer governing the two steeds, irritability *(thymos)* and appetite *(epithymia)*, dates to the *Phaedrus* 246. For Evagrius and the tripartite model of the soul, see his *KG* (*Patrologia Orientalis* 28) 3.35; 4.73; 6.13, 85.

78. See, for example, Dionysius's handling of the powers or activities of purification, illumination, and perfection as applied to the angelic hierarchy in *CH* 8, 205B-D (p. 27, l. 4–p. 28, l. 12), to the individual intellect whether angelic or human in 10.3, 273C (p. 40, l. 23–p. 41, l. 6), and to the orders of the Church (clergy, monks, laity) in *EH* 5.1, 500D-501A (p. 104) and esp. 504A-C (p. 106, ll. 4-23), wherein the actions and physical placement are those which obtain during the celebration of the services.

79. *EH* 1.3, 373C (p. 66, l. 5-6); see also *CH* 12.3, 293B (p. 43, ll. 12-19) on "holy men" as, like angels, receiving the title of divinity by participation.

80. *EH* 3.3.7, 533CD (p. 86, ll. 7-16).

81. For *naos* in Malachi 3:1 and its importance for the reading of Dionysius's use

the "condition of mind [*hexis*]" of the saint, bring us to our second set of textual pairings. We begin with the passage from Dionysius's *Celestial Hierarchy* 1.3:

> It would not be possible for the human intellect [*nous*] to be ordered with that immaterial imitation and contemplation of the heavenly hierarchies [i.e., angels] unless it were to use the material guide that is proper to it [the liturgy, thus:], reckoning the visible beauties as reflections of the invisible splendor, the perceptible fragrances as impressions of the intelligible [*noetos*] distribution, the material lights an icon of the immaterial gift of light, the sacred and extensive teaching [of the scriptures] [an image] of the mind's intelligible fulfillment, the exterior ranks of the clergy [an image] of the harmonious and ordered habit of mind [*hexis*] which leads to divine things, and [our partaking] of the most divine Eucharist [an icon] of our participation in Jesus.[82]

The text speaks first of all about the earthly liturgy as an imitation and revelation of the one in heaven. Secondly, though, it also states that our hierarchy, specifically the ranks and order of the clergy, is an image of that inward state or condition of the *nous* that allows for the vision of God — in other words, just what we found out of order in Demophilus. The visible liturgy and outward church are an icon of the liturgy celebrated in the perfected soul. In short, there are as it were three "liturgies" going on here, three "churches": the heavenly church, the earthly church, and the "little church" of the soul. The first two meet in the third, in the perfected soul of the "hierarch" — as we saw above — but this is not to say that the middle term or earthly cult is unnecessary. It is instead essential. It mediates and reflects the eternal and unseen presence of heaven in the saint. Everything here below is icon or symbol of a pervasive and invisible reality that is discovered at the end of the passage, in the Eucharist and in Jesus. The image of the Church outside reveals and enables the reality present both in heaven and within the soul, but the soul does not and cannot become aware of this reality, cannot find the indwelling presence of Christ, without the "material guide" given from above.

In his fourteenth *Ethical Discourse*, Symeon wonders about the true meaning of great and elaborate liturgical solemnities. "How," he asks, can the

---

of *exaiphnes* in *Epistle* 3 (1069B, p. 159), see my article, "The Mysticism of Dionysius Areopagita: Platonist or Christian?" *Mystics Quarterly* 19:3 (1993), esp. pp. 108f.

82. *CH* 1.3, 121C-124A (p. 8, l. 18–p. 9, l. 6).

man who has "seen the Master" and who knows himself as naked and poor "take pride in beauty, or pay great attention to the multitude of candles and lamps, or fragrances and perfumes, or an assembly of people, or a rich . . . table?"[83] The wise man, he replies, does not look to the visible, but to the eschatological "events which are present in the rites being celebrated," and he will therefore celebrate the feast "in the Holy Spirit with those who celebrate in heaven."[84] This does not mean that Symeon discourages the visible liturgy — "God forbid! On the contrary, I both advise and encourage you to do these things" — but he does want to point out what the things done "in types and symbols really mean."[85] In explaining the latter, he displays his debt to the Areopagite. The function, he says, of the lamps in church is "to show you the intelligible light" (Dionysius's "immaterial gift of light").[86] The perfumes and incense (Dionysius's "perceptible fragrances") suggest the "intelligible perfume of the Holy Spirit"; the crowds reveal "the ranks of the holy angels," friends and dignitaries "the saints," and the refreshments laid out for the people "the living bread . . . Who comes to you in and through what is perceptible" (Dionysius's "most divine Eucharist").[87] These comparisons follow fairly closely the sequence of the text from the *Celestial Hierarchy*. The order is a little different from Dionysius's, with lights preceding perfumes and the crowds and dignitaries instead of the order of the clergy, but the overall debt Symeon owes the Areopagite in these passages seems to me to be clear. So is the general idea. For both men the earthly church at worship is the image of the new man transfigured in Christ. It reflects both heaven and the saint and, more, connects the latter to the former. Neither for Symeon nor for Dionysius is the icon, here preeminently the Eucharist, a mere pointer or empty memorial. Rather, it conveys the presence that it signifies. Dionysius tells us in the *Ecclesiastical Hierarchy* that the Eucharist is the "sacrament of sacraments" (*telete teleton*), which first illumined his own perceptions and by whose light he was "led up in light to the contemplation of the other sacred things."[88] It is in the same

83. *Discourse* 14 (SC 129:424, ll. 26-35).
84. *Discourse* 35-44.
85. *Discourse*, p. 428, ll. 87-92.
86. *Discourse* 93-94 and following.
87. *Discourse*, p. 430, l. 106–p. 432, l. 139 for the fragrances, p. 432, ll. 140-53 for the crowds, and p. 436, l. 211–p. 458, l. 223 for the Eucharist. The sequence light, fragrances, crowds is repeated in p. 436, l. 194–p. 438, l. 223.
88. *EH* 3.1, 424C (p. 79, l. 3) for *telete teleton*, and 425AB (p. 80, ll. 2-4) for Dionysius's personal witness.

spirit that Symeon addresses his reader at the end of *Discourse* 19.1f, he says, you truly celebrate the feast and partake worthily

> . . . of the divine mysteries, all your life will be to you one single feast. And not a feast, but the beginning of a feast and a single Pascha, the passage and emigration from what is seen to what is sensed by the intellect, to that place where every shadow and type, and all the present symbols, come to an end.[89]

The Roots of an Image: Evagrius, Macarius, and the *Liber Graduum*

The three-cornered relationship between Dionysius, Symeon, and Nicetas is therefore no paradox and certainly not the fault of sloppy thinking on Nicetas's part. At this point I should like to take a look at the roots that all three, and particularly the Areopagite, have in the ascetic literature of the fourth and fifth centuries. Here I have especially in mind the two authors, Evagrius and the anonymous source of the *Macarian Homilies,* with whom we saw Father John linking, respectively, Dionysius and the New Theologian.

For both Evagrius and Macarius, the theme of the microcosm plays an important role, and that in ways that contributed significantly to the three men whom we have been discussing. Evagrius inherits and makes important use of Origen's myth of a precosmic fall. In part as the result of this inheritance, though the idea has deep roots, he reads the phenomenal world as, in effect, the human being writ large. To borrow a phrase from David Evans's summary of the Evagrian scheme, the present human realities of body, soul, and *nous* represent "moments in the knowledge of God."[90] The universe created to house the fallen *noes* is thus a kind of giant school-book or lesson plan, and ultimately a sacrament. For the person who contemplates it, it carries the knowledge of one's soul, of Christ who created

---

89. *Discourse* 14 (p. 443, ll. 280-90). In this eschatological context, see Dionysius, *DN* 1.4, 592BC (Suchla, p. 114, l. 1–p. 115, l. 5) with its sequence "now," i.e., in this world, "but then," i.e., in the world to come.

90. D. B. Evans, *Leontius of Byzantium* (Washington, DC, 1970), esp. pp. 89-111. For Evans's — as well as everyone else's — source, see Guillaumont, *Les "Kephalaia Gnostica,"* pp. 15-43 for an analysis of Evagrius's doctrine and, for the text of the *Kephalaia* that Guillaumont established and edited for *Patrologia Orientalia* 28, see ibid., pp. 200-258.

the soul's temporary housing, of the eternal realm of the intellects, and, at the last, leads to the "essential knowledge" of the Trinity.[91] One does one's lessons by ascending the three stages of the ascetic life, moving from mastery of the passions crowned by *apatheia* and love, then to illumination with regard to the *logoi* investing both the visible and invisible worlds, and finally to the vision of God.[92] The world as icon, as in a way "church" and "sacrament," therefore fulfills a function analogous to the one that we have seen the visible Church serving for Dionysius, Symeon, and Nicetas. It points the way toward, and communicates, the reality that is already present within the believer. But the imagery of church and liturgy, especially as expressed in the Old Testament language of Exodus, particularly chapters 19 and 24, is important for Evagrius, too. The account of the theophany at Sinai, itself influenced by the Temple liturgy and paradigmatic in turn for subsequent descriptions of God's manifestation in both public cult and personal experience, serves Evagrius well in a number of key texts. He is, indeed, one of the first — if not the first — to internalize it. Hence his description on several occasions of the "place of God" within the *nous* as "like a sapphire," a clear borrowing from the account of the Shekhinah, the divine presence that Moses and the elders encounter on the Mountain in Exodus 24:10.[93] In a passage from his *Kephalaia Gnostica*, he also makes explicit use of temple imagery in order to describe the innermost reality of the human soul as the "place" of encounter with the Trinity:

91. For the *praktike* as precondition, see *KG* 2.6-9; for the physical universe as (temporary) sign, 3.57 and 70; for the (again temporary) necessity of the body as sign, 4.60 and 62; for motion as original sin 3.22; for Christ as the maker and meaning of the (temporary) physical world, but not the Word and the *telos* of creation, 3.2-3, 24, 57; 4.8-9, 60-62, 80, and 6.14; for the "essential science" of the Trinity as beginning and end of the cycle, 3.6 and 15; 4.18; 5.60, 77-88; and especially 6.10.

92. For the *Praktikos*, see *Traité Pratique* (SC 171 and 172) and Guillaumont's "Introduction," SC 171:38-62 and 113-24. For Evagrius's own words, *Praktikos* 1-3 (pp. 498-501) and on *apatheia*, 63-70 (pp. 646-57). For the contemplation of the *noeta*, see *KG* 2.19 and 6.55.

93. See the sixty chapters supplementary to the *KG*, whose Syriac translation was edited and retranslated into Greek by W. Frankenberg, *Evagrius Ponticus* (Berlin, 1912), esp. ch. 2 (Frankenberg, p. 425). See also *Letters* 29 (p. 587), 33 (p. 589), and esp. 39 (p. 593). In the last, Evagrius identifies the vision of God within the *nous* with both Sinai and Zion and calls it "another heaven" (recall Nicetas and Symeon above). For the Zion motif, an implicit reference to the Temple, see also *KG* 5.88 and 6.49.

The intelligible temple is the pure intellect which now possesses in itself the "Wisdom of God, full of variety"; the temple of God is he who is a beholder of the sacred unity, and the altar of God is the contemplation of the Holy Trinity.[94]

Thus again, as in the three later writers, we find our theme of the holy man as the true temple and altar of the divine presence.

The equation of the inner man with, specifically, the liturgy and even the hierarchy of the Christian Church appears in unmistakeable form in a remarkable passage from the *Macarian Homilies*, though not from the usual collection of fifty homilies, but in the longer version edited by H. Berthold for *GCS*.[95] The text in question is *Homily* 52, and it begins on a note which by now should be quite familiar to us:

> The whole visible arrangement [*oikonomia*] of the Church of God came to pass for the sake of the living and intelligible being [*noera ousia*] of the rational soul [*logikes psyches*] . . . which is the living and true Church of God. . . . For the Church of Christ and Temple of God and true altar and living sacrifice is the man of God.[96]

Thus, he continues, just as the Old Dispensation was the shadow of the New, "so is the present and visible Church a shadow of the rational and true inner man."[97] Neither does Macarius mean by this that the present Church and its liturgy is "mere symbol": "The Savior granted through the Apostles that the Comforter Spirit should be present and take part in all the liturgy of the Holy Church of God."[98] The same Spirit is truly communicated to faithful believers in the sacraments, though It stays "far away from the unworthy."[99] Ultimately, however, which is to say in the perspective of the eschaton:

---

94. *KG* 5.84.

95. *Makarios/Symeon. Reden und Briefe: Die Sammlung I des Vaticanus Graecus 694 (B)*, ed. H. Berthold (Berlin, 1973), 2:138-42.

96. Ibid., p. 138, ll. 1-8.

97. Ibid., ll. 10-11.

98. Ibid., p. 139, ll. 7-9.

99. Ibid., ll. 26-27. Recall Symeon above in *Discourse* 1.4, together with his emphasis in the *Letter on Confession* on the necessity of the holy man being illumined. So, too, Dionysius in *Epistle* 8 on the *aphotistos hiereus*.

> The living activity of the Holy Spirit is to be sought from God in living
> hearts, because all visible things and all the [present] arrangement [of
> the Church] will pass away, but hearts alive in the Spirit will abide.[100]

Macarius concludes this section with a repetition of the theme of the church
as icon *(eikon)* noting that the Savior came and that the icon of the Church
was formed *(diatyposis)* in order that "faithful souls might . . . be made
again and renewed and, having accepted transformation [*metabole*], be
enabled to inherit life everlasting."[101] The reference to change or transformation is quite in line with the parallel between the liturgy and the Christian soul. The term *metabole*, after all, carries the distinct echo of the
eucharistic change at the liturgy's consecratory prayer.[102] The consecration
of the sacred elements is an anticipation of the eschatological transformation of the believer and of the world.

It is therefore to the service itself that Macarius turns his attention
next. He begins by restating his points above in a way that should alert us
still more clearly to the themes in Dionysius, Symeon, and Nicetas with
which we have been occupied:

> Because visible things are the type and shadow of hidden ones, and the
> visible temple [a type] of the temple of the heart, and the priest [a type]
> of the true priest of the grace of Christ, and all the rest of the sequence
> [*akolouthia*] of the visible arrangement [a type] of the rational and
> hidden matters of the inner man, we receive the manifest arrangement
> and administration [*oikonomia kai dioikesis*] of the Church as an illustra-
> tion [*hypodeigma*] of [what is] at work in the soul by grace.[103]

By sequence *(akolouthia)* and arrangement *(oikonomia)* Macarius means,
respectively, the sequence of the liturgy and the hierarchical ordering of the
faithful and of the sacramental ministers. Beginning with the first, he observes that the two parts of the eucharistic liturgy, the *synaxis* ("liturgy of
the word") and *anaphora* (offertory, consecration with the *epiklesis* of the
Spirit, and communion), are incomplete without each other. The whole

100. Ibid., ll. 27-29.
101. Ibid., p. 139, l. 30–p. 140, l. 2.
102. See Lampe, *A Patristic Greek Lexicon* (Oxford, 1961), p. 850 for *metabole*
and p. 848 for *metaballo*. The sources cited for the former begin as early as Justin Martyr.
103. *Makarios/Symeon*, p. 140, ll. 3-8.

rule *(kanon)* of the first must be completed in order for the consecration to follow and, conversely, the *synaxis* is "incomplete and in vain" without the sacramental communion.[104] Just so, he argues, is it the case for the individual Christian. The latter must have the full complement of "fasting, vigil, psalmody, ascesis, and every virtue" for the "mystical activity of the Spirit" to be "accomplished by grace on the altar of the heart."[105] This interior order, *kosmos,* of the Spirit's activity *(energeia)* corresponds to the visible order and glory of the sacrament.[106]

Turning to the order of the Church's hierarchy, Macarius's remarks bring very sharply to mind what both Dionysius and Nicetas, each in his respective eighth epistle, had had to say about the physical place of each of the respective ranks of the Church. Those believers, Macarius says, who "do not sin and who make progress . . . come to the priesthood, and they are transferred from some outer place [*apo topou tinos exoterou*]" — presumably referring to the narthex or nave — "up to the altar [*epi to thysiasterion*] so that they may be God's ministers and assistants [*leitourgoi . . . kai paredroi*]."[107] The latter term suggests the throne, the *hedra,* of the bishop who, as Ignatius of Antioch wrote, occupies the place of God.[108] This spatial arrangement of clergy and laity — "according to this example" — is then taken and applied to the "Christians who are moved by grace."[109] Whoever sins must confess and repent in order to come again under the oversight — *episkopes,* an evident play on *episkopos,* bishop — of the Spirit.[110] As for the soul that makes continual progress in the struggle for the virtues:

> It is made worthy of transference [or promotion, *metathesis*] and of spiritual dignity [*axiomatos*], and of being transferred from divine to

---

104. Ibid., ll. 8-19.

105. Ibid., ll. 21-23.

106. Ibid., p. 141, ll. 1-2. Note the use of *kosmos,* and recall Nicetas and Symeon above.

107. Ibid., ll. 13-15. Recall Dionysius in *Epistle* 8, esp. 1088D-1089A (p. 176, l. 9–p. 177, l. 8), on the physical placement of clergy, monks, and laity, and likewise Nicetas's *Epistle* 8 (pp. 280-86), esp. 8.3 (p. 283).

108. See Ignatius, *Polycarp* 6 along with *Ephesians* 6; *Magnesians* 6-7; *Trallians* 1-2; *Philadelphians* 4; *Smyrnaeans* 8. Lampe, *Lexicon,* p. 406 cites *hedraioma* for the bishop's throne and indicates *Polycarp* 6 for *paredroi,* p. 1030.

109. *Makarios/Symeon,* p. 141, l. 16.

110. Ibid., p. 142, l. 1.

heavenly mysteries [i.e., from the sacraments here below to the Kingdom] . . . and thus, having reached the perfect measure of Christianity through both its own freely willed ordeal and with help from on high, the soul will be inscribed in the Kingdom among the perfect workers and with the blameless ministers and assistants [*leitourgous kai paredrous*] of Christ.[111]

The spatial ordering of clergy and faithful is the icon of both the *taxis* of heaven and of the illumined soul. We are back, in short, to the version of hierarchy that Nicetas would offer us in greater detail seven hundred years later. In between stand his elder, Symeon, and, for both master and disciple, the *Corpus Dionysiacum*.

Given this text, and reckoning it as of the same late fourth-century provenance as the other *Macarian Homilies*,[112] we can surely take it as shedding new light on Dionysius's supposed "originality." It allows us to see the Areopagite as something other than the lonely meteor crossing the night sky of patristic thought that some have taken him for, and gifted moreover in consequence of his pseudonym with an otherwise inexplicable authority. *Homily* 52 by itself shows up Dionysius as part of an already extant tradition.[113] But the homily is not alone, neither in the Macarian *corpus* nor even in a wider context. The whole thrust of the Macarian writings, in the words of Father Georges Florovsky, is "the soul as throne of God."[114] The famous first *Homily* in the more familiar and widespread collection of fifty opens with the vision of God from Ezekiel 1, itself of course with deep roots in the Temple cult, and goes on to speak of the soul as the true resting place of the divine glory.[115] In this same vein, and

111. Ibid., p. 142, ll. 9-16.
112. If, as no one questions, the *Homilies* are by the author that wrote the *Great Letter*, they can be no later than Gregory of Nyssa's *On Christian Perfection*, and therefore the 380s stand as the *ad quem* in dating their composition. For a brief survey of the question and of Macraius's alleged "Messalianism," see G. Maloney's Introduction to *Pseudo-Macarius: The Fifty Spiritual Homilies and the Great Letter* (New York, 1992), esp. pp. 7-11.
113. See my article, "The Mysticism of Dionysius Areopagita," pp. 105f.
114. G. Florovsky, *Byzantine Ascetic and Spiritual Writers* (Belmont MA, 1987), p. 154. "And it is there," Florovsky adds, "that a certain secret light flashes out." The light is Christ, and this sudden flash recalls to me, once again, Dionysius's *Epistle* 3: "suddenly," there is Christ.
115. *Homily* 1.1-3 and 9, in *Die 50 geistlichen Homilien des Makarios*, ed. H. Dör-

scattered througout the rest of the homilies, in whatever collection, we can find references to the soul as temple or as "little church."[116]

The theme of the "little church" is not confined to the Macarian writings. Taking its start from St. Paul's *logia* in 1 Corinthians 3:16 and 6:19-20 that the Christian is the "temple of the Holy Spirit," we discover that this motif is well established in the Syriac Christian tradition from at least the same time as Macarius. We find it chiefly in the *Liber Graduum*. Thought by some scholars earlier this century to have been the Messalian *Ascetikon* condemned at Ephesus in 431,[117] the *Liber* appears in fact to be the work of a writer, one perhaps somewhat embattled by ecclesiastical authorities, who is at pains to distance himself and his community from the charge of neglecting the visible Church.[118] The work as a whole does not breathe the atmosphere of sectarianism, and its account of the relation between the inner and outer Church bears striking resemblance to what we have just seen in Macarius, as well as to the themes we picked out in Evagrius — under whose name, interestingly enough, it seems often to have circulated.[119]

I should like first of all to point to the hierarchy of believers that the book presumes throughout: those being purified, the righteous (laity), and the perfected (ascetics).[120] This triad certainly seems to echo at least the

---

ries, E. Klostermann, and M. Kroeger (Berlin, 1964), pp. 1-5 and ,10. For English, see *Pseudo-Macarius* (Maloney) pp. 37-38 and 42. For the Transfiguration in Macarius as both foreshadowing the body's eschatological transformation and as an image for the soul's inner reality even now, see esp. *Homily* 8, specifically 8.3 (Dörries, pp. 78-80; Maloney, pp. 81f.), and 15.38 (Dörries, pp. 149f.; Maloney, pp. 122f.). Again recall *DN* 1.4. For the *nous* (here in place of *kardia!*) as the throne of God, see for example 6.5 (Dörries, pp. 68f.; Maloney, p. 77).

116. See the references collected and cited by R. Murray, *Symbols of Church and Kingdom: A Study in Early Syriac Tradition* (Cambridge, 1975), pp. 269-71; C. Stewart, *"Working the Earth of the Heart": The Messalian Controversy in History, Texts, and Language to A.D. 431* (Oxford, 1991), pp. 218-20.

117. A thesis advanced in particular by M. Kmosko in his Praefatio to his edition of the *Liber Graduum* in *PS* III. A. Vööbus replied to the contrary in *History of Asceticism in the Syrian Orient* (Louvain, 1958) I:178-84, and was seconded more recently by A. Guillaumont, "Situation et significance du 'Liber Graduum' dans la spiritualité syriaque," in *Symposium Syriacum 1972, Orientalia Christiana Analecta* 197 (Rome, 1974), pp. 311-25.

118. So Murray, *Symbols*, pp. 263-69.

119. Vööbus, *History of Asceticism* I:184, n. 31.

120. Ibid., pp. 190-93, though the *Liber* concentrates on the second two, the

lay orders of Dionysius's own hierarchy, as well as having established roots in the Syriac tradition.[121] Secondly, though, and more importantly for our argument, there is the picture drawn in the *Liber's Discourse* 12, "On the Ministry of the Hidden and Manifest Church."[122] The writer is anxious to insist on the necessity of the visible Church and its liturgy. The Lord himself, he tells us, "established this Church, altar, and baptism, which can be seen by the body's eye" and did so in order that,

> by starting from these visible things, and provided that our bodies become temples and our hearts altars, we might find ourselves in their heavenly counterparts . . . migrating there and entering in while we are still in this visible Church.[123]

The latter's "priesthood and its ministry," as we just saw in Macarius, act "as fair examples for all those who imitate there the vigils, fasting, and endurance of our Lord."[124] To despise this visible Church, however, means that our body

> . . . will not become a temple, neither will our heart become an altar. . . . Nor shall we have revealed to us that Church on high with its altar, its light, and its priesthood, where are gathered all the saints who are pure in heart.[125]

The Church in heaven is shown forth in the "likeness" that is the earthly Church,[126] and it is the latter that makes of each believer "that body and heart where the Lord dwells . . . in truth a temple and an altar."[127] As we

---

righteous (laity) and the perfect (ascetics). See also A. Persic, "La Chiesa di Siria e i 'gradi' della vita Christiana," in *Per Foramen Acus* (Milano, 1986), pp. 208-63, esp. pp. 214ff.

121. The idea of a kind of triad can be found in Ephraem, too. See M. Schmidt, who underlines this and moreover draws an explict connection with Dionysius, "Alttestamentliche Typologien in den Paradieshymnen von Ephräm dem Syrer," *Paradeigmata*, ed. F. Link (Berlin, 1989), p. 78.

122. Kmosko, *PS* III:285-304. The translation is by S. Brock, *The Syriac Fathers on Prayer* (Kalamazoo, 1987), pp. 45-63.

123. Brock, p. 46, l. 2 (Kmosko, p. 288, l. 23–p. 289, l. 1).

124. Brock, p. 46 (Kmosko, p. 289, ll. 2-4).

125. Kmosko, p. 289, ll. 14-22.

126. Brock, p. 48 (Kmosko, p. 292, ll. 13-16).

127. Kmosko, p. 292, ll. 7-10.

noted above in discussing *Celestial Hierarchy* 1.3, there are therefore "three churches, and their ministries possess Life."[128] The earthly Church enables the Christian to "find himself in the Church of the heart and in the Church on high."[129] All three churches, all three liturgies, are necessary and all three are necessarily coordinated, though only the second (the heart) and the third (the heavenly original) will abide the eschaton.[130] There, "on the mountain of the Lord," which is the Church in heaven, "shines the light of the countenance of our Lord," and there alone is he "seen openly."[131]

Some Conclusions

To return to the point where we began, Father John was both correct and quite wrong. He was absolutely right to see Symeon and Nicetas carrying on a tradition inherited from the Areopagite. He was right, furthermore, in seeing the understanding of hierarchy as linked to the notion of the charismatic ascetic. He was wrong, however, in failing to note the eschatological character of this linkage and in reading Dionysius's hierarchy as "standing between the individual Christian and God," and thus as carrying over into Christian language the rigid system of Neoplatonist mediation. The Areopagite's hierarchy does not stand between — in the sense of blocking — anything, save in the way that we saw the earthly Church "standing between" heart and heaven in Macarius and the *Liber Graduum*. It is the necessary and, through Christ, divinely given image of both heart and heaven, the icon, in the sense of Hebrews 10:1, as opposed to the "shadow" of the Law.[132] On this issue, as so often happens to all of us in academia, Father John was following the scholarly consensus, and the consensus with regard to the *Areopagitica* was, and largely continues to be, insensitive to

---

128. Brock, p. 49, l. 4 (Kmosko, p. 294, ll. 23-24).

129. Kmosko, p. 296, ll. 8-10.

130. Thus recall, again, *DN* 1.4.

131. Brock, p. 7, ll. 42-43 (Kmosko, p. 301, l. 15–p. 304, l. 11). Note the "Mountain of the Lord" (Kmosko, p. 304, ll. 17-20), citing Ps. 24:3-5, and adding: "This is the heavenly Church," and recall Sinai in *MT* I.3 together with our observations concerning Evagrius in note 103 above.

132. See Dionysius on the relationship of the "Legal" to the "Ecclesiastical Hierarchy" in *EH* 3.3.5, 432B (p. 84, ll. 15-21) and esp. 5.1.2, 501B-D (p. 104, l. 15–p. 105, l. 21).

important elements in the tradition out of which Dionysius came. The monks, I think, have always known better.

As for the issue of ecclesiological (and sacramental) "subjectivism" that Father John raised with respect to all three of our authors, there, indeed, he pointed to a real problem. I have no intention of trying to maintain that Dionysius — or Symeon or Nicetas for that matter — has solved it. The notion of hierarchy as I believe we find it in the Areopagite oscillates or, perhaps better, shimmers somewhere between objective and subjective realities. If we push Dionysius too hard in either direction, then, certainly, we do end up in difficulties. It is clear, empirical fact that clerical office holders are not always, or even often, holy men. On the other hand, if we were to push the "charismatic" option to its limits, as Symeon almost does, then we would end up dissolving the visible structures of the Church quite entirely. The key, though, is that "almost." Neither the New Theologian, nor his disciple, nor Dionysius do push their logic to the limits. They are content with ambiguity, and they are thus very wise. Wise, too, is the Orthodox tradition, because it has never sought to resolve an ambiguity that constitutes, in fact, one of the fundamental antinomies of Christian existence *in statu via*.[133] The tension between charisma and institution, or *Geist* and *Amt,* does not admit of any resolution this side of the eschaton. The fact of this strain between the pneumatic and institutional facets of the Church's life was one of Father John's own favorite themes. He upheld it, together with its resulting ambiguities, consistently and approvingly.[134] It is one of the lessons that I received most gratefully as his student and that I hope I have served to illustrate in this essay, offered as a tribute to the man who introduced me to the Fathers, who was also patron and friend, and whom I look forward to greeting — God being merciful to me, a sinner — in the liturgy of heaven. *Lux perpetua luceat ei.*

133. Murray, *Symbols,* pp. 275f., makes the same point regarding Macarius and the *Liber Graduum.*

134. See, for example, his two essays, "The Holy Spirit as God" and "St. Basil, the Church, and Charismatic Leadership," in *The Byzantine Legacy in the Orthodox Church* (Crestwood, 1982), pp. 153-65, esp. 162-65, and pp. 197-215, esp. 204-15, respectively.

SCRIPTURE AND EXEGESIS

Which Paul? Observations on the Image of the Apostle in the History of Biblical Exegesis

KARLFRIED FROEHLICH

For the understanding of the Christian tradition as a whole, the history of biblical interpretation is as important as the biblical texts themselves. No one can do biblical exegesis or make the transition from text to application without being mindful of the filter of centuries of Christian commitment to these texts. This insight, which seems to have become a commonplace in hermeneutical discussion today, renders the contemporary task of exegesis at the same time more complex than is often assumed in the theological community and more rewarding in the context of our ecumenical situation. East and West, North and South approach the task in their own framework of experience and form the ongoing agenda of their biblical faith on this basis. The biblical text is shared by all, and interpretation of it reflects the history of our divisions, both in their troubling dimension of estrangement and separation and in the promise of enriching diversity. We need to know what decisions were made, what switches were thrown, and what options were chosen by those generations to which we look as parents in our various faith communities in order to realize what it will take to live in closer church fellowship with each other in the future. Father John Meyendorff has done more than others in fostering this knowledge and in raising consciousness about the shared basis of our faith as well as the differences in outlook. The following essay is dedicated to him as a tribute to his spirit and the model he has set before us.

When we think of competent biblical exegesis in the academic world today, we probably have a fairly clear idea of what it is. It is the attempt to find out exactly what a particular author said, using all the tools available to literary scholars when they study a text: linguistic analysis, literary criticism, history, the social sciences. The Greek term ἐξήγησις meant just that. As a technical term, it belongs in the context of secondary education in the Hellenistic world in which the appropriation of the literary heritage, especially Homer and the ancient poets, was the goal.[1] "Exegesis" was the third step of the curriculum taught by the high school teacher, the γραμματικός. It followed textual reconstruction (διόρθωσις) and reading and declamation (ἀνάγνωσις). This third step involved the basic explanation of the text with a focus on vocabulary, grammar, syntax, and the rudiments of mythology, which one had to know in order to understand the ancient poems. One can easily see that in this sense "exegesis" was the matrix of the literary genre of "commentary" in the Hellenistic world. Commentaries were schoolbooks — tools for textual study and nothing more.[2] But this painstaking philological work was not all to which a student was exposed. The curriculum included one further step, the μέρος κριτικόν, "critical" interpretation. The idea was that the teacher would apply the classical texts to the present by introducing the students to the values and the ethos of the Homeric world, which was at the root of the self-understanding of Greek society. The μέρος κριτικόν was meant to explain *why* Homer was a classic and why all the drudgery of textual exegesis was a worthwhile enterprise. At the hands of a good teacher, this exercise in social adjustment may well have been the exciting part of the school experience for many students.

The Christian biblical commentary included this "critical" step from the very beginning. No Christian teacher would investigate the details of an Old Testament text without considering the meaning of the Jewish Scriptures in the framework of the new Christian self-understanding. Otherwise, why should one burden Gentiles with the study of the books of the Jews? The reason is easy to comprehend: For Christians, the task of "exegesis," of finding out what the biblical author meant, was determined by the conviction of the divine origin of "all scripture" (cf. 2 Tim. 3:16),

---

1. For the following, see Henri-Irénée Marrou. *A History of Education in Classical Antiquity* (New York: Sheed and Ward, 1956), pp. 166ff.

2. Rudolf Pfeiffer, *History of Classical Scholarship from the Beginnings to the End of the Hellenistic Age* (Oxford: Clarendon, 1968); Karlfried Froehlich, "Bibelkommentare — zur Krise einer Gattung," *Zeitschrift für Theologie und Kirche* 84 (1987), pp. 465-92.

the real author of both "Testaments," the Old and the New, being none other than God. Nothing reveals this hermeneutical framework more clearly than the legend of the origin of the Septuagint, the standard Greek translation of the Hebrew Bible, which Greco-Roman Christianity regarded as even more "inspired" than the Hebrew original. In its pre-Christian form, recorded at length in the pseudepigraphical *Letter of Aristeas* (ca. 140-120 B.C.),[3] the story told of a third-century Ptolemaic king who wanted to include Greek translations of all important writings of the world in his library at Alexandria and asked the Jerusalem authorities for help. Seventy-two emissaries, six from each tribe of Israel, went to work on the translation of the Pentateuch. Their drafts were compared, and the whole work, finished in seventy-two days, was endorsed by the Jewish community in Alexandria. The later Christian version, following Philo, greatly enhanced the miraculous aspect of the event. Irenaeus pictured seventy translators working in total isolation from each other, each in his own cell, and emerging with exactly the same text, this time of the entire Old Testament.[4] Undoubtedly, as Augustine emphasized, the author of *this* text was God.[5] Nothing quite comparable could be said about the Hebrew Bible. It is no surprise, then, to hear of near-riots in a church of Augustine's neighborhood when the bishop introduced Jerome's new Vulgate translation, based on the Hebrew, in the chanted readings of the liturgy instead of the Old Latin version, which derived from the Septuagint.[6] For Christians, exegeting a biblical text, especially from the Old Testament, asking what the author was saying simply had to include the question of *God's* intention, of the *theological* meaning of the text. Even today, biblical exegesis as a meaningful exercise in the church cannot exclude the μέρος κριτικόν, the question of how the text speaks to us today, how, through it, the Word of the God of all times and places may become perceptible as "Word of God for us" in our world. What else can be the task of a preacher who is supposed to wrestle with a text in preparation of his or her sermon?

3. Translated by R. J. H. Shutt in James H. Charlesworth (ed.), *The Old Testament Pseudepigrapha* (Garden City, NY: Doubleday, 1983) II, pp. 7-43.

4. Irenaeus, *Adversus haereses* 3.31.

5. Augustine, *De doctrina Christiana* 3.15.22; *De civitate Dei* 18.42-43.

6. Augustine, *Epistola* 71.3.5. The case concerned the rendering of the name of the plant under which the prophet Jonah was resting (Jonah 4:6); Jerome replaced "gourd" by "ivy" on the evidence of the Hebrew and other Greek translations. Cf. his defense and Augustine's final comment in *Epistola* 75.7.22 and 82.5.36.

Over the centuries, the Epistles of Paul have served as a major resource, perhaps *the* major resource, for this task of Christian preachers and Bible readers. Along with the Gospel, we read the "Epistle" in our worship services, and most of these texts come from the Epistles of Paul. They often provide the theological key for the meaning of the Gospel and the Old Testament lesson under the theme of the day. In the West, commentaries on the Epistle to the Romans have more than once become the vehicles of major syntheses and breakthroughs in theology. Here is the place where theological decisions have been made, switches thrown, and the deepest issues of truth and value raised. Augustine immersed himself in Romans at the time of his final conversion and again during his study leave before he took up his duties at Hippo Regius. Abelard articulated his ethics of intentionality most powerfully in his commentary on Romans. Martin Luther's theology found its decisive shape during his first lecture course on Romans. Karl Barth wrote his *Römerbrief* as a theological indictment of the prevalent values of the culture-Protestantism of his day. Barth's commentary has been criticized for being all *krisis* and offering little *exegesis*. But even the most important recent Romans commentary by a professional Protestant exegete, Ernst Käsemann, displays this daring, this genuine theological passion that the study of Paul's Epistle to the Romans has so often triggered.[7] Käsemann's commentary gives the reader a strong dose of the more pedestrian fare, the philological and historical exegesis of textual details. But it engages one's full attention precisely at the points where the author turns "theological" — fighting the dangers of certain modern theologies that claim to rest on Paul but actively disparage central tenets of the Pauline message. Behind the critical discussion in each of these instances the reader senses the author's passionate concern for a theology of Christian freedom that he thinks must be defended against the straitjackets of a supposed Pauline mysticism, sacramentalism, and institutionalism, but also a supposed Pauline subjectivism, moralism, and pietism. The blows fall densely to the right and to the left, one after another. One is reminded of the powerful image of Jude 9, the archangel Michael contending with the devil and disputing over the body of Moses — a fight of truly cosmic dimensions. Käsemann wages his battle in the

---

7. Ernst Käsemann. *An die Römer* (Handbuch zum Neuen Testament; Tübingen: Mohr, 4th ed., 1980), translated as *Commentary on Romans* (Grand Rapids: Eerdmans, 1980).

name of the true Paul of Romans. But Käsemann's Paul is not a dead body, a corpse out of the past. His Paul challenges the reader to hear the voice of God in the living word of the ancient writer. Käsemann's Paul? Can one say that? Käsemann has been criticized for presenting nothing more — at best a "typically Lutheran" Paul, at worst an idiosyncratic Paul who reflects more the personality of the author of the commentary than that of the author of the letter. Which Paul? Is there a "true" Paul anywhere, at least in Romans? The question is not new. The fight over the true Paul goes all the way back to the Christian beginnings when the Pauline Epistles were canonized. Even more significantly, the process itself of the reception of Paul into the canon reflects the struggle over the very definition of what may be claimed to be authentic Christianity and what may not. Let me illustrate by pointing to three major disputes over the meaning of the "true" Paul in the Early Church.

The first is the Marcionite crisis in the middle of the second century.[8] Marcion was a layman of some means who at first joined the church at Rome but then founded his own counter-church when the Roman congregation became suspicious of his theology and excluded him from its ranks. Marcion seems to have been the first to "canonize " a collection of Pauline Epistles and to claim their substance as the authoritative basis for his understanding of the true Christian religion. His Paul was the only authentic apostle of Christ and of the unknown, good God whom Jesus Christ proclaimed. While we do not have the actual text of the corpus of his Pauline letters, the very arrangement of his collection reveals its polemical thrust: Galatians, not Romans, leads the list — the letter in which Paul argues most vividly against "Judaizers," that is, the advocates of the inferior Old Testament God and his evil laws, according to Marcion. The anti-Marcionite writers of the later second century, especially Irenaeus of Lyons, fought not only against Marcion's rejection of the Jewish scriptures for Christians but

---

8. Our main source is the anti-Marcionite polemic of the church fathers, especially Tertullian. Adolf von Harnack's magisterial monograph of 1921, *Marcion: Das Evangelium vom fremden Gott,* collected a wealth of material and argued for a more sympathetic appreciation of Marcion's reforming spirit and his Paulinism. This latter point is shared by R. Joseph Hoffmann, the author of the most recent monograph: *Marcion: On the Restitution of Christianity. An Essay on the Development of Radical Paulinist Theology in the Second Century* (AAR Academy Series, 46; Chico, CA: Scholars, 1984), who attempts, however, to alter the scholarly direction of post-Harnack research in most other respects.

accused him also of arbitrariness in dealing with the Gospels, of which he retained only a purged form of Luke. Irenaeus was the first to use an enlarged Pauline corpus that included the Pastoral Epistles, implying that they existed before Marcion's time and were kept out by him because they contradicted the Marcionite interpretation of Paul. Both the early date, however, and the implication are highly doubtful. In fact, some scholars have postulated an anti-Marcionite origin for the Pastorals, seeking their author in a Lucan circle in Asia Minor or in the person of the martyr bishop Polycarp of Smyrna.[9] Of even greater interest is the Paul whom Tertullian defends against the Marcionites at the beginning of the third century. In Tertullian's writings we see the consequences of having to advocate a canonical Paul whose works included the Pastoral Epistles as authentic. Tertullian did honor Paul as an apostle, even as a special vessel of God's election, drawing on the Epistles as well as the Book of Acts. But he clearly reacted against the super-authoritative Paul of the Marcionites. Paul for him was an apostle alongside the Twelve, to whom he was "posterior" by his own admission. At one point, Tertullian called him "the apostle of the heretics" *(haereticorum apostolus).*[10] The term does not disqualify Paul as an apostle altogether, but it certainly does not qualify him as *the* apostle either. Tertullian's interpretation of Galatians 1–2 simply ignored the thrust of verses in which Paul insists that he does not owe his gospel to any human authority (1:11-17). Tertullian emphasizes instead that Paul needed and was granted approval for his mission from the Jerusalem apostles. Thus, according to Tertullian, Paul's opposition to Peter at Antioch (Gal. 2:11-14) was the overreaction of a recent convert, to put it mildly, rather than a necessary correction.[11] Against Marcion, Tertullian also tries to minimize Paul's seeming criticism of the Law, especially in Romans. Law and Gospel, he holds, are not antithetical, as if they came from two different Gods. What was abolished with the coming of Christ were the "burdens" *(onera legis),* the ceremonial law, not the decalogue and the moral precepts of God.

A second front that saw the clash of rival understandings of Paul was the fight over Christian Gnosticism in the second and third centuries. Elaine

---

9. See Hans von Campenhausen. *Polykarp von Smyrna und die Pastoralbriefe* (Sitzungsberichte der Heidelberger Akademie der Wissenschaften, Philosophisch-historische Klasse, Jahrgang 1951:2; Heidelberg: Winter, 1951).

10. *Adversus Marcionem* 3.5.4.

11. *Adversus Marcionem* 1.20; 4:3.

Pagels has shown that the Valentinian Gnostics developed the descriptive grid by which they presented their cosmology and soteriology as Christian from terminology they found in Paul's letters: "outer" and "inner" person; "flesh," "soul," and "spirit"; "spirit" and "letter"; "gnosis," "wisdom," etc. Obviously, for them Paul was a normative teacher.[12] Irenaeus did not challenge the Valentinian use of Christian writings or of the Pauline Epistles as such, but he rejected their claim to possess a truer understanding than that of other readers. Their Gnostic Paul, he held, was a secondary construct, deliberately distorting the message of the Apostle about Christ and salvation to fit their preconceived systems. Gnostics were like people who take apart the beautiful mosaic of a king and reassemble the pieces into the picture of a wild dog or some horrible monster.[13] The anti-Gnostic front still dominated the Pauline interpretation of theologians in the third century as far as we can judge from the scant evidence. It is even possible that the first running commentaries on the Pauline Epistles, those of Origen, of which the Romans commentary is preserved,[14] were actually written to refute similar Gnostic attempts by carefully retracing the Apostle's argument sentence by sentence.

The purpose of writing a detailed commentary in order to prove a particular use of Paul's letters wrong must probably be assumed also in the third instance of a clash between rival understandings of the Apostle, the amazing "Renaissance of Paul" among Western theologians of the late fourth century and their opponents. The term refers to the phenomenon that, after a total Western silence during the earlier centuries, no less than six major Latin commentaries on the Pauline corpus were written during the fifty years between A.D. 360 and 410, those of Marius Victorinus, the so-called Ambrosiaster, Jerome, Augustine, Pelagius, and the Budapest *anonymus*.[15] These commentaries have nothing to do with the Pelagian

---

12. Elaine Pagels, "The Valentinian Claim to Esoteric Exegesis of Romans as Basis for Anthropological Theory," *Vigiliae Christianae* 26 (1972), pp. 241-58; *The Gnostic Paul: Gnostic Exegesis of the Pauline Letters* (Philadelphia: Fortress Press, 1975).

13. *Adversus Haereses* 1.8.1; 1.9.4.

14. See the recent edition by Caroline P. H. Bammel, *Der Römerbriefkommentar des Origenes. Kritische Ausgabe der Übersetzung Rufins, Buch 1-3* (Vetus Latina. Aus der Geschichte der lateinischen Bibel, vol. 16; Freiburg: Herder, 1990).

15. The last-mentioned text was identified and published by H. J. Frede: *Ein neuer Paulustext und Kommentar* (2 vols., Vetus Latina, 7-8; Freiburg: Herder, 1973-74). Frede dated it to about A.D. 396 to 405.

controversy; even Pelagius' own commentary antedates the beginning of that struggle, contributing to its rise rather than being its fruit. Some of them reveal no obvious polemical purpose. One scholar has pointed to the parallel phenomenon of several exegetical tracts on the book of Job that were written at that time, and he wonders whether the interest in both Paul and Job may reflect the replacement of an earlier naive triumphalism among Christians by a new mood of gloom and the resulting preoccupation with theodicy — the problem of God's power in a world of human failure — and the nature of evil.[16] For the early Augustine, however, a much more specific polemical front must be acknowledged. We have from his pen three pieces of Pauline commentary, all dating from the first years of his tenure at Hippo: a brief exposition of Galatians, a miscellany of eighty-four "propositions," mainly on Romans 7–9, and a long fragment on the opening lines of Romans. Paula Fredriksen Landes, the latest editor and translator of the Romans materials,[17] has demonstrated that Augustine developed his Paulinism in antithesis to the Manichean Paul he had encountered while being a member of this powerful religious movement. Manicheans were not only dualists in their cosmology and anthropology. Like Marcion, their leaders in North Africa rejected the Old Testament and used the Pauline Epistles to argue against the "unspiritual law" in all its forms. Paul was their main religious hero after Mani, their founder. Polemic against the Manichean Paul in the wider context of the fight against fatalism can also be discerned behind the first of this group of new commentaries, the one by Marius Victorinus. Victorinus was the great Neoplatonic philosopher whose public turn to Christianity had such a decisive influence on Augustine's conversion. Recent close inspection of his works has revealed additional polemical intentions.[18] As a professional philosopher, Victorinus wanted

16. Wilhelm Geerlings, "Hiob und Paulus: Theodizee und Paulinismus in der lateinischen Theologie am Ausgang des vierten Jahrhunderts," *Jahrbuch für Antike und Christentum* 24 (1981), pp. 56-66.

17. *Augustine on Romans: Propositions from the Epistle to the Romans, Unfinished Commentary on the Epistle to the Romans* (SBL Texts and Translations, 23; Chico, CA: Scholars, 1982).

18. W. Erdt, *Marius Victorinus Afer, der erste lateinische Pauluskommentator* (Europäische Hochschulschriften, Ser. 23, Theologie, 135; Bern: Lang, 1980). The Latin text of the three extant commentaries (the Romans commentary is lost) is available in *Marii Victorini Afri commentarii in epistulas Pauli ad Galatas, ad Philippenses, ad Ephesios*, ed. Albrecht Locher (Bibliotheca Teubneriana; Leipzig: Teubner, 1972).

to refute pagan philosophical polemicists such as Porphyry and Emperor Julian who poured out their contempt for Paul. He also tried to establish Nicene orthodoxy against the use of Paul by the Arians. His argument was meant to be "professional," that is, philosophical. For this purpose he used quite deliberately the genre of the detailed commentary of an authoritative text, in this case Paul. It was a proven method of philosophical demonstration that he himself had used in commentaries on Cicero and other authors. One could argue that the example of this highly respected commentator triggered the attempts of other Latin authors to develop the true Christian philosophy against detractors of all kinds by writing commentaries on Paul in the wake of the Western acceptance of anti-Arianism as orthodoxy in the middle of the fourth century.

Our three examples of clashes between rival interpretations of Paul in the Early Church should have made several things quite clear as we think of "Paul and the Legacies of Paul." William Babcock, the editor of a recent volume with this title, takes great pains to combat a "distressingly stereo-typed pattern" prevalent among Protestants, a pattern that finds the true legacy of Paul only in marginal or ultimately heretical versions of early Christianity while claiming that the mainline church ignored Paul. He characterizes it as a tendency that praises the Western Augustine for his advocacy of justification by grace and faith apart from works while despising the Greek and Eastern tradition.[19] Babcock is certainly correct in his criticism. But is this tendency the only possible misconstruction? While the theory of a marginal Paul who was belittled, suppressed, and misunderstood by the mainstream Church until Augustine and Luther came along is untenable, the contrary theory of a smooth, linear reception of Paul into the theology of the early church is equally doubtful.[20] It assumes that from the beginning Paul was a dominant factor in the formation of Christian thought and identity, that his letters were collected early on, and that they were later enriched by deutero-Pauline materials representing a Pauline "school" that tried to protect the master from unwarranted conclusions others drew from his writings. Thus, these scholars hold, while an unintentional adaptation

19. Introduction, in: William S. Babcok, ed. *Paul and the Legacies of Paul* (Dallas: Southern Methodist University, 1990), pp. xiii-xxviii; here pp. xiii-xv.

20. I think, e.g., of the important study by Karl Hermann Schelkle, *Paulus, Lehrer der Väter: Die altkirchliche Auslegung von Römer 1–11* (Düsseldorf: Patmos, 1956), or Otto Kuss, *Paulus. Die Rolle des Apostels in der theologischen Entwicklung der Urkirche* (Regensburg: Pustet, 1971).

of Pauline theology to the needs of later generations may have been at work in these efforts and while the absorption of the Pauline theology into a mainline frame of mind may have obscured parts of the real Paul, true Paulinism has always been effective in interpretation.

I submit that we may have to reckon with a far more confusing situation, a constant back and forth of assertions and reactions, endorsements and rejections, in short, a much more colorful palette of normative images of Paul. Which Paul influenced the beginnings of Christian theology? Which Pauline "school" upheld the true Paul against distortions? To which church was which Pauline theology adapted? There are no easy answers to these bewildering questions.

Focusing on the Pauline Epistles, we should not forget that there is early evidence of reticent, if not outright critical, reactions coming from various quarters. There is the caution expressed in 2 Peter 3:16, a document basically sympathetic to Paul: "So also our beloved brother Paul wrote to you according to the wisdom given him, speaking of this as he does in all his letters. Some things in them are hard to understand, which the ignorant and unstable twist to their own destruction. . . ." Or the well-known passage about faith and works in James 2:14-26. It may well be that the author of James does not intend to attack the teachings of Paul's letters directly, but he certainly argues against some kind of "Paulinists." We also have the phenomenon of an early Jewish Christian antagonism to Paul. It has been treated recently by Gerd Lüdemann in a book entitled, *Opposition to Paul in Jewish Christianity.*[21] The centerpiece of evidence here is the pseudo-Clementine literature, a sentimental Christian novel about the accidental separation of a Christian family and its final reunion. The oldest source used in these writings constantly attacks the person and the letters of Paul under the name of Simon the Magician, whose evil plots against the apostles are reported in Acts 8.

I for one still wonder about the alleged universal impact of Paul's letters on Christians in the second century. Fifteen years ago, Ernst Dassmann surveyed the material once more and concluded that "a large number of writings of all kinds and genres of early Christian literature betray a knowledge of the person and work of Paul."[22] Dassmann's discus-

---

21. Gerd Luedemann, *Opposition to Paul in Jewish Christianity,* tr. Eugene Boring (Minneapolis: Fortress, 1989).

22. Ernst Dassmann, *Der Stachel im Fleisch: Paulus in der frühchristlichen Literatur bis Irenaeus* (Münster: Aschendorff, 1979), p. 316.

sion was balanced and allowed for variety in the attitudes toward Paul. With regard to Paul's letters, however, I am still impressed by the large number of writings that demonstrate no knowledge or interest in Paul's letters at all: the Acts of the Apostles, the Didache, the Epistle of Barnabas, 2 Clement, Hermas, Papias, Hegesippus, Aristides the Apologist. One can cite good reasons for their silence. Nevertheless, it seems clear that reliance on the Pauline Epistles and their theology did not belong to the indispensable conditions of early Christian theologizing.

With Dassmann and others, we may even have to distinguish between knowledge of Paul's *work* and knowledge of his *person* among early Christians, the Paul of the Epistles and the Paul of tales and legends. It seems that the tradition of a Pauline legend glorifying the great preacher, missionary, and miracle worker antedates the epistolary collection by a considerable margin. Small collections of some Pauline letters may have circulated locally after the Apostle's death, but the legendary Paul had a life independent of such material. A number of apocryphal writings of the late second and early third centuries bear witness to a popular veneration of Paul that was nourished by independent traditions unrelated to the Epistles. The most interesting piece is the *Acta Pauli,* which tell with rhetorical flourish the story of Paul's missionary triumphs in Asia Minor, including the conversion of Saint Thecla, and of his final exploits. In a study published in 1983, Dennis MacDonald linked the development of the Pauline legend to two unusual hypotheses.[23] First, he assumed that the *Acta Pauli* rested on older oral traditions. Taking his cue from the prominence of Paul's convert Thecla and the theme of chastity throughout the text, he claimed a Pauline circle of ascetic women as the most likely matrix for these tales and thus for the legendary Paul of the *Acta.* The second hypothesis introduced the Pastoral Epistles. Macdonald suggested that they were composed precisely in reaction to this sectarian image of the Apostle by presenting Paul as a conservative leader who wanted to silence the tale-telling women. For evidence supporting this interpretation he appealed to 1 Tim. 4:7, which the RSV translated: "Have nothing to do with godless and silly myths." "Silly myths" is certainly not what the Greek has here: μύθοι γραώδεις. The adjective γραώδεις is derived from γραῦς, "old woman": the stories or "myths" are those told by old women. The NRSV has vindicated

---

23. Dennis R. MacDonald, *The Legend and the Apostle: The Battle for Paul in Story and Canon* (Philadelphia: Westminster, 1983).

MacDonald on this point. It translates: "Have nothing to do with profane myths and old wives' tales."

While the basis for these bold hypotheses is slim, there are some implications worth pondering. It is an undisputed fact that the archaeological and liturgical evidence for a veneration of Paul (apart from his pairing with Peter in Rome) is extremely meager, even in places such as Ephesus, Salonica, Philippi, and Corinth where one would think he would be remembered.[24] Perhaps he was not, or not favorably. In Asia Minor, the Thecla cult of Seleucia vastly outdistanced any traces of veneration for Paul. In the iconography of Paul and Thecla, the Apostle appears more as a companion figure of the female saint, not as the main subject.[25] To those groups of ascetic women it was perhaps Thecla, not Paul, who was really important as a Christian heroine and role model. Should one conclude that neither Paul's Epistles nor his reputation as a holy man in themselves were impressive enough to secure him special love and respect in this area? A second implication that imposes itself is this: We cannot simply *assume* that the Pastoral Epistles were the legitimate second-century heirs of the Pauline heritage. They are important witnesses to *one* of the ongoing Pauline traditions, but for the second century we have to reckon with a plurality of "Pauls," all of whom had their supporters and detractors in various circles of Christians. The theory of a single "Pauline school" is probably insufficient. Pauline pluralism was fed, on the one hand, by an appropriation of his legendary image with regional variations. On the other hand, more importantly, it was fed by the many unreconciled strands and the general versatility of Paul's own theologizing in the surviving remnants of his correspondence. What the historical Paul fervently desired but never accomplished the epistolary Paul finally achieved: It was he who became "all things to all people" (1 Cor. 9:22).

This insight holds true even for the time of the fully canonized Paul of later centuries. Ernst Benz, one of the finest Protestant interpreters of Eastern Orthodoxy in his generation, made a similar point fifty years ago in a discussion of the differences between East and West.[26] In a general

24. Ernst Dassmann, "Archäologische Spuren frühchristlicher Paulusverehrung," *Römische Quartalschrift* 84 (1989), pp. 271-98.

25. Ernst Dassmann, *Paulus in frühchristlicher Frömmigkeit und Kunst* (Rheinisch-Westfälische Akademie der Wissenschaften; Geisteswissenschaftliche Vorträge, G 256; Opladen: Westdeutscher Verlag, 1982).

26. Ernst Benz, "Das Paulusverständnis in der morgenländischen und abendländischen Kirche," *Zeitschrift für Religions- und Geistesgeschichte* 3 (1951), pp. 289-309.

sense, Benz said, Western theology was always concerned with the juridical aspect of the relationship between humanity and God, with law and gospel, covenant and human obligation. The East, on the other hand, stressed soteriological themes such as θεῶσις, rebirth, new creation, resurrection, and the glorification of human nature. Consequently, the Eastern churches on the whole remained less receptive to the thematic field of justification as Paul had laid it out in Romans, and they never developed a specific "doctrine of justification." Instead, the East took up and deepened the mystical impulses of Pauline theology, the themes of christology, the sacraments, the Holy Spirit, and the spiritual gifts that the West never fully pursued except in a partial, muted, and ecclesiastically oriented form. As proof of his observation, Benz pointed to the history of Pauline exegesis: The great interest in Romans in the West from the fourth century on was not shared in the East. None of the great Eastern Fathers of the fourth century produced a commentary on Romans; Didymus the Blind wrote on the Corinthian Epistles, Galatians, and Ephesians, but not on Romans. When John Chrysostom and some of the later Antiochene exegetes included an interpretation of Romans, it was more for the sake of completeness; the central themes of the Epistle found little echo here. Benz concluded that, roughly speaking, "the East could be described as having accepted the Paul of Corinthians, the West the Paul of Romans" (p. 291).

Today we would have to question Benz's proof from the distribution of commentaries. From fragments preserved in exegetical chains we know that, just as in the West, there were Arianizing and anti-Arian commentaries on Romans written by Greek theologians of the late fourth century, and the sustained interest in Romans among the theologians of the Antiochian school demands an explanation. But Benz's basic point remains an intriguing invitation for further exploration.[27] Compared with the East, the interest in Romans and its theological themes has been much greater than in the West. A recent author counted more than fifty Romans commentaries in the Latin Middle Ages produced before 1300.[28] Of course, not all of these

27. Benz's thesis was sympathetically reviewed by Dassmann in 1986: "Zum Paulusverständnis in der östlichen Kirche," *Jahrbuch für Antike und Christentum* 29 (1986), pp. 27-39.

28. See the appendix in Werner Affeldt, *Die weltliche Gewalt in der Paulusexegese: Römer 13,1-7 in den Römerbriefkommentaren bis zum Ende des dreizehnten Jahrhunderts* (Forschungen zur Kirchen- und Dogmengeschichte, 22; Göttingen: Vandenhoeck und Ruprecht, 1969), pp. 256-85.

writings offered new and independent interpretations. From the sixth to the eleventh century, "commentaries" were mostly collections of older expositions making available the heritage of patristic exegesis for Christian education in the barbarian civilizations of early medieval Europe. The monasteries were centers of schooling. It is to the humble work of monks and nuns nourished in the spirit of Saint Basil, Saint Benedict, and Cassiodorus that we owe the preservation of most of the Latin texts I have mentioned so far. Monastic schooling and writing made possible the new ferment of the scholastic age, in which the methods and routines of modern academic life have their root. The twelfth century already saw a tremendous upsurge in commentary production; no less than twenty unpublished Romans commentaries from that period alone are known to exist. Much work still needs to be done here, and surprises are to be expected. It has become clear, for example, that an anonymous commentary from the latter half of the twelfth century, much used in the thirteenth, served as an agent in spreading Peter Abaelard's innovative Romans interpretation to a much wider audience than scholars had hitherto realized.[29]

Incidentally, this standard commentary from the school of St. Victor in Paris bears the title *Allegoriae in Novum Testamentum*. For the treatment of the Pauline Epistles this title is quite incorrect. There is no allegorization to speak of. This should not be a surprise. A reader who expects medieval exegetes to expound their texts regularly according to the so-called fourfold method of literal, allegorical, tropological, and anagogical sense, or at least a twofold method of literal and spiritual interpretation, will find that this multiplicity is practically absent in medieval commentaries on the Pauline Epistles. They all pursue one sense, the literal. The reason probably is quite simple and has to do with the perceived role of Paul in the biblical canon. Medieval theologians no longer regarded "allegory" as synonymous with "spiritual interpretation" in general, as had been the case in earlier centuries. In its precise technical sense, allegory meant the interpretation of Old Testament passages in New Testament terms or, more comprehensively, of

---

29. See these studies by Rolf Peppermüller: *Abaelards Auslegung des Römerbriefs* (Beiträge zur Geschichte und Philosophie des Mittelalters, Texte und Untersuchungen, n.s., 10; Münster: Aschendorff, 1972) and "Zum Fortwirken von Abälards Römerbriefkommentar," in *Pierre Abélard — Pierre le Vénérable. Les courants philosophiques, littéraires et artistiques en occident au milieu du XIIe siècle* (Paris: CNRS, 1975), pp. 557-68. The commentary was printed among the works of Hugh of St. Victor in J. P. Migne's *Patrologia Latina*, vol. 175, cols. 879-904.

any scripture in terms of the system of Christian doctrine.[30] In the texts of the Old Testament and in Jesus' stories and parables this doctrine was "hidden"; the Old Testament writers proclaimed the mysteries of Christ under a veil. The apostles and evangelists, however, declared the full truth without cover.

As the obvious latecomer, Paul was the last of the inspired canonical writers. In this sense, he stood at the end of a line. At the same time, however, he was the first *doctor evangelii*, God's chosen teacher of the nations, opening the long line of biblical interpreters after him. Paul's letters were therefore regarded as *manifesta expositio*. In their own literal sense, they contained the full truth about the Old Testament and the story of Christ without any cover needing to be lifted and with no further allegory to be supplied. In the East, John the apostle and evangelist was called ὁ θεόλογος, the theologian. In the West, the theologian was Paul. He was the dove that first carried the sprouting olive twig of the nascent doctrine of Christ to the ark, the symbol of the Church from all nations. He was the steward at the Wedding Feast of Cana, the first to serve to the wedding guests the new, superior wine into which the Lord had changed the old water. If Peter was given the key of the kingdom, Paul received the key of knowledge, which opens the meaning of the law and the prophets. Historians agree that the development of "theology" as an academic discipline in the Middle Ages began with exegetical *quaestiones* being added to the exposition of biblical books in the schools of the twelfth century.[31] We probably need to be even more specific: these "questions" were added to the exposition of the *Pauline Epistles*, primarily Romans, and this was done in the work of Peter Abelard and his school. Here Paul became the model teacher of the new dialectic and thus of the new way of doing theology. His language provided the norm, the purest expression of the truth that any theological formulation of Christian doctrine was intended to convey.

Thomas Aquinas wrote a Romans commentary himself. His interpretation exemplifies the central role that Paul had assumed for the whole

---

30. Hugh of St. Victor, *Didascalicon* 6.4, English tr. in Jerome Taylor, *The Didascalicon of Hugh of St. Victor* (New York: Columbia University, 1961), pp. 139-44.

31. See, e.g., G. R. Evans, *Old Arts and New Theology: The Beginnings of Theology as an Academic Discipline* (Oxford: Clarendon, 1980). Much of the pioneering work in this field is contained in the eight volumes of Arthur Maria Landgraf's *Dogmengeschichte der Frühscholastik* (Regensburg: Pustet, 1952-56).

enterprise of scholastic theology.[32] Thomas's commentary begins with a *laudatio* of Paul, for which he selected a Bible verse to serve as the theme, as was the custom at Paris. He chose Acts 9:5: *"Vas electionis est mihi iste"* — "this one is a vessel of election for me, to carry my name before nations and kings and before the people of Israel." Vessels have a purpose. They contain something and allow it to be carried to distant places. Paul was destined by God to carry the name of Jesus, the very sum of redemptive doctrine, to all people, present, absent, and future by handing on the Christ of Scripture in his teaching. Among the books of the Old Testament, the Psalms are most frequently used in the Church. Among the books of the New Testament it is the Epistles of Paul. The reason is — so Thomas — that both authors, David and Paul, speak as forgiven sinners or, even more plausibly because "these two books contain almost the entire teaching of all theology."[33]

This image of Paul must be placed in the context of Thomas's self-understanding as a teacher, to which he gave vivid expression in his inaugural lecture as a young university master. Legend claims that Thomas received the Scripture verse for this address from an angel: *"Rigans montes"* — "Watering the mountains from his heights, the earth will be satisfied by the fruit of your works" (Ps. 103:13).[34] The mountains are the teachers. Theirs is an exposed, elevated position. They are placed high. The illumining rays of the sun in the morning touch them first. The vital waters from above drench first the peaks and from them run down in streams to moisten and fructify the plains. Teachers are the essential mediators of the life-giving truth, and Paul was the first of them.

In a delightful essay, Otto Hermann Pesch has described Aquinas's Paul as "the professor among the apostles."[35] Indeed, Thomas saw in the

---

32. I have used the text published in the Parma Edition, vol. 13. There is no English translation as yet. A thorough analysis of the commentary was published by Thomas Domanyi: *Der Römerbriefkommentar des Thomas von Aquin: Ein Beitrag zur Untersuchung seiner Auslegungsmethoden* (Basler und Berner Studien zur historischen und systematischen Theologie, 39; Bern: Lang, 1979).

33. Thomas Aquinas, *Opera Omnia* (Parma ed.), vol. 13, p. 2b.

34. An English translation may be found in *Albert and Thomas: Selected Writings*, tr. and ed. Simon Tugwell, O.P. (Classics of Western Spirituality; New York: Paulist, 1988), pp. 355-60.

35. Otto Hermann Pesch, "Paul as Professor of Theology: The Image of the Apostle in St. Thomas' Theology," *The Thomist* 38 (1974), pp. 584-605.

Paul of the Epistles not only the teacher of the *content* of Christian doctrine but also the master of its scholastic *presentation,* the professional role model for the precocious teacher's own aspirations. Each chapter of his Romans commentary begins with a detailed analysis of the rhetorical disposition: main theme, subthemes, sub-subthemes, etc. Thomas never tired of marveling at Paul's skills. He saw the Apostle handling the rules of effective rhetoric with such subtlety, and applying the requirements of formal logic with such expertise, that the interpreter could never hope to do more than carefully trace the Apostle's argument for his or her own enjoyment and for the instruction of others. Thus, reading and interpreting Paul's Epistles became the sublime training ground for proper theological argumentation and systematization among medieval theologians. The second point is of particular importance. What Maurice Wiles observed with regard to the early commentators applies even more to the medievals:[36] They regarded Paul's thought as uniform throughout and used all their skill to reduce his multiple affirmations to a wholly self-consistent system, the very system of Christian truth that they themselves were engaged in teaching to ever new generations.

Contrary to the impression of many modern biblical scholars, one cannot fault medieval exegetes for inattentiveness to the Pauline text or for reading their own ideas into it. They were careful, meticulous readers precisely because they looked to Paul as the one who provided them with the content as well as the terminological tools of Christian theology.[37] I would be prepared to argue that the course of Western medieval theology itself was to a large extent dictated by the vocabulary of Paul's Epistles. Their text presented the basic pool of language that determined the concepts, themes, and formulations deemed worthy of discussion and refinement in the ongoing theological work of the schoolmen.

Of course, the medieval reading of Paul in the West labored under serious handicaps. There was first of all the problem of the Vulgate. It was the Latin Paul who suggested the terms of the theological agenda, not the Paul of the Greek originals. This can make a huge difference at crucial points; it still

36. Maurice F. Wiles. *The Divine Apostle: The Interpretation of St Paul's Epistles in the Early Church* (Cambridge: Cambridge University, 1967), p. 139.

37. For support of this statement see my article "Romans 8:1-11: Pauline Theology in Medieval Interpretation," in John T. Carroll, Charles H. Cosgrove, and E. Elizabeth Johnson (eds.), *Faith and History: Essays in Honor of Paul W. Meyer* (Atlanta: Scholars, 1991), pp. 239-60.

does, and the problem carries over into English, which derives most of its theological terminology from the Latin. A striking example is the medieval reading of Paul's doctrine of justification. The word *iustificatio*, in its very etymology as a Latin compound, suggests a specific model of reading our salvation in Christ. In the words of Augustine: *"iustificare est iustum facere"* — to justify means to make righteous, to transform a sinner into a righteous person. *"Ex impio fit pius"* — "the godless becomes a godly person."[38] There is no other way to read the word. The entire Latin tradition down to the Council of Trent understood justification as a process of transformation. Paul's Greek word, δικαιοῦν, δικαιοῦσθαι, is able to evoke other models as well: forensic (we are declared righteous), putative (we are regarded as righteous), external (we are clothed with Christ's righteousness) — models that the Protestant Reformers of the sixteenth century took up and developed.[39]

Another problem was the state of the commentary tradition. Almost no Greek Fathers were available to the Western exegetes. Augustine, on the other hand, seemed omnipresent, at least in the form of excerpt collections. Along with Augustine's interpretations, however, Pelagius's commentaries on the Pauline Epistles remained standard tools used by everyone without any suspicion. Three different versions, two of them insufficiently revised, were circulating under perfectly orthodox names — Jerome and Primasius — and were regularly consulted.[40] If one adds the observation that the important anti-Pelagian decisions of the regional Synod of Orange in A.D. 529 were simply forgotten in the Middle Ages because they failed to be copied into the early collections of the church's canon law, one realizes that the Pelagian Paul with his strong imperatives of "working out one's own salvation with fear and trembling" (Phil. 2:12) was alive and well throughout the period.[41]

---

38. Augustine, *De spiritu et littera* 9.15-16; 26.45.

39. For further discussion of this topic see the "Common Statement" in H. George Anderson, T. Austin Murphy, and Joseph A. Burgess (eds.), *Justification by Faith: Lutherans and Catholics in Dialogue VII* (Minneapolis: Augsburg, 1985), pp. 17-74.

40. On the attempted revision by Cassiodorus and his students, see David W. Johnson, "The Myth of the Augustinian Synthesis," in Mark S. Burrows and Paul Rorem (eds.), *Biblical Hermeneutics in Historical Perspective* (Grand Rapids: Eerdmans, 1991), pp. 100-114.

41. See Karlfried Froehlich, "Justification Language and Grace: The Charge of Pelagianism in the Middle Ages," in Elsie Anne McKee and Brian G. Armstrong (eds.), *Probing the Reformed Tradition: Historical Studies in Honor of Edward A. Dowey, Jr.* (Louisville: Westminster/John Knox, 1989), pp. 21-47, here pp. 28-30.

What then happened in the Protestant Reformation? Certainly the rediscovery of the Greek Paul in the circles of the humanists revolutionized the reading of Paul, and the new translations of the Greek Fathers that became rapidly available with the spread of the printing press added immensely to a fuller grasp of the range of Pauline traditions. The humanists admired Paul's Greek and continued to praise him as a master rhetorician. More importantly, they discovered the individual behind the text, Paul the towering human genius whom they could celebrate and strive to imitate. Marsilio Ficino understood Paul as the great mystic whose ascent into the third heaven (2 Cor. 12:2-4) gave him the vision of the same eternal truth to which Plato had access and that Marsilio himself felt called to proclaim in a bold synthesis of classical and Christian ideas.[42] On the other hand, Erasmus's widely read *Paraphrases* of Romans and Galatians promoted the image of an anticlerical Paul whose teaching of Christ's philosophy was aimed at a simple piety of the heart. This Paul was for everyone. All true theology, Erasmus argued, must be for everyone. It never is for the scholastic theologians only.[43]

I mentioned at the beginning that Martin Luther's central theological insights were inextricably linked to his reading of the Epistle to the Romans. He was aware of the parallel to Augustine. As a late medieval theologian, he still saw Paul primarily as the normative systematician, the one whose teaching provided the proper framework for theological discourse and opened the true meaning of all Scripture. His discovery was a new christocentric form of the Pauline key to this meaning, which he, too, formulated in language nourished by the traditional Latin Paul: *Christus pro nobis, simul iustus et peccator,* law and gospel, the theology of the Cross. Why then did the Paul of Luther's reading sound so different from the scholastic Paul, who was teaching medieval theology? I think the strength of Luther's reading, just as that of the Romans commentators of the early church, was its polemical, antiheretical bias. In Luther's eyes, church and theology of his time had succumbed to the Pelagian error. The Paul he found in the texts was the anti-Pelagian Paul whose contours Augustine had never fully drawn

42. Josef Nolte, "Pauli Mysteria. Zur theologischen Erkenntnislehre des Marsilio Ficino anhand von dessen Proömium einer Pauluskommentierung," in *Wort Gottes in der Zeit. Festschrift für Karl Hermann Schelkle* (Düsseldorf: Patmos, 1973), pp. 274-87.

43. The *Paraphrases* are available in an annotated English translation by John B. Payne, Albert Rabil, Jr., and Warren S. Smith, Jr., edited by Robert D. Sider, in the *Collected Works of Erasmus,* vol. 42 (Toronto: University of Toronto, 1984).

out exegetically. The task had been left unfinished, and it had become ever more difficult with the development of the medieval exegetical tradition. Measured by the standards of his day, Luther's new reading revealed to him a startling truth: "Here you have Paul, the most heretical of all heretics; his heresy is unheard of — dead to the law in order to live for God" (Gal. 2:19).[44]

Which Paul? Was Luther's "heretical" Paul the real Paul? Luther still had no sense of the historical situation of the Epistles. Romans, he claimed, "was written to Christian believers of a congregation that was in need of a witness of its faith and doctrine from the pen of this great Apostle in their fight against Jews and pagans in Rome."[45] In the same vein, Melanchthon's commentary on Romans called the Epistle "a compend of Christian theology" and proceeded to subject it in Ciceronian fashion to an analysis by *loci* that systematized its content into a handbook of Lutheran orthodoxy. True, Melanchthon and many Reformers with him eagerly drew on the rich tradition of the Eastern Fathers, whom they loved and respected; in this way, their work opened up ecumenical horizons that could have, but tragically did not yet lead to the new solidarity of a world church that would reunite East and West.[46] This task is still before us. Thinking of Paul today, we all will be uncomfortable with any blatant disregard for the historical

44. *In Epistolam Sancti Pauli ad Galatas* (1535), *Luthers Werke* (Weimar Edition), vol. 40/I, p. 267:8.

45. *In Epistolam Sancti Pauli ad Romanos* (1515-16), *Luthers Werke* (Weimar Edition), vol. 56, p. 160:5f.

46. Several publications by Ernst Benz deal with attempts to establish contacts between the churches of the Lutheran Reformation and the Patriarchate of Constantinople and with the Greek translation of the Augsburg Confession that Melanchthon prepared in 1559: *Wittenberg und Byzanz: Zur Begegnung und Auseinandersetzung der Reformation und der östlich-orthodoxen Kirchen* (Marburg: Elwert, 1949); "La Confession d'Augsbourg et Byzance au XVIe siècle," *Irénikon* 29 (1956), pp. 390-405; "Tübingen und Byzanz," *Zeitschrift für Religions- und Geistesgeschichte* 13 (1961), pp. 368-72. More recently, Dorothea Wendebourg published *Reformation und Orthodoxie: Der ökumenische Briefwechsel zwischen der Leitung der Württembergischen Kirche und Patriarch Jeremias II. von Konstantinopel in den Jahren 1573-1581* (Göttingen: Vandenhoeck und Ruprecht, 1986). Melanchthon drafted a letter in Greek to the Patriarch, who had asked for information, in which he emphasized that his Lutheran church was "devoutly preserving the dogmatic canons of the holy synods and the teachings of your Fathers: Athanasius, Basil, Gregory, Epiphanius, Theodoret, Irenaeus, and those who agree with them."

Paul. If one thing is clear, it is that the real Paul was *not* a professor of systematic theology as medieval exegetes firmly believed and Luther and Melanchthon still assumed. What then, who then was he? In trying to answer this question today, we must decide which Paul we are finally looking for in our exegetical endeavors: the author of some first-century literature whose personality will probably remain as elusive as ever, or the Apostle who helped the Church of all ages in East and West fight the good fight of the faith in the midst of the ever changing challenges of unfaith and distortion. I hope we can settle for the latter.

The Old Testament Canon in the Orthodox Churches

HAROLD P. SCANLIN

The first Bible translation in English to receive the approval of the Orthodox Church was *The New Oxford Annotated Bible with the Apocrypha, Expanded Edition: An Ecumenical Study Bible, Revised Standard Version,* first published in 1977. It may be hard for the churches of the West to imagine that a church with over six million adherents in English-speaking countries has flourished without an officially approved translation of its entire canonical Scriptures until the 1970s and that the translation that has finally filled this need was prepared primarily by Protestant translators. One should not assume, however, that the Bible is less important to the Orthodox nor that they lack a commitment to the centrality and uniqueness of the Scriptures in worship and doctrine. But this situation does suggest that Orthodox belief regarding canon is different from that in the West.

The Orthodox canon is not so narrowly defined by conciliar declaration or Reformation affirmation, but does nevertheless include a prescribed list of certain books. Every Old Testament canon list throughout the history of the Orthodox churches has included the books of the protocanon, although discussion of the canonicity of Esther continued for a number of centuries. The Orthodox Churches today also accept the books designated by the Roman Catholic Church as Deuterocanonical (Tobit, Judith, Wisdom, Sirach, 1 and 2 Maccabees, the Greek version of Esther [with its longer text], the additions to Daniel, and Baruch along with the Letter of Jeremiah [= Baruch 6 in some editions]). Several additional books included in the "Apocrypha" by Protestants, namely 1 and 2 Esdras and

The Prayer of Manasseh, are also accepted by the Orthodox and included in their designation "Deuterocanonical." Added to this collection are Psalm 151, Psalm 153, and 4 Maccabees, although 4 Maccabees is not accorded the same status as the other books. The use of the term "Deuterocanonical" should not, however, be construed as meaning that the Orthodox view of these books corresponds precisely to that of the Roman Catholic Church.

To some, statements regarding the Old Testament canon by theologians of the Eastern Churches may seem ambiguous, or even contradictory. Father John Meyendorff, whose memory and contribution to the faith and life of the church we honor in this volume, wrote, "In spite of the fact that the Byzantine patristic and ecclesiastical tradition almost exclusively uses the Septuagint as the standard Biblical text, and that parts of the 'longer' canon — especially Wisdom — are of frequent liturgical use, Byzantine theologians remain faithful to a 'Hebrew' criterion for Old Testament literature, which excludes texts originally composed in Greek."[1] On the other hand, Elias Oikonomos begins his essay on the Deuterocanonicals in the Orthodox Church by saying, "Both Judaism and Christianity began by simply using the deuterocanonical writings as part of the biblical canon."[2] He bases this assumption on the supposed actions of the Council of Jamnia: "The end of the period of unquestioning use of the deuterocanonical writings in Judaism is marked by the Synod of Jamnia (100 C.E.), where on the basis of philological and historical arguments, a catalog of Old Testament writings binding on Judaism, was drawn up for the first time."[3] However, the very existence of a Synod (or now more generally, Council) of Jamnia that decided on the matter of the Old Testament canon has been questioned in recent years. The origin of the theory that the Jewish Elders decided on the closing of the canon of the Hebrew Bible, especially the third division, the Kethubim, can be traced to a specific proposal first made by Heinrich Graetz in an Appendix to his commentary on Qoheleth.[4] This theory was popularized by H. E. Ryle in *The Canon of the Old Testament* in connection with his theory regarding the closing of the third division of

1. *Byzantine Theology: Historical Trends and Doctrinal Themes* (2nd ed., New York: Fordham University, 1979), p. 7.
2. Elias Oikonomos, "The Significance of the Deuterocanonical Writings in the Orthodox Church," in *The Apocrypha in Ecumenical Perspective,* ed. Siegfried Meurer (UBS Monograph Series, 6; Reading and New York: United Bible Societies, 1991), p. 17.
3. Ibid.
4. *Kohelet* (Leipzig: Winter, 1871), pp. 163-66.

the Jewish canon.[5] It should be noted that Ryle's statements were quite cautious: The closing of the canon "may, indeed, very well have happened at this, or at some similar, gathering about that time. In the absence of precise information . . . we can only say that, at the time at which the Synod of Jamnia was held, and apparently the subjects which occupied its discussions, are favourable to the conjecture, that there is no reason for objecting to it."[6] Blenkinsopp summarizes the situation: ". . . there is no evidence that the canon as a whole was ever officially established during [the first century], and that such a decision was made by the Jewish leadership at Javneh (Jamnia) at the end of the first century of the era is a myth of Christian scholarship without documentary foundation."[7]

Jack Lewis's article, "What Do We Mean by Jabneh?" describes what actually transpired there.[8] Jabneh (or Jamnia) became a main center for Jewish religious discussion after the fall of Jerusalem in A.D. 70. The record of religious thought and decisions made over a period of years covered a wide range of issues. In all these discussions there remains a record of only two matters of discussion regarding the canon, debating the status of Qoheleth and Song of Songs, both of which, it was decided did "defile the hands," that is, they were divinely inspired and considered part of Holy Scripture. It should be noted, however, that the question of the status of these two books continued to be a subject of debate among Jewish leaders.

Sid Z. Leiman offers another perspective on the concept of authority and canon in first-century Judaism: "A canonical book is a book accepted by Jews as authoritative for religious practice and/or doctrine, and whose authority is binding upon the Jewish people of all generations."[9] By this definition both Scripture and the hakakhic codes of the Mishna and the Talmud are canonical and authoritative. But, Leiman argues, there is another way of categorizing religious texts, namely inspiration: The inspired canonical literature consists of Hebrew Scripture, believed by the Tannaim and Amoraim to have been composed under divine inspiration. That still leaves the category *uninspired canonical,* to which the Mishna and Talmud

5. 2nd ed.; London: Macmillan, 1904, pp. 181-83.

6. Ibid., p. 183.

7. *Prophecy and Canon: A Contribution to the Study of Jewish Origins* (Notre Dame: University of Notre Dame, 1977), p. 3.

8. *Journal of Bible and Religion* 32 (1964), pp. 125-32.

9. *The Canonization of Hebrew Scripture: The Talmudic and Midrashic Evidence* (Hamden, CT: Archon, 1977), p. 14.

belong. Although Leiman's theory has not gained wide acceptance, it does offer an insight into categories of thinking in the first century A.D.

It is important to recognize that the Eastern Churches approach the issue of biblical canon from their own perspective. First, Eastern Churches are autocephalous, that is, each national church tradition can make autonomous decisions, including decisions regarding the biblical canon. Significant differences are seen in the Old Testament canon of the Ethiopian Orthodox Church, one of the non-Chalcedonian Orthodox Churches, and hence not in communion with the autocephalous Chalcedonian Orthodox Churches.[10] Further, the relationship between Scripture and tradition is considered differently than Scripture-Tradition discussions in the West. A related issue is the Eastern hermeneutic, characterized in the term *thēoria* (to be discussed below).[11] Finally, it is important to recognize the crucial role of liturgical use of Scripture.

There is a broad consensus in favor of the Jewish Palestinian canon among the Eastern Fathers, although there are some minor differences in the extant lists. It is not altogether surprising, since they were more likely to be conversant with the Jewish tradition. In their debate with Jewish opponents, they were keenly aware of the Jewish charges of distortions and variations among the various Greek translations of the Hebrew Bible. While earlier Jewish records speak positively about the legitimacy of the translation enterprise, for example, in the *Letter to Aristeas,* Jewish religious leaders became increasingly skeptical, especially in light of the appropriation of the Septuagint by Christianity, with its exegetical tradition in passages such as Isaiah 7:14. The *Letter to Aristeas* commends the work of the seventy(-two) translators of the Septuagint. Later elaborations and emendations of the legend by Christians tend to exaggerate the claims of divine superintendence, while Jews relied more and more on the exclusive authority of the Hebrew original. Text-critical and editorial activity on Old Greek translations in the first centuries of the era relate to these tendencies. Not only did Aquila produce a painfully literal translation, but there is evidence in

---

10. See G. A. Mikre-Sellassie, "The Bible and Its Canon in the Ethiopian Orthodox Church," *The Bible Translator* 44 (1993), pp. 111-23, for a helpful survey. See also Roger Beckwith on "The Canon in the Early Ethiopian Church" in his *The Old Testament Canon of the New Testament Church* (Grand Rapids: Eerdmans, 1985), Appendix 5, pp. 478-505.

11. Bradley Nassif provides an extensive treatment of *thēoria* in his essay " 'Spiritual Exegesis' in the School of Antioch," in this volume, pp. 343ff.

the famous Naḥal Ḥever Greek manuscript of the Minor Prophets, probably
to be dated to the first century A.D., of adjustment of the Old Greek to the
proto-Masoretic Hebrew text.[12] Origen's text-critical activity, which resulted in his multi-column comparison of the Greek translations extant in
his day with the Hebrew text, was certainly motivated, in part, by his
awareness of the Jewish-Christian debate.[13]

Orlinsky[14] concludes that Origen's motive for his Hexapla was ped-
agogic; he intended to provide a tool for his fellow Christians to arm
themselves with a knowledge of Hebrew. John Wright, in one of a collection
of important papers from a symposium on Origen,[15] maintains that
Origen's rationale was the preparation of an exegetical resource for a wide
range of applications. According to Oikonomos,[16] Origen's comments on
the Old Testament canon should be seen within the context of the Jewish-
Christian debate as tactical, not theological. Origen, in his *Letter to Afri-
canus,* said that it was important to note differences in the canon and variant
textual readings, "so that in our debates with the Jews we do not quote
passages which are lacking in their texts, and so we can make use of those
which are in their texts but not in ours."[17] In examining early statements
on the Old Testament canon, it is always necessary to be aware of the context
of the statements, including the audience, and the motivation of the author.

The earliest extant statement of an Eastern Father on the Old Testa-
ment canon is from Melito of Sardis (died ca. 180) and is preserved in
Eusebius's *Ecclesiastical History* (4.26.14): "When, therefore, I went to the
East and came to the place where these things were preached and done, I

12. Dominique Barthélemy, *Les devanciers d'Aquila* (Supplements to Vetus Testa-
mentum, 10; Leiden: Brill, 1963). See also the official publication of this manuscript by
Emanuel Tov, et al., *The Greek Minor Prophets Scroll from Nahal Hever (8HevXIIgr) (The
Seiyal Collection I)* (Oxford: Oxford University, 1990).

13. See N. R. de Lange, *Origen and the Jews* (Cambridge: Cambridge University,
1977) for a full discussion of the issues, including the Old Testament canon.

14. "The Columnar Order of the Hexapla," *Studies in the Septuagint: Origins,
Recensions, and Interpretations,* ed. Sidney Jellicoe (New York: KTAV, 1974), pp. 369-81.

15. "Origen in the Scholar's Den: A Rationale for the Hexapla," in *Origen of
Alexandria: His World and His Legacy,* ed. Charles Kannengiesser and William L. Petersen
(Notre Dame: University of Notre Dame, 1988), pp. 48-63.

16. Oikonomos, "The Significance of the Deuterocanonical Writings in the Orthodox Church," p. 20.

17. De Lange, *Origen and the Jews,* p. 50, however, maintains that this quotation
alone is insufficient to support the apologetic theory for the Hexapla.

learned accurately the books of the Old Testament; and I send you the list in order."[18] Melito then lists all the books of the proto-canon and includes Wisdom from the deutero-canon. Origen himself, in the preface to his commentary on Psalms (again preserved for us in the *Ecclesiastical History*) enumerates "the twenty-two books according to the Hebrews," listing only the books of the proto-canon. He then adds, "and, outside of these, there is Maccabees." There has been some discussion of the precise meaning of Origen's phrase ἔξω δὲ τούτον, some maintaining that it can be translated, "besides these," but Jurgens convincingly argues that the phrase could actually be rendered "*excluded* from these, however . . ." (1:204, n. 4).

Origen's reference to "the twenty-two books" occurs in a number of the canonical lists of the Eastern Church. The phrase most likely alludes to the well-known statement of Josephus in *Against Apion* 1.8 (1:38 in the Loeb edition): "We do not posses myriads of inconsistent books, conflicting with each other. Our books, those which are justly accredited (τὰ δικαίως πεπιστευμένα), are but two and twenty." Josephus comments no further on the significance of the number twenty-two, but in later Rabbinic thought this number was considered significant since there are twenty-two letters in the Hebrew alphabet, representing the completeness of the number of sacred books as well.

The Council of Laodicea (between 343 and 381), Canon 60, numbers the twenty-two "books of the Old Testament which ought to be read."[19] They are the books of the proto-canon, with one exception; books attributed to Jeremiah and his circle are counted as one, including Baruch and Letter(s), in addition to Jeremiah and Lamentations. This statement illustrates a pattern seen in other Eastern canon lists. There is a desire to conform to the number twenty-two, and any departure from the Palestinian Jewish canon generally includes books of the deutero-canon whose authorship or historical connection is firmly tied to the books of the proto-canon.

Clement of Alexandria (150-211/216), in his *The Instructor of Children*, introduces a lengthy quote from Baruch 3:16-19 with the statement, "Divine Scripture . . . says most excellently." Athanasius (295-373), in his *Thirty-Ninth*

---

18. This and the following patristic quotations are taken from William A. Jurgens (ed. and tr.), *The Faith of the Early Fathers*, 3 vols. (Collegeville, MN: Liturgical, 1970-79).

19. The actual list of books is generally considered by scholars to be a later addition. See Bruce M. Metzger, *The Canon of the New Testament* (Oxford: Clarendon, 1987), p. 210.

Festal Letter, also says that there are twenty-two books in the Old Testament, "which also, I have heard, is traditionally the number of written characters used by the Hebrews." Again, he adds to the proto-canon only Baruch and the Letter of Jeremiah, counting them as one with Jeremiah and Lamentations. After his discussion of the books included in the canon of the Old Testament and New Testament, he goes on to comment on the existence of "other books beside the aforementioned, which, however, are not canonical. Yet they have been designated by the Fathers to be read by those who join us and who wish to be instructed in the word of piety." This category includes the book of Esther, in addition to Wisdom, Sirach, Tobit, and Judith of the deutero-canon. Nothing at all is said of Maccabees. He concludes with, "Those which I mentioned earlier [the twenty-two books], beloved, are included in the canon, while these latter are but recommended for reading."

Cyril of Jerusalem (ca. 315-386), in his *Catechetical Lectures,* commends the use of the Septuagint since "the translation was effected by the Holy Spirit," but goes on to warn, "read the twenty-two books, but have nothing to do with the apocrypha." In Cyril's list Jeremiah includes Baruch and the Letter, reckoned as one book. Gregory of Nazianzus (ca. 330-389) also reckons the number of books as twenty-two, but his list does not offer sufficient detail to know what was included in Jeremiah. Amphilochius of Iconium (ca. 340/345–post-394) limits his list of Old Testament books to the proto-canon and offers a few additional details. He lists "angel twice-named Malachi," a statement supported by the Septuagint with the title Malachi and ἄγγελος in the first verse. The Old Testament list ends with "to these some add Esther." He concludes the entire passage on the canon with the Greek phrase κανών . . . τῶν θεοπνεύστων γραφῶν, perhaps the earliest known use of this phrase in a technical sense.

Virtually every known statement on the canon from the East up to the closing of the fourth century limits the Old Testament canon to the Hebrew canon, and where there are specific comments beyond mere enumeration, they usually offer a negative valuation of other books, with the notable exception of books associated with Old Testament personalities of the proto-canon. On the other hand, there are positive statements about the inspiration and validity of the Septuagint. In the specific canon lists this reverence for the Septuagint does not extend to the additional deuterocanonical books of the Septuagint, but it probably established the Old Greek editions of Esther and Daniel.

The situation in the West was different, although the evidence goes back only as far as the latter part of the fourth century. Hilary of Poitiers, in his *Prologue to the Commentary on Psalms,* knows of the twenty-two–book tradition, based on the number of letters in the Hebrew alphabet, but adds Tobit and Judith to bring the number to twenty-four, "the number of letters used by the Greeks." The *Acts of the Council of Rome* (382) includes a decree, known as the *Decree of Damasus,* named for Pope Damasus I, who is best known for his appointment of Jerome to revise the Latin Bible. The second decree, later incorporated in the *Gelasian Decree,* dating to the end of the fifth century, lists "the divine Scriptures: what the universal Catholic Church [receives] and what she must shun." The list corresponds precisely with the full Old Testament canon of the Roman Catholic Church.

There has been much debate about the views of Jerome. It is clear that he was greatly influenced by Jewish biblical scholars when he moved to Palestine to study Hebrew and continue his translation work. In his *Prologue to the Book of Kings* in the Vulgate he begins, "Just as there are twenty-two letters by which we can write in Hebrew anything we say . . . so there are twenty-two books," and ends, "thus we may be certain that whatsoever is not among these is to be placed among the apocrypha *(apokrifa)*." There may be some uncertainty as to the precise meaning of *apokrifa* here, whether it is used in the traditional sense of "hidden" or in the more technical sense of "excluded." However Jerome goes on in the same passage to say that Wisdom, Sirach, Tobit, and Judith are not in the canon *(non sunt in canone).* In the West even the words of the highly revered Jerome, however, cannot negate the word of the councils and the enormous influence of Augustine, who in *Christian Instruction* (2.8.13), enumerates the forty-four books of the Roman Catholic Old Testament canon, with the authority of "the greater part of the Catholic Churches," while realizing that there are some books "which fewer Churches of lesser authority" do not accept.

The general preference for the Palestinian Jewish canon in the East, did, nevertheless, leave certain aspects of the question open. As we have seen, even within the twenty-two book limitation there was some room for variation. Also, the positive preference for the Septuagint as an "inspired" translation is stated in several contexts. It can also be added that in actual practice the Eastern Fathers cited the books of the deutero-canon. Franz Stuhlhofer has compiled a statistical profile of patristic citations of the deuterocanonical books.[20] His statistics are calculated by number of cita-

---

20. *Der Gebrauch der Bibel von Jesus bis Euseb: Eine statistische Untersuchung zur Kanongeschichte* (Wuppertal: Brockhaus, 1988), esp. chs. 12 and 13.

tions divided by book length. The protocanonical books of the Kethubim rate highest, primarily because of the great number of citations of the Psalms. Citations of the deuterocanonical books are lowest, approximately equal to the ratings of the historical books of the proto-canon. Stuhlhofer charts a trend in the increased rating of citations of deuterocanonical books between the second and third centuries (0.22 to 0.38), while citation ratings for the proto-canon remained more constant (e.g., the Pentateuch remained 1.9, and the Kethubim increased from 1.4 to 1.7).

In 691 the Trullan Synod confirmed the canons of the local synods and Church Fathers. Unity was required regarding the primary writings, but diversity was permitted for the deuterocanonical books, which occupied a "second place." That seems to have settled the issue in the East until Cyril Lucar, Patriarch of Constantinople, published his views on the Old Testament canon in 1629. Cyril was greatly influenced in his thinking by the Protestant Reformation and adopted the Reformed view of the Old Testament canon: "those which we call Apocrypha, we distinguish by this name, because they have not the like authority from the All-holy Spirit, as have the properly and undoubtedly Canonical Books."[21] The Synod of Constantinople (1642) rejected Cyril's Calvinist tendencies as well as his view of the Old Testament canon, describing the deuterocanonical writings as not canonical but, "because of their 'good and virtuous' content [they] are not to be rejected."[22]

Scripture, Tradition, and the Orthodox Hermeneutic of *Thēoria*

We now need to examine the other factors in the understanding of Scripture in the Eastern Churches to gain an appreciation for their concept of canon, which appears to tolerate a degree of difference when compared to attitudes in the West.

The Orthodox Church is keenly aware of the continuity of history and a reverence for the principles of patristic interpretation. Ultimately all exegesis is christological, and the proper locus for the interpretation of the

21. *The Acts and Decrees of the Synod of Jerusalem*, tr. J. N. W. B. Robertson (New York: AMS, 1969, reprint of the 1899 London edition), pp. 211f.

22. Oikonomos, "The Significance of the Deuterocanonical Writings in the Orthodox Church," p. 23.

Word of God, the eternal Logos of God, is the church. Traditionally, this has meant a certain skepticism toward the historical-critical method, which has been the cornerstone of biblical study in the West since the Enlightenment. In recent years biblical scholars in the Orthodox tradition have pursued the historical-critical method as a means for recovering the literal meaning of the ancient text, but have continued to pursue a more traditional approach to the discovery of the spiritual meaning of the Word of God, the true reason for appropriating the Holy Scriptures for the life of the church. The hermeneutical method of the Fathers was typology and the aim was *thēoria,* "an inspired vision of the presence and purpose of God within history and within the Church."[23]

The patristic concept of *thēoria* holds that Scripture contains both a literal and a spiritual sense. The literal sense is essentially authorial intent, that is, the message that the writer sought to communicate to his readers. The spiritual sense refers to "the Word which God speaks *through the written text* in each present moment of the Church's life."[24] The hermeneutical approach of typology bridges the literal (original) meaning to the spiritual, the conceptual revelation evoked by the event. The interconnectedness of the ancient historical moment with the contemporary moment(s) of revelation is what distinguishes typology from allegory in Orthodox hermeneutics. This historical and conceptual interconnectedness is also emphasized by Protestant advocates of typology such as L. Goppelt and others.

Orthodox *thēoria* recognizes Scripture as canonical, that is, as normative for the faith and life of the church, but it also stresses the role of the revelation of the living Word of God in a synergistic, dynamic revelation. Accordingly, canon is defined in terms of function; all Scripture that functions in the dynamic relationship of God's revelation may be said to possess canonical authority. The use of Scripture in the liturgy and worship of the church is, accordingly, that which defines the extent of the canon.

Liturgical Authority

The liturgical traditions of the Orthodox Church integrate many Scripture quotations and allusions. Inclusion in the liturgy means that any translation

---

23. John Breck, "Orthodoxy and the Bible Today," *Sourozh* 46 (1991), p. 13.
24. Ibid., p. 14.

designed for use by the Orthodox will need to contain the books of the
deutero-canon so used. But we have seen that use in the liturgy actually
helps to define what is canonical. According to a survey of Scripture in
Greek Orthodox worship prepared by Demetrios Constantelos,[25] the following deuterocanonical books are used in the liturgy (arranged in order
of frequency of use): Wisdom, Judith, Sirach, Song of the Three Children,
Tobit, Baruch, Susanna, 4 Maccabees, 3 Maccabees, 1 Esdras, 1 Maccabees
and 2 Maccabees. Although no passages from the Letter of Jeremiah or Bel
and the Dragon are incorporated in the liturgy, the early lists of canonical
books compiled by the Eastern Fathers do include these books, the Letter
of Jeremiah as part of the "works" of the prophet Jeremiah, and Bel as part
of the Greek version of the book of Daniel.

Georges Barrois, in *Scripture Reading in Orthodox Worship*,[26] has an-
alyzed the use of Scripture in the Orthodox liturgy, particularly as used in
the Russian Orthodox Church. While there are some minimal divergences
in Scripture use in the Greek Orthodox liturgy, the principle of use and the
authority inherent in Scriptures so used is the same in both traditions. The
Russian Orthodox Church also uses the Prayer of Manasseh, even though
it is not generally found in the historical canonical lists.

Conclusion

The concept of canon in the Eastern Orthodox Churches, while not defined
as in the West, is crucial to the life and worship of the church. Canon is
functional rather than descriptive; it is the church's recognition that the
sacred texts accepted as canonical function as the means of divine revelation, both as a historical event as well as a spiritual bridge linking past and
present. The liturgy functions within the worshipping community as a
mode of communication, and scriptural texts used in that context are, by
definition, canonical. This corpus of Old Testament books, which the
church regards as sacred texts fulfilling these functions, corresponds more
nearly to the larger canon of the Roman Catholic Church, with the inclusion
of books from the Protestant Apocrypha as well. Yet within the framework

25. "The Holy Scriptures in Greek Orthodox Worship," *The Greek Orthodox
Theological Review* 12 (1966), pp. 7-83.
26. Crestwood, NY: St. Vladimir's Seminary, 1977.

of this larger canon there has been a historical recognition that the authority of some books is derivative.

The issue of canon relates not only to the number of books but also to the form of the books. The Greek text form of the books of the proto-canon has generally been regarded to have an exegetical primacy over the Hebrew text by the contemporary Eastern Churches.[27] Elsewhere I have described the variety of forms of texts in existence at the turn of the era.[28] The Orthodox community, in choosing to maintain the witness of the Septuagint translation as their Old Testament, is dealing with a textual witness that stood side-by-side with the proto-Masoretic text in the early stage of development, before and during the period when the proto-Masoretic/early Rabbinic text emerged as the standard form of the Old Testament text. The Old Testament manuscripts discovered in recent decades in the area of the Dead Sea, and especially at Qumran, has confirmed the existence of Hebrew text forms that were previously known only in the Old Greek (Septuagint) translation. The extensively preserved Psalm scroll found in Cave 11 at Qumran (11QPs[a]) includes Psalm 151, as well as other Psalms that are not included in any canonically recognized Psalter collection. The textual issues involved in weighing the Qumran and Dead Sea evidence are complex. Some manuscripts, for example, while offering a Hebrew witness to Old Greek readings also offer other readings as well. Some scholars have also raised the question whether the Cave 11 Psalm scroll was considered a canonically delimited collection or a hymn and worship collection for general use. Nevertheless, scholars are now aware of the complexity of the textual tradition that existed immediately prior to the emergence of more stable text forms emerging by the end of the first Christian century. Orthodox exegetes who may have exhibited a degree of

27. Paul N. Tarazi, *The Old Testament: An Introduction. Volume 1: Historical Traditions* (Crestwood, NY: St. Vladimir's Seminary, 1991), combines a knowledge of the Western historical-critical method with the Eastern emphasis on the *collective* reading of Scripture that recognizes the continuity of the Church's understanding and interpretation of its Sacred Book. While Tarazi follows the larger canon of the Septuagint and includes a discussion of 1 and 2 Maccabees, the Old Testament historical traditions are described without specific recourse to the textual and exegetical traditions of the Septuagint.

28. Harold P. Scanlin, "What Is the Canonical Shape of the Old Testament Text We Translate?" in *Issues in Bible Translation*, ed. Philip C. Stine (UBS Monograph Series, 3; London/New York/Stuttgart: UBS, 1988), pp. 207-20.

naiveté regarding the complexities of historical and textual criticism are now in a position to formulate their discussion of Old Testament canon within the context of a new corpus of evidence. The new textual evidence may not always lend support to traditional Eastern views regarding the superiority of the Old Greek version of the Old Testament, but Western definitions of canon may need to be refined as well, with a renewed appreciation for the functional, dynamic dimension of canon. Continued East-West dialogue can only be mutually enriching, especially in the field of Bible translation.

Theodoret's Commentary on Isaiah: A Synthesis of Exegetical Traditions

METROPOLITAN DEMETRIOS TRAKATELLIS

I. Introduction

The biblical exegesis offered by the Fathers of the Church of the first five centuries A.D. is a fascinating phenomenon that constantly attracts scholarly investigation and study. The reasons for such a perennial attraction are easy to understand. The patristic exegetes involved here are the most brilliant theologians of the church. And their exegetical work constitutes a monumental body of literature that breathes originality and dynamism and is unique in its theological depth, aesthetic quality, literary wealth, and historical perspective.

This unique body of literature, though highly appreciated, seems somehow to have suffered from stereotyped and oversimplified classifications. Biblical patristic exegesis of the first five centuries, for instance, has been conveniently divided into schools of exegesis, basically the Alexandrian and the Antiochene. Such a division and classification, justifiable to a certain degree, is, nonetheless, inadequate if not misleading.[1]

---

1. Dr. Bradley Nassif, the editor of the present volume, was kind enough to place in advance at my disposal his stimulating essay " 'Spiritual Exegesis' in the School of Antioch," published in this volume. It offers an excellent review of the scholarly work on the "Antiochene *thēoria*," among other things, and shows the need for more intensive and systematic discussion of specific issues of patristic biblical exegesis and for studies that go beyond the very general classifications of the type "Antiochene exegesis" or

One could argue, for instance that this classification tacitly or overtly assumes that a status of polarity or disagreement exists among those schools of exegesis, and that their methods of interpretation, represented by terms like "historical," "literal," "allegorical," "metaphorical," "figurative," "mystical," "spiritual," and the like, are in strong opposition or tension to each other. Is this really the case?

Furthermore, one could argue that a great number of patristic exegetical works cannot be classified under the categories of either the Alexandrian or the Antiochene schools. The works are either sophisticated and nuanced enough to resist an easy categorization, or they display such an eclectic exegetical attitude that any attempt at placing them within a rigid taxonomic scheme becomes an exercise in futility.[2]

We could add that in various instances there are differences of exegetical methods and approaches not only within each school but even within the works of the same author. Chrysostom's exegetical work on the Book of Genesis, to mention an example, is different from his work on the Book of Psalms in terms of interpretative techniques and principles. If Chrysostom is an Antiochene exegete, then how does his Antiochene exegesis on the Book of Genesis compare to his Antiochene exegesis on the Book of Psalms?

The inadequacy of the polarized and rigid categorization of patristic exegetical works[3] becomes more recognizable in the fact that such catego-

---

"Alexandrian exegesis." On the last point see also Bertrand de Margerie, *Introduction à l'histoire de l'exégèse. I: Les Pères Grecs et Orientaux* (Paris: Cerf, 1980), pp. 188f.

2. Fr. John Breck, in his book *The Power of the Word in the Worshiping Church* (Crestwood, NY: St. Vladimir's Seminary, 1986), pp. 49-92, offers an insightful general survey of the exegetical schools of Alexandria and Antioch. It is significant for our study that in his survey Fr. Breck (a) warns against stereotyping the exegetical schools, (b) limits himself to clearly defined representatives of the two schools, thus purposely omitting important patristic exegetes who simply cannot be classified under those schools, and (c) points out the lack of homogeneity even within the same school, giving as a telling example the names of John Chrysostom and Theodore of Mopsuestia (p. 68).

3. The rigid categorization into Alexandrian and Antiochene schools is inadequate even when it is presented by means of a sophisticated analysis and reinterpretation of the data. This is the case, for instance, with the article by Frances Young, "The Rhetorical Schools and Their Influence on Patristic Exegesis," in R. Williams (ed.), *The Making of Orthodoxy* (Festschrift for H. Chadwick; Cambridge: Cambridge University, 1989), pp. 189-99. Young plausibly argues about the influence of the philosophical schools on the Alexandrian exegesis in contradistinction to the influence of the rhetorical schools on

rization seems to ignore a development that occurred as we moved from the third to the fifth centuries. This was a development toward an increased mixture of exegetical methods, toward a phenomenon of converging lines of interpretation, and, finally, toward a synthesis of various exegetical traditions. Such a development was facilitated, in all probability, by the prevalence of the christocentric hermeneutical principle as the absolute and ultimate principle of biblical exegesis performed within the realm of the church.

This process toward a synthesis of exegetical traditions in patristic biblical interpretation, beyond its significance for reevaluation of stereotyped classifications, is also important in itself as a central phenomenon in the history of biblical exegesis and definitely deserves a thorough study.

In the pages that follow, I intend to offer a few basic observations as a contribution to such a study. I will proceed with the examination of a very concrete case that may give us plausible evidence and data about the exegetical synthesis that seems to have occurred in the course from the third to the fifth centuries. This is the case of Theodoret of Cyrus, specifically of his *Commentary on Isaiah*.[4]

Theodoret's *Commentary on Isaiah* is a lengthy one, written sometime before A.D. 447.[5] Theodoret composed this work at an age of maturity as the last but one of his commentaries on the prophetic books of the Old Testament. Because of the nature of the Book of Isaiah, which contains history and prophecy with indisputable messianic references, a commentator like Theodoret working with it was forced to show his exegetical methods, his interpretative tendencies and choices, and his hermeneutical principles. There are, however, additional considerations that make focusing on Theodoret's *Commentary on Isaiah* extremely fruitful for our task. We are in

---

the Antiochene exegesis. There is an interesting point here, but it is very limited and insufficient as a major criterion for differentiation and categorization.

4. Theodoret of Cyrus, Ἑρμηνεία εἰς τὸν προφήτην Ἡσαΐαν. In this article I am using the critical edition of the text of Theodoret's *Commentary on Isaiah* in Jean Noël Guinot, *Théodoret de Cyr Commentaire sur Isaie* (3 vols., Sources chrétiennes 276, 295, and 315; Paris: Cerf, 1980, 1982, 1984). I will cite this commentary under the abbreviation Theodoret, *Isaiah*, giving in parentheses the corresponding pages in the Guinot edition.

5. Guinot, *Théodoret de Cyr Commentaire*, I, pp. 16-18, offers persuasive evidence for a date of composition of the commentary between 435 and 447, preferring a date closer to 447 rather than to 435.

the advantageous position of having at our disposal three other important commentaries on Isaiah that preceded Theodoret's work. They come from Eusebius of Caesarea,[6] John Chrysostom,[7] and Cyril of Alexandria.[8] It could be safely assumed that Theodoret knew well these three commentaries, which were in existence and circulation when he composed his own.[9] How does Theodoret's commentary compare with those written by Eusebius, Chrysostom, and Cyril, which seem to represent differing exegetical traditions? Can we discern in his case a synthesis that creatively combines substantive elements coming from those traditions? Can we see there a work, which by critically and selectively using existing exegetical approaches established or followed by important interpreters of the Scriptures, offers an exegesis that is more inclusive and more multifaceted and appears more as a synthesis resistant to stereotyped classifications? Can we then go a step backward and detect elements of similar tendencies of inclusiveness and synthesis already in the works consulted by Theodoret, namely, in the commentaries on Isaiah by Eusebius, Chrysostom, and Cyril? The answer to these questions seems to be yes, and such an answer is neither unjustifiable nor implausible,[10] as the present study will attempt to show.

6. Eusebius of Caesarea, Ὑπομνήματα εἰς τὸν Ἡσαΐαν. In this article I am using the critical edition of the text of Eusebius's *Commentary on Isaiah* in Joseph Ziegler, *Eusebius Werke: Der Jesajakommentar* (Griechischen christlichen Schriftsteller; Berlin: Akademie, 1975). I will cite this commentary under the abbreviation Eusebius, *Isaiah*, giving in parentheses the corresponding pages in the Ziegler edition.

7. John Chrysostom, Ἑρμηνεία εἰς τὸν προφήτην Ἡσαΐαν. In this article I am using the critical edition of the text of Chrysostom's *Commentary on Isaiah* in Jean Dumortier, *Jean Chrysostom Commentaire sur Isaie* (Sources chrétiennes 304; Paris: Cerf, 1983). An English translation of the commentary is in Duane A. Garrett, *An Analysis of the Hermeneutics of John Chrysostom's Commentary on Isaiah 1–8 with an English Translation* (Lewiston, NY: Mellen, 1992). I will cite Chrysostom's commentary under the abbreviation Chrysostom, *Isaiah*, giving in parentheses the corresponding pages in the Dumortier edition and in Garrett's English translation.

8. Cyril of Alexandria, Ἐξήγησις Ὑπομνηματικὴ εἰς τὸν προφήτην Ἡσαΐαν. In this article I am using the text of Cyril's *Commentary on Isaiah* from J. P. Migne's *Patrologia Graeco-Latina (PG)*, vol. 70. I will cite this commentary under the abbreviation Cyril, *Isaiah*, giving in parentheses the corresponding columns in the *PG* edition.

9. See pertinent data in Guinot, *Théodoret de Cyr Commentaire* I, pp. 24-33. For the connections between Theodoret and Eusebius see Ziegler, *Eusebius Werke, Der Jesajakommentar*, p. xlix.

10. D. S. Wallace-Hadrill, in his monograph *Christian Antioch: A Study of Early*

This study is dedicated to the memory of the unforgettable friend and colleague Father John Meyendorff, the outstanding Orthodox theologian and scholar who clearly saw that consistency, continuity, and synthesis were among the major forces in the history of patristic theological work.

I will start with a brief presentation of the textual, literary, and historical elements found in Theodoret's exegesis of Isaiah. Then I will proceed with a comparison of his exegesis with the exegeses of Eusebius, Chrysostom, and Cyril in their commentaries on Isaiah. The comparison will be focused on the exegesis of three characteristic pericopes, chapters 1, 6, and 7 of Isaiah. Since Chrysostom's commentary does not go beyond Isaiah 8, I have chosen the characteristic examples only from the section Isaiah 1–8 in order to have Chrysostom included in the comparative study.

II. Textual, Literary, and Historical Elements in Theodoret's Exegesis of Isaiah

a) Theodoret in his *Commentary on Isaiah* appears as an exegete who pays high attention to the text and tries by all means to clarify its meaning through all tools available to him.

The biblical text that he is using is the Septuagint in its Lucianic recension. When he speaks of the Septuagint ('Εβδομήκοντα) he means a specific Lucianic recension that was available to him.[11] He is, however, not limited to the Septuagint version of Isaiah.

Theodoret quite frequently quotes other Greek translations of the Book of Isaiah. More specifically, he mentions Aquila, Symmachus, and Theodotion many times and presents quotations from their respective texts. Sometimes, he does not mention their names and uses expressions like "the

---

Christian Thought in the East (Cambridge: Cambridge University, 1982), p. 29, when discussing Antiochene biblical interpretation, makes the following eloquent statement: "presented with an anonymous piece of typological interpretation it might be possible to identify it as coming from the pen of John Chrysostom or Theodoret in Antioch or Cyril in Alexandria or Eusebius between the two at Caesarea."

11. As Guinot notes (*Théodoret de Cyr Commentaire* I, p. 43), the Lucianic version used by Theodoret is not in its purest form. Cf. J. Ziegler, *Septuaginta, Vetus Testamentum graecum. XIV: Isaias* (Göttingen, 1967[2]), pp. 80f.; G. W. Ashby, *Theodoret of Cyrrhus as Exegete of the Old Testament* (Grahamstown: Rhodes University, 1972), pp. 13-15.

other interpreters" or simply "the other" (οἱ ἄλλοι ἑρμηνευταί, οἱ ἄλλοι), "the three interpreters" or simply "the three" (οἱ τρεῖς ἑρμηνευταί, οἱ τρεῖς), or "the rest of the interpreters" or simply "the rest" (οἱ λοιποὶ ἑρμηνευταί, οἱ λοιποί).[12] He cites them in order to clarify the meaning of particular passages, to offer different semantic possibilities for given words or phrases, or simply to evaluate critically and reject or accept the cited translation vis-à-vis its Septuagintal counterpart.

In addition to the Septuagint and the translations of Aquila, Symmachus, and Theodotion, Theodoret uses and mentions in several instances the Hebrew text of Isaiah. He calls it "the Hebrew" (ὁ Ἑβραῖος) or "the Hebrew Scripture" (ἡ Ἑβραϊκὴ γραφή).[13] His objective in such quotations is to discuss words or phrases that appear in the Hebrew but not in the Septuagint text or to explain the precise meanings of difficult terms.

In a few instances, Theodoret cites a Syriac translation of Isaiah under the name of "the Syriac" (ὁ Σῦρος).[14] J. N. Guinot has argued that the designation probably refers to the Syriac translation known as the Peshitta.[15] Here again the reason for the quotation is the semantic clarification of a term or a passage.

Theodoret mentions one more category of texts in the Book of Isaiah that he utilizes in a few instances. He makes reference to them by using the formula "some of the copies (or texts)" or "some copies" (ἔνια τῶν ἀντιγράφων, ἔνια ἀντίγραφα).[16] What we seem to encounter here is not another Greek version of Isaiah but some manuscripts, either isolated or in groups, that offer a variant reading on specific passages.

The picture created by this brief survey is that of an exegete who pays serious attention to the textual, literary, and semantic questions related to the Book of Isaiah. He basically works with the Septuagint version of Isaiah in its Lucianic recension, but keeps a constant eye on the Hebrew original, the Syriac translation (Peshitta), the three additional translations of Aquila,

12. E.g., Theodoret, *Isaiah*, on Isa. 3:2 (Guinot I, 212); 6:5 (Guinot I, 264); 8:16-18 (Guinot I, 312-14); 10:3-4 (Guinot II, 22); 27:3 (Guinot II, 222); 33:4-8 (Guinot II, 310-14); 49:6-7 (Guinot III, 80-82); 61:3 (Guinot III, 270), etc.

13. E.g., Theodoret, *Isaiah*, on Isa. 8:8-9 (Guinot I, 304-6); 23:1 (Guinot II, 170); 60:8 (Guinot III, 250), etc.

14. Theodoret, *Isaiah*, on Isa. 23:13 (Guinot II, 178); 30:33 (Guinot II, 286).

15. Guinot, *Théodoret de Cyr Commentaire*, I, pp. 48-50.

16. Theodoret, *Isaiah*, on Isa. 8:21 (Guinot I, 316); 45:4-5 (Guinot III, 20); 59:4 (Guinot III, 226), etc.

Symmachus, and Theodotion, and some free circulating manuscripts in which variant readings are encountered. He not only keeps an eye on them, but constantly quotes from them.[17]

In this case, Theodoret is not using a new and unknown exegetical approach in writing a commentary on an Old Testament book. Being an Antiochene, he was familiar with a tradition that was sensitive to the literary and textual aspects of the biblical text.[18] Chrysostom, however, who also was an Antiochene, did not present in his commentary on Isaiah the type of developed and methodical handling of the textual, literary, and semantic aspects of the text that we encounter in Theodoret's commentary. It is the non-Antiochene Eusebius, who in his commentary on Isaiah gives us a picture of a textual work somehow similar to that of Theodoret, especially in using Aquila, Symmachus, Theodotion, and the Hebrew. Eusebius, as it is well known, follows very closely Origen's (lost) commentary on Isaiah.[19] Theodoret in this case seems to move along the lines of Eusebius, in combination with a textual tradition represented by Lucian, Diodore of Tarsus, and Theodore of Mopsuestia. Here we can perhaps speak of the development of a specific exegetical tradition of a textual nature that originated in Alexandria, was cultivated in Antioch, and found itself fully integrated in the exegetical synthesis of Theodoret.

b) Theodoret's eagerness to offer an exegesis based on all data coming from the text of Isaiah is revealed in his way of using grammatical, etymological, and semantic information as well as information related to the natural sciences and to history. J. N. Guinot in his introduction to Theodoret's *Commentary on Isaiah* discusses all these aspects and provides the reader with ample relevant evidence.[20] One could mention by way of

17. In three instances he also mentions the Septuagint version found in the *Hexapla.* See his comments on Isa. 45:4-5 (Guinot III, 20); 60:8 (Guinot III, 250); and 63:11-12 (Guinot III, 296).

18. The names of Lucian, Diodore of Tarsus, and Theodore of Mopsuestia are indicative of such a tradition. Cf. Breck, *The Power of the Word*, pp. 71, 72, 81; Dimitri Z. Zacharopoulos, *Theodore of Mopsuestia on the Bible* (New York: Paulist, 1989), pp. 118-23.

19. See Ziegler, *Eusebius Werke, der Jesajakommentar*, xxxi-xxxiv; J. Quasten, *Patrology*, vol. III (Utrecht: Spectrum, 1966), p. 338.

20. Guinot, *Théodoret de Cyr Commentaire*, I, pp. 57-68. Similar aspects of exegesis are encountered also in Theodore of Mopsuestia. Cf. Breck, *The Power of the Word*, p. 81.

example many occasions when Theodoret speaks of grammatical phenomena like the change from singular to plural within a passage, the unexpected usage of a possessive pronoun, the appearance of a verb in the future tense instead of the expected past or in the passive voice instead of the active, the change of subjects and verbs within a sentence, the transposition of an accent from one syllable to another resulting to a transformation of the meaning, and the like.[21]

From the realm of the sciences, Theodoret on many occasions brings into his effort to explain the text of Isaiah examples and information from medicine, psychology, botany, zoology, and physics.[22] He seems to be particularly fond of geography, as one readily sees in his frequent notes related to geographical issues, usually determining locations mentioned by Isaiah.[23]

The most important area from which Theodoret draws constantly is history.[24] In interpreting his biblical text, he is very attentive to all historical data provided by it. Such an effort is facilitated by the very nature of the book of Isaiah, which has an obvious historical basis. Theodoret's attitude, nonetheless, is explainable not so much by the nature of the biblical text as it is by his own respect for history as a basis for exegesis. In the final analysis he appears to be eager to show that the messianic prophecies in Isaiah have a strong and undeniable foundation on history.

The commentaries on Isaiah by Eusebius, Chrysostom, and Cyril have, in various degrees, elements of exegesis based on the sort of information that Theodoret uses. This is clearly observable in the area of history. None of them, however, provides the amount of data and information found in Theodoret's commentary. Here again, Theodoret seems to have worked with a particular tradition of exegesis and to have advanced it, making it more systematic, more extensive, and more substantive in the task of understanding the biblical text. Behind such systematization and enhancement of an existing exegetical method lies perhaps Theodoret's

21. Theodoret, *Isaiah*, on Isa. 19:19 (Guinot II, 142); 40:9 (Guinot II, 400); 1:4 (Guinot I, 154); 9:20 (Guinot II, 20); 30:10 (Guinot II, 270); etc.

22. Theodoret, *Isaiah*, on Isa. 38:20-21 (Guinot II, 384); 30:26 (Guinot II, 280f.); 1:30-31 (Guinot I, 184); 7:22 (Guinot I, 296-98); 11:6 (Guinot II, 46); 13:21 (Guinot II, 78); 40:26 (Guinot II, 410-12).

23. Theodoret, *Isaiah*, on Isa. 49:12 (Guinot III, 88); 14:13 (Guinot II, 88); 63:13-14 (Guinot III, 298); 60:9 (Guinot III, 252); 43:3 (Guinot II, 452).

24. For details on this subject see Guinot, *Théodoret de Cyr Commentaire*, I, pp. 61-68.

conviction that the exegete must use any available technical information in order to render the meaning of a scriptural pericope or passage clear and complete.[25] Here one can see the emergence of an exegesis characterized by discernible tendencies toward inclusiveness and synthesis. This, perhaps, could be better seen in the following study of the specific passages from Isaiah as they have been interpreted by Theodoret and by the three patristic commentators who preceded him, namely, Eusebius, Chrysostom, and Cyril.

III. Isaiah 1

The first text that could be used as a study case is Isaiah 1. What are the characteristics of the exegesis offered here by Theodoret? And how does this exegesis relate and compare to the exegesis of the same pericope by Eusebius, Chrysostom, and Cyril?

a) Eusebius after a short prologue starts with a verse-by-verse exegesis of Isaiah 1. In his exegesis we do not encounter grammatical, linguistic, or stylistic observations. We encounter, however, textual observations in the form of quotations from Aquila, Symmachus, and Theodotion and one from the Hebrew text of Isaiah 1:21.

Eusebius, being a well-known Church historian, is aware of the historical nature and dimensions of the text that he is interpreting. He draws attention to the fact that there is a need for an extensive and precise special knowledge in order to see at what specific period of time a particular prophecy applies.[26]

In interpreting Isaiah 1, however, Eusebius does not spend time in showing the application of the concrete prophetic words in the course of ancient Hebrew history. In almost all instances, he sees the fulfillment of a prophecy in Christ, or he simply reads the historical references in Isaiah 1 in a christocentric mode. Thus "the Lord" in Isa. 1:2 and 4 is Christ; the

---

25. As Fr. Breck (*The Power of the Word*, p. 89) succinctly put it, "a master in virtually every area of biblical science, Theodoret attempted to develop a hermeneutic which could elucidate the deepest meaning of Scripture."

26. Eusebius, *Isaiah*, introductory comments (Ziegler, 4): πολλῆς δεῖσθαι καὶ ἀκριβοῦς ἐπιστήμης τῷ μέλλοντι διαιρεῖν καὶ εἰς χρόνους ἀφορίζειν τὴν τῶν ἐμφερομένων διάνοιαν καὶ ταῖς πράξεσι ταῖς καθ᾽ ἑκάστην βασιλείαν πεπραγμέναις τὴν προφητείαν ἐφαρμόζειν.

one against whom the Jewish people rebelled, according to the same verses, is Christ; the hands of people are full of blood (1:15) because they have killed Christ; and the commandment "wash yourselves clean" (1:16) is a prophecy of what Christ said in John 3:5, "unless one is born of water and the Spirit, he cannot enter the kingdom of God."[27] The christological understanding here has dominated the perception of history to a degree that has caused a discernible diminishing of a real interest for the historical events closely related to the time of Isaiah and to the Jewish history as such.

This, nonetheless, does not mean that historical exegesis has vanished from the scene. It is present, but is focused on the christological realm of history. Eusebius reads Isaiah 1 as history, but history prophetically predicted by Isaiah and realized in Christ. The exegetical key here is the idea of prophecy and fulfillment.

Is Eusebius's exegesis of Isaiah 1 free from allegorical elements? Not at all. Already in the opening lines of his prologue he acknowledges the need for an allegorical interpretation when symbols, specific words, and names in a text suggest another meaning.[28] In Eusebius's exegesis of Isaiah 1, we encounter several examples of this type of allegorical interpretation. The "land" in 1:19, for instance, is the human soul, the "silver" in 1:22 is the word of the Jewish teachers, the "return from the captivity" in 1:27 (Septuagint) is the conversion from error to the truth of God, etc.[29]

The main line of Eusebius's exegesis of Isaiah 1, however, is not allegorical in the strict sense, not ahistorical. For him, Isaiah 1 is history, but history fully realized in Christ and in the time of the church.

b) John Chrysostom's exegesis of Isaiah 1 is different from that of Eusebius. In his commentary there are no observations referring to literary or textual aspects of the text. There are no quotations from any biblical version or translation other than the Septuagint in its Lucianic recension.[30]

---

27. Eusebius, *Isaiah,* on Isa. 1:4 (Ziegler, 5); 1:11-15 (Ziegler, 8); 1:16 (Ziegler, 9).

28. Eusebius, *Isaiah,* introductory comment (Ziegler, 3): Τὸ πνεῦμα τῷ προφήτῃ ἐδείκνυ ποτὲ μὲν σαφῶς τὰ δηλούμενα ὡς μὴ δεῖσθαι τρόπων ἀλληγορίας . . . ποτὲ δὲ διὰ συμβόλων ἑτέρων πραγμάτων, ἐμφαντικοῖς ῥήμασί τε καὶ ὀνόμασιν ἑτέραν ὑποβαλλόντων διάνοιαν.

29. Eusebius, *Isaiah,* on Isa. 1:19 (Ziegler, 9f.); 1:21-22 (Ziegler, 11); 1:27 (Ziegler, 12f.).

30. Garrett, *An Analysis of the Hermeneutics of Chrysostom,* p. 188, notes that "nowhere in the commentary does Chrysostom comment on variant readings of the Greek text of Isaiah."

Chrysostom offers a concise verse-by-verse exegesis that looks like an amplified paraphrase of the text of Isaiah. He consistently stays with the strict literal-historical meaning of Isaiah 1, and applies it to the Jewish people whom the prophet was addressing. There are no substantive christological references or interpretations here. Chrysostom does not say that such references should be excluded, but he does not mention them. The frequent interpretations of Eusebius, for instance, of passages in Isaiah 1 as referring to the killing of Christ by the Jewish people are not to be found in Chrysostom's interpretation of Isaiah 1. Beginning with the exegesis of Isaiah 2, Chrysostom will gradually introduce aspects of christological and ecclesiological interpretations when he sees that the biblical text allows such interpretation. In Isaiah 1, however, he presents us with a purely and strictly literal-historical exegesis.

It goes without saying that such exegesis has no room for allegory. Chrysostom in Isaiah 1 does not attack allegory; he simply ignores it as an exegetical tool. Even in cases where he could explain a passage in a metaphorical way, he avoids doing so. As an example we could mention his exegesis of the phrase "Hear, O heaven and give ear, O earth" (Isa. 1:2), where Chrysostom sees God speaking to the natural inanimate elements (ἀναίσθητα φύσει στοιχεῖα) because he could not speak to the people because of their utter depravity.[31] Other exegetes, such as Eusebius, understood "heavens" and "earth" in Isa. 1:2 allegorically, namely, as terms indicating spiritual entities.

One specific example shows Chrysostom's exegetical attitude vis-à-vis some allegorical-metaphorical interpretations. When he comes to Isa. 1:22, "Your silver has become dross," "your wine mixed with water," he notes that some exegetes have understood this passage allegorically, thinking that here silver is the words of God and wine the teaching. "I am not dishonoring such an interpretation (οὐκ ἀτιμάζω ταύτην τὴν ἐξήγησιν)," says Chrysostom, "but I think that the other one that I propose is more true," namely, that the prophet here speaks about greed and fraudulence in transactions.[32]

---

31. Chrysostom, *Isaiah*, on Isa. 1:2 (Dumortier, 50; Garrett, 42).
32. Chrysostom, *Isaiah*, on Isa. 1:22 (Dumortier, 82; Garrett, 55): Ἀλλά τινες οὐ συνιέντες τὴν ἄφατον τοῦ Θεοῦ φιλανθρωπίαν, κατ' ἀναγωγὴν τὸ εἰρημένον ἐξέλαβον. . . . Ἐγὼ δὲ οὔτε ταύτην ἀτιμάζω τὴν ἐξήγησιν, καὶ τὴν ἑτέραν ἀληθεστέραν εἶναί φημι. Garrett's English translation of the phrase οὔτε ταύτην ἀτιμάζω τὴν ἐξήγησιν is incorrect.

Chrysostom's reluctance to engage in an allegorical-metaphorical exegesis and his strong adherence to the literal-historical interpretation certainly are the results of his appreciation for a well-known Antiochene tradition of Old Testament exegesis. One could suggest, however, that Chrysostom's insistence on literal-historical exegesis also has to do with his intense socio-ethical sensitivities. It should not be viewed as accidental that in his prologue to the *Commentary on Isaiah*, Chrysostom speaks at length about the immense and unbearable pain that Isaiah and the great prophets felt when facing the social decadence and the moral corruption of the people of their times.[33] The deep pain in view of such a situation and the inescapable need for a radical change, things terribly important for Chrysostom, could not be better depicted than by exegesis that pays the highest attention even to the details of the historical facts contained in the text of Isaiah.

c) Cyril's commentary on Isaiah 1 is lengthy and offers an elaborate verse-by-verse exegesis. In his prologue he explains that the prophetic word is obscure and filled with hidden concepts. Therefore the task of the interpreter is to find out the precise historical facts and, at the same time, the interpretation or application of the spiritual *theōria*.[34] Following these programmatic exegetical statements, Cyril begins his work with a historical review of the lives and attitudes of the kings mentioned in Isa. 1:1, and closes the review with the statement that Isaiah remembers throughout his prophetic utterances the redemption through Christ. Hence for Cyril, Isaiah "is at the same time prophet and apostle, and the words of his prophetic work are not lacking the joyfulness of the evangelical preaching."[35]

Cyril's exegesis of Isaiah 1 reflects the above-quoted statements. He reads Isaiah as a prophet who speaks at a certain historical period, sharply criticizing Israel for its abandonment of the Lord and for its moral and religious depravity. As he proceeds with a verse-by-verse analysis of Isaiah 1, Cyril brings in passages and texts from other Old Testament prophets as well as from various Old Testament books that display the same unmiti-

---

33. Chrysostom, *Isaiah*, prologue (Dumortier, 36-40; Garrett, 35): (Ἡσαΐας) ἤλγει καὶ ἐδάκνετο καὶ πικρότερον τῶν ἁλόντων ὠδύρετο. . . . Οὗτοι (i.e., the prophets) τῶν ἀρχομένων ὑπεραπέθνησκον, ὀδυρόμενοι, θρηνοῦντες, κακῶς πασχόντων αὐτῶν τὸν Θεὸν παρακαλοῦντες, συναπαγόμενοι, κοινωνοῦντες τῶν δεινῶν, πάντα καὶ ποιοῦντες καὶ πάσχοντες. . . .

34. Cyril, *Isaiah*, prologue (*PG* 70:9).

35. Cyril, *Isaiah*, prologue (*PG* 70:13).

gated criticism of Israel. As becomes obvious, Cyril goes beyond the specific time of Isaiah and includes later Jewish generations in the indictments pronounced by Isaiah 1. Then, quite naturally, in most instances of his exegesis of Isaiah 1, he concludes with the time of Christ and sees the full application of Isaiah's prophetic indictment of Israel in the Jewish religious rulers and people of the period of Jesus. When he reaches this point, he very frequently quotes various New Testament texts containing words of Jesus or of the apostles.

Such exegesis is a mixture of an awareness of history and of an awareness of a total fulfillment of everything historical and spiritual in Christ. Cyril, writing from the vantage point of the revelation in Christ, probably feels that his exegesis is legitimate because it respects the text of Isaiah in its historical context without necessarily being limited by it. The "spiritual *theōria*" and exegetical possibilities offered by the full knowledge of the truth through the incarnation of God in Christ gives Cyril a legitimate way of unlocking the text of Isaiah with the interpretative key of the New Testament.

Cyril does not use allegory in a noticeable manner. In the few instances in Isaiah 1 when he uses an allegorical interpretation, he does so in a limited way and with application to rather secondary issues. This is the case, for instance, in his exegesis of Isa. 1:5, 7, 9, and 13.[36] In fact, when he interprets verse 2, "hear O heavens, and give ear O earth," he offers a series of exegetical possibilities ranging from the literal to the allegorical, inclusively rather than exclusively.[37]

d) Theodoret's commentary on Isaiah 1[38] gives us an exegetical picture that coincides and at the same time departs from the exegetical pictures presented by Eusebius, Chrysostom, and Cyril.

In the prologue of his commentary Theodoret announces the subject of the prophecy of Isaiah (Ὑπόθεσις τῆς Ἡσαΐου προφητείας) and explains how he understands his exegetical task. According to Theodoret all the prophets not only declared what would happen to Israel, but also

36. Cyril, *Isaiah,* on Isa. 1:5 (*PG* 70:21); 1:7 (*PG* 70:25); 1:9 (*PG* 70:29); 1:13 (*PG* 70:36).

37. Cyril, *Isaiah,* comment on Isa. 1:2 (*PG* 70:16-17).

38. A handsome English translation of Theodoret's commentary on Isaiah 1 is Anton Vrame, "Theodoret, Bishop of Kyros as an Exegete of Isaiah 1," *Greek Orthodox Theological Review* 34 (1989), pp. 127-47. Vrame makes an interesting comparison between Theodoret's exegesis and modern exegesis of Isaiah 1.

indicated the salvation of the nations and predicted the appearance of the Lord. More than anyone else, it was Isaiah who was entrusted with this prophetic function, since he foretells everything about Christ.[39] Theodoret gives a long list of what he means by "everything," including all the major christological events, even Christ's second coming.[40]

The things that Isaiah wrote, continues Theodoret in his prologue, are not all on the same level of language. Some are clear and have an evident meaning, while some are expressed metaphorically (τροπικῶς εἰρημένα) and need interpretation. Theodoret promises to be very brief with the former and more elaborate with the latter, trying always to remain concise.[41]

His exegesis of Isaiah 1 is concise and brief, limited to the very basic elements needed for establishing a meaning with clarity. In some instances he quotes the variant readings from Symmachus, Aquila, and Theodotion. He follows the text verse by verse, speaking first about the historical circumstances related to the specific passages. He offers a literal-historical exegesis, almost simply paraphrasing the biblical text. There is no doubt that he does nothing that would show disrespect for the literal or historical value of Isaiah 1. But then, almost in all cases, he sees the full force of the prophetic words applied to the time of Christ. Viewed from this angle, his exegesis becomes christocentric. He reads, for instance, Isa. 1:2-4 as finally applied to the events of the crucifixion, 1:7 as originally realized at the time of Nebuchadnezzar but ultimately at the time of the Roman emperors Titus and Hadrian, and 1:16-18 as eventually applied to Christian baptism.[42] He sees the severe judgment against the Jewish people realized only in part at the time of the original utterance of the prophecy of Isaiah 1, but fully at the time of Christ.

39. Theodoret, *Isaiah*, prologue (Guinot I, 142): Ἅπαντες οἱ θεσπέσιοι προφῆται οὐ μόνον τὰ τῷ Ἰσραὴλ συμβησόμενα ὑπηγόρευσαν, ἀλλὰ καὶ τῶν ἐθνῶν τὴν σωτηρίαν ἐθέσπισαν καὶ τὴν δεσποτικὴν προεμήνυσαν ἐπιφάνειαν· πάντων δὲ μάλιστα ὁ θειότατος Ἡσαΐας. . . . Σαφῶς γὰρ ἅπαντα προλέγει.

40. Theodoret, *Isaiah*, prologue (Guinot I, 142-44): προλέγει (i.e. Isaiah) . . . τὴν ἐκ παρθένου γέννησιν τοῦ σωτῆρος καὶ τὰς παντοδαπὰς θαυματουργίας . . . καὶ τὸ πάθος, καὶ τὸν θάνατον καὶ τὴν ἐκ νεκρῶν ἀναβίωσιν καὶ τὴν εἰς οὐρανοὺς ἄνοδον . . . πρὸς τούτοις καὶ τὴν δευτέραν τοῦ Θεοῦ καὶ σωτῆρος ἡμῶν ἐπιφάνειαν.

41. Theodoret, *Isaiah*, prologue (Guinot I, 144).

42. Theodoret, *Isaiah*, on Isa. 1:2-4 (Guinot I, 148-54); 1:7 (Guinot I, 156); 1:16-18 (Guinot I, 170-74).

Such an exegetical attitude was not encountered in Chrysostom, as we have seen, but rather in Cyril. Thus, with Theodoret, a prominent Antiochene himself, exegesis goes beyond a strict literal-historical understanding of the prophetic text. There is a synthesis discernible here, combining the Antiochene exegetical tradition with other exegetical traditions.

The tendency toward a synthesis is also discernible in that Theodoret does not hesitate to use metaphorical-allegorical approaches in dealing with certain passages. A clear example is Isa. 1:5-6,[43] where Theodoret offers an allegorical interpretation similar to the one proposed by Cyril, whereas Chrysostom in the same instance follows a strictly historical interpretation. Another equally telling example is 1:22,[44] which Theodoret interprets allegorically-metaphorically, in contradistinction again to Chrysostom's exegesis, which is historical, although the latter clearly knows the specific allegorical interpretation of the passage, since he mentions it.

IV. Isaiah 6

We now proceed to the study of the exegesis of another text from Isaiah namely, Isaiah 6, the chapter where the prophet describes his call by God. What is the exegesis offered here by Theodoret in view of the parallel exegesis offered by Eusebius, Chrysostom, and Cyril?

a) Eusebius's interpretation of Isaiah 6 follows the methods and principles of exegesis that we encountered in his interpretation of Isaiah 1. We find again a few philological observations (e.g., the meaning of the word "seraphim" in Greek)[45] and a few variant readings of certain passages from Symmachus, Aquila, and Theodotion. We also find that he shows an awareness of the historical facts presupposed by Isaiah 6. The reader of Eusebius's commentary on Isaiah 6, gets the impression that the author deals with a biblical text that is undeniably historical and that he is conscious of such a historical perspective.

---

43. Theodoret, *Isaiah*, on Isa. 1:5-6 (Guinot I, 154-56): Κεφαλὴν καλεῖ τοὺς βασιλέας καὶ ἄρχοντας, καρδίαν δὲ τοὺς ἱερέας καὶ διδασκάλους.

44. Theodoret, *Isaiah*, on Isa. 1:22 (Guinot I, 176-78): οὐδὲ καπήλων οὐδὲ ἀργυραμοιβῶν ποιεῖται κατηγορίαν ἀλλ᾽ ἱερέων καὶ διδασκάλων τὸν θεῖον νοθευόντων νόμον.

45. Eusebius, *Isaiah*, on Isa. 6:6 (Ziegler, 41).

The main line for Eusebius's exegesis, however, in Isaiah 6, as it was in Isaiah 1, is christological. He begins his exegesis of Isaiah 6 by flatly declaring that the Lord whom Isaiah saw (6:1) is the "only begotten God who is in the bosom of the Father . . . who made himself visible and comprehensible to human beings." It was precisely this God whom Isaiah saw, and the glory that the prophet beheld in this instance was "the glory of our Savior Jesus Christ."[46]

The angelic beings who sing the hymn "holy, holy, holy" (Isa. 6:3) address it to Christ, and the hymnic expression "the whole earth is full of his glory" is an outburst of a joyful foreseeing of the glory of God's Son in his incarnation.[47] The burning coal with cleansing power in 6:6-7 is an anticipation of the work of Jesus who will "baptize you in the Holy Spirit and in fire" (Matt. 3:11).[48] Isa. 6:9-10 clearly refers to the Jewish people at the time of Jesus. In this instance Eusebius addresses Isaiah, in a rhetorical fashion: "The Lord whom you have seen, O prophet, and whom you have heard, the very same Lord, this people will also see and hear at some time, but this people will not listen to him nor will accept his grace."[49] Eusebius here simply echoes the very clear comments on Isa. 6:9-10 presented in Matt. 13:13-15 and Mark 4:12 (cf. also Luke 8:10).

Finally, Eusebius reads Isa. 6:11-12 as a prediction of the catastrophies that befell Israel because of its resistance to Christ at the times of the Roman emperors Vespasian and Hadrian.

In Eusebius's exegesis of Isaiah 6, there are some instances of an allegorical interpretation, especially in the passage dealing with the angelic powers (Isa. 6:2-3).

b) Chrysostom in his commentary on Isaiah 6 remains faithful to his method of literal-historical exegesis that we encountered in his interpretive work on Isaiah 1. He interprets Isaiah's call to the prophetic office in a way that is predominantly historical. This we see from the very beginning of his exegesis of Isaiah 6, when he speaks about King Uzziah, giving the pertinent historical data and explaining why the death of Uzziah is mentioned here.

---

46. Eusebius, *Isaiah*, on Isa. 6:1 (Ziegler, 36).

47. Eusebius, *Isaiah*, on Isa. 6:3 (Ziegler, 39-40): (the seraphim) προγνώσει τοῦ μέλλοντος ὑπερεθαύμαζον. . . . Ἐπειδὴ γὰρ ἑώρων αὐτοῦ (i.e. Christ's) τὴν δόξαν ἐπὶ γῆς μέλλουσαν ἐκλάμπειν . . . εἰκότως ἀνεβόων τὸ ἅγιος, ἅγιος, ἅγιος Κύριος σαβαώθ. . . .

48. Eusebius, *Isaiah*, on Isa. 6:6-7 (Ziegler, 41).

49. Eusebius, *Isaiah*, on Isa. 6:9-10 (Ziegler, 42).

Moving over to the phrase "I saw the Lord sitting upon a throne" (Isa. 6:1), Chrysostom notes that according to Christ "no one has ever seen God; the only begotten Son, who is in the bosom of the Father, he has made him known" (John 1:18). Having said that, he does not engage in a christological exegesis like the one we found in Eusebius. He simply states that Isaiah saw what was possible to see as an image of God, in a way similar to various visual appearances of God described in the Old Testament.[50] There are no traces here of an exegesis that goes beyond the strict data provided by the text of Isa. 6:1 and the other Old Testament books. There is no attempt to introduce a christological understanding of the passage.

Chrysostom continues along the same lines of literal-historical exegesis of Isaiah 6. In some instances he is eager to show that he insists on a historically oriented exegesis versus an allegorical, metaphorical, or spiritual interpretation. An eloquent example comes in his exegesis of verses 6 and 7, where he states: "Some say, that the altar, the fire, the serving angel, the placing into the mouth, the cleansing of the sins are symbols of the future mysteries; however, I stick to the history and say why all that happened."[51] The statement clearly reveals Chrysostom's exegetical attitude and his insistence on interpreting the facts as they are and within their own context.

When he reaches the end of Isaiah 6 and comes sto verses 11-13 he applies them to Israel at the time of Isaiah, more specifically to events related to the Assyrian king Sennacherib, about whom Isaiah himself speaks (Isa. 36:1ff; also 2 Kings 18:13–20:19). And the "holy seed" of Isa. 6:13 is again the very same people of the very same time.[52] Once again there are no traces of a suggestion that verses 11-13 should be interpreted as related to the people of Israel at the time of Jesus or that the catastrophy predicted in the same passage is the result of their wrong attitude toward Christ.

There are, however, instances in Chrysostom's exegesis of Isaiah 6 when he introduces elements of a theological, spiritual, or christological nature. They are very brief and limited, yet they are unmistakably clear.

When, for instance, Chrysostom interprets the angelic hymn "holy,

---

50. Chrysostom, *Isaiah*, on Isa. 6:1 (Dumortier, 256; Garrett, 124): γυμνὴν γὰρ τὴν θεότητα καὶ ἀκραιφνῆ τὴν οὐσίαν οὐδεὶς ἐθεάσατο πλὴν τοῦ Μονογενοῦς· ὁ δὲ προφήτης τὴν αὐτῷ δυνατὴν ἰδεῖν ἀπαγγέλει. Οὐδὲ γὰρ αὐτὸς ὅπερ ἐστίν ὁ Θεός ἰδεῖν ἠδυνήθη, ἀλλὰ σχηματισθέντα αὐτὸν θεωρεῖ.

51. Chrysostom, *Isaiah*, on Isa. 6:6 (Dumortier, 272-74; Garrett, 130): ἡμεῖς δὲ τέως τῆς ἱστορίας ἐχόμεθα καὶ λέγομεν τίνος ἕνεκεν τοῦτο γεγένηται.

52. Chrysostom, *Isaiah*, on Isa. 6:11-13 (Dumortier, 284-88; Garrett, 135-36).

holy, holy," (Isa. 6:3), he asks "why they [the angels] did not say it ["holy"] once . . . or twice . . . but three times? Is it not very clear that they did so because they referred the hymn to the Trinity?" He further asks, "When was the whole earth full of his glory?" and answers, "when this hymn came down to earth and human beings became co-dancers with the heavenly powers. . . . And if the Jewish people refuse to accept this explanation, then let them show us at what time such a thing happened."[53]

Further down, Chrysostom reads Isa. 6:4 as a prophecy announcing the end of the Temple and of the Old Testament: "This was a sign of the desolation and of the destruction of the Temple; the Temple having been destroyed, all other things were destroyed too. The New Testament put an end to the Old."[54]

In interpreting Isa. 6:9-10, Chrysostom brings in passages from the New Testament (e.g., Acts 28:25-26; John 11:43-53; John 12:38-40), saying that he does not need to interpret the passage in Isaiah since the New Testament authors have already done so.[55] Here Chrysostom works with the tacit assumption that if there is in the New Testament an interpretation of an Old Testament passage, such an interpretation is valid. This assumption, however, raises questions regarding a pure historical exegesis of the Old Testament.

c) Cyril's interpretive work on Isaiah 6 is characterized, as his work on Isaiah 1, by an elaborate exegesis in which he tirelessly cites passages from both Testaments to explain the meaning of the Isaianic text. He also is eager to provide in special cases all possible historical information that helps create the proper understanding of the passages under discussion. As a telling example we could mention his extensive information about King Uzziah (Isa. 6:1), covering almost two columns in Migne's edition of the commentary. In this case, Cyril cites verbatim 2 Kings 15:1-5; 2 Chron. 26:16-20; Ezek. 3:26; and Amos 1:1, that is eleven full verses from biblical texts other than Isaiah, to provide historical information.[56]

53. Chrysostom, *Isaiah*, on Isa. 6:3 (Dumortier, 268-70; Garrett, 128-29).

54. Chrysostom, *Isaiah*, on Isa. 6:4 (Dumortier, 270; Garrett, 129): Ἐρημώσεως γὰρ τουτὶ τὸ σημεῖον ἦν, καὶ ἀνατροπῆς τοῦ ναοῦ· τοῦ ναοῦ δὲ ἀφανισθέντος, καὶ τἄλλα συγκατελύετο πάντα. Καὶ ἵνα μάθῃς ὅτι ἡ Καινὴ (i.e., Διαθήκη) τὴν Παλαιὸν ἔπαυσεν.

55. Chrysostom, *Isaiah*, on Isa. 6:9-10 (Dumortier, 280; Garrett, 133).

56. Cyril, *Isaiah*, on Isa. 6:1-5 (*PG* 70:169, 172).

The main feature, however, in Cyril's exegesis of Isaiah 6 is, again, his christological orientation. His hermeneutical key is the revelation in Christ, which constitutes the point of ultimate convergence of all meanings.

After establishing the historical facts related to the time of Isaiah's call to the prophetic office, Cyril flatly states that the Lord whom Isaiah saw was the Son in the glory of God the Father.[57] Cyril supports his statement by citing John 12:41: "Isaiah said this, because he saw his [Christ's] glory and spoke of him."

Again the expression "the whole earth is full of his glory" in Isa. 6:3 is, according to Cyril, a prediction of the mystery of the economy brought about by Christ. "Because the only begotten Logos of God became a human being, the whole earth has been filled with his glory."[58]

The clauses "the foundations of the thresholds shook" and "the house was filled with smoke" (Isa. 6:4) indicate, in Cyril's understanding, the final destruction of the Temple because of the negative attitude of the Jewish people toward Christ: "Because they did not accept the one who came from heaven in human form, having being announced by the Law and the prophets, or rather because they killed the giver of life, he abandoned his house [i.e., the Temple]. . . . The land became desolate and the Temple was burned."[59]

The entire scene described in Isa. 6:6-7 becomes for Cyril a rich mine out of which he extracts a number of christological applications.

Finally, Isa. 6:9-10 has, according to Cyril, its full application in the case of the Jewish religious leaders and people vis-à-vis Jesus Christ. The same also holds true for verse 13, which Cyril reads as a prophecy fulfilled in the times of the Roman emperors Vespasian and Hadrian.[60]

Elements of an allegorical exegesis are very few in Cyril's comments on Isaiah 6, limited mostly to verses 4 and 6-7. And it is characteristic that Cyril introduces the specific allegorical exegesis on verse 4 as a second interpretive option with a tentative qualification: "And if someone would like to understand these [words] in another way."[61]

d) Theodoret displays in his exegesis of Isaiah 6 the basic characteris-

---

57. Cyril, *Isaiah*, on Isa. 6:1 (*PG* 70:172-73): Ὅτι μέν οὖν τὸν Υἱὸν ὁ προφήτης τεθέαται ἐν τῇ δόξῃ τοῦ Θεοῦ καὶ Πατρός, οὐκ ἂν ἐνδοιάσειέ τις. . . .

58. Cyril, *Isaiah*, on Isa. 6:3 (*PG* 70:176): ἐπειδὴ δὲ γέγονεν ἄνθρωπος ὁ μονο-γενὴς τοῦ Θεοῦ Λόγος, πεπλήρωται τῆς δόξης αὐτοῦ πᾶσα γῆ.

59. Cyril, *Isaiah*, on Isa. 6:4 (*PG* 70:176).

60. Cyril, *Isaiah*, on Isa. 6:9-10 (*PG* 70:185); 6:13 (*PG* 70:189).

61. Cyril, *Isaiah*, on Isa. 6:4 (*PG* 70:177); 6:6-7 (*PG* 70:181).

tics that we encountered in his exegesis of Isaiah 1. He is concise and precise, combining brevity and clarity of exposition.

And here again we see him as an exegete who is conscious of the historical facts and who is trying to interpret the text within its historical context. He begins with the story of Uzziah the king in order to place the attached prophecy in the proper time frame and perhaps in order to "underline the historicity of the prophecy," as J. N. Guinot suggests.[62] As he proceeds with his exegesis of Isaiah 6, Theodoret will often connect particular verses of that chapter with the story of Uzziah,[63] thus maintaining the historical character of the entire pericope.

Theodoret seems to follow the line of Chrysostom in his exegesis of the phrase "I saw the Lord" in Isa. 6:1. He mentions the words of Christ in John 1:18 and 6:46 in order to argue that Isaiah could not have seen the very essence or nature of God.[64] What happened to Isaiah was something similar to what happened to Moses, Micah, Daniel, and Ezekiel. Theodoret stops here, and he does not go the direction that Cyril and Eusebius went as they argued that Isaiah saw the preexistent Logos–Son of God.

To the end of Isaiah 6, Theodoret consistently reads the prophet's words as applying first to Isaiah's own time and to Isaiah's contemporaries. Theodoret's adherence to a historically oriented exegesis does not prevent him, however, from interpreting the prophetic text in a christological key too, since Christ is part of the developing history.

Thus, the phrase "the whole earth is full of his glory" (Isa. 6:3) is ultimately fulfilled through the incarnation of God in Christ. Verses 6-7 prefigure the remission of sins obtained through the dominical body and blood. And the phrase "hear and hear, but do not understand; see and see, but do not perceive" (6:9), has an immediate application in the time of Isaiah, though its final realization occurs in the time of Jesus.[65]

The same holds true for Theodoret's exegesis of Isa. 6:11-13. The catastrophies described in the passage occur in full force during Roman

---

62. J. N. Guinot, *Théodoret de Cyr Commentaire sur Isaie,* I, 254-55.

63. As two characteristic examples one could cite Theodoret's exegesis of Isa. 6:5 and 6-7 (Guinot I, 264-66) where he mentions Uzziah in connection with impurity due to leprosy and cleansing from leprosy. Cf. Ashby, *Theodoret of Cyrrhus,* p. 125.

64. Theodoret, *Isaiah,* on Isa. 6:1 (Guinot I, 256-58): Εἰδέναι δὲ χρή, ὡς ('Ησαΐας) οὐκ αὐτὴν εἶδε τοῦ Κυρίου τὴν φύσιν.

65. Theodoret, *Isaiah,* on Isa. 6:3 (Guinot I, 262); 6:6-7 (Guinot I, 266); 6:9 (Guinot I, 268).

times, ending with the total annihilation of Jerusalem by Emperor Hadrian after the Bar Kochba insurrection.[66]

Theodoret's christological exegesis of Isaiah 6 is not like that of Cyril or of Eusebius. It is not elaborate and does not use a rich and extended christological vocabulary. Theodoret is very restricted, almost laconic when he introduces christological aspects, and he does so in a way that does not give the impression that he has left the historical field. This, however, is an exegesis filled with clear and explicit christological references. Such an exegesis would not be like exegesis in the strict Antiochene mode of Diodorus of Tarsus or Theodore of Mopsuestia. Theodoret clearly has taken a step ahead and seems to offer a synthesis, including christological aspects of exegesis found in some of his non-Antiochene fellow exegetes.

V. Isaiah 7:10-17

Our final passage is Isaiah 7:10-17, which contains the famous Immanuel prophecy. This prophecy, being of a messianic type, will help us to have one more look at Theodoret's exegesis in comparison to the exegeses of Eusebius, Chrysostom, and Cyril.

a) Eusebius in this case offers an exegesis that pays high attention to the details of the text, to textual problems, and to questions of translation.

He speaks extensively about the meaning of the term "sign" (σημεῖον) in verses 11 and 14, illustrating his points with the help of passages from various Old Testament books (e.g., Ps. 135:9; Exodus 8–10; Ps. 78:45-48; 1 Sam. 28:7-25).

He also speaks extensively about the name Immanuel, and insists on the variant reading "καὶ καλέσεις τὸ ὄνομα αὐτοῦ Ἐμμανουήλ" (Isa. 7:14, Septuagint) instead of "καὶ καλέσουσι . . . ," which appears in Matt. 1:23, because, Eusebius argues, this was an order given to Ahaz and not to the people in general.[67]

He mentions the terms "virgin" or "young woman" in Isa. 7:14, noting that the Septuagint text has παρθένος while the other ancient translators have νεᾶνις, but he feels that neither term changes the essence of the meaning, which still reveals a miraculous event.

66. Theodoret, *Isaiah*, on Isa. 6:11-13 (Guinot I, 270-74).
67. Eusebius, *Isaiah*, on Isa. 7:14 (Ziegler, 49).

In his exegesis of Isa. 7:10-15, Eusebius frequently cites passages from the translations of Aquila, Symmachus, and Theodotion, a fact indicative of his decision to offer as many options as possible for a full and clear understanding of difficult passages. The same fact is also indicative of his sensitivity to the literary-linguistic aspects of the text.

The heart of the prophecy is, of course, messianic and this is obvious in Eusebius's handling of Isa. 7:10-17. It is interesting, therefore, to see how he applies the Immanuel prophecy to Ahaz. He argues that what Ahaz was given was the possibility to pray to a God who would be with him. Invoke Immanuel, that is, God who is with us, and you will be saved from the threat of your enemies, says Eusebius, addressing himself to Ahaz. And he adds: "call upon Immanuel, the one who will be born at a certain time from a virgin, but who already is God and is with us, hence able to do great things for your salvation."[68]

Eusebius further interprets Isa. 7:14-16 as proclaiming the birth of the saviour from the holy Virgin and the real humanity and divinity of Immanuel. The humanity of Christ is suggested by the mention of food, whereas the divinity is stated in the phrase related to the knowledge of the good and the evil (verse 15).[69] The pure christological statements of Eusebius in his exegesis of verses 10-15 are clear and unequivocal, but brief. His main objective is the clarification of the text in its essentials not the offering of elaborate christological interpretations.

b) Chrysostom's exegesis of Isa. 7:10-17 analyzes very carefully the text within its historical context, paying also particular attention to some of its literary characteristics.

Chrysostom deals extensively with the short dialogue between the Lord and king Ahaz (verses 10-13), showing how wrong the king was in refusing to ask for a sign from the Lord and how this attitude did not cancel the plans of God. In fact, Chrysostom indicates through his exegesis that the king's refusal makes the Lord turn to the house of David and to the Jewish people in general and offer to them the sign (σημεῖον). At this point Chrysostom, by drawing attention to the usage of personal pronouns in

---

68. Eusebius, *Isaiah,* on Isa. 7:14 (Ziegler, 49): Ἐμμανουήλ κάλει καὶ τῆς τῶν πολεμίων ἐλευθερίας ἐπιγράφου τοῦτον αἴτιον, ἐκ παρθένου μὲν γενησόμενόν ποτε, ἤδη δὲ θεόν ὄντα καὶ μεθ' ἡμῶν ὄντα, ἐντεῦθέν τε ἤδη τὰ μεγάλα σοι πρός σωτηρίαν χαριούμενον.
69. Eusebius, *Isaiah,* on Isa. 7:15-17 (Ziegler, 50).

verse 14, demonstrates the transition from Ahaz to the people as recipients of the sign.[70]

Then Chrysostom proceeds to the exegesis of the phrase "Behold the virgin . . ." (verse 14). He strongly insists that the prophecy speaks here about a miraculous event, namely, a virgin giving birth to a child: "if she was not a virgin, then there was no sign."[71] He further observes that Isaiah here does not speak about "a virgin" (ἰδοὺ παρθένος) but "*the* virgin" (ἰδοὺ ἡ παρθένος), making by means of the definite article a very formal (ἐπίσημον) and unique (καὶ μόνην) statement. At this point Chrysostom adduces examples from John 1:1, 19-25 in which the usage of the definite article for Christ functions in a way similar to that encountered in Isa. 7:14 for the virgin.[72]

Chrysostom spends some time in talking about the name Immanuel, arguing that this name was not given to Christ by someone, but by the very reality. It was in Christ that God has been with us, appearing on earth and associating himself with the people.[73]

Chrysostom's careful handling of Isa. 7:10-15 is focused almost exclusively on christological issues. After the initial observations about Ahaz, he engages in a step-by-step discussion of the issues raised by the succeeding verses with respect to Christ. The virgin birth, the role of the Holy Spirit in the conception of Christ, the name Immanuel as indicative of the reality of the incarnation, the human nature of the child born of the virgin, and the divine nature of the same child are themes with which Chrysostom deals in a very natural way, because he sees them in the text.

In a particular case, when he talks about the name Immanuel, Chrysostom becomes elated and highly inspired and offers a beautiful text that actually sings the astonishing results of the incarnation of God in the person of Christ, the real Immanuel.[74]

c) Cyril opens his exegesis of Isaiah 7 with a very interesting statement

---

70. Chrysostom, *Isaiah,* on Isa. 7:14 (Dumortier, 314; Garrett, 146): Διὰ τοῦτο γάρ, φησί, δώσει, οὐχὶ σοί, ἀλλ ὑμῖν σημεῖον.

71. Chrysostom, *Isaiah,* on Isa. 7:14 (Dumortier, 314; Garrett, 146): Εἰ δὲ μὴ παρθένος ἦν, οὐδὲ σημεῖον ἦν. D. A. Garrett, *An Analysis of the Hermeneutics of Chrysostom,* 224-26, presents seven more arguments adduced by Chrysostom in his exegesis of Isa. 7:14-16 in support of the messianic interpretation of the passage.

72. Chrysostom, *Isaiah,* on Isa. 7:14 (Dumortier, 314-16; Garrett, 146).

73. Chrysostom, *Isaiah,* on Isa. 7:14 (Dumortier, 318; Garrett, 147-48).

74. Chrysostom, *Isaiah,* on Isa. 7:14 (Dumortier, 318-20; Garrett, 147-48).

about the importance of the historical exegesis of the biblical text. He says that the spiritual *theōria* (θεωρία πνευματική) is good and useful, but when Scripture offers to us historical accounts (ἱστορικῶς πεπραγμένα) we must gather from them whatever is profitable, so that we take every salvific and edifying element provided by the God-inspired text.[75] This statement coming from an Alexandrian exegete is significant indeed.

Cyril, faithfully following what he said, proceeds with a very detailed, historically oriented exegesis of the first nine verses of Isaiah 7. When he reaches verses 10-17, he spends some time interpreting verses 10-14a and concludes with the decision of the Lord to give Israel a sign of salvation in spite of the wrong attitude of King Ahaz. Then he proceeds with the exegesis of the core of the prophecy, which is the sign of Immanuel.

Cyril's exegesis of the crucial verses 14b-17 is rather brief. He discusses the virgin–young woman (παρθένος-νεᾶνις) terminology, showing that no matter what the specific term is, the essence of the matter is an unusual and immeasurable sign.[76] He offers a few remarks about the name Immanuel, applying it to Christ, who being above the whole created world, came to be with us.[77] And he concludes his exegesis with a few christological observations on the human and the divine natures of the Logos who became flesh. Here, Cyril the exegete lets Cyril the theologian take over and offer some beautiful christological formulations. His commentary on Isa. 7:10-17 becomes strongly theological, whereas his commentary on the first verses of the same chapter was more historical.

d) Theodoret's commentary on Isa. 7:10-17 is the briefest among those of the four exegetes examined in the present essay. Brevity, however, does not prevent him from presenting all the data that contribute to the full understanding of the passage. For that purpose, among other things, he repeatedly quotes from Aquila, Symmachus, and Theodotion in a critical

75. Cyril, *Isaiah*, on Isa. 7:1 (*PG* 70:192): Θεωρία μὲν γὰρ πνευματικὴ καλή τε καὶ ὀνησιφόρος, καὶ τῆς διανοίας τὸν ὀφθαλμὸν εὖ μάλα καταλαμπρύνουσα νουνεχεστάτους ἀποτελεῖ. Ὅταν δέ τι τῶν ἱστορικῶς πεπραγμένων διὰ τῶν ἱερῶν ἡμῖν Γραμμάτων εἰσφέρηται, τότε δὴ τότε τὸ ἐκ τῆς ἱστορίας χρήσιμον θηρᾶσθαι πρέπει, ἵνα πανταχόθεν ἡμᾶς ἡ θεόπνευστος Γραφὴ σώζουσά τε καὶ ὠφελοῦσα φαίνηται.

76. Cyril, *Isaiah*, on Isa. 7:11 (*PG* 70:204).

77. Cyril, *Isaiah*, on Isa. 7:14 (*PG* 70:205): Ὅτε γὰρ πέφηνε καθ' ἡμᾶς ὁ μονογενὴς τοῦ Θεοῦ Λόγος, τότε καὶ γέγονε καὶ μεθ' ἡμῶν. Ὁ γὰρ ὑπὲρ πᾶσαν τὴν κτίσιν, γέγονε καθ' ἡμᾶς.

manner that, depending on the case, is either approving or disapproving of their translations. Theodoret clearly is eager to keep his exegesis of Isa. 7:10-17 fully informed in terms of literary and historical data.[78]

On the other hand, he does not hesitate to engage in a thoroughly christological interpretation. He starts with a few concise and insightful comments on the dialogue between the Lord and Ahaz and then spends most of his time analyzing verse 14b, focusing on the virgin birth. He attacks the Jewish exegetes who advocate the term "young woman" instead of "virgin," arguing that such a reading is not reliable because it is based on the translations by Aquila, Symmachus, and Theodotion, which were composed after the appearance of Christ and were, at points like this, truly biased. The reading "virgin" on the other hand is to be found in the Septuagint, a translation produced with the assistance of divine grace long before Christ by venerable Jewish exegetes, and is therefore truly reliable.[79] Regardless of the specific terminology, however, the essence here is that we deal with a sign, argues Theodoret, and a sign that is of the largest proportions.

The next point of concentration for Theodoret in his exegesis of Isa. 7:14b is the name Immanuel. Here he offers two very interesting christological comments. First he relates the name to verse 11, "ask a sign of the Lord your God; let it be deep as Sheol or high as heaven."[80] "It was Immanuel," argues Theodoret, "who went down to Hades and who went up to heaven and who brought up to heaven Adam, the one lying in Hades."[81] The comment is quite interesting because of its particular christological application and soteriological language. The second comment deals with the signification of the name Immanuel, and is formulated in christological language reflecting the theological debates and creedal statements of Theodoret's time: "The name [Immanuel] signifies the God who is with

78. It is characteristic that Theodoret does not hesitate to relate the phrase "sign . . . deep as Sheol or high as heaven" of Isa. 7:11 to historical events that occurred in the life of King Hezekiah (Theodoret, *Isaiah*, on Isa. 7:11, Guinot I, 284).

79. Theodoret, *Isaiah*, on Isa. 7:14 (Guinot I, 286-88).

80. The Septuagint text uses in Isa. 7:11 the phrase εἰς βάθος ἢ εἰς ὕψος ("in depth or in height"). Theodoret, by citing Theodotion's and Aquila's versions, is able to use here the terminology of Hades and heaven.

81. Theodoret, *Isaiah*, on Isa. 7:14 (Guinot I, 286): Ὁ δὲ Ἐμμανουὴλ καὶ εἰς τὸν ᾅδην κατελήλυθε καὶ εἰς τὸν οὐρανὸν ἀνελήλυθε καὶ τὸν εἰς τὸν ᾅδην κείμενον Ἀδὰμ εἰς οὐρανὸν ἀναβίβασεν.

us, the God who became a human being, the God who has assumed human nature, the God who was united to it, the form of God and the form of the servant known in the one Son."[82]

These two statements are perhaps the result of Theodoret's desire to offer with clarity his christological ideas, since he has been at the center of christological debates for a long time and has suffered considerably on account of them. But they may equally have been the result of his decision to use more freely and literally an advanced and sophisticated christological language in his exegesis. Having secured the literary-historical aspects of exegesis of Isa. 7:10-17, Theodoret introduces his interpretation, which moves along the lines of the parallel interpretations by Eusebius, Chrysostom, and Cyril. One can see in this instance the converging lines of patristic exegesis, the combination or synthesis of the literary-historical exegetical methods with the christological-theological interpretive approaches. Such a combination already is detectable in Eusebius's, Chrysostom's, and Cyril's exegesis of Isa. 7:10-17, but is more visible in Theodoret's interpretive work on the same pericope.

VI. Concluding Observations

a) On the basis of the preceding analysis one might justifiably conclude that the three major commentaries on Isaiah by Eusebius, Chrysostom, and Cyril are respectful of the historical facts of the text of Isaiah. They do not offer an ahistorical exegesis and they do not engage in a loose, arbitrary allegorical interpretation. In the case of Chrysostom, the adherence to the historical facts of the text is very pronounced and dominant, a phenomenon explainable by his Antiochene origin. Eusebius and Cyril, on the other hand, despite their connection with Origen and Alexandria, display no less eagerness to have their exegesis built on solid historical facts. There is of course a difference here between Chrysostom and the other two exegetes, but this is a difference of degree not of a radical nature.

b) In the commentaries of Eusebius and Cyril we found several in-

---

82. Theodoret, *Isaiah*, on Isa. 7:14 (Guinot I, 290): Δηλοῖ δὲ τοὔνομα τὸν μεθ᾽ ἡμῶν Θεόν, τὸν ἐνανθρωπήσαντα Θεόν, τὸν τὴν ἀνθρωπείαν φύσιν ἀνειληφότα Θεόν, τὸν ἑνωθέντα ταύτῃ Θεόν, τὴν τοῦ Θεοῦ μορφὴν καὶ τὴν τοῦ δούλου μορφὴν ἐν ἑνὶ υἱῷ γνωριζομένην.

stances of metaphorical or allegorical exegesis. We noticed, however, that such exegesis was limited and related to rather secondary points and not to crucial passages. Elements of metaphorical exegesis we encountered in Chrysostom too, but they were rather scant.

c) In all three commentaries we observed a basic common phenomenon, namely, a christocentric or christologically oriented exegesis. This, we noticed, was the dominant characteristic of Cyril's and Eusebius's interpretation of Isaiah, but Chrysostom was also clear in following the same path, though in a more restricted way. What we have here is not exactly a typological exegesis of the type-antitype schema, but rather an exegesis presupposing an extension of the applicability of Isaiah's prophecy. Thus the prophetic word is applicable to Isaiah's own time, to the time which follows, and finally to the time of Christ. Such an interpretation is possible because of the revelation in Christ. Eusebius, Cyril, and Chrysostom simply read Isaiah *sub specie Novi Testamenti*. This kind of reading preserves the integrity of the original historical facts related to Isaiah's prophecy but is not confined to them.

The conclusion, then, is that the commentaries on Isaiah by Eusebius, Chrysostom, and Cyril display two significant common characteristics, namely, respect for the historical facts presented by the text and christocentric exegesis. Allegorical interpretation plays no noticeable role in Chrysostom and a restricted role in Eusebius and Cyril. Hence, when one carefully reads the three commentaries in parallel, one can detect in them a consistent distancing from extremist exegetical positions (e.g., purely historical, predominantly allegorical) and an increasing tendency toward converging methods of interpretation, by which the exegetical notions are enhanced and multiplied. In this case, traces of a developing exegetical synthesis become more and more discernible.

d) In Theodoret's *Commentary on Isaiah* the developing exegetical synthesis is clearly observable. It consists, as the data indicate, of the integration of four major exegetical facets or methods coming from various interpretive traditions.

The first is the textual-philological aspect of exegesis. As we have seen, Theodoret is employing the Lucianic recension of the Septuagint, but he is constantly quoting from Aquila, Symmachus, and Theodotion, from the Hebrew and the Syriac, and from the Septuagint in the Hexapla. He is eager to have in his commentary the best text of Isaiah and the best variants of it. In addition, throughout his exegesis he frequently offers observations related to grammatical, syntactical, stylistic, and semantic issues. The textual-philological tradition in exegesis comes from both Alexandria and Antioch, but in Theodoret it appears fully developed and consistently applied. It remains, however, subservient to the main objective of interpretation, which is the disclosure of the theological meaning of the text.

The second major exegetical facet in Theodoret's exegesis of Isaiah is his strong adherence to the historical facts of the text. In every step of his interpretation, his primary concern is the presentation of the real and undisputable data provided by the verses, pericopes, or chapters of Isaiah. He reads the prophetic words as clearly applicable to the people and circumstances indicated by the historical information contained in the text. One could suggest that even the medical, botanical, zoological, psychological, and, mostly, geographical notes dispersed throughout his commentary are expressions of Theodoret's effort to be as close as possible to the historical truth contained in Isaiah.

The exegetical tradition of a strong respect for the historical facts of the biblical text comes to Theodoret mainly, but not exclusively, from Antioch. In his case, however, this tradition is expressed in a concise and refined form. Theodoret's historical exegesis is neither crude nor polemical nor absolutist. Contrary to what happened to Diodore of Tarsus or even Theodore of Mopsuestia, Theodoret's historical exegesis can comfortably coexist with other important methods of exegesis.

The third major aspect in Theodoret's exegesis is metaphorical-allegorical interpretation. One should note that in his commentary this type of exegesis is not encountered in a degree comparable to historical or literary exegesis. It is, however, there, and Theodoret employs it, even though not as frequently, but without hesitation. This kind of exegesis certainly does not belong to the tradition of Antioch, but comes from Alexandria. Theodoret uses it because, as he states in his prologue, he believes that the very text of Isaiah imposes it. Nonetheless, the inclusion of the metaphorical exegetical approach in the acceptable methods of interpretation by an Antiochene exegete constitutes a rather bold step, a step revealing a synthesis in the making.

The final, and by far more significant, major exegetical aspect is Theodoret's christocentric principle of exegesis. Some scholars speak in this case of a typological interpretation or Antiochene *"theōria."*[83] This,

---

83. The article of Bradley Nassif published in this volume constitutes an excellent guide for a solid basic acquaintance with the whole issue of Antiochene *"theōria."*

however, is an issue too big and complicated to be discussed here. The basic fact in this instance is, to put it in oversimplified terms, that the person of Christ, the revelation in Christ, and the ecclesial reality established by Christ constitute the fundamental and indispensable hermeneutic principle and method for the complete and perfect interpretation and understanding of the prophecy of Isaiah and of any other Old Testament prophecy. The christocentric principle and method for interpreting Old Testament prophetic books like Isaiah does not appear to be fully and decisively operative in the exegesis of the Antiochene interpreters. Even Chrysostom is hesitant to apply it beyond the explicitly messianic pericopes in Isaiah. We encountered it fully developed and dominating in the exegesis of Cyril[84] and of Eusebius. Theodoret in all probability is influenced by them, but he does not allow his christocentric exegesis to produce an interpretation loaded with heavy and elaborate theological language. His christocentric exegesis is presented in a precise and concise language, controlled by and integrated with the other major exegetical methods. In Theodoret's *Commentary on Isaiah,* christocentric exegesis belongs to a synthesis of interpretative traditions.[85]

This synthesis constitutes a remarkable achievement. It makes Theodoret's exegetical work extremely valuable not only for the study of patristic biblical exegesis but also for the study of modern hermeneutical problems. It is not accidental that G. W. Ashby concludes his monograph on Theodoret's exegesis of the Old Testament with a very revealing long citation from a programmatic article on Old Testament hermeneutics by G. von Rad.[86] Ashby, after presenting von Rad's basic points in eight prop-

---

84. Points of exegetical similarities between Cyril and Theodoret are to be detected not only in their respective commentaries on Isaiah but in other commentaries as well. As D. S. Wallace-Hadrill, *Christian Antioch,* p. 39, states, "We have already noted that in their treatment of the minor prophets Theodore and Theodoret do not always agree, and that the latter sometimes stands nearer to Cyril than to Theodore." Cf. G. W. Ashby, *Theodoret of Cyrrhus,* p. 158.

85. Theodoret's striking ability for critical evaluation and synthesis of theological and/or philosophical traditions is visible not only in his exegetical works like the *Commentary on Isaiah,* but in other of his works as well. A good example is his apologetic book Ἑλληνικῶν θεραπευτικὴ παθημάτων. Cf. Paul Crego, *A Translation of and Commentary on Theodoret of Cyrus'* Ἑλληνικῶν θεραπευτικὴ παθημάτων, *Book Five:* Περὶ φύσεως ἀνθρώπου (Ph.D. Dissertation, Boston College, 1993).

86. Gerhard von Rad, "The Typological Interpretation of the Old Testament," in

ositions or theses, adds: "Strange as it may seem, von Rad never mentions one church father in connection with his argument, though he does mention Near Eastern ancient use of types and Reformation application of these methods. Yet what he says might well be the canon of exegesis of Theodoret of Cyrrhus."[87] The last sentence eloquently suggests the refreshing openness of hermeneutical perspectives offered by the study of a patristic exegete like Theodoret of Cyrus.

K. Westermann (ed.), *Essays in Old Testament Interpretation* (London: SCM, 1963), pp. 35-39.

87. G. W. Ashby, *Theodoret of Cyrrhus*, pp. 150-53.

"Spiritual Exegesis" in the School of Antioch[1]

BRADLEY NASSIF

To write about "spiritual exegesis" in the School of Antioch will appear to many readers as a historical curiosity. Understandably, this curiosity stems from the prevailing caricature of Antiochene exegesis. Traditional scholarship on patristic exegesis has been content to emphasize the thesis that "Antiochene exegesis of Scripture was historical, and, unlike Alexandria, looked not for a hidden meaning in the text, but for the sense intended by its inspired writer."[2] On the other hand, in antithetical reaction, Jacques Guillet earlier maintained that historians had sharpened this divergence implausibly: "Between the two schools there is not, therefore, an opposition; rather, there is a very large area of agreement on traditional exegesis. In this agreement, however, there is a special insistence on different points of view."[3]

While these interpretive theories have attempted to either divide or

---

1. In anticipation of this memorial volume, a longer version of this essay appeared in *Anglican Theological Review* 70/4 (1993), pp. 437-70: "The 'Spiritual Exegesis' of Scripture: The School of Antioch Revisited." Clarifications and omissions have been made for the abbreviated form presented here.

2. "Antiochene Theology," in *The Oxford Dictionary of the Christian Church*, 2nd ed. by F. L. Cross and E. A. Livingstone (London: Oxford University, 1974), p. 66. This conventional portrayal is a symbolic representation of what can be found in countless textbooks on church history, the history of exegesis, and hermeneutical studies.

3. Jacques Guillet, S.J., "Les exégèses d'Alexandria et d'Antioche. Conflit ou malentendu?" *Recherches de science religieuse* 34 (1947), pp. 257-302.

unite the exegetical orientations of Antioch and Alexandria, neither adequately reflects the results of a narrowly focused investigation into Antiochene exegesis that has been conducted in a relatively obscure, numerically scant, and linguistically scattered form since the end of the nineteenth century. A small but highly skilled group of international scholars (to be discussed below) have attempted to demonstrate over the course of the past hundred years that behind the Antiochene Fathers' search for the literal meaning of Scripture lies a deceptively simple hermeneutic that governed their efforts to bridge the spiritual and historical approaches to biblical interpretation. This "spiritual" hermeneutic, known as *theōria* ("vision, insight, contemplation"), lies at the center of the Antiochenes' dual concern for a historical and yet christological reading of the Bible. It not only permitted but required them to find "mystical" interpretations that were based upon and congruent with the literal sense of the text. In short, *theōria* specified the content and character of a distinctly Antiochene form of mystical exegesis.

Credit for the originality of this thesis rightly belongs to two scholars from the late nineteenth and early twentieth centuries, Henrich Kihn and Alberto Vaccari. In researching the books and essays that have been published over the past hundred years, I was astonished to discover that no full-scale history of critical scholarship on Antiochene *theōria* had previously been written. A comprehensive survey of the most significant participants, views, and problems related to *theōria* remains to be synthesized in order to provide a synopsis of the major issues that have surrounded it in the history of exegesis. The task of this essay, then, is to fill a lacuna in the literature by introducing contemporary historians, theologians, and biblical exegetes to the theological issues, interpretive debates, and hermeneutical assessments that have emerged from the study of Antiochene *theōria* over the past century. It is important to emphasize at the outset that in tracing the scholarship, neither those authors nor I wish to advocate a radical revision of the prevailing view of Antiochene interpretation as being marked chiefly by its stress on the historical meaning of the Bible. Instead, I wish to clarify how the exegetes of the fourth-century School of Antioch interpreted Scripture not only according to the letter of the text, but also according to the Spirit.

I seek to achieve four goals: (1) to demonstrate how the Antiochene Fathers applied *theōria* to their interpretation of the Bible (as much as that is possible), (2) to examine the various ways in which scholars have defined *theōria* in relation to the other types of Scriptural senses, i.e., the literal, allegorical, and typological senses and the *sensus plenior,* (3) to summarize the current state of research so that new directions may be undertaken to advance the field in the light of where scholarship has been and where it needs to go, and (4) to encourage a moderate revision of the stereotyped portrayal of Antiochene exegesis that presently dominates the secondary literature.

I. History of Primary Scholarship from 1880 to the Present

The history of scholarship on Antiochene *theōria* began most clearly with Heinrich Kihn in 1880 and continues in the work of the present author. As far as I can determine, the subject has been studied at length by only nine scholars over the past century. There are three different yet complementary lines along which they have understood the hermeneutic: *exegetically* as a *literal method of messianic exegesis, theologically* as a *typological or mystical type of textual meaning,* or *etymologically* as a *spiritual illumination in the mind of the biblical author, prophet, or later interpreter.* A combination of one or more of these approaches were found, in varying degrees, in the exegetical literature of Julian of Eclanum, Diodore of Tarsus, Theodore of Mopsuestia, John Chrysostom, Severian of Gabala, Jerome, Theodoret of Cyrus, and others. For the most part, researchers have focused on the biblical commentaries of Julian of Eclanum, Theodore of Mopsuestia, and Diodore of Tarsus, in whose writings *theōria* was interpreted almost exclusively as a method of messianic exegesis.

The historiographical evolution of the study of Antiochene *theōria* began in Germany. In a pioneering article entitled "On *Theōria* and *Allēgoria* According to the Lost Hermeneutical Writings of the Antiochenes,"[4] the great German patrologist Heinrich Kihn attempted to revise the prevailing views of much of nineteenth-century scholarship, which had mistakenly identified Antiochene *theōria* with Alexandrian *theōria* or allegory. The views of three scholars became the special object of rebuttal for Kihn: those of Ernesti, Munter, and Augusti.[5] These men had argued that Diodore of

---

4. H. Kihn, "Über '*Theōria*' und '*Allēgoria*' nach den verlorenen hermeneutischen Schriften der Antiochener," *Theologische Quartalschrift* 20 (1880), pp. 531-82.
5. The style of documentation in nineteenth-century Germany did not provide full citation of their works. See Kihn, pp. 554ff., for sources noted.

Tarsus and Theodore of Mopsuestia equated *allēgoria* with *theōria* and therefore rejected both terms as signifying one and the same exegetical abuse. The basis for their views was Facundus's remarks concerning Theodore's mystical exegesis and especially the earlier ecclesiastical historians Socrates and Sozomen, who defined *theōria* exclusively in terms of Alexandrian allegory.[6] Kihn replied that Ernesti, Munter, and Augusti had made false generalizations about the semantic range of the term in the School of Antioch by failing to distinguish it from *allēgoria*. Although, to be sure, the two words were regarded as essentially synonymous within the Alexandrian School, they were not so regarded in Antioch. Kihn proved his hypothesis through a diachronic word study from Plato through the early Church Fathers. As he deepened his research, Kihn discovered that in their condemnations of Alexandrian allegory the Fathers of Antioch did not eliminate *theōria* as a legitimate approach to biblical exegesis. The Antiochenes qualified, rather than opposed, the "deeper mystical sense" of Scripture by placing *theōria* within the framework of a literal hermeneutic. By *allēgoria* the Antiochenes meant "arbitrary exegesis," whereas *theōria* "drew a distinction between allegory and the justified higher sense."[7] Kihn believed that the function of *theōria* in Theodore's exegesis was "to elucidate the meaning of the typological prophecies of Scripture."[8] He concluded his essay with a definition:

> *Theōria* is actually the investigation of the objectively verifiable but hidden meaning of Scripture. It is of two types: The first is the figurative type, in which the meaning of a word is somewhat hidden; in the second the meaning is what one arrives at through the study of history and doctrine, a typical-mystical meaning based on reality and relating to the dogmas of the New Testament, improvement of the ethical life, and life after death.[9]

---

6. Socrates, *Ecc. Hist.* 6.3 (following translations supplied): "Diodorus . . . wrote many treatises, in which he limited his attention to the literal sense of Scripture, avoiding that which was mystical *(tas theōrias autōn)*" (Nicene and Post-Nicene Fathers, vol. II, p. 139); Sozomen 8.2: "Diodorus . . . explained the significance of the sacred words and avoided allegory" (Nicene and Post-Nicene Fathers, vol. II, p. 399).

7. Kihn, "Über 'Theōria' und 'Allēgoria,'" p. 536.

8. Ibid., p. 571.

9. Ibid., p. 582.

The chief value of Kihn's work lies in the terminological clarification he made between the Antiochene and Alexandrian schools of exegesis. He sounded the death knell to the prevailing view of his day that had wrongly assumed that *allēgoria* and *theōria* were synonyms in the writings of the Antiochene Fathers. Important a clarification as this was, many questions were left unanswered. Were the New Testament writers reading messianic meanings into Old Testament prophecies that the original authors did not intend? What role did the prophet's consciousness play in the recording of his prediction? Did the prophet himself have a full comprehension of the present and future fulfillment of his prophecy? It would be left to future scholars to grapple with these and other critical questions.

Due to the paucity of evidence, it is quite difficult, if not impossible, to trace the history of the reception of Kihn's essay in the four decades that followed its publication. Between 1880 and 1920, research on Antiochene *theōria* was conducted in a somewhat parenthetical fashion via the study of individual personalities linked with the Antiochene School, though no substantial contribution appears to have been made.[10]

It was not until 1920 that Kihn's earlier monograph finally began to impact the world of patristic scholarship. Alberto Vaccari, the eminent patrologist from Italy, read Kihn and was persuaded that he had made a far-reaching discovery. Of special interest was the connection Kihn had made between *theōria* and the prophetic portions of Scripture. This connection inspired Vaccari to expanded on Kihn's work in conjunction with G. Morin's reconstruction of Julian of Eclanum's exegesis. In what turned out to be a landmark essay on the subject, Vaccari made a fresh study of the sources and published his findings in an article entitled, "*Theōria* in the Exegetical School of Antioch."[11]

Vaccari maintained that *theōria* operated as a way to resolve the dilemma that the Antiochene authors faced when confronted with the *historia* of a biblical text and its later christological meaning. It sought to

10. The one notable exception in this period was Adolf von Harnack, *History of Dogma* vol. III, tr. James Miller (Oxford: Williams and Norgate, 1897), pp. 201-2, n. 2. He recommends "above all, the works of Kihn." See also the brief remarks on Diodore's treatise, "On the Difference between *Theōria* and Allegory," O. Bardenhewer, *Geschichte der altkirchlichen Literatur* (Freiburg, 1912), vol. 3, pp. 307-8.

11. A. Vaccari, "La '*teōria*' nella scuola esegetica di antiochia," *Biblica* 1 (1920), pp. 3-36. Credit belongs to Professor Aida Ricci of Fordham University for her careful translation of Vaccari's articles used here.

steer a middle course between the excesses of allegory, which the Antiochenes believed led to an unbridled dehistoricizing of the text, and the
literalism of Judaism, which deprived Scripture of its mystical and eschatological significance. *Theōria* was viewed as an attempt to do justice simultaneously to the original historical setting of the predictive words of a
prophet and to their future christological meaning. Depending on its use
in a given context, *theōria* could refer to one or all of the following: (a) the
prophetic vision itself, (b) the prophet's recording of both the original
historical and future messianic meanings under one literal but hyperbolic
mode of expression, and/or (c) a specific method of apostolic or even
post-apostolic exegesis.

In Vaccari's estimate, the clearest example of *theōria* could be found
in Julian of Eclanum (ca. 380-455). Of critical importance for understanding the function of *theōria* in messianic prophecy was Vaccari's discovery
of an obscure but priceless definition of it given by Julian in the *Commentarii in prophetas minores tres*. Only the Latin has survived of what originally
was from a Greek/Antiochene provenance: "*Theōria est autem, ut eruditis
placuit, in brevibus plerumque aut formis aut causis earum rerum quae po-
tiores sunt considerata perceptio*" ("*Theoria*, however, as the erudite are
pleased to understand it, is for the most part a considered perception of
either brief forms or causes of those things which are of greater importance.")[12] Vaccari believed that every word of this precious definition had
been carefully crafted. Its origin played an important role in defining its
hermeneutical characteristics:

> Who is the author of this definition? Julian himself says that it is from
> other people; "*ut eruditis placunt*," he says. It is written by learned people.
> Who are those scholars? From all we know about Christian literature of
> the fourth century we can frankly say without fear of being mistaken:
> the Antiochenes.[13]

Julian's definition may have been obtained from Theodore of Mopsuestia, with whom Julian lived during his exile from Italy between 421 and
428. Its exact meaning was debated piecemeal soon after Vaccari first discovered it. The exegetical difficulties centered upon whether or not the

---

12. Vaccari, "La '*teōria*' nella scuola esegetica di antiochia," p. 14; *Patrologia Latina*,
ed. J. Migne, 21:971B.
13. Vaccari, "La '*teōria*' nella scuola esegetica di antiochia," p. 15.

expression *considerata perceptio* was an indication that the prophet was conscious of the messianic import of his words;[14] whether *eruditis* referred, as Vaccari held, to the Antiochene Fathers or to the rhetorical teachers from whom the Antiochenes derived their technical vocabulary;[15] and whether the terms *formis* (i.e., the rhetorical device of hyperbole by which messianic events were prophesied through the historical medium of Israel) and *causis* (i.e., their messianic fulfillment) were to be taken separately on the basis of the conjunctions *aut . . . aut*, thus dividing the prophecy into two separate parts,[16] or whether *formis* and *causis* were to be joined as one generic prophecy with two distinct fulfillments.[17]

As an outgrowth of the definition, Vaccari identified four essential marks of *theōria* that subsequent scholars would refer to time and again: (1) *Theōria* presupposed the historical reality of the events described by the biblical author; those events functioned like a mirror imaging a different reality. (2) In addition to the historical reference, *theōria* simultaneously embraced a second future reality that was ontologically linked to the first. (3) The first or near historical event stood in relation to the second as the mediocre to the perfect, the small to the large, or a sketch to the finished work of art. (4) Both the present and future events together were described as direct objects of *theōria* but in different ways. The present functioned as the less significant vehicle through which the prophet knowingly described a greater future event in human history through the use of hyperbolic language.

Vaccari applied these four characteristics to the Antiochenes' interpretation of selected messianic texts in the Old Testament. The commentary by Theodore of Mopsuestia on Zechariah 9:9-10 was a good example. The

14. Paul Ternant (n. 24 below) with Henri de Lubac maintained that the definition remained ambiguous on the question (H. de Lubac, " 'Typologie' ad 'Allegorism,'" Recherches de science religieuse 34 [1947], p. 210), while Vaccari and Seisdedos (n. 23 below) affirm a clear consciousness.

15. "It is possible, however, that the *'eruditi'* may rather have been those rhetorical teachers from whom the Antiochenes derived their technical equipment." N. Bate, "Some Technical Terms of Greek Exegesis," *Journal of Theological Studies* 23 (1923), p. 63. Ternant and de Lubac remained undecided.

16. P. J. Bover, "La *'teoria'* antioquena definida por Julian de Eclano," *Estudios Eclasiasticos* 12 (1933), pp. 405-15.

17. Alberto Vaccari's rejoinder to Bover, "La *'teōria'* esegetica antiochena," *Biblica* 15 (1934), p. 95.

passage predicted Israel's coming king riding on a donkey, which Matthew 21:25 and John 12:15 interpret as fulfilled in the ministry of Jesus of Nazareth.

> It is clear that these things are said here about Zerubbabel. But I am amazed at the ideas of those people who follow bizarre interpretations by applying a certain part to Zerubbabel, then again another part to Christ the Lord, which is nothing else than dividing the prophecy between Zerubbabel and Christ the Lord. . . . Thus many of the things that are confusing and are said either about the people or about those chosen for them, the Scripture speaks about them in a most hyperbolic way so that the text is not true in terms of its immediate historical reference; but these things are discovered to be true whenever they are interpreted in reference to the Lord Christ. . . . Here it is therefore said concerning Zerubbabel, while the sense is limited to him concerning about whom what was written is said, but in the Gospels it is said concerning Christ. . . . On the other hand, to say that a part of it is said concerning Christ, but for those returning to be changed to Zerubbabel, and back to Christ from him, and back to Zerubbabel from Christ the Lord . . . equally dividing the written sayings between the steward and the Lord . . . is a sign of extraordinary nonsense and lack of skill in interpreting the divine Scriptures.[18]

The exegetical point Vaccari drew from the commentary was this: Theodore interpreted the Zechariah passage as a single prophecy that contained two fulfillments. The prophecy applied at the same time both historically (to Zerubbabel) and eschatologically (to Christ). The first fulfillment was the less important event that foreshadowed a second greater reality to come by sharing a historical resemblance with that eschatological event. Both events were generically or ontologically combined into one prediction by the Old Testament prophet without division (*indivisum*). Through the rhetorical device of hyperbole, the biblical author predicted the future through exaggerated expressions that applied first to Israel and second to the Messiah. Hence, *theōria* could be defined as that prophetic vision whereby the prophet saw and recorded both the present historical and future messianic meanings under one literal and

---

18. *Patrologia Graeco-Latina*, ed. J. Migne [hereafter *PG*], 66:556, in Vaccari, "La 'teōria' nella scuola esegetica di antiochia," pp. 18-19.

hyperbolic mode of expression, without division, in its historic and later messianic sense.

Vaccari turned next to Julian of Eclanum. Julian interpreted Paul's use of the prophecy in Hosea 1:10 ("and it will come about that in the place where it is said to them, 'You are not my people,' it will be said to them, 'You are the sons of the living God.'") in Romans 9:26 as reference to both the release of the Jews from their Babylonian captivity and the future adoption of the Gentiles as sons of God.

> St. Paul declares that the joy allowed by those words will be fulfilled in the time of the gospel. . . . By this Paul does not want to negate . . . the prophecy that also promises the release from the Babylonian captivity; but the apostle wants to show us which rule we must follow in the interpretation of the prophetic books. It is this: When we hear the prophets speaking about the Jews and something is promised that goes beyond the small circle of people, yet we see it partly fulfilled in that nation, we know from *theōria (per theoriam)* that the promise is given for all people. . . . It will not be appropriate to say that the recall from the Babylonian captivity is predicted according to history and the liberty given by Christ according to allegory. No. The prophet predicted both things together at one time, jointly *(cum sermo propheticus solide utrumque promiserit)*, in order that the mediocrity of the first fulfillment would predict the abundance of the second. . . . So what Hosea was saying about Babylonian times, Paul attributes to the facts of the Savior.[19]

Vaccari maintained that if Julian had been correct in asserting that the messianic prophecies contained double fulfillments, then the prophet himself actually foresaw and recorded the personalities and facts of both eras. The modern interpreter, therefore, will understand the close relationship between the two objects of the prophecy that are described jointly and will interpret that single expression in proportion to the near or distant referents. Since allegory was defined by the Antiochenes in its classical *rhetorical* sense as "a continued metaphor," such was ruled out as being inconsistent with the prophet's intent. *Theōria* reflects a literal sense, not a double literal or even additional secondary meaning, as in allegory or typology proper. Through an inspired *excursus* of the mind, the prophet

---

19. *Patrologia Latina* 21:971B, in Vaccari, "La '*teōria*' nella scuola esegetica di antiochia," pp. 20-22.

perceived the antitype by means of the type and announced the former
through the latter.

The relation between typology and *theōria* became an important issue
in the later history of scholarship. Vaccari made the brief but significant
observation that *theōria* belonged to one of two kinds of typological
prophecies:

> Now a typological prophecy, which includes those we are studying, could
> be understood in two ways: Either the prophet under inspiration did not
> see or indicate by his words that the first object, the type, contains the
> antitype; or the prophet foresaw both objects . . . and through the first
> wished to announce the second; here properly consists *theōria*. . . . In
> those *excursus* [mystical revelations] the eye of the inspired prophet does
> not abandon the first object but penetrates it more deeply; his sight, fixed
> on the future, goes beyond the first horizon and embraces a larger hori-
> zon without changing his field of vision.[20]

On the basis of his discussion of these passages and other, similar
passages, Vaccari identified two criteria for modern biblical exegetes to
follow when determining if *theōria* was to be discerned in the prophetic
portions of Scripture: (1) the presence of hyperbolic traits in the text that
would indicate a double reference to the original historic and future messianic age and (2) an explicit "theoretic" exegesis of the Old Testament in
the New, as Hosea 1:10 in Romans 9:26 or Joel 2:28 in Acts 2:17. Consequently, "*Theōria*, according to its etymological meaning, was first a *vision*
in the mind of the prophet, which later becomes a *hermeneutical rule* in
the hand of the interpreter."[21]

Twenty years passed until the decade of the 1950s, when scholars
resumed the subject by adding technical refinement to Kihn and Vaccari's
work. An article entitled, "Antiochene *Theōria*" by the Spaniard Francisco
Seisdedos essentially duplicated Vaccari's insights.[22] However, Seisdedos's

20. Vaccari, "La '*teōria*' nella scuola esegetica di antiochia," pp. 22, 26.

21. Ibid., 28, emphasis original.

22. F. A. Seisdedos, "La '*teōria*' antioquena," *Estudios Biblicos* 11 (1952), pp. 31-67.
It should not go unnoticed that Seisdedos relied heavily on Vaccari's work, sometimes
without explicit reference. Compare, for example, Seisdedos's verbatim restatement of
Vaccari's definition of *theōria* as "the perception of grandiose things by means of other
less illustrious objects" (p. 62 with Vaccari, "La '*teōria*' nella scuola esegetica di antiochia," p. 36).

discussion of the similarities and differences between typology and *theōria* brought increased clarity to the distinction. He pointed out that the Antiochenes were terminologically imprecise and sometimes even used the same words to designate typological and figurative meanings in the Bible. The distinctions between *theōria* and typology became a very subtle and difficult matter that explains why confusion existed even among the Antiochenes themselves: "All in all, the explanation of *theōria* certainly does not seem to have a very marked difference from a type. From this, the confusion among the Antiochenes themselves is verified."[23] Hence, with Vaccari, Seisdedos grouped *theōria* under one of two types of typology. In one form (typology proper), the prophet neither saw nor intended to bespeak the future antitype. In the other *(theōria)*, the prophet did, in fact, see the antitype (albeit imperfectly) by divine revelation through the historical circumstances of his own day. The future eschatological reality shaped the language utilized by the prophet to address his contemporaries, and the present, in turn, became a vehicle for the prophet to intentionally announce future messianic realities. The prophet had both objects of his prophecy in mind when penning his words, and it was this double vision that constituted *theōria.*

By far the most extensive analysis of the Antiochene hermeneutic was undertaken in a three-part monograph by a Jesuit, Paul Ternant, entitled, "The *Theōria* of Antioch in the Framework of the Senses of Scripture."[24] Along with the works of the previous authors, Ternant's articles are now outdated in some respects by the recent advances made in biblical criticism. They are also limited by the number of patristic authors treated. Nevertheless, for a general survey of how several of the Antiochenes employed *theōria* in their Scriptural exegesis Ternant's articles remain the most systematic and critically interactive treatment in all the history of scholarship to date. Writing in the days of the patristic revival among French Catholics, Ternant was convinced that, despite Kihn and Vaccari's foundational works, *theōria* was still a "forgotten and badly misunderstood" hermeneutic. He conceded that Vaccari had misdefined Alexandrian allegory by following the *rhetorical* tradition of the Antiochenes themselves, who identified an allegory as "a continued meta-

---

23. Seisdedos, "La '*teōria*' antioquena," p. 60.
24. P. Ternant, "La '*theōria* d'Antioche dans le cadre des sens de l'Ecriture," *Biblica* 34 (1953), pp. 135-58, 354-83, 456-86.

phor." In some sense, then, it was true that the opposition between Antioch and Alexandria was artificially created, but only partially so. A real difference in exegesis still existed in the two schools, and a proper understanding of *theōria* could help explain it. Ternant's task coincided with the titles of his three-part study: "The Nature of *Theōria* and Its Place within the Framework of the Scriptural Senses," "Scholarly Objections against *Theōria* and the Criteria for Applying Its Principles," and "A Survey of the Use of *Theōria* in the Course of History from the Fourth Century to the Present."

Ternant advanced the history of scholarship on three fronts. First, taking Kihn and Vaccari as his point of departure,[25] he incorporated into his research the results of specialized studies on individual Antiochene authors that had been published over the past thirty years since Vaccari's 1920 article. The most important monographs were done on Theodore and Diodore by Schweizer, Maries, and Devreesee.[26] Second, Ternant contributed to the then current debates over the value of precritical exegesis for modern historical critical interpretation of the Bible by directly addressing the question of the relation of *theōria* to typology, allegory, and the *sensus plenior* — issues that had been hotly debated among Catholics. Eager to root the hermeneutic in the mainstream of the Church, he traced the use of *theōria* in the history of exegesis from the fourth century to the 1950s, focusing chiefly on the Roman Catholic tradition. Third, Ternant wed the insights of biblical criticism to the Antiochene *theōria* by adding a third criteria (given below) to Vaccari's previous two for knowing when and how to identify a theoretic prophecy.

Unlike Vaccari, Ternant relied chiefly on Diodore of Tarsus rather than Julian as a better source for providing a definition of *theōria*. Diodore declared:

25. "It is to the merit of Vaccari who revived the interest of exegetes in this methodology by specifying and completing the data of an article by Kihn" (Ternant, "La '*theōria* d'Antioche dans le cadre des sens de l'Ecriture," p. 136). Seisdedos's article was unknown to Ternant until only "after we had finished our work" (p. 475, n. 3).

26. E. Schweizer, "Diodor von Tarsus als Exeget," *Zeitschrift für die neutestamentliche Wissenschaft* 40 (1941), pp. 33-75; L. Maries, "Études préliminaires à l'édition de Diodore de Tarse 'sur les Psaumes,'" *Recherches de science religieuse* 22 (1932), pp. 385-408; R. Devreesee, "La méthode exégétique de Theódore de Mopsueste," *Revue Biblique* 53 (1946), pp. 207-41.

The prophets, predicting the events in advance, have adapted their discourse to the eras which they are pronouncing for contemporary and future times by hyperbolic expressions which are in perfect agreement and proportion to the prophecies.[27]

Throughout his discussion, Ternant was careful to point out that *theōria* was properly speaking a "literal" hermeneutic that always corresponded to the original intent of the biblical author. Everywhere that such prophecies were to be found the text always had a singular, not plural, meaning. How, then, are we to understand the relation of *theōria* to typology and the *sensus plenior* of Scripture? Ternant argued that the Antiochenes saw no opposition between *theōria* and typology since both were similar but distinct methods of exegesis. Although they sometimes overlapped in a common exegetical vocabulary (e.g., *typos, alētheia*), and there may be an element of the typological *sensus plenior* in *theōria*,[28] the distinguishing feature between *theōria* and typology was that *theōria* functioned as a form of direct verbal prophecy that was attached to the predictive words of Scripture. In typology proper, however, all futurity was in the type itself, that is, in persons, events, or institutions that the prophet generally did not consciously foresee or predict.

In comparing the *sensus plenior* with Antiochene *theōria* the problems became more delicate since the former had not gained a consensus acceptance among biblical scholars. Ternant claimed that since *theōria* presupposed a conscious awareness on the part of the prophetic writers it should not be thought of as a "plenary," "literal plenary" or "double literal" sense, but quite plainly "literal." The essential difference between *theōria* and the *sensus plenior* was simply the "conscious knowledge" that was possessed by the prophet concerning the messianic import of his words. For this reason, if one used the expression "spiritual sense" to refer to exegetical conclusions that were not historical, then "*theōria* does not seek to discover a spiritual sense because its goal precisely aims at unveiling the whole spectrum of a prophet's horizon in a given text."[29]

27. Ternant, "La '*theōria* d'Antioche dans le cadre des sens de l'Ecriture," 145-46, quoting Maries's translation in *Recherches de science religieuse* 9 (1919), p. 97.

28. Ternant, "La '*theōria* d'Antioche dans le cadre des sens de l'Ecriture," p. 143.

29. Ternant, "La '*theōria* d'Antioche dans le cadre des sens de l'Ecriture," p. 155, cited the support of J. Coppens, *Les harmonies des deux Testaments* (Casterman, Tournai, 1949), p. 60. For a refutation of Roland Murphy and A. M. Dubarle's rejection of this approach on psychological and exegetical grounds, see Ternant, pp. 357ff.

Vaccari's two-fold canon of interpretation accounted for many theoretic texts. But critical refinement was still needed to address the advances made by modern Old Testament scholars. Hence, Ternant added a third rule (derived more from the methodological principles of *theōria* than from the Antiochenes themselves): *theōria* could sometimes be applied in cases where a biblical redactor adapted a previously historical text for a messianic purpose. The compositional intent of the redactor, rather than the original intent of the author or personages described, was to compile existing texts into a final form that would point to the future messianic hope. An analysis of the Chronicler's use of 2 Samuel 7 in 1 Chronicles 17 indicated that the author functioned as both prophet and historian. Through an inspired vision *(theōria)* the Levite knowingly communicated the coming Messiah through the person of Solomon, who was the ancestor and image of Christ. He superimposed, not substituted, the Messiah on the son of David by means of one and the same prophecy.

> It seems, therefore, that one must admit even apart from all New Testament attestations and particularly hyperbolic formulas, a *third criteria* for applying the Antiochene system: If after a serious literary study of an Old Testament text one should establish a messianic and eschatological perspective that had been *superimposed* by an inspired author upon an originally non-messianic text, and those historical and messianic meanings had been consciously intended in the mind of a later redactor who expressed them under one formula, then one is obliged to interpret the text *kata theōrian*.[30]

For all practical purposes interest in the Antiochene method came to a halt in the late 1950s and early 1960s after Catholic biblical scholars rejected it as a viable method for modern exegesis. Once again, twenty to thirty years would pass before further research would commence. In the decade of the 1980s scholars returned to the field and plowed decidedly new ground in two directions. First, new precision was added to the criteria for interpreting *theōria* as a method of exegesis when the hermeneutic made

---

30. Ternant, "La 'theōria d'Antioche dans le cadre des sens de l'Ecriture," pp. 382-83, emphasis original. See also his brief discussion of *theōria* in Thomas Aquinas, *Quodlibet* vii, art. 15.5 (we might also add *Summa Theologiae* 1a q.1, a.8-10), and Nicholas of Lyra, *Postilles Biblia sacra cum glossa ordinaria*, pp. 460ff. Even Roland Murphy admitted that Aquinas's exegesis of Psalm 72 included "the heart of *theōria*."

its strongest appeal to conservative Protestant circles through the Old Testament scholar Walter Kaiser, Jr. Having only a general awareness of Vaccari's article in the history of patristic scholarship, Kaiser built mostly on Willis Beecher's theory of interpreting messianic prophecy as a single-meaning hermeneutic: "Such a solution is very close to the concept of *theōria* posed by the Antiochene school of interpretation."[31] Kaiser then added what amounted to a fourth criteria for discerning *theōria:* the discovery in prophetic texts of common theological and grammatical distinctives. These included the presence of collective singular nouns in Hebrew, which might convey simultaneously a singular and plural connotation, and the frequent shift in prophetic passages between singular and plural pronouns or pronominal suffixes. Kaiser is the most creative apologist for the use of *theōria* as a method of messianic exegesis in biblical studies today.

A second new direction was pursued when two important studies no longer viewed *theōria* principally in terms of a *method of exegesis,* but also as a *type of textual meaning viewed from the perspective of fulfilled prophecy.* The first was by a Roman Catholic theologian, Bertrand de Margerie, the second from an Eastern Orthodox scholar, John Breck. Under their direction, recent scholarship widened its comprehension of the hermeneutic and renewed its proposal of *theōria* as a viable solution to the gap that exists between the historical and christological approaches to exegesis.

In 1980, Bertrand de Margerie published an important three-volume series entitled, *Introduction to the History of Exegesis.* In volume one, on *The Greek and Oriental Fathers,* de Margerie devoted a whole chapter to *theōria* entitled "History, *Theōria,* and Tradition in the Antiochene School."[32] The

---

31. Walter Kaiser, Jr. *The Uses of the Old Testament in the New* (Chicago: Moody, 1985), p. 71, developing Willis Beecher, *The Prophets and the Promise* (Grand Rapids: Baker, 1963 reprint of 1905 ed.), p. 130. Other interpreters of prophecy before Kaiser had also proposed a similar theory, but Kaiser added the critical refinement that seemed lacking in previous attempts. Within conservative Protestantism, controversy continues over the principle of double fulfillment. Other terms that are interchangeable with "double fulfillment" are "near and far view," "double sense," "multiple fulfillment," "gap prophecy," "foreshortening," "generic prophecy," etc. The leading proponents include A. H. Strong, Berkeley Mickelsen, Dwight Pentecost, John Walvoord, Bernard Ramm, C. L Feinberg, and Charles Ryrie. In the absence of a clear definition of the method and because of the concern to distinguish descriptive from prescriptive principles of apostolic exegesis, many conservatives today have rejected the validity of double fulfillment.

32. Bertrand de Margerie, "*Theōria*' et tradition dans l'École d'Antioch," *Introduction à l'histoire de L'exégèse,* vol. I (Paris: Cerf, 1980), pp. 188-213.

very existence of a special chapter given over to the Antiochene *theōria* by a
leading scholar of de Margerie's stature underscores the importance of the
subject. Much of his treatment depended on the earlier work done by Vaccari,
Maries, and especially Ternant, whose work was quoted time and again in the
footnotes and even in the subheadings of the chapter. De Margerie made no
special effort to compare his conclusions with the prior history of scholarship
that we have already surveyed, but he provided a general introduction to the
issues for the nonspecialist and offered new and creative insights that argued
for the rightful acceptance of *theōria* in biblical exegesis today. The major
achievements of this study demonstrated not only how the Antiochene
Fathers understood prophetic activity as both history and contemplation
(theōria), but that *theōria* succeeded at preserving the delicate union in
revelation between the words and events of Scripture.

Along with previous specialists on the subject, de Margerie maintained that the Antiochene exegetes believed that the prophets were conscious of both the historical and eschatological applications of their oracles.
They were "contemplative historians" of their own time and age as well as
of the glorious messianic future. Diodore's commentary on Psalm 68 supported this assertion:

> The words of the psalms are at the same time both history and prophecy.
> Words are uttered, from the historical point of view, with "hyperbole"
> (that is to say that they go beyond the historical situation that occasions
> them), but the same words, from the prophetic point of view, are realized
> in truth.[33]

Moreover, de Margerie explained that such predictions were consistent with
the literal meaning of the sacred text:

> The prophet, according to the Antiochene exegetes, is fully aware of the
> figurative value of the primary object his words intend to convey. . . . We
> could say, too, that the *theōria* or contemplation of the Antiochenes is
> properly speaking a literal sense. . . . This in no way introduces a duality
> of literal senses. The adequate literal sense is no more than one, but, if
> the expression may be pardoned, it is virtually double. *"There is a single
> prediction only, which is twice fulfilled: the first time partially, the second*

33. Ibid., pp. 190-91.

time fully". . . . for this School, the two aspects of the literal sense were both historical.[34]

On the debated question of the relation of typology to *theōria*, de Margerie maintained that the Antiochenes appeared to be divided. On the one hand, Theodore of Mopsuestia flatly denied their identity, since typology was based on a correspondence between two persons or events whereas prophecy was said to predict the future by means of words in their literal or figurative senses. On the other hand, John Chrysostom merely distinguished verbal prophecy from typological prophecy, inferring that the biblical author was not always explicitly aware of the typological value of the events he was recording. Thus, "there is no rigorous uniformity within the Antiochene School."[35]

Of critical importance was de Margerie's shift away from the question of *prophetic intention* on to a new focus that defined *theōria* more in terms of *prophetic fulfillment.*

> It would appear then that it is not so easy to find an example of *theōria* proposed by an Antiochene author which fulfills all the conditions supposedly laid down by the School. Can we overlook in particular the fact that Theodore of Mopsuestia does not say that Zechariah had a clear vision into the future of Zerubbabel and Jesus and that he saw Jesus in Zerubbabel? . . . What interested them was not so much the subjective awareness of the biblical writers as the objective fulfillment of what they announced.[36]

Too much attention had been focused on the Old Testament writers by insisting that they had a literal foreknowledge of the future. The key to acquiring a better understanding of *theōria* among the Antiochenes was to observe how, from the perspective of fulfilled prophecy, the hermeneutic functioned as a christological reading of the biblical text.

> Without wishing to state our case absolutely, we are not clearly aware of a single case of genuine *theōria* attributed by the Antiochene authors to Old Testament prophets with a foundation in the New Testament and in

34. Ibid., p. 191, emphasis original.
35. Ibid., p. 194. See Theodore's exegesis of Ps. 15:10 (LXX) and John 12:41 on pp. 200-204.
36. Ibid., p. 204.

the sense of a conscious two-stage prophecy. With the research we have done, it seems likely that the *theōria* of Antioch was intended to allude to a twofold objective realization of a prophecy rather than to a subjective awareness of a two-stage prophecy. This would be true at least in a great number of cases.[37]

The move away from authorial intent to prophetic fulfillment opened the way for viewing *theōria* as a hermeneutic that maintained the balance in revelation between the words and events of recorded Scripture without resorting to the traditional *sensus plenior* approach. Its theological relevance seems to be a promising solution to the question of whether the recorded "words" or "events" are the locus of inspiration in revelation, but the author stops short of drawing out the implications for us.

Antioch can make a contribution by its insistence that we never separate words from the institutions and events to which they refer. . . . In our judgment, then, the Antiochene notion of *theōria* is not identical to the *sensus plenior* we speak of today, but . . . the School of Antioch challenges us today to transpose the *theōria* of events to words, while not forgetting the link that binds the latter with the former.[38]

De Margerie's emphasis on the fulfillment side of prophecy became the springboard for developing fresh insights on *theōria* in the work of John Breck. Like de Margerie, Breck's interaction with the history of scholarship was minimal but his conclusions were still very significant. In 1986 Breck published a collection of essays in his book *The Power of the Word in the Worshiping Church*. Three articles written on *theōria* between 1975 and 1983 were entitled "The Hermeneutic Problem," "The Patristic Setting for 'Theoretic' Hermeneutics," and "*Theōria*: An Orthodox Hermeneutic."[39] His stated goal was to address the contemporary hermeneutical crisis over how to bridge a past biblical text with the pressing needs of the current human situation via the Eastern Orthodox tradition.[40]

37. Ibid., p. 205. De Margerie seems self-contradictory. Earlier in his chapter he postulated that the prophets were fully cognizant of their two-stage prophecies (see n. 34 above), but here he denies it.

38. Ibid., pp. 211-12.

39. John Breck, *The Power of the Word in the Worshiping Church* (Crestwood, NY: St. Vladimir's Seminary, 1986), parts I, II, and III, pp. 25-116.

40. Ibid., pp. 9-10.

Our purpose is to suggest an Orthodox answer to what biblical scholars call the "hermeneutic problem," an answer that gives full weight to the need for a rigorously scientific approach to biblical studies, while remaining faithful to Orthodox convictions concerning inspiration and the relationship between Holy Scripture and Holy Tradition.[41]

From Breck's perspective, neither the Protestant emphasis on "the Word" nor the Roman Catholic stress on "the Church" as a papal institution could resolve the current crisis in exegesis. The most promising resource for overcoming such problems was a thoroughgoing application of Orthodox pneumatology. Breck's distinctive contribution to scholarship, therefore, was to focus on the role of the Holy Spirit in revelation and to interpret *theōria* within that context as a hermeneutic of *spiritual illumination*.

The crucial question for determining the continuing validity of *theōria* is this: does *theōria* depend upon discernment by the biblical author of the *spiritual* as well as the literal sense of the event he is describing? . . . Such conscious intention, however, becomes quite unimportant when we consider the secondary meaning of *theōria:* the intuitive perception of spiritual meaning not by the author, but by the *later interpreter.* . . . We would argue, then, that this discernment by the interpreter . . . is in fact the *primary* sense of *theōria*.[42]

In agreement with Ternant, Breck emphasized that *theōria* was not to be confused with allegory or the *sensus plenior* with regard to the *words* of Scripture. Rather, one can look for a *sensus plenior* of typological *events* while avoiding the dehistoricizing tendency of allegory. "We mean by the 'spiritual sense,' then, a *sensus plenior,* unperceived by the prophet but discerned by the interpreter *within the event itself* by means of *theōria*."[43] Breck differed from Ternant, however, who with Vaccari had conceived *theōria* too narrowly by merging the literal and spiritual senses. Such a view fails to accommodate the fuller significance of typological events implied in *theōria*.

By identifying the spiritual with the literal sense, Fr. Ternant virtually eliminates the antitype which fulfills the original type or prophetic image.

---

41. Ibid., p. 26.
42. Ibid., pp. 96f., emphasis original.
43. Ibid., p. 103.

In some way, then, the spiritual sense must be regarded as distinct, if not separate, from the literal sense. . . . Refusal to accept a spiritual sense in these terms often leads to a confusion of *theōria* with the exegetical method of typology. To be exact *theōria* is not a "method" at all; it is a spiritual perception or divination *inspired by the Spirit,* which discerns the existence of a typological relationship between two persons, objects, institutions, or events.[44]

In 1990 Breck developed these themes further in an article on "Orthodoxy and the Bible Today."[45] The patristic principle of *theōria* helped to form a specifically Orthodox approach to modern biblical studies.

We can summarize the enduring value of *theōria* by the following points. 1) A "theoretic" approach to Scripture avoids the Fundamentalist fallacies of inerrancy and verbal inspiration by insisting on the "synergistic" process by which Scripture is composed and interpreted. . . . 2) By seeking meaning in persons, objects, institutions and events, *theōria* affirms the *historical* ground of the biblical witness. . . . 3) With its emphasis on a "wholistic" reading of Scripture, *theōria* validates, and therefore can legitimately appropriate, such new approaches to biblical interpretation such as "canonical" and "reader-response" criticism. . . . 4) *Theōria* as a hermeneutic principle understands that divine revelation is contained in the Scriptures but is not limited to them. *Theōria* perceives the work of the Spirit in the Church today. . . . 5) Finally, the greatest contribution *theōria* can make to the Church is perhaps to restore to biblical interpretation its *doxological* quality. . . . The function of *theōria,* and of Orthodox hermeneutics as a whole, then, is to provide biblical criticism with what is needed to enable us to hear the voice of God, and to respond to that voice with faithfulness and joy.[46]

A brief response to these articles is required because of their significance in the history of scholarship and potential value to the modern theological community. While Breck relegates authorial intent to a subordinate role in exegesis through a typological use of *theōria,* he admits at the same time that a divergence existed between apostolic and Antiochene

---

44. Ibid., pp. 102-3.
45. In *The Legacy of St. Vladimir's,* ed. J. Breck, J. Meyendorff, and E. Silk (Crestwood, NY: St. Vladimir's Seminary, 1990), pp. 141-57.
46. Ibid., pp. 155-57.

exegesis. In passages such as John 12:41; 8:56; Acts 2:31; and 1 Peter 1:10-12, "to the Antiochenes the prophets were conscious of the precise way in which their prophecies would be realized." Yet, for the New Testament authors "their prophetic vision surely consisted of no more than a mere apercue or glimpse of an eternal reality which would become incarnate in history at some future time."[47] This leads one to question whether the Antiochene authors themselves would have agreed with Breck's deemphasis of the authorial intent of Scripture under the rubric of *theōria*, since it leaves unresolved the hermeneutical problem that the Antiochenes had to reckon with in their efforts to reconcile the historical and christological meanings of Old Testament prophetic texts. Moreover, an emphasis on historical events as the supreme medium of divine revelation runs the risk of over-looking that God also gives the meaning of his saving acts in the divine words of Scripture as part of revelation itself. While Breck acknowledges the truth of this in his discussion on the nature of Scripture, it does not seem to affect his exposition of the Antiochene *theōria*. Without the inter-pretation of God's redemptive acts provided in the verbal revelation of Scripture, how else would one know which historical events in all of human experience were salvific?

Though Breck does not make the connection, we might add that the Protestant tradition has also had a rich history of applying its equivalent to *theōria* through the doctrine of "spiritual illumination." *Theōria*, defined as the illuminating work of the Holy Spirit, extends also to the conviction of the Reformers and Protestant scholastics who developed in a more advanced way the *testimonium internum Spiritus Sancti* (internal testimony of the Holy Spirit) as that which is necessary to the subjective receipt of the truth of Scripture and which ratifies that truth without adding any new revelations to the biblical text. Here is where the Antiochene *theōria* corre-lates with the pneumatology of such reformers as John Calvin and what the twentieth Anglican Article of Religion calls "God's Word written." Both the Fathers and Reformers possessed what may be called an "intuitional hermeneutical approach" to interpretation. The fundamental difference between them, however, is in how the Orthodox and Protestant traditions conceive the relationship between ecclesiology and pneumatology in bibli-cal exegesis. A recent effort has been made to examine various facets of this by comparing the two hermeneutical approaches. An emerging frontier of

47. Breck, *Power of the Word*, p. 101.

contemporary interest has begun to focus on comparative theology between the Orthodox and Protestant evangelical traditions. Although important differences exist and should not be minimized, the convergences yield a strikingly similar vision of theological values.[48]

Returning to our historical survey, it is significant to observe that almost all the major authors from 1880 until the present have focused their work more generally upon portions of selected commentaries by various Antiochene Fathers as opposed to a specific writer. Two exceptions include a 1949 doctoral dissertation by Francis Rossiter on *theōria* in Theodoret of Cyrus[49] and the 1991 dissertation by the present author. [50] I think it would be appropriate at this point to summerize my own research in this review of the history of scholarship, hopefully as a modest contribution to the discussion at hand.

The purpose of my dissertation was to conduct a study of Antiochene *theōria* in the New Testament homilies of John Chrysostom. After analyzing every occurrence of the term with the help of the *TLG* database, I concluded that *theōria* was *a distinct but not prominent feature* of his exegesis. In the clear instances where it does appear, Chrysostom knew *theōria* as the divine *revelation* of God's Word given to prophets, or the *illumination* of a text's deeper meaning given by the Holy Spirit in the act of interpretation or homiletical discourse. He does not employ *theōria* as a method of double prophecy. Quite unlike Theodore of Mopsuestia's or Diodore of Tarsus's hyperbolic method of messianic prophecy, Chrysostom generally uproots such prophecies as Zechariah 9:9 from their historical setting and interprets them as direct prophecies of Christ. However, like Diodore, his exegetical tutor, Chrysostom applied *theōria* to typologi-

---

48. See Grant Osborne, "The Many and the One: The Interface between Orthodox and Evangelical Protestant Hermeneutics," *St. Vladimir's Theological Quarterly* (forthcoming, 1995). The Society for the Study of Eastern Orthodoxy and Evangelicalism also has a series of unpublished papers from their annual meetings at the Billy Graham Center in Wheaton College, Wheaton, Illinois, now being collected into a volume. For an analysis of how evangelicals may study Orthodox theology today see my chapter on "Orthodox Theology" in *New Dimensions in Evangelical Theology* (Grand Rapids: Baker, forthcoming).

49. Francis S. Rossiter, "Messianic Prophecy According to Theodoret of Cyrus and Antiochene 'Theōria'" (Ph.D. diss., Pontifical Gregorian University, Rome, 1949). I have been unable to consult this work.

50. Bradley Nassif, "Antiochene *Theōria* in John Chrysostom's Exegesis" (Ph.D. diss., Fordham University, New York, 1991).

cal relationships or a broad range of narrative statements and figures of speech in Scripture. Metaphors, proverbs, parables — virtually any figures of speech — were capable of expressing the fuller meaning of a text whose spiritual sense *(theōria)* was determined by the particular literary vehicles that the sacred authors employed.[51] Due to his veneration of the historical nature of revelation and profound respect for the reality of the Incarnation, Chrysostom pursued the spiritual content of the text through a contemplative exegesis of the literal sense. *Theōria* helped resolve apparent discrepancies among the Gospel writers at the literary level[52] and revealed the spiritual treasures that were hidden in etymologies. By penetrating the deeper meaning contained in the etymological components of biblical names and places, the exegete could discover the mystical depths of divine revelation.[53]

Chrysostom heightened the importance of illumination *(theōria)* that was needed to interpret biblical types. That emphasis was possibly the distinctive mark that set him apart from others in the Antiochene School. In his typological interpretation, *theōria* became a means of processing the historical and theological patterns of unity between the Testaments in the types and antitypes that were prefigured and fulfilled. Through the enlightening power of *theōria*, Chrysostom discerned the deeper revelatory function of the shadow *(skia)* of the historical events *(hē dia pragmatōn prophēteia)* as images of their antitypes. Hence, the goal of theoretic exegesis was to comprehend the whole of the divine activity in Scripture through an integrated understanding of its parts. By means of *theōria*, Chrysostom beheld in Scripture the Spirit's activity in supplying historical words and events with soteriological significance.[54] To his flock in Antioch he declared that St. Paul had obtained such salvific truth by "theorizing" or "divining" the deeper soteriological import of the prophets' oracles, and so also should they:

> Hence we find him [Paul] continually appealing to the testimony of the prophets, and theorizing *(theōrounta)* into their writings. Paul, then, applies this to reading, for it is no small gain that is to be reaped from

51. *Expos. in Ps.* 9 (*PG* 55:126, 127); *Hom. in Jn.* 34 (*PG* 59:194).
52. *Hom. in Mt.* 36 (*PG* 57:413).
53. *Hom. in Mt.* 4 (*PG* 57:41).
54. *In Ep. ad Heb. hom.* 15 (*PG* 63:118), and *hom.* 12 (*PG* 63:97). For the role of *theōria* in liturgical exegesis, see Nassif, "Antiochene *Theōria* in John Chrysostom's Exegesis," pp. 248-56.

the Scriptures. But we are indolent, and we hear with carelessness and indifference. What punishment do we not deserve![55]

Finally, Chrysostom made discreet homiletical use of *theōria* when he applied the Scriptures to the moral and spiritual needs of his flock. Since *theōria* often referred to the deeper theological truths of God's revelation, he *rarely* spoke of the spiritual treasures that lay hidden in the text, simply because his congregation was spiritually unprepared for receiving them. Part of the pastoral task of *theōria* required Chrysostom to administer redemptive truths to his flock in the same patient and gradual manner in which God had revealed himself in holy Scripture.[56]

II. Antiochene *Theōria* in the Secondary Literature

For all the advances made by the specialists discussed above, Antiochene *theōria* today remains an unfamiliar, understudied, and misunderstood principle of patristic exegesis. Any mention of it is at best confined to sketchy or incidental remarks buried in the narratives of a few specialized books and articles. Three reasons can be suggested to explain why this is so. First, lacunae exist in some of the extant primary sources, such as the lost hermeneutical writings of Diodore of Tarsus. Undoubtedly, this was due to his posthumous condemnation by the Fifth Ecumenical Council in 553. Second, a general lack of awareness or acknowledgment of *theōria* by biblical, historical, and patristic scholars has *de facto* minimized its importance to the theological community simply because of the relative silence that has pervaded the literature. Third, whenever Antiochene *theōria* has been seriously discussed, it has generally been confused with allegory, typology, or the *sensus plenior* of Scripture. In such cases, *theōria* acquired a false hermeneutical classification, thereby adding more confusion because of its erroneous identification with one of the other scriptural senses.

The following discussion will assess the ways in which *theōria* has been presented in a wide number of secondary and tertiary works and will offer a hopefully constructive evaluation of their accuracy as judged by the norms and criteria of the specialists that have been surveyed above. The

55. *In Ep. 1 ad Tim. hom.* 13 (*PG* 62:566).
56. *Hom. in Jn.* 7 (*PG* 59:85).

central question over which there has been the greatest disagreement among students of patristic exegesis concerns the relationship between Antiochene *theōria* and allegory, typology, and the *sensus plenior* of Scripture.

Allegory

The first American historian to have introduced English readers to the Antiochene hermeneutic was Robert Grant. His special contribution was to draw attention to *theōria*'s use in Theodore, Diodore, and Chrysostom's exegesis and to show how it survived into the ninth-century School of Antioch, which flourished at Nisibis, Persia, in the Syriac author Isho-dad of Merv.[57] Further discussion came a few years later from a biblical exegete, Raymond Brown,[58] in the context of the *sensus plenior* debate. Brown identified five areas of contrast and comparison between Antiochene *theōria* and Alexandrian allegory: (1) Both schools respected the obvious meaning of the biblical text. (2) Both schools agreed that certain passages have a secondary, more profound sense. (3) The search to find that secondary sense was not identical between them; Antioch sought to obtain the intentions of the human authors whereas Alexandria pursued the thoughts of the Holy Spirit. (4) Both schools were defective in solving the basic problem of establishing a clear criteria for determining the spiritual sense of Scripture. (5) The Alexandrian School exercised a greater influence on subsequent exegesis in the Middle Ages than did the literalism of Antioch.[59]

Brown succeeded at distinguishing allegory from *theōria*. Unfortunately, there were in his analysis inaccurate or misleading statements that do not square with the findings of the specialists on the hermeneutic. In particular, Brown's third point introduced a distinction between Antioch and Alexandria to which the Antiochenes themselves would have objected as being artificial.

57. Robert Grant, *A Short History of the Interpretation of the Bible* (New York: Macmillan, 1948; revised edition co-edited with David Tracy, 1984), pp. 91-94.

58. Critical issues surrounding *theōria* were exposed simply by virtue of Brown's interaction with the work of Ternant, Seisdedos, and Vaccari in his book *The "Sensus Plenior" of Sacred Scripture* (Baltimore: St. Mary's University, 1955).

59. Brown, *"Sensus Plenior,"* pp. 49f. Later Brown confuses *theōria* with allegory in the *Jerome Biblical Commentary* (1968), p. 612, and the *New Jerome Biblical Commentary* (1990), p. 1154: "But Antioch also proposed a more-than-literal exegesis that involved *theōria*, for all practical purposes a close equivalent of Alexandrian *allēgoria*."

They insisted that there was a higher meaning conveyed by the Spirit in the Scriptures, and it was precisely that meaning that they sought to obtain through a reconstruction of the historical context and authorial intent of the text. In addition, the affirmation in point four that neither school established criteria for determining a legitimate spiritual sense cannot be sustained from the conclusions of Vaccari and Ternant. As we have seen, these scholars clearly identified at least two and possibly three criteria used by the Antiochenes for determining the use of *theōria*. Thus, Brown's distinction between Alexandrian allegory and Antiochene *theōria* failed to assimilate fully the conclusions of the specialists upon whom he himself had relied.

The problem subdivides when we ask whether allegory and *theōria* differ in degree or in kind of exegesis. On the one hand, scholars who support Guillet's older theory of "degree"[60] have *collapsed the distinction* between "historical" and "spiritual" types of meaning into a single herme-neutical continuum. They have maintained that the real differences between Alexandrian allegory and Antiochene *theōria* were not in their principles of exegesis but in their application. Alexandria sought to obtain higher celestial truths while Antioch extracted primarily moral applications from the text. Karlfried Froehlich posits that

> the difference between Alexandria and Antioch seems to reflect more the methodological emphases and priorities of the schools than soteriologi-cal principles. . . . The anagogy of Alexandrian *allēgoria* led the soul into a realm of true knowledge where the vision of intelligible truth would crown the road to salvation. The anagogy of Antiochene *theōria*, convey-ing glimpses of the one God of All, led humans into a truly moral life which would continue into all eternity as an existence free of sin.[61]

On the other hand, *theōria* scholars affirm with one voice that a discernibly different "kind" of textual meaning existed in the schools of Antioch and Alexandria, and this difference evoked correspondingly dis-

---

60. See n. 3 above.

61. Karlfried Froehlich, *Biblical Interpretation in the Early Church* (Sources of Early Christian Thought, 5, ed. William Rusch; Philadelphia: Fortress Press, 1984), pp. 20, 23. Except for a few lines on p. 32, Joseph Trigg unfortunately fails to include any serious discussion of Antiochene *theōria* in his otherwise excellent collection of primary texts illustrating early Christian exegesis. Joseph Trigg, *Biblical Interpretation* (Message of the Fathers of the Church, 9; Wilmington: Glazier, 1988). See also Manlio Simonetti, *Biblical Interpretation in the Early Church*, tr. John Hughes (Edinburgh: Clark, 1994).

tinct searches for the deeper meaning of the biblical text.[62] Alexandria's exclusion of metaphorical language as part of its definition of the literal sense[63] differed from Antioch's inclusion of metaphor in the literal meaning. Different textual theories led to different exegetical goals and their accompanying spiritual exegesis.

I am reasonably certain that no extensive research has been done on *theōria* as a term borrowed from the technical vocabulary of the classical rhetorical tradition. Frances Young has recently shown how the quests of classical rhetoric reappear in Antiochene exegesis in such terms as *mimēsis, historikē, methodikē, oikonomia,* and *hypothesis.* But her examination of *theōria* is confined only to a passing reference.[64] A check of the standard German reference books on rhetorical literature suggests that *theōria* was not a significant rhetorical term in the classical schools.[65] Yet this *may* be due to a lack in rhetorical studies since Liddell and Scott include at least one reference to its rhetorical use as an "explanatory preface to a *meletē*" in the writings of a sixth-century C.E. rhetorician named Choricius.[66] As

---

62. So also Georges Florovsky, *The Eastern Fathers of the Fourth Century,* tr. Catharine Edmunds (Belmont, MA: Büchervertriebsanstal, 1987), p. 261.

63. "To the Alexandrians the literal meaning of a text did not include its metaphorical meaning. . . . At Antioch, on the other hand, the meaning of a passage, its 'theory' included both metaphor and simple statement." Robert Grant, "History of the Interpretation of the Bible. I: Ancient Period," in *The Interpreter's Bible,* ed. G. A. Buttrick, et al., vol. 1 (New York and Nashville: Abingdon, 1951), p. 111.

64. Frances Young, "The Rhetorical Schools and Their Influence on Patristic Exegesis," in Rowan Williams (ed.), *The Making of Orthodoxy: Essays in Honour of Henry Chadwick* (Cambridge: Cambridge University, 1989), pp. 182-99. Young is to be commended for illustrating the parallels between the pagan literary tradition and patristic methods of exegesis. Her thesis that "the Origenist tradition adopted the allegorical techniques of the philosophical schools, and the Antiochene reaction was the protest of rhetoric against such a way of handling texts" (p. 188) is convincing. Nevertheless, she seems to overstate the case when she rightly corrects the *exclusively* theological or historical interpretation that is given to explain the traditional (but, I believe, still valid) exegetical orientations. To say also that "There was no genuine historical criticism in antiquity" (p. 189) minimizes the original sources cited by Robert Grant in his numerous works on early Christianity, and especially D. S. Wallace-Hadrill, *Christian Antioch: A Study of Early Christian Thought in the East* (Cambridge: Cambridge University, 1982), pp. 30-51.

65. Heinrich Lausberg, *Handbuch der Literarischen Rhetorik* (Munich: 1960), vol. 2, p. 861. Josef Martin, *Antike Rhetorik: Technik und Methode* (Munich: Beck, 1974).

66. H. G. Liddell and R. Scott, *A Greek-English Lexicon,* 9th ed. by H. S. Jones, et al. (Oxford: Clarendon, 1940; supplement, 1968), p. 797, col. a.

previously noted, Henrich Kihn traced it back to the philosophical tradition of Plato and Aristotle, but Norman Bates traced it to the rhetoriticians (see note 15). It is apparent that illustrative parallels between the philosophical and rhetorical traditions and the Antiochene exegetical practice of *theōria* remain to be demonstrated.

Typology

The relationship between typology and *theōria* forms a *crux interpretum* within the history of exegesis. Theologians have constructed widely divergent schemes to address the role of typology in biblical interpretation. The few who have applied *theōria* to the prophetic literature often have either classified it as a type of direct prophecy or confused it with typology proper. Few, if any, have classified *theōria* as a subset of typology as have Vaccari and Seisdedos. This lack of precision accounts for much of the ancient and modern misunderstandings of *theōria* and its association with typology. The complicated views of the relation between *theōria* and typology can be conveniently classified under two groupings.

One group of authors has tended to equate (or confuse) *theōria* with typology proper. De Margerie claims that the Antiochene School was divided on the issue but points out that Theodore of Mopsuestia flatly denied their identity; J. N. D. Kelly identifies typology proper with *theōria* and implies that the latter was not the same as foretelling prophecy:

> The true key to its deeper spiritual message where this was not already fully explicit, as in genuine prophecy, was what they [the Antiochenes] called "insight" *(theōria)*. By this they meant the power of perceiving, in addition to the historical facts set out in the text, a spiritual reality to which they were designed to point. Thus they accepted typology proper — indeed the classic definition of a type as "a prophecy expressed in terms of things."[67]

But Kelly's equation of *theōria* with typology proper fails to recognize the verbally predictive elements in *theōria* that was also sometimes used by the Antiochenes.

67. J. N. D. Kelly, *Early Christian Doctrines* (3d ed., New York: Harper and Row, 1978), p. 76.

A second group has suggested that *theōria* can be viewed as a subspecies of typology that is distinct from typology proper. In typology proper the prophet did not see or intend to prophesy future antitypes; but *theōria* does both through the symbolic imagery of the prophet's present circumstances. *Theōria* is to be distinguished, though not separated, from typology proper based on its classification as a literal sense, considerations about the conscious nature of the prophetic experience, and the verbal and hyperbolic mode of predictive discourse. This is the view held by some of the *theōria* specialists surveyed above.[68] In this way, *theōria* functions as "an *intended* type" in the mind of the prophet. Through the shadow of an intended type, the prophet knowingly predicts the future in its immediate and messianic senses through hyperbolic language.

Rowan Greer leans toward this view by averring that Theodore's interpretation of Zechariah 9:9 was an example of double typology under the literary device of hyperbole *(theōria)*, rather than direct prophecy: "It is fair to say that this double typology is a method of exegesis."[69] Greer more closely conforms to Vaccari and Seisdedos, who grouped *theōria* as an alternate form of typology, but does not clarify his position.

This ancient distinction seems to offer a new way of viewing the New Testament's use of the Old. Biblical exegetes may profit from evaluating and perfecting it as a valid hypothesis to account for certain prophetic texts that seem to function in that capacity. In fact, some biblical interpreters have already inadvertently proposed *theōria* as a solution to portions of the New Testament's exegesis of the Old Testament while unaware of its Antiochene antecedents and its potential relation to typology. C. K. Barrett, for example, acknowledges that typology has been viewed not as a "fulfillment of a prediction" but as "the recurrence of a pattern." He adds that

---

68. See my earlier description of Vaccari's and Seisdedos's views; Kihn, Ternant, de Margerie, and Breck, however, have not made this important distinction. For them, *theōria* can be the means of perceiving typological correspondences, but some have failed to clarify its difference from typology proper. Ternant stressed the literal feature as a distinguishing mark, de Margerie emphasized the absence of exegetical uniformity among the Antiochenes, and Breck denied their identity altogether.

69. James Kugel and Rowan Greer, *Early Biblical Interpretation* (Philadelphia: Westminster, 1986), p. 181. Earlier Greer stated that *theōria* is "presumably, in some sense, typology." Rowan Greer, *Theodore of Mopsuestia: Exegete and Theologian* (London, 1961), p. 93. See also A. Puech, *Histoire de la litterature grecque chrétienne* (Paris, 1930), vol. 3, p. 456.

"the distinction is useful, but it is probably true that the most characteristic New Testament estimate of the Old sees in it a combination of typology and prophecy."[70] Barrett's suggestion that the New Testament's use of the Old Testament often involved a "combination of typology and prophecy" echoes both the verbal and symbolic features of the Antiochene method in its effort to explain prophetic passages in their historical and predictive dimensions (that is, as intended types).

Sensus Plenior

The spotlight shone briefly on *theōria* during the *sensus plenior* debates of the 1950s. The *sensus plenior* theory in general viewed certain texts as containing a "double sense," that is, a literal meaning and also a fuller spiritual meaning that could surpass the original intent of the biblical author. The issues between *theōria* and the *sensus plenior* centered on the extent and nature of the human author's intention signified in the words of the biblical text. The views of Raymond Brown, a dominant voice in the discussion, vacillated over the years when comparing the two, as reflected in the following classifications.

First, there are those scholars who include *theōria* as a prophetic expression of the *sensus plenior* if a definition of the latter allows the biblical writer at least a vague awareness of the future import of his words.[71] Second, *theōria* has been viewed as a typological expression of the *sensus plenior* of divine acts rather than a *sensus plenior* of words, thereby eliminating the problem of the extent and nature of the human author's intention.[72] A third position is that which sees *theōria* and the *sensus plenior* as separate hermeneutical principles since there is no clear criteria in the methodology of the *sensus plenior* for determining the biblical author's mental relationship to the fuller meaning of his words. Brown frankly acknowledges the shift in his position:

70. C. K. Barrett, "The Interpretation of the Old Testament in the New," in P. R. Ackroyd and C. F. Evans, *The Cambridge History of the Bible. I: From the Beginnings to Jerome* (New York and Cambridge: Cambridge University Press, 1970), pp. 410f. See also the interpretation of Daniel 12:1-2 by E. F. Sutcliffe in *The Old Testament and the Future Life* (Oxford: Burnes Oates and Washbourne, 1946).

71. Brown's original position in 1955, *"Sensus Plenior,"* p. 110.

72. De Margerie, "*'Theōria'* et tradition dans l'École d'Antioch," pp. 211f.; Breck, *The Power of the Word,* p. 74f.

In 1955 we defined the SP of a text as a deeper meaning "intended by God, but not clearly intended by the human author." Our definition neither insisted on consciousness nor ruled it out. . . . We admit now that such explanations as the *theōria* of the Antiochenes are totally out of the question. But we believe more firmly than ever that there are many factors that make it virtually impossible to characterize exactly the human author's mental relationship to that richer meaning which his words would be seen to possess at a future time.[73]

To summarize part II of this article, few modern presentations in the secondary literature that analyze the Antiochene *theōria* have reflected an integrated understanding of the areas of agreement and disagreement that have been expressed by the specialists over the last hundred years. It is hoped that the above attempt to clarify the issues has also mapped out the alternatives for future reflections on the subject.

III. Conclusion

We close our study with a succinct summary of the current state of the field given by Bertrand de Margerie:

> The complexity of the material available undoubtedly shows that we still await the definitive work which will give us an exact understanding of the meaning of Antiochene *theōria,* and the different meanings of the hermeneutic found in the authors of the School of Antioch, and even within a single author.[74]

The diverse ways in which *theōria* was employed as a *terminus technicus* in Antiochene exegesis makes it impossible to construct a single model of the hermeneutic that was uniformly applied. Whether it was used *exegetically* as a *literal method of messianic exegesis; theologically* as a *typological or mystical type of textual meaning; etymologically* as a *spiritual illumination in the mind of the biblical author, prophet, or later exegete,* or all three depends on which particular Antiochene author and passage one

---

73. Raymond Brown, *Catholic Biblical Quarterly* 25 (1963), pp. 264, 276, contra Ternant, "La '*theōria* d'Antioche dans le cadre des sens de l'Ecriture," p. 155.

74. De Margerie, "*Theōria*' et tradition dans l'École d'Antioch," p. 194.

consults. Indeed, the central point that has caused so much confusion over the past hundred years among those who have tried to nail down the precise meaning of *theōria* in Antiochene exegesis boils down to this: In many cases the spiritual sense *was* the historical sense, but sometimes it *was not.* This diversity has made it extremely confusing for anyone who works casually with the material, and challenging for the specialist who has the responsibility of sorting it all out. The common fallacies that generalists and specialists have fallen into are methodological. They have either *overgeneralized the extent of hermeneutical unity* among the Antiochenes, *dichotomized the data* to fit into the "literal" versus "more-than-literal" categories, gone to the opposite extreme of *collapsing the distinction* between "historical" and "spiritual" types of meaning into a single hermeneutical continuum (see "Allegory" above in section II), or *emphasized only one of the three possible meanings of theōria* (method of exegesis, type of textual meaning, or spiritual illumination) to the exclusion of the others. Except for overgeneralizing the hermeneutical unity, the other approaches of dichotomizing the data, collapsing the distinction, or delineating three distinguishable technical meanings of the term are not wrong in and of themselves. They become methodological fallacies whenever scholars propose only one strand as "the" exclusive approach that was taken by the Fathers, and then impose that interpretation on their readership as if it were the only legitimate way to understand the nature of spiritual exegesis in the School of Antioch.

Future research will need to avoid the exegetical fallacies that have been committed in the past, but also build on the foundation that has been laid. A great deal of specialized work still needs to be done in monographs or doctoral dissertations. As we look ahead, we find ourselves standing at the start of a new and potentially fruitful field of inquiry in patristic exegesis. If asked where one might want to begin advancing the field, the answer is that it needs to be pursued virtually anywhere and everywhere in history that the principles of Antiochene exegesis made their influence. In particular, I would suggest that future studies of Antiochene *theōria* may profitably proceed in at least six directions.

First, the Antiochene Fathers themselves need separate monographs or dissertations. Their work is foundational for all else that follows. Graduate students and researchers should focus primarily on the Fathers' use of *theōria* in their biblical commentaries, but also on how the Antiochene principle was carried over to their liturgical exegesis of the church's sacramental rites in liturgical commentaries and catechetical literature.[75] Possible connections should also be examined between the Antiochene School and North African exegesis.[76]

Second, scholars need to investigate whether *theōria* was used as part of the technical vocabulary of the rhetorical schools and, if so, what influence those schools had in that regard on patristic exegesis.

Third, more attention should be given to the Syriac literature and to the Greek Fathers whose writings survive only, or primarily, in Syriac translations, none of which has ever been explored in great depth. The area in which the Syriac literature may prove most valuable is in its use of *theōria* as a double historical method of messianic exegesis. A fascinating project that awaits investigation is a history of the influence of John Chrysostom and Theodore of Mopsuestia's legacy of *theōria* on the Syriac tradition of biblical exegesis. The works of Theodore, who was known as "the exegete" par excellence, were destroyed by Justinian in the sixth century and survive only in Syriac translations. A notable start on Chrysostom's influence in this direction can be seen in Cornelia Molenberg's doctoral dissertation on Iso bar Nun.[77]

A fourth line of inquiry needs to discover the influence that the Antiochene methods of messianic interpretation exerted on Irish exegesis in the West from the seventh to the twelfth centuries. Diodore and

---

75. Liturgical studies on the Antiochene *theōria* will expand on the initial work that has been done by R. Bornert, *Les commentaires byzantins de la divine liturgie du VIIe au XVe siècle* (*Archives de l'Orient chrétien*, 9; Paris: *Institut francias d'études byzantines*, 1966). For an application of Bornert's thesis to the Byzantine iconoclastic controversy see Robert Taft, S.J., "The Liturgy of the Great Church: An Initial Synthesis of Structure and Interpretation on the Eve of Iconoclasm," *Dumbarton Oaks Papers* (1980-81), pp. 34f. See also Marie-Josephe Rondeau, "Les Commentaires Patristiques Du Psautier (IIIe-Ve siecles)," *Orientalia Christiana Analecta* 220:2 (1982), esp. pp. 260-346, 408-9, n. 1143.

76. For a close equivalent of Antiochene *theōria* in North African exegesis, see the "species and genus" type of prophecy in Rule 4 of Tychonius's *Book of Rules* in Pamela Bright, *The Book of Rules of Tychonius: Its Purpose and Inner Logic* (Notre Dame: University of Notre Dame, 1988), pp. 69-76.

77. Cornelia Molenberg, *The Interpreter Interpret: Iso Bar Nun's Selected Questions on the Old Testament* (Groningen: Rijksuniversiteit Groningen, 1990), esp. pp. 359-81. Dr. Molenberg has informed me that *theōria* was also used by Mar Aba of Kaskar, who patterned his exegetical homilies after Chrysostom (preserved in the Gannat Bussame by G. J. Reinink, *CSCO* 414, Subs. 57 and *CSCO* 502). Note also Isho-dad of Merv according to Grant, *A Short History of the Interpretation of the Bible*, pp. 91-94.

Theodore's theory of a twofold historical sense clearly reappears in early Irish scholars.[78]

Fifth, Medievalists may profitably expand upon Ternant's initial observation that the double historical sense occurs in the christological exegesis of scholastic theologians Thomas Aquinas and Nicholas of Lyra.[79] And Reformation theologians will want to examine the potential continuities of Antiochene *theōria* in the christological exegesis and pneumatology of the Reformers and Protestant scholastics in order to discover the patristic origins and parallel exegetical patterns with the School of Antioch.

Sixth, contemporary biblical scholars will need to determine the extent to which *theōria* may enrich their interpretive methods by evaluating the recent advances made by patristic experts in this field. While some exegetes in the jury have passed an earlier negative judgment based exclusively on its double fulfillment principle of interpreting prophecy, the specialists on *theōria* have begun to show us how to appropriate and perfect its methodological and hermeneutical implications.[80] While every precaution must be taken against uncritically accepting *theōria* as a panacea for the current problems that beleaguer biblical scholarship, or even of exaggerating the originality of this deceptively simple principle of patristic exegesis, fruitful applications await development.

The end result of these researches will widen our comprehension of how the Antiochene *theōria* was employed throughout Christian history. It will trace the pneumatology underlying the Antiochene interpreters and

---

78. "Theodore's approach had no lasting success, except in the extreme East in the Syrian Church and in Ireland in the West. . . . Both commentary and Epitome enjoyed a central place in Irish Psalms exegesis from the beginning right down to the twelfth century, and through it Irish Psalms exegesis is strongly Antiochene. . . . In fact it appears that the early Irish scholars worked out their own peculiar theory of a twofold historical sense." James P. Mackey, *An Introduction to Celtic Christianity* (Edinburgh: Clark, 1989), pp. 428f.

79. See n. 30 above.

80. I attempt to do this in a very small way with structuralism, genre criticism, and canonical criticism in the last chapter of "Antiochene *Theōria* in John Chrysostom's Exegesis," pp. 301-6, 315-19. For a suggestive modern approach to interbiblical interpretation that is analogous to the Antiochene *theōria* in its adaptation of previous Scripture for a messianic purpose see John Sailhammer, "1 Chronicles 21:1 — A Study in Inter-Biblical Interpretation," *Trinity Journal* 10 (1989), pp. 33-48, compared with Ternant's observations, p. 356 above.

their successors, who understood Scripture both according to the letter and according to the Spirit. It will also uncover more of the Antiochenes' approach to the unity of the Testaments, and it will enable us to define more precisely the meaning of the *sensus literalis* of Scripture in the history of exegesis.

Select Bibliography of Works
by John Meyendorff

John Meyendorff's writings have appeared in at least twelve languages. He himself wrote in English, French, and Russian. The following is a selection of his most important scholarly books in English. Numerous articles in other languages can be found in a complete bibliography forthcoming in the *St. Vladimir's Theological Quarterly*.

Byzantine Hesychasm: Historical, Theological and Social Problems: Collected Studies. London: Variorum Reprints, 1974.

Byzantine Theology: Historical Trends and Doctrinal Themes, 2d ed. with revisions. New York: Fordham, 1983.

Byzantium and the Rise of Russia: A Study of Byzantine-Russian Relations in the Fourteenth Century. Cambridge: Cambridge University Press, 1981.

Catholicity and the Church. Crestwood, NY: St. Vladimir's Seminary Press, 1983.

Christ in Eastern Christian Thought. Washington, DC: Corpus Books, 1969.

Christian Spirituality: High Middle Ages and Reformation, ed. with J. Raitt and B. McGinn. New York: Crossroad, 1987.

Christian Spirituality: Origins to the Twelfth Century, ed. Bernard McGinn and John Meyendorff in collaboration with Jean Leclerq. New York: Crossroad, 1985.

Christian Spirituality: Post-Reformation and Modern, ed. Louis Dupré and Don E. Saliers in collaboration with John Meyendorff. New York: Crossroad, 1989.

Imperial Unity and Christian Divisions: The Church 450-680 A.D. Crestwood, NY: St. Vladimir's Seminary Press, 1989.

Living Tradition. Crestwood, NY: St. Vladimir's Seminary Press, 1978.

Marriage: An Orthodox Perspective, 3d rev. ed. Crestwood, NY: St. Vladimir's Seminary Press, 1984.

Orthodoxy and Catholicity. New York: Sheed and Ward, 1966.

St. Gregory Palamas and Orthodox Spirituality. Crestwood, NY: St. Vladimir's Seminary Press, 1974.

The Byzantine Legacy in the Orthodox Church. Crestwood, NY: St. Vladimir's Seminary Press, 1982.

The Legacy of St. Vladimir, ed. J. Breck, J. Meyendorff, and E. Silk. Crestwood, NY: St. Vladimir's Seminary Press, 1990.

The Orthodox Church: Yesterday and Today, 3d rev. ed. Crestwood, NY: St. Vladimir's Seminary Press, 1981.

The Primacy of Peter: Essays in Ecclesiology and the Early Church, ed. Nicholas Afanasieff, John Meyendorff, et al., rev. ed. St. Vladimir's Seminary Press, 1992.

A Study of Gregory Palamas, 2d ed. Crestwood, NY: St. Vladimir's Seminary Press, 1974.

The Triads: Gregory Palamas, ed. with introduction. New York: Paulist Press, 1983.